D1570382

OXFORD STUDIES IN
MODERN EUROPEAN HISTORY

General Editors

SIMON DIXON, MARK MAZOWER,

and

JAMES RETALLACK

The Plough that Broke the Steppes

Agriculture and Environment on Russia's Grasslands, 1700–1914

DAVID MOON

OXFORD
UNIVERSITY PRESS

Great Clarendon Street, Oxford, OX2 6DP,
United Kingdom

Oxford University Press is a department of the University of Oxford.
It furthers the University's objective of excellence in research, scholarship,
and education by publishing worldwide. Oxford is a registered trade mark of
Oxford University Press in the UK and in certain other countries

British Library Cataloguing in Publication Data

Data available

ISBN 978-0-19-955643-4

Printed in Great Britain by
MPG Books Group, Bodmin and King's Lynn

Dedicated to my father, Derek James Moon, and to the memory of my mother, Marie Theresa Moon (née McMahon) (1925–2012)

Morning breaking over the limitless steppes shows a dreary prospect, – a level earth stretching away unbroken to the horizon . . . One turns to a book to forget it.

Michael Myers Shoemaker, *The Great Siberian Railway: From St. Petersburg to Pekin* (New York, 1903), 40.

Contents

Preface and Acknowledgements

In May 2003, I was invited to join an expedition of botanists from Rostov-on-Don to the Rostov steppe *zapovednik* (scientific nature reserve) in the south-east of the steppe region. When we arrived, after dark, my companions warned me that, when it got light the following morning, I would feel ill at ease in the flatness of a landscape without trees. I was puzzled and wondered if they were teasing me (we had whiled away the long drive exchanging stories and telling jokes). But when, early the next morning, I got up and went outside, I did indeed feel disorientated, exposed, and overwhelmed by the vastness of the sky overhead. Over the next few days, we saw some sad specimens of trees that had been planted on sandy soil, but for the most part only uninterrupted flatness and the salt lake Manych-Gudilo. The landscape was so flat it seemed two-dimensional. But I did start to get accustomed to it and could honestly admit I thought it beautiful in its own way. I also learned a great deal about the steppe environment and how scientists go about studying it. I would like to acknowledge *zapovednik* Director Aleksei Valentinovich Chekin for permitting my visit. I am very grateful to Antonina Shamareva, Zhanna Shishlova, and their colleagues from the Rostov Botanical Garden for taking a visiting historian from far-off Scotland along with them, and for their good humour (at least I think it was humour) in telling me that their archive—the steppe—was preferable to reading old documents in 'stuffy archives'.

Shortly after my visit, I accepted an invitation from the Geography Faculty of Rostov State University (now the Southern Federal University) to join a field trip to Veshenskaya in northern Rostov region. After another long drive, I saw and learned about a rather different environment of high steppe, cut through by the river Don and ravines. There were more trees, but they were mostly in the river valley and the ravines, as well as a forestry plantation we visited. I would like to express my thanks to the staff and students of the Geography Faculty. I am also grateful to the director and staff of the Teberdinskii *zapovednik* in the Caucasus mountains, which I visited (for contrast as well as another long drive through the steppes and the foothills of the mountains) in June 2003, and Director Yurii Petrovich Krasnobaev and his colleagues at the Zhigulevskii *zapovednik*, near Samara, which I visited in August 2005. My thanks are due also to Dr Ivan Ivanovich Moysiyenko of Kherson State University for a tour of the Oleshkivs'ki (Aleshkovskie in Russian) sands on the left bank of the river Dnepr, and to *zapovednik* Director Viktor Semenovich Gavrilenko and his colleagues at the Askaniya Nova *zapovednik*, both of which I visited on a trip to southern Ukraine in May 2011.

Researching and writing this book have been an adventure, intellectually and otherwise, spread over several years. In the process, I have accrued many debts to many people and institutions that I cannot possibly repay. I hope my expressions of sincere gratitude, both those above and those to follow, may in some way suffice.

Most of the research was conducted on visits to Russia, Finland, and Ukraine. The trips to Russia would not have been possible without the support of the institutions that kindly agreed to invite me. I am very grateful to Dean Igor Mironovich Uznarodov of the History Faculty of Rostov State University (now the Southern Federal University); Dean Aleksandr Abakarevich Kudryavtsev of Stavropol' State University; Vice Rector Petr Serafimovich Kabytov of Samara State University; Director Eduard Izrailovich Kolchinskii of the Institute for the History of Science and Technology of the Russian Academy of Sciences in St Petersburg; and Dr Julia Aleksandrovna Lajus and Dr Aleksandra Viktorovna Bekasova of the European University in St Petersburg. I am grateful also to their colleagues and counterparts at neighbouring institutions who willingly offered assistance, in particular Viktor Apryshenko, Gennadii Magakov, Andrei Pushkar-enko, Elena Ryabenkaya, and Vladimir Sagalaev in Rostov-on-Don; Elena Kalinina, Eduard Kempinskii, Tat'yana Nevskaya, and Tat'yana Plokhotnyuk in Stavropol; Nina Narykova, formerly of Stavropol' State University and now the St Petersburg State Agrarian University; Vera Dubina, Mikhail Leonov, Nadezhda Rogozhina, Peter Savel'ev, and Nina Ustina in Samara. I am also grateful to Olena Sinyavs'ka and Olena Smyntyna in Odessa; Mikhail Podrainyi and Sergei D'yachenko in Kherson; and Zhanna Kormina, Boris Mironov, and Volodya Somov in St Petersburg. (I express my thanks to other colleagues in St Petersburg below.)

I am very grateful to the directors and archivists of (in order of my first visits for research for this book): the State Archive of Rostov Region; the Russian State Historical Archive in St Petersburg; the State Archive of Stavropol' Region; the State Archive of Samara Region; the St Petersburg branch of the Archive of the Russian Academy of Sciences; and the State Archive of Odessa Region. I have benefitted greatly from the assistance of the librarians at: the Russian National Library in St Petersburg; the Slavonic Library of the National Library of Finland in Helsinki, in particular Irina Lukka; the Don State Public Library in Rostov, including my namesake, Deputy Director Mikhail Moon; the Samara Region Universal Scientific Library; the Stavropol' Region Universal Scientific Library; the Odessa State Scientific Library. I am grateful also to the archivists and librarians at the Library of Congress in Washington, DC; the Minnesota Histor-ical Society, St Paul; and the Firestone Library and the Library of the Institute for Advanced Study in Princeton.

I have tried out ideas, abandoned many of those that didn't stand up to scrutiny, and taken away many new ones when presenting papers at conferences and seminars at: the Ohio State University, Columbus; the Annual Convention of the American Association for the Advancement of Slavic Studies in Toronto; the Institute of History of the Russian Academy of Sciences, Moscow; Joensuu

University, Finland; the World Congresses of the International Council for Central and East European Studies in Berlin and Stockholm; Samara Municipal Institute of Administration; the Annual Meeting of the Social Science History Association in Minneapolis and Southwest Minnesota State University in Marshall, Minnesota; Georgetown University, Washington, DC; the University of Nebraska-Lincoln; The Kobe Institute, Japan; the Institute of the History of Science and Technology of the Russian Academy of Sciences and the European University in St Petersburg; the Institute for Advanced Study, Princeton; the Harriman Institute, Columbia University, New York; the University of Texas at Austin; the University of Kansas, Lawrence; Trinity College Dublin; Braga, Portugal; Helsinki; the Annual Convention of the Association for Slavic, East European, and Eurasian Studies, Los Angeles; the Rachel Carson Center, Munich; the Radcliffe Institute for Advanced Study, Harvard University; Yale University; and in the UK at the universities of Stirling, Strathclyde, Birmingham, Cambridge (Annual Conferences of the British Association for Slavonic and East European Studies), York, Glasgow, the West of England in Bristol (a paper invited by the Royal Historical Society), Nottingham (the Study Group on the Russian Revolution), Newcastle, and Sunderland. In addition, I presented papers at the first six conferences of the European Society for Environmental History: St Andrews, Scotland, 2001; Prague, 2003; Florence, 2005; Amsterdam, 2007; Copenhagen (also the first World Congress), 2009; and Turku, Finland, 2011. My sincere thanks to all who have come to listen to what I had to say, ask questions, and share their expertise.

Scholars with whom I have participated in conference panels and seminars on several occasions, from whom I have learned a great deal, and to whom I owe my particular thanks, include: Aleksandra Bekasova, Nicholas Breyfogle, Catherine Evtuhov, Anastasiya Fedotova, Julia Lajus, Marina Loskutova, Jonathan Oldfield, and Denis Shaw. I am grateful also to Seymour Becker, Deborah Coen, Peter Holquist, Jonathan Israel, Stephen Kotkin, Robert Layton, Jonathan Oldfield, Hamish Scott, Susan Smith-Peter, and Richard Wortman, who offered detailed comments on draft chapters, and an anonymous reader for Oxford University Press. There are many others I would like to thank, but to acknowledge everyone who assisted in some way would exclude too many from being invited to review this book. I hope they know who they are and will accept my thanks anonymously.

I would like to pay tribute to the memory of three scholars of great distinction and generosity who offered advice, assistance, and encouragement: Pavel Dolukhanov, Aleksei Karimov, and Richard Stites. Richard suggested the title.

None of this would have been possible without grants and fellowships from several institutions, to all of which I am truly grateful: the University of Strathclyde in Glasgow, which supported the early stages of my research; The Leverhulme Trust, for a Study Abroad Fellowship, which I held in Rostov-on-Don; The British Academy, for three of their irreplaceable small grants, which funded research trips to Russia and Finland; the Carnegie Trust for the Universities of

Scotland, which funded my visit to Samara; the Kennan Institute of the Wood-row Wilson International Center for Scholars, Washington, DC, for a short-term grant; the Institute of Advanced Study in Princeton, where I was Felix Gilbert member in 2008–9; and the UK Government Arts and Humanities Research Council for a fellowship and funding my visit to southern Ukraine in 2011.

I am very grateful to the city councils of Glasgow and Rostov-on-Don for 'twinning' their cities, and to my former colleagues at the University of Strath-clyde for setting up an exchange with what was then Rostov State University. It was this that determined my choice of region in Russia for this study. Although it is not customary among scholars to do so, I would like to thank the Russian authorities for permitting me to visit their country, and travel about it 'without let or hindrance', on many occasions. I came to realize that I was dividing much of my time researching this book between St Petersburg in northern Russia and Helsinki in Finland, both of which are in forested regions with plentiful supplies of water, and various locations in the steppe region, in which trees and water are in short supply. I should like to acknowledge these two contrasting environments for helping me shape my argument.

In order to meet my obligations to the institutions that have employed me to submit work to the periodic assessments that determine research funding at UK universities, I have published several articles and chapters based on the research for this book. Permission has been granted by the editors and publishers of *Istoriko-biologicheskie issledovaniya/Studies in the History of Biology* and the *Russian Review* to use revised versions of articles in chapters 3 and 4, and the *Slavonic and East European Review* to use parts of an article in chapter 2. (Full references to the articles may be found in the relevant chapters.) Some passages in different parts of this book have been based on paragraphs in 'The Environmental History of the Russian Steppes: Vasilii Dokuchaev and the Harvest Failure of 1891', *Transactions of the Royal Historical Society*, 6th series, 15 (2005), 149–74 (published by Cambridge University Press) and 'Agriculture and the Environment on the Steppes in the Nineteenth Century' in Nicholas Breyfogle, Abby Schrader, and Willard Sunderland (eds.), *Peopling the Russian Periphery: Borderland Coloniza-tion in Eurasian History* (Abingdon and New York: Routledge, 2007), 81–105. The editors and publishers have allowed me to use the passages in this book.

I would also like to thank Christopher Wheeler of Oxford University Press for inviting me to submit a proposal for this book, the series editors, in particular Simon Dixon, for their encouragement and advice, Stephanie Ireland and the production team at the Press, and copy-editor Elizabeth Stone of Bourchier for their assistance.

Anything of merit in what follows is due to those I have thanked. My contribution is the rest.

David Moon

St Petersburg

List of Illustrations

List of Maps

List of Tables

List of Abbreviations

DAOO	Derzhavnyi arkhiv Odes'koi oblasti, Odessa
ES	*Entsiklopedicheskii slovar'*, 82 vols (Spb: Brokgauz and Efron, 1890–1907)
GARO	Gosudarstvennyi arkhiv Rostovskoi oblasti, Rostov-on-Don
GASK	Gosudarstvennyi arkhiv Stavropol'skogo kraya, Stavropol'
GASO	Gosudarstvennyi arkhiv Samarskoi oblasti, Samara
IOPDMGI	*Istoricheskoe obozrenie pyatidesyatiletnei deyatel'nosti ministerstva gosudarstvennykh imushchestv, 1837–1887*, 5 vols (Spb, 1888)
IRGO	*Izvestiya Russkogo Geograficheskogo Obshchestva*
JGO	*Jahrbücher für Geschichte Osteuropas*
LZh	*Lesnoi zhurnal*
MDGSR	*Materialy dlya geografii i statistiki Rossii, sobrannye ofitserami general'nogo shtaba* (Spb, 1860–8)
PERSKh	*Polnaya entsiklopediya russkogo sel'skogo khozyaistva i soprikasayushchikhsya s nimi nauk*, 12 vols (Spb, 1900–12)
PFA RAN	Sankt-Peterburgskii filial arkhiva Rossiiskoi Akademii Nauk, St Petersburg
PSUPpR	*Polnoe sobranie uchenykh puteshestvii po Rossii*
PSZ	*Polnoe sobranie zakonov Rossiiskoi imperii*, 3 series: 1st series, 45 vols (Spb, 1830); 2nd series, 55 vols (Spb, 1825–81); 3rd series, 33 vols (Spb, 1881–1916)
RGIA	Rossiiskii Gosudarstvennyi Istoricheskii arkhiv, St Petersburg
RGVIA	Rossiiskii Gosudarstvennyi Voenno-Istoricheskii arkhiv, Moscow
RR	*Russian Review*
SOVDSK	*Sbornik oblastnogo Voiska Donskogo statisticheskogo komiteta*
SEER	*Slavonic and East European Review*
SKhiL	*Sel'skoe khozyaistvo i lesovodstvo* (continues *Zhurnal Ministerstva gosudarstvennykh imushchestv* from 1865)
Spb	St Petersburg
SR	*Slavic Review*
SSSpSG	*Sbornik statisticheskikh svedenii po Samarskoi gubernii. Otdel khozyaistvennoi statistiki* (Samara, 1883–90)
TESLD	*Trudy Ekspeditsii, snaryazhennoi Lesnym Departmentom, pod rukovodstvom professora Dokuchaeva* (Spb, 1894–8)
TVEO	*Trudy Vol'nogo ekonomicheskogo obshchestva*
VIET	*Voprosy istorii estestvoznaniya i tekhniki*

VRGO	*Vestnik Russkogo geograficheskogo obshchestva*
VSORI	*Voenno-statisticheskoe obozrenie Rossiiskoi imperii* (Spb, 1848–58)
ZhMGI	*Zhurnal Ministerstva gosudarstvennykh imushchestv*
ZIOSKhYuR	*Zapiski imperatorskogo obshchestva sel'skogo khozyaistva yuzhnoi Rossii*
ZRGO	*Zapiski Russkogo geograficheskogo obshchestva*

ABBREVIATIONS IN ARCHIVAL CITATIONS

f.	*fond* (collection)
op.	*opis'* (inventory)
d.	*delo* (file) (Russian)
sp.	*sprava* (file) (Ukrainian)
l.	*list* (folio)
ob.	*obrorot* (verso)

Glossary

This glossary contains both English translations or explanations of Russian terms and the original Russian for English translations that are used in the text. I have generally preferred English to Russian terms in the text.

Appanage Department	*Udel'nyi departament* (the government department that managed estates belonging to the imperial family)
ataman	Cossack headman, at all levels from settlement to Host. By the nineteenth century, the atamans of Cossack Hosts were the equivalents of provincial governors
Cossack Host	*Voiska* (the official term for the individual cossack groups, for example the Don Cossacks)
cossack settlement	*stanitsa*
district	*uezd* or *okrug* (sub-divisions of provinces and regions/cossack territories respectively)
governor	*gubernator*
gulley	*balka*
Ministry of State Domains	*Ministerstva gosudarstvennykh imushchestv* (the ministry founded in 1837 that was responsible for managing state lands. It was re-formed as the Ministry of Agriculture in 1894)
province	*guberniya*
ravine	*ovrag* or *buerak*
region (as an administrative unit)	*oblast'*
territory (as an administrative unit)	*zemlya* (the administrative term used until the late nineteenth century for regions inhabited largely by cossacks)
township	*volost'*
zapovednik	scientific nature reserve
zemstvo (pl. *zemstva*)	Elected councils set up at district and provincial levels from 1864

Russian Units of Measure

I have generally used the units of measure given in the sources, providing equivalents in imperial and metric measures where appropriate.

Russian	Imperial	Metric
arshin	28 inches	71 cm
chetvert' (dry measure)	5.77 bushels	210 litres
desyatina (state)	2.7 acres	1.1 hectares
pud	36 lb	16.38 kg
sazhen	7 feet	2.13 cm
vershok	1¾ inches	4.45 cm
versta (pl. *versty*)	0.66 miles	1.07 km

A Note on Transliteration and Proper Nouns

The British Standard system (without diacritical marks) has been used for transliterating Russian and Ukrainian into the Roman alphabet. I have anglicized the names of the tsars (e.g. Alexander not Aleksandr), and the main cities (e.g. St Petersburg not Sankt-Peterburg). With some exceptions, whenever possible, most other proper nouns are given in their original languages in the standard forms in use in the period covered by this book. Therefore, and without wishing to give offence, place names in present-day Ukraine have been given in the Russian forms in use at the time (e.g. Odessa not Odesa, Nikolaev, not Mykolaiv). In most cases, the names of people of non-Russian or Ukrainian origin are given in the original languages. Thus I have endeavoured to use the German spellings for the names of the many Germans, including Baltic Germans, who appear in this book. In the notes, however, authors' names are given in the language in which they appear in the publication. There are cases, therefore, when names are given in German in the text, but transliterated from a Russian spelling in the notes if I have cited a Russian edition of their works. For example, the Baltic German leader of one of the Russian Academy of Sciences expeditions of 1768–74 is referred to as Johann Anton Güldenstädt in the text, but sometimes appears as I. Ya. Gil'denshtedt in the notes. Likewise, the Mennonite elder Johann Cornies is spelled thus in the text, but when I have cited contemporary Russian translations of his work, as I. Kornis in the notes. I have used the German spelling, Molotschna, in preference to the Russian Molochna, for the colony where he lived in order to convey the extent to which it differed from the surrounding area.

Introduction

This book seeks to explain why, after worrying for a long time about the lack of trees on the steppes and how to rectify this omission, Russians went on instead to devise modern soil science, settlers on the steppes, in particular Mennonite communities, came up with techniques to conserve scarce moisture in the fertile black earth, and why this story eventually takes us to North America. These things happened because people moved from one type of environment to another, displaced the indigenous population, and replaced one way of using the natural resources with a different way. In the Russian Empire, from the early eighteenth century, growing numbers of agricultural settlers moved from regions with significant areas of forest, adequate supplies of water, but in many cases soil that was moderately fertile. They settled in the steppe region, which was predominantly grassland, with a semi-arid climate, periodic droughts, but extremely fertile soil. Many of the settlers and their descendants, however, supported themselves in much the same way that they or their forebears had done in their previous homelands: they ploughed up the land and cultivated grain. The people they displaced, in contrast, were mostly nomadic and grazed large herds of livestock on the grassland.

The central theme of this book is how, when people have moved between regions with such different natural conditions, but persisted with their previous way of life, there have been consequences both for themselves and the new environment they have settled in. In time, as the consequences for the new environment have become apparent, such people have engaged in critical reflection on the non-human world and the impact of human activity on that world. Some have gone on to develop conceptual and practical innovations for understanding and managing the relationship between the human and non-human worlds. In the process, they have raised questions about what we would now term 'conservation' and 'sustainability'. Russia's steppes, like settler societies in other parts of the world—such as parts of the Americas and Australasia—thus provide very fertile ground for investigating the ways in which people have understood the environment of which they are a part.[1]

---

[1] On the steppes as a 'settler empire', see Denis J. B. Shaw, *Russia in the Modern World: A New Geography* (Oxford, 1999), 4–9. The term 'settler society' has been used for regions where migrants of European origin became numerically dominant over indigenous peoples. See Tom Griffiths and Libby Robin (eds), *Ecology and Empire: Environmental History of Settler Societies* (Edinburgh, 1997).

In 1865, the Russian botanist L. Chernyaev wrote that the steppes were 'so special' that they were a 'separate world'. He identified their distinguishing characteristics as the absence of forests, the scarcity of running water, the aridity of the climate, the summer heatwaves, the winter cold, and the flatness of the landscape. He also noted the fertile black earth (*chernozem*).[2] A few years earlier, Ivan Palimpsestov had written: 'Our steppes, without forests and water, cannot be presented to migrants as . . . the United States, which is so rich with all the gifts of nature.'[3] Palimpsestov was a native of the steppes: born in Saratov on the Volga, he later moved to Odessa on the coast of the Black Sea. He was a tireless advocate of agricultural development in the steppe region. He pronounced his verdict on his native region to an anniversary meeting of the Southern Russian Agricultural Society in Odessa. By emphasizing the environmental constraints on agriculture in the region, Palimpsestov was using a rhetorical device to accentuate what the society had achieved. By highlighting the lack of forests and water, he was describing the steppe environment by drawing attention to what was not there.[4]

Writers in the Russian Empire regularly contrasted the steppes with the forested world they, or their forebears, were accustomed to. In 1870, S. A. Zabudskii, an agricultural specialist from Kazan', wrote:

Comparing the black-earth steppes in the south with lands in the north, we find that in the north, which is abundant in water and forests, the soil is lacking in productive force for grain crops, and requires artificial fertilization and intelligent labour; in the south, where the black earth is extremely productive, it lacks rain and moisture. There are no lakes, marshes, fast rivers . . . , dense or extensive forests from which evaporated moisture could irrigate the millions of *desyatiny* of steppes that have been sown with grain and suffer from drought in the spring and summer.[5]

Visitors from elsewhere in Europe also noted unfamiliar aspects of the steppe environment. At the start of the twentieth century, a professor from Breslau in south-eastern Germany (now Wrocław in Poland) cast his unaccustomed eye over the steppe. He noted that the 'southern Russian plain' was of great interest to the farmer, 'thanks to the peculiar quality of the soil, to which is attributed wondrous, inexhaustible fertility'. He continued:

[2] L. Chernyaev, 'Ocherki o stepnoi rastitel'nosti', *SKhiL*, 88 (1865), 2nd pagn, 33.
[3] I. Palimpsestov, 'Rech', proiznesennaya sekretarem obshchestva I. Palimpsestovym', *ZIOSKhYuR*, 12 (1856), appendix, 9. On Palimpsestov, see below, p. 52.
[4] In his classic study of another semi-arid grassland, Walter Prescott Webb considered how 'the white man' triumphed over an environment in which the timber and water the settlers had relied on in their previous homes were absent: *The Great Plains* ([1931], Lincoln, NE, 1981).
[5] S. A. Zabudskii, 'O zasukhakh na yuge i o sredstvakh k sokhraneniyu i uvelicheniyu syrosti v nashikh stepyakh', *TVEO*, 1 (1870), 8.

Undoubtedly . . . one's first impression is the endlessness brought about by the remarkable uniformity of the steppe. Travelling day and night in a train or . . . hundreds of *versty* by carriage, the eye of the traveller wanders across the plain, meeting neither hill nor forest, nothing that would limit the horizon.[6]

Settlers had moved south and south-east onto the steppes from the sixteenth century, if not earlier, but large-scale migration began in the eighteenth century. Most settlers were Slavs, mainly Russians and Ukrainians,[7] including cossacks,[8] peasants, and estate owners. Their previous homes had been to the north and north-west in the forest and forest-steppe regions. In the latter, areas of woodland were interspersed with grasslands. Many of the migrants from the forest-steppe had moved there, or were descended from migrants, from the forest region.[9] From the mid-eighteenth century, they were joined by foreign colonists, who had responded to invitations from the Russian government that offered them land and other privileges. Many came from German lands, which were also forested.[10]

While the natural conditions on the steppes contrasted to varying degrees with what the settlers had been accustomed to, the famed black earth—among the most fertile soils in the world—was a major attraction as it yielded bumper harvests in good years. In time, growing grain in the fertile soil became the largest part of the steppe economy, and arable fields came to occupy much of the land in the region. In seeking to exploit the fertile soil, however, the settlers had to endure recurring droughts that led to crop failures and, in the worst years, famines. Serious damage to crops was also done by pests, in particular burrowing rodents and insects, most dramatically locusts.[11] The main focus of this book, however, is on arable farming in conditions of relatively low and unreliable supplies of water.

[6] F. Gol'defleis, 'O yuzhno-russkoi stepi', *ZIOSKhYuR*, 5–6 (1905), 92, 98–9.

[7] The terms 'Ukraine' and 'Ukrainian' came into wider usage over the nineteenth century. I have consciously used them anachronistically for lack of appropriate alternatives.

[8] On cossack ethnicity, see Peter Holquist, 'From Estate to Ethnos: The Changing Nature of Cossack Identity in the Twentieth Century', in Nurit Schleifmann (ed.), *Russia at a Crossroads: Historical Memory and Political Practice* (London, 1998), 89–123.

[9] On the origins of migrants and settlement of the steppe region, see 'Obozrenie mer po pereseleniyu gosudarstvennykh krest'yan', *ZhMGI*, 52 (1854), 2nd pagn, 1–20; D. I. Bagalei, *Ocherki iz istorii kolonizatsii i byta stepnoi okrainy moskovskogo gosudarstva* (Moscow, 1887); Bagalei, 'Kolonizatsiya Novorossiiskogo kraya i pervye shagi ego po puti kul'tury', *Kievskaya starina*, 25 (1889), 27–55, 438–84 and 26 (1889), 110–48; M. K. Lyubavskii, *Obzor istorii russkoi kolonizatsii s drevneishikh vremen i do XX veka* (Moscow, 1996), 312–427; S. I. Bruk and V. M. Kabuzan, 'Migratsiya naseleniya v Rossii v XVIII–nachale XX veka (chislennost', struktura, geografiya)', *Istoriya SSSR*, 4 (1984), 41–59; David Moon, 'Peasant Migration and the Settlement of Russia's Frontiers, 1550–1897', *Historical Journal*, 40 (1997), 859–93.

[10] See 'Istoriya i statistika kolonii inostrannykh poselentsev v Rossii', *ZhMGI*, 52 (1854), 2nd pagn, 35–78; Roger P. Bartlett, *Human Capital: The Settlement of Foreigners in Russia, 1762–1804* (Cambridge, 1979).

[11] See, for example, G. Kulesha, 'Suslik i drugie vredniye gryzuny', *PERSKh*, ix (1905), 623–43; V. Morachevskii, 'Bor'ba zemstv s vragami polevodstva', *SKhiL*, 193 (1899), 183–208; 194 (1899), 193–225.

The growing settler population thus changed the prevailing land use in the steppe region from pasture, when the region had been the domain of pastoral nomads, to arable fields. In the process, they removed the native vegetation, mostly wild grasses, and felled much of the small areas of woodland that did exist in parts of the region. The settlers also drove away larger fauna, for example wild horses and saigaki (steppe antelopes).[12] Some contemporaries believed that the changes made by the settlers were having wider environmental consequences. The climate appeared to be becoming more variable, with more frequent droughts. Soil erosion, including dust storms, seemed to be increasing. Attempts were made to understand the processes of change, and to differentiate between human (anthropogenic) and non-human (autogenic) causes. It was easy to work out who was to blame for removing the wild grasses and chopping down trees; it was harder to understand whether the climate was changing or soil erosion increasing, and if so, who or what was to blame. Contemporaries also tried to work out what was to be done to deal with the changes and cope with the vagaries of the steppe environment from the perspective of arable farming. The key problem was the low and unreliable supplies of the water that was so critical for farmers.

For a book that purports to be about steppes, trees and forests will feature prominently. Indeed, to a far greater extent than I imagined when I embarked on this odyssey onto Russia's grasslands, the steppes will often be observed through the trees of Russia's forests. The fact that most of the settlers came from forested, or partly forested, environments is only part of the explanation. Perhaps a more significant factor is that forests have loomed large in Russian life, culture, and identity. A great deal has been written about Russia and forests. Russians used the products of the forest to meet a large number of their everyday needs. They used timber for many purposes, including building their homes and churches, making agricultural implements and carts, and fashioning household items from bowls to spoons. They used firewood for fuel, and the fruits, mushrooms, and wildlife of the forest to supplement their diets. Russians' lives were inconceivable without trees and forests.[13] Their importance was reflected in the ways Russians incorporated images of trees on the icons in their churches and conjured up spirits of the forest in their folklore.[14] For many people, the depictions of forests in Ivan

[12] For reasons of concision, consideration of the wildlife of the steppes is outside the scope of this study. For some discussion, see David Moon, 'The Russian Academy of Sciences Expeditions to the Steppes in the Late-Eighteenth Century', *SEER*, 88 (2010), 222–6.

[13] See, for example, Stephen Brain, *Song of the Forest: Russian Forestry and Stalinist Environmentalism, 1905–1953* (Pittsburgh, PA, 2011), 4–9; R. A. French, 'Russians and the Forest', in J. H. Bater and R. A. French (eds), *Studies in Russian Historical Geography*, 2 vols (London, 1983), i. 23–44; R. E. F. Smith, *Peasant Farming in Muscovy* (Cambridge, 1977), 47–79.

[14] See Valerie Kivelson, *Cartographies of Tsardom: The Land and its Meanings in Seventeenth-Century Russia* (Ithaca, NY, 2006), 110–12; Linda J. Ivanits, *Russian Folk Belief* (Armonk, NY, 1989), 64–70; N. A. Krinichnaya, *Krest'yanin i prirodnaya sreda v svete mifologii: bylichki, byval'shchiny i pover'ya russkogo severa* (Moscow, 2011), 17–74, 163–317.

Shishkin's landscape paintings of the late nineteenth century *are* Russia.[15] At around the same time as the artist was painting forests, the historian Vasilii Klyuchevskii was portraying their role on the canvas of Russia's history. He noted that until the mid-eighteenth century, the life of the majority of the Russian people was associated with the forest region where they lived. Until this time, the steppe intruded on Russian life only in malicious episodes such as incursions by the nomadic Tatars and cossack rebellions.[16] The foreign colonists who moved from German lands, moreover, also came from a landscape and culture in which forests played a key role.[17]

The large part played by forests in the life, and imagined life, of the Russian Empire can be illustrated by the children's book *Tales about God, Man, and Nature* published in St Petersburg in 1849. The authors were Vladimir Odoevskii, a writer and public figure, and Andrei Zablotskii-Desyatovskii, an official of the Ministry of State Domains. They were born, respectively, in Moscow, in the forest heartland of Russia, and Chernigov in northern Ukraine, in the forest-steppe region. The book portrays an idealized world of peasant villages with buildings and bridges built from wood, and with nearby orchards and forests. Trees feature routinely in the tales—apart from those about the life of Jesus in the 'Land of Israel (which is far from us in the East)'—in a world created by a god who, on the third day of creation, covered the earth with trees and grasses (in that order),[18] and placed people in a garden with trees bearing fruits.

The section of the book on natural history contains stories about nature walks a group of village children are taken on by their teacher or parish priest. The first walk is to the orchard. The forest proper is left for the fourth walk. The teacher describes the trees and explains their uses, such as for building houses, ships, and barges, and making tar and charcoal. Acorns are good feed for pigs and can be used to make a sort of coffee, and birch sap makes a tasty juice. Pine trees grow on sand, which is useful because they bind the loose soil. (This was a current issue and recurs later in this book.) The children's attention is also drawn to the berries and mushrooms that grow on the forest floor. The village children enjoy the walk in the woods so much that they ask if they can go back. They return early in the morning to hear the birds singing and see the wild animals. The children are taken on shorter, and less exciting, walks to see the crops in the fields and to the meadow. They are not, however, taken to see the steppe, where they could have admired the beautiful carpet of wild flowers or the iconic feather grass waving in

[15] See Christopher Ely, *This Meagre Nature: Landscape and National Identity in Imperial Russia* (DeKalb, IL, 2002), 199–206.

[16] V. O. Klyuchevskii, *Sochineniya v devyati tomakh*, 9 vols (Moscow, 1987–1990), i. 83–5; 'Les i step' v russkoi istorii po V. Klyuchevskomu', *LZh*, 35/4 (1905), 676–81.

[17] See Simon Schama, *Landscape and Memory* (London, 1996), 75–134.

[18] In Genesis 1:11–12, grass comes before fruit trees. See the text of the Old Church Slavonic Bible (a 1900 edition) at <http://lib.ru/HRISTIAN/BIBLIYA/old/gen.pdf> (accessed 16 April 2012).

the wind in the spring. The children learn about the forces of nature: they are warned not to shelter under trees during thunderstorms. No advice is given to the children on how to protect themselves during dust storms. A brief mention of droughts serves only to prompt a long explanation of clouds and rain.[19]

The third walk includes mountains, which would have been difficult for teachers and priests in most of Russia—which is a plain—to replicate. This betrays the fact that Odoevskii and Zablotskii-Desyatovskii adapted the book from a 'first school book' by Eduard Wüst. He was a protestant preacher from Württemberg, in southern Germany, where mountains, but not steppes, were nearby. (The Russian authors stated that they had revised the book to suit Russia, but did not seem to notice or consider important the absence of steppes.)[20] But the fact that the book was German in origin indicates the key role played by trees and forests in German as well as Russian culture. Wüst came to the Russian Empire in 1845 to serve as pastor to a German colonist community on the steppe not far from the Mennonite colony of Molotschna in Tauride province. He became acquainted with the Mennonites, who were well known to the Ministry of State Domains, which probably explains how his book came to Zablotskii-Desyatovskii's attention.[21]

Thus, many of the inhabitants of the steppe region in the period covered by this book, the officials who administered them, the specialists and scientists who advised them, and the wider intelligentsia who took an interest in them were, or were the descendants of, people for whom trees and forests were an important part of everyday life. When confronted with the steppes, many seem to have viewed the different environment as one bereft of trees. Even people who were natives of the steppes, such as Palimpsestov, were obsessed with trees and forests. Thus arboreal vegetation, and its scarcity or absence, had a profound influence on the way many of the authors of the sources for this book—mostly educated inhabitants of the Russian Empire—thought about the steppes.

THE STEPPE REGION

The steppe region of southern and south-eastern European Russia and Ukraine is part of a vast belt of semi-arid grassland that extends for over five thousand miles from the Hungarian *puszta*, across present-day Romania, Moldova, Ukraine, Russia, Kazakhstan, Mongolia, and into northern China. Since the eighteenth century, naturalists and scientists have researched the characteristic features of

---

[19] B. Odoevskii and A. Zablotskii, *Rasskazy o boge, cheloveke i prirode: chtenie dlya detei, doma i v shkole* (Spb, 1849), 5, 7, 16–18, 32, 83–4, 94–6, 105, 134, 139, 142, 145–7, 151–69, 178–204. On the authors, see *ES*, xlii (1897), 748–9; *ES*, xxiii (1894), 86.

[20] Odoevskii and Zablotskii, *Rasskazy*, vi. 178–204.

[21] James Urry, *None but Saints: The Transformation of Mennonite Life in Russia, 1789–1889* (Winnipeg, 1989), 169–72.

'steppes',[22] and developed a conception of a natural region that is defined by its native vegetation, climate, landscape, and soil. The main vegetation is, of course, wild grasses. The climate is temperate, that is, the mean annual temperature is cool, but continental, with hot summers and cold, freezing winters. It is also semi-arid: precipitation is low, averaging between 325 and 400 mm a year in most of the region outside the North Caucasus (where it is higher), and unreliable, varying sharply from year to year. More moisture evaporates, moreover, than falls in precipitation. The landscape is flat. The soil comprises various types of black earth (*chernozem*) and dark chestnut soils (*temno-kashtanovye pochvy*), with some areas of salty soils (*solontsy*). Over the period covered by this book, scientists came to understand that all these aspects of the steppe environment are interconnected.

Geobotanists have identified sub-zones inside the steppe region. The climate is more continental, and more arid, to the south and east. There are corresponding changes in the soil, from black earth to chestnut soils, and in vegetation, as feather grasses (*kovyl', Stipa*) and fescues (*tipchak, Festuca*) give way to worm-wood (*polyn', Artemisia*). In the more arid south and east of the steppes, the predominant types of vegetation are those capable of growing on more alkaline soils and better able to withstand shortages of moisture and droughts. Steppes have evolved, moreover, at certain latitudes. To the north and west, where the climate is wetter, is the forest-steppe, with areas of woodland and grassland. Further north, where more water is available, is the vast forest region that extends from the heartland of the Russian state around Moscow to the north and east and across Siberia. To the south and south-east of the steppes, in areas with more arid climates, are semi-deserts that merge into the deserts of Central Asia.[23]

Contrary to the views of some naturalists and scientists in the period covered by this book, the environment of the steppes encountered by the first waves of migrants was not a 'pristine' world that had evolved independently of human action. Later research confirmed the suspicions of some earlier specialists, such as Palimpsestov, that the treeless grassland was to some extent created by human activity. For many centuries, the indigenous, nomadic population burned the steppe to encourage the growth of fresh grasses for their herds of livestock to graze on. The combined effects of fire and grazing contributed to the evolution of the grassland, restricting the spread of trees and shrubs from those parts of the landscape where they grew naturally.[24]

---

[22] I have generally used the term 'naturalists' for specialists working in the eighteenth and early nineteenth centuries, and 'scientists' for those active from the mid-nineteenth century.

[23] See A. A. Chibilev, *Stepi Severnoi Evrazii: ekologo-geograficheskii ocherk i bibliografiya* (Ekaterinburg, 1998); A. A. Chibilev and O. A. Grosheva, *Ocherki po istorii stepevedeniya* (Ekaterinburg, 2004), 5–106; E. M. Lavrenko, Z. V. Karamysheva, and R. I. Nikulina, *Stepi Evrazii* (Leningrad, 1991), 12–21, 26–32. For a classic work on landscape science, see L. S. Berg, *Natural Regions of the U.S.S.R.*, trans. O. A. Titelbaum (New York, 1950).

[24] See C. V. Kremenetski, 'Human Impact on the Holocene Vegetation of the South Russian Plain', in John Chapman and Pavel Dolukhanov (eds), *Landscapes in Flux: Central and Eastern Europe in Antiquity* (Oxford, 1997), 275–87; M. N. Stroganova (ed.), *Zapovedniki evropeiskoi chasti*

The region analysed in this book is the steppes in the European part of the Russian Empire. This comprised the region below the southern boundary of the forest-steppe in the basins—from west to east—of the rivers Dnestr, Bug, Dnepr, Don, Volga, and Ural, together with the North Caucasus, which is drained by the Kuban' and Terek rivers. The southern boundary of the steppe region was the northern and north-eastern shores of the Black Sea, the Sea of Azov, and the Caspian Sea, and the Caucasus mountains. From the nineteenth century, many schemes have been devised to divide the Russian Empire (and later the Soviet Union and post-Soviet states) into regions. Most have relied on a combination of environmental and economic factors.[25] The region that is the subject of this book is defined largely by its environment (see Map 1).

The administrative boundaries of provinces (*gubernii*), regions (*oblasti*), and cossack territories (*zemli*) in the Russian Empire did not coincide exactly with environmental boundaries. According to the administrative borders of the first half of the nineteenth century, the steppes in the region covered by this book were situated wholly or partly in—again from west to east—the provinces of Kherson, Tauride, and Ekatinerinoslav (known as 'New Russia', today's southern Ukraine); the Don Cossack territory (from 1870 the Don region); and the Caucasus (later Stavropol') province in the North Caucasus; Saratov province on the Volga; and Orenburg province towards the southern Urals. Changes in administrative boundaries led to the creation in 1851 of Samara province on the left, or eastern, bank of the Volga from parts of Saratov and Orenburg provinces, and in 1860, the Kuban' and Terek regions from the western and south-eastern parts of Stavropol' province respectively. There were areas of forest-steppe in northern Saratov and Samara provinces. The wooded foothills of the Caucasus mountains were in southern Stavropol' province and the Terek region. The southern end of the densely forested Ural mountains were in Orenburg province. Moreover, there were areas of steppe in Bessarabia (today's Moldova), and southern Podolia, Kiev, Poltava, Khar'kov (before 1835 known as Slobodsko-Ukraine), and Voronezh provinces. In Astrakhan' province, on the lower reaches of the Volga, the steppe merged into semi-desert (see Map 2).[26]

RSFSR: ii (Moscow, 1989), 26–7; I. Palimpsestov, *Stepi yuga Rossii byli-li iskoni vekov stepami i vozmozhno-li oblesit' ikh?* (Odessa, 1890).

[25] See Judith Pallot and Denis J. B. Shaw, *Landscape and Settlement in Romanov Russia, 1613–1917* (Oxford, 1990), 112–35; Nailya Tagirova, 'Mapping the Empire's Economic Regions from the Nineteenth to the Early Twentieth Centuries', in Jane Burbank and David L. Ransel (eds), *Russian Empire: Space, People, Power, 1700–1930* (Bloomington, IN, 2007), 125–38; Marina Loskutova, '"Nauka oblastnogo masshtaba": ideya estestvennykh raionov v rossiiskoi geografii i istoki kraevedcheskogo dvizheniya 1920-kh gg.', *Ab Imperio*, 2 (2011), 83–122.
[26] See P. Semenov, *Geografichesko-statisticheskii slovar' Rossiiskoi imperii*, 5 vols (Spb, 1863–85), i. 148–53; ii. 111–16; iii. 673–81; iv. 408–18, 472–83, 723–9; v. 399–406; V. P. Semenov (ed.), *Rossiya: Polnoe geograficheskoe opisanie nashego otechestva*, 11 vols (Spb, 1899–1914), ii. *Sredne-russkaya chernozemnaya oblast'*, map facing 32, 57; vii. *Malorossiya*, map facing 24; xiv. *Novorossiya i Krym*, map facing 48, 72–7. On administrative boundaries, see V. E. Den, *Naselenie Rossii po V revizii*, i (Moscow, 1902), 163–83.

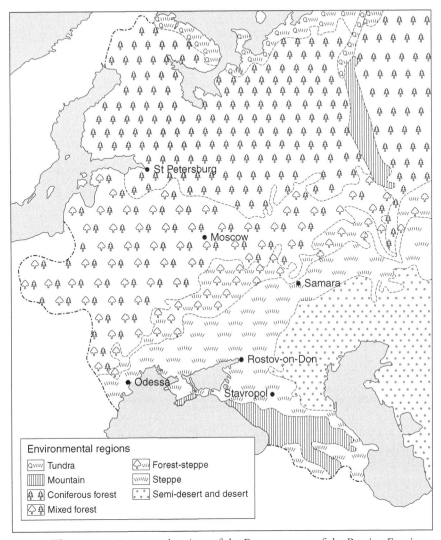

Map 1. The main environmental regions of the European part of the Russian Empire

Adapted from Judith Pallot and Denis J. B. Shaw, *Landscape and Settlement in Romanov Russia, 1613–1917* (Oxford and New York, 1990), xv. Used with the permission of the authors and copyright holders.

Map 2. Administrative borders in the European part of the Russian Empire (late nineteenth century)

Adapted from Gregory Freeze (ed.), *Russia: A History* (Oxford, 1997), 427.

THE RUSSIAN CONQUEST AND INTEGRATION
OF THE STEPPE REGION

The Russian conquest of the steppe region began in earnest in the 1550s, when Tsar Ivan the Terrible defeated the Tatar Khanates of Kazan' and Astrakhan'. Moscow thus gained control of the entire length of the river Volga that flowed from the forest heartland through the steppes to the Caspian Sea. From the late sixteenth century, Moscow also extended its power into the North Caucasus, and east across the steppes to the Ural mountains and beyond, in time towards Central Asia. But for a long time expansion across the steppes to the Black Sea to the south was blocked by the Khanate of Crimea. The Crimean khans controlled not just the Crimean peninsula, but also the steppes to the north and north-east of the Black Sea and Sea of Azov. The Khan was a vassal of the Ottoman Sultan, who proved more than a match for the Russian tsars into the eighteenth century. Peter the Great took the fortress of Azov on the delta of the river Don in 1696, but held it only until 1711. Peter's successors inched their way across the steppes to the Black Sea. The decisive victories over the Ottomans were achieved by Catherine the Great in wars of 1768–74 and 1787–92. In between, in 1783, Catherine annexed the Khanate of Crimea. She sent Grigorii Potemkin to develop her new southern lands and visited them herself in 1787. The Russian conquests were part of the partition of the Eurasian steppes between the Russian, Ottoman, Persian, and Chinese empires.

The Russian state did not conquer the steppes by military force alone, but used a variety of methods to annex, incorporate, and subjugate parts of the region and its inhabitants. It took part in steppe politics, manipulating rivalries between the various peoples. The tsars periodically allied with a particular people, for example the Kalmyks or Nogai, against others, such as the Bashkirs, Kazakhs, and even rebellious cossacks. The Russian state co-opted the elites of indigenous peoples by granting them noble status in return for oaths of allegiance, tribute, and service. A series of defensive lines was built right across the Russian steppe frontier. In the mid-seventeenth century, the Russian authorities constructed the Belgorod and Simbirsk lines along the southern boundary of the forest-steppe. The initial purpose of the lines was to defend the Russian heartland and population against raids by the Crimean Tatars and steppe nomads. Over time, the lines became starting points for further expansion onto the steppes. New lines were built ever further south and east, across the North Caucasus and the steppes of today's Kazakhstan. Behind the lines, settlers moved in and cultivated the newly secured land.

These issues are explored by Michael Khodarkovsky in his book on Russia's steppe frontier. He argued that 'Russia's expansion to the south and east' was a policy of 'deliberate aggrandizement and conscious transformation of the new territories and subjects'. He compared Russia's 'making of a colonial empire' on the steppes with the earlier Spanish reconquest of the Iberian Peninsula. Both involved encounters between the Christian and Islamic worlds, but Russia's steppe frontier had also separated settled and nomadic populations, agriculture and herding, and a sovereign state and tribal confederations. Khodarkovsky did not, however, consider the environmental dimension of the steppe frontier.[27]

'Colonization and empire on the Russian steppe' is the subject of Willard Sunderland's monograph, which focuses on 'empire building, state building, society building, and nation building' on the steppe. His analysis involved bureaucrats and cartographers, Slav and foreign colonists, cossacks and steppe nomads, that is, colonizers and colonized. He explored the relationship between the centre and periphery, the long ambiguity over whether the steppes were part of or distinct from central Russia. Sunderland acknowledged the importance of the steppes as a distinct environment, and considered discussions of human impact on that environment. But at the centre of his analysis were the people who lived in the steppe region and thought about its identity.[28]

The population of the steppe region, both indigenous and settler, has been the subject of much recent research on particular groups, for example: cossacks,[29] Kalmyk nomads,[30] peasants,[31] and German and Mennonite colonists.[32] Two recent books, by John R. Staples and Leonard Friesen, have traced how these different groups interacted, how settlers adapted to the steppe environment, and how the society and economy of the region developed from the late eighteenth

[27] Michael Khodarkovsky, *Russia's Steppe Frontier: The Making of a Colonial Empire, 1500–1800* (Bloomington, IN, 2002), 2–3 (quotations). See also Brian L. Davis, *Warfare, State and Society on the Black Sea Steppe, 1500–1700* (London, 2007). For a classic study, see William H. McNeill, *Europe's Steppe Frontier, 1500–1800* (Chicago, 1964). For the perspective from the other end of the Eurasian steppe, see Peter C. Perdue, *China Marches West: The Qing Conquest of Central Eurasia* (Cambridge, MA, 2005).

[28] Willard Sunderland, *Taming the Wild Field: Colonization and Empire on the Russian Steppe* (Ithaca, NY, 2004), especially 3–5, 172–3, 202–6.

[29] Thomas M. Barrett, *At the Edge of Empire: The Terek Cossacks and the North Caucasus Frontier, 1700–1860* (Boulder, CO, 1999); Brian J. Boeck, *Imperial Boundaries: Cossack Communities and Empire-Building in the Age of Peter the Great* (Cambridge, 2009); Shane O'Rourke, *Warriors and Peasants: The Don Cossacks in Late Imperial Russia* (New York, 2000).

[30] Michael Khodarkovsky, *Where Two Worlds Met: The Russian State and the Kalmyk Nomads, 1600–1771* (Ithaca, NY, 1992).

[31] See Brian Boeck, 'Containment vs Colonization: Muscovite Approaches to Settling the Steppes', in Nicholas Breyfogle, Abby Schrader, and Willard Sunderland (eds), *Peopling the Russian Periphery: Borderland Colonization in Eurasian History* (Abingdon, 2007), 41–60; Willard Sunderland, 'Peasants on the Move: State Peasant Resettlement in Imperial Russia, 1805–1830s', *RR*, 52 (1993), 472–85; Willard Sunderland, 'An Empire of Peasants: Empire-Building, Interethnic Interaction, and Ethnic Stereotyping in the Rural World of the Russian Empire, 1800–1850s,' in Jane Burbank and David L. Ransel (eds), *Imperial Russia: New Histories for the Empire* (Bloomington, IN, 1998), 174–98.

[32] See, for example, Fred C. Koch, *The Volga Germans in Russia and the Americas, from 1763 to the Present* (University Park, PA, 1977); Dmytro Myeshkov, *Die Schwarzmeerdeutschen und ihre Welten, 1781–1871* (Essen, 2008); Urry, *None but Saints*. I am grateful to Professor Urry for his advice and for a copy of an unpublished manuscript on Mennonite agriculture by David G. Rempel.

century. Staples offered a micro-study of the Molochna river basin in eastern Tauride province. Friesen presented a broader interpretation of New Russia that paid attention to the growth of industry and cities, as well as agriculture. Both books highlight the significant part played by Mennonites.[33] Many earlier studies, especially those by Soviet historians, focused on the settlement and economic development of the region.[34] The environment is implicit or explicit in most of these studies, but in this book the environmental history of the steppe region is at the centre of the stage.

THE ENVIRONMENT IN RUSSIAN HISTORY

In offering an environmental history of the steppe region, this book makes a contribution to a wider body of writing on the environment in Russian history. For a long time, such discussions drew heavily on the environmental-determinist views of nineteenth-century historians Sergei Solov'ev and Vasilii Klyuchevskii.[35] These views persisted among western scholars,[36] and were revived by Russian historians, for example Leonid Milov, in the 1990s.[37] While there is no doubt that on the steppes, and elsewhere, the natural environment has played a role in shaping the lives of the people who have lived there—or rather, people have taken the environment into account when making decisions about their lives— crude environmental-determinist interpretations are not sustainable.[38] Another trend in writing on the environmental history of this part of the world has been to emphasize the enormous ecological damage caused by the Soviet regime, including such disasters as the explosion at the Chernobyl' nuclear power station

[33] John R. Staples, *Cross-Cultural Encounters on the Ukrainian Steppe: Settling the Molochna Basin, 1783–1861* (Toronto, 2003); Leonard Friesen, *Rural Revolutions in Southern Ukraine: Peasants, Nobles, and Colonists, 1774–1905* (Cambridge, MA, 2009).

[34] See, for example, E. I. Druzhinina, *Severnoe Prichernomor'e v 1775–1800 gg.* (Moscow, 1959); E. I. Druzhinina, *Yuzhnaya Ukraina v 1800–1825 gg.* (Moscow, 1970); E. I. Druzhinina, *Yuzhnaya Ukraina v period krizisa feodalizma 1825 1860 gg.* (Moscow, 1981); A. P. Pronshtein, *Zemlya Donskaya v XVIII veke* (Rostov-on-Don, 1961); A. P. Pronshtein (ed.), *Don i stepnoe Predkavkaz'e: XVIII-pervaya polovina XIX veka: Zaselenie i khozyaistvo* (Rostov-on-Don, 1977); P. A. Shatskii, 'Sel'skoe khozyaistvo Predkavkaz'ya v 1861–1905 gg.', in S. A. Chekmenev (ed.), *Nekotorye voprosy sotsial'no-ekonomicheskogo razvitiya yugo-vostochnoi Rossii* (Stavropol', 1970), 3–320. See also P. I. Savel'ev, *Puti agrarnogo kapitalizma v Rossii: XIX vek (Po materialam Povolzh'ya)* (Samara, 1994).

[35] S. M. Solov'ev, 'O vliyanii prirody russkoi gosudarstvennoi oblasti i na ee istoriyu', *Otechestvennye zapiski*, 69 (1850), 2nd pagn, 229–44; on Klyuchevskii, see n. 16. See also Mark Bassin, 'Turner, Solov'ev, and the "Frontier Hypothesis": The Nationalist Significance of Open Spaces', *Journal of Modern History*, 65 (1993), 473–511.

[36] See, for example, Richard Pipes, *Russia under the Old Regime*, 2nd edn (London, 1995), 1–24.

[37] L. V. Milov, *Velikorusskii pakhar' i osobennosti rossiiskogo istoricheskogo protsessa* (Moscow, 1998).

[38] See David Moon, 'Review of Milov', *Kritika*, 3 (2002), 537–45; David Moon, 'Land and Environment', in Simon Dixon (ed.), *The Oxford Handbook of Modern Russian History* (Oxford, forthcoming).

in northern Ukraine and the drying up of the Aral Sea in Central Asia in the late twentieth century.[39] The pioneering environmental historian of Russia, Douglas Weiner, has traced the origins of the attitudes that led to such damage to deep into Russia's pre-Soviet history.[40] On the other hand, as Weiner has also argued, from the late nineteenth century, Russian scientists were among the pioneers of the theory and practice of nature conservation.[41] The network of scientific nature reserves (*zapovedniki*) throughout the lands of the former Soviet Union and Russian Empire—some of which I visited while researching this book—have their origins in the work of Vasilii Dokuchaev and other Russian scientists in the late nineteenth and early twentieth centuries.[42] Contemporary notions of 'sustainable development', moreover, can be traced back to the work of Russian scientists such as Dokuchaev.[43]

This book seeks to mediate between these differing approaches in offering a contribution to the growing body of research on the environmental history of the vast areas of Eurasia that have been ruled by Russian, Soviet, and post-Soviet states.[44] Important work on topics related to this book has been produced by British historical geographer Denis Shaw individually,[45] and in collaboration with Judith Pallot,[46] and Jonathan Oldfield.[47] Pioneering studies of the environmental history of parts of the forest-steppe and steppe regions have been produced by Zack Deal, Ihor Stebelsky, Tat'yana Nevskaya, and Andrei

[39] See, for example, Murray Feshbach and A. Friendly, *Ecocide in the USSR: Health and Nature under Siege* (London, 1992); Murray Feshbach, *Ecological Disaster: Cleaning up the Hidden Legacy of the Soviet Regime* (New York, 1995); Paul Josephson, 'Industrial Deserts: Industry, Science and the Destruction of Nature in the Soviet Union', *SEER*, 85 (2007), 294–321.

[40] Douglas Weiner, 'The Genealogy of the Soviet and Post-Soviet Landscape of Risk', in Arja Rosenholm and Sari Autio-Sarasmo (eds), *Understanding Russian Nature* (Helsinki, 2005), 209–36.

[41] Douglas R. Weiner, *Models of Nature: Ecology, Conservation and Cultural Revolution in Soviet Russia*, 2nd edn ([1988], Pittsburgh, PA, 2000); Douglas Weiner, *A Little Corner of Freedom: Russian Nature Protection from Stalin to Gorbachev* (Berkeley, CA, 1999).

[42] Feliks Shtilmark, *The History of Russian Zapovedniks, 1895–1995*, trans. G. H. Harper (Edinburgh, 2003).

[43] Jonathan D. Oldfield and Denis J. B. Shaw, 'Revisiting Sustainable Development: Russian Cultural and Scientific Traditions and the Concept of Sustainable Development', *Area*, 34 (2002), 391–400.

[44] For a survey of this literature, see Andy Bruno, 'Russian Environmental History: Directions and Potentials', *Kritika*, 8 (2007), 635–50. For a pioneering work, see A. V. Dulov, *Geograficheskaya sreda i istoriya Rossii: konets XV–seredina XIX v.* (Moscow, 1983).

[45] See, for example, Denis J. B. Shaw, 'Southern Frontiers of Muscovy, 1550–1700', in Bater and French (eds), *Studies*, i. 118–42; Denis Shaw, 'The Settlement of European Russia during the Romanov Period', *Soviet Geography*, 30/3 (1989), 207–28; Denis Shaw, 'Settlement and Landholding on Russia's Southern Frontier in the Early Seventeenth Century', *SEER*, 69 (1991), 232–56; Denis Shaw, 'Mapmaking, Science and State Building in Russia before Peter the Great', *Journal of Historical Geography*, 31 (2005), 409–29.

[46] Pallot and Shaw, *Landscape and Settlement*.

[47] See, for example, Denis J. B. Shaw and Jonathan Oldfield, 'Landscape Science: A Russian Geographical Tradition', *Annals of the Association of American Geographers*, 97/1 (2007), 111–26.

Pushkarenko.[48] Shane O'Rourke and Thomas Barrett gave serious consideration to environmental history in their monographs on cossacks.[49] The environment plays a key role in an innovative study of Nizhnii Novgorod province—which straddled the forest and forest-steppe regions—by Catherine Evtuhov.[50] A new generation of scholars is producing original studies that approach the environmental history of the Eurasian steppes from various angles, including the history of science.[51]

The growing body of research to which this book contributes goes some way to answering calls for more work on Russian environmental history by specialists on other parts of the world. In 2003, John McNeill pointed out that 'the sweep of Russian frontier expansion' is 'cry[ing] out . . . for the attention of environmental historians'.[52] A few years later, Joachim Radkau asserted that 'Russian environmental history is still largely unexplored'. He added, perceptively, that this was paradoxical, since Russia had been the 'birthplace of modern soil study'.[53] Russia's steppe frontier with its fertile soil offers an ideal location,

[48] Zack Deal, *Serf and State Peasant Agriculture: Kharkov Province, 1842–1861* (New York, 1981); I. Stebelsky, 'Agriculture and Soil Erosion in the European Forest-Steppe', in Bater and French (eds), *Studies*, i. 45–63; T. A. Nevskaya, 'Kul'tura zemledeliya v XIX–nach. XX v. i ekologiya', in A. A. Anikeev (ed.), *Istoriya i ekologiya: Mezhvuzovskii sbornik nauchnykh trudov* (Stavropol', 1994), 61–70; A. A. Pushkarenko, 'Prirodookhrannaya deyatel'nost' v Oblasti Voiska Donskogo vo vtoroi polovine XIX–nachale XX vv.' (Candidate dissertation, Rostov State University, 2000); A. A. Pushkarenko, G. P. Dolzhenko, and Ya. A. Perekhodov, *Okhrany prirody v oblasti voiska donskogo (vtoraya polovina XIX—nachalo XX v.)* (Rostov-on-Don, 2000.)

[49] Barrett, *At the Edge of Empire*, 57–83; O'Rourke, *Warriors and Peasants*, 63–101.

[50] Catherine Evtuhov, *Portrait of a Russian Province: Economy, Society, and Civilization in Nineteenth-Century Nizhnii Novgorod* (Pittsburgh, PA, 2011).

[51] See, for example, Sarah Cameron, 'The Hungry Steppe: Soviet Kazakhstan and the Kazakh Famine, 1921–1934' (Ph.D. dissertation, Yale University, 2010) (I am grateful to Dr Cameron for a copy of her dissertation); Ian Campbell, 'Knowledge and Power on the Kazakh Steppe, 1845–1917' (Ph.D. dissertation, University of Michigan, 2011); Marc Elie, 'Dessicated Steppes: Droughts, Erosion, Climate Change, and the Crisis of Soviet Agriculture, 1960s–1980s', unpublished paper presented at a conference on 'Eurasian Environments: Nature and Ecology in Eurasian History', Ohio State University, 16–17 September 2011 (I am grateful to Dr Elie for permission to cite his unpublished paper); Anastasia A. Fedotova, 'The Origins of the Russian Chernozem Soil (Black Earth): Franz Joseph Ruprecht's "Geo-Botanical Researches into the Chernozem" of 1866', trans. David Moon, *Environment and History*, 16 (2010), 271–94 (first published as A. A. Fedotova, 'Geobotanicheskie issledovaniya o chernozeme F. I. Ruprekhta', *VIET*, 1 (2008), 22–34); A. A. Fedotova, 'Izuchenie stepnoi rastitel'nosti evropeiskoi Rossii (1850–1917): stanovlenie geobotaniki' (Candidate dissertation, St Petersburg branch of the Institute of the History of Science and Technology of the Russian Academy of Sciences, 2012) (I am grateful to Dr Fedotova for providing me with a copy of her dissertation); Nina Sergeevna Tsintsadze, 'Demograficheskie i ekologicheskie aspekty posledstviya krest'yanskoi reformy 1861 goda v Tambovskoi gubernii', *Vestnik Tambovskogo Gosudarstvennogo Universiteta*, 87/7 (2010), 240–7 (I am grateful to Dr Tsintsadze for sending me a copy of this and other articles).

[52] J. R. McNeill, 'Observations on the Nature and Culture of Environmental History', *History and Theory*, 40 (2003), 30, 41–2.

[53] Joachim Radkau, *Nature and Power: A Global History of the Environment*, trans. Thomas Dunlap (New York, 2008), 183.

therefore, for a study that seeks to help fill the lacunae identified by McNeill and Radkau.

THE STEPPE REGION: SETTLEMENT AND LAND USE

Large-scale agricultural settlement of the steppe region took off in the eighteenth century. As a result of mass migration and the high fertility of the settlers, the region's population increased considerably between the early eighteenth and early twentieth centuries. Changes in administrative borders and in the ways the population was counted, as well as doubts over the reliability of some of the data, mean it is possible to trace only general trends (see Table I.1.)

The total population of the steppe region in the European part of the Russian Empire, around 90 per cent of whom lived in rural areas, increased more than eightfold over the eighteenth century, nearly trebled over the first half of the nineteenth century, and trebled again by 1914. The rate of growth far exceeded that of the empire as a whole, and was part of the relocation of the centre of gravity of the population from the old forest heartland to the south. Boris Mironov calculated that in 1719, 2.6 per cent of the population of the European part of the Russian state lived in the steppe region. By 1795, this had more than doubled to 6.7 per cent. It increased twofold again over the first half of the nineteenth century, and had reached 21.2 per cent by 1914.[54] The permanent population was supplemented by large numbers of seasonal migrant labourers who came to work on commercial farms in the region each year.[55]

The dramatic increase in the rural population of the steppe region was accompanied by an equally dramatic change in land use. A primarily pastoral, and partly nomadic, economy was replaced by settled, arable farming. Pasture was ploughed up and transformed into fields of grain. The two developments went hand in hand as growing grain generates several times more calories per unit of land than livestock husbandry, and many times more than nomadic pastoralism. Thus, the change in land use to arable farming meant that the region could support a far larger, and settled, population. The nomads were compelled to settle or to leave.

---

[54] B. N. Mironov, *Blagosostoyanie naseleniya i revolyutsiii v imperskoi Rossii: XVIII–nachalo XX veka* (Moscow, 2010), 334–40.

[55] See David Moon, 'Peasant Migration, the Abolition of Serfdom and the Internal Passport System in the Russian Empire, *c.*1800–1914', in David Eltis (ed.), *Free and Coerced Migration: Global Perspectives* (Stanford, CA, 2002), 339–45, 354–7.

Table I.1 Population of the Steppe region of the European part of the Russian Empire, 1719–1914

Year	Total	Index
1719	380,000	100
1762	1,385,000	364
1795	3,120,000	821
1850	8,442,000	2,221
1897	14,051,000	3,698
1914	25,296,000	6,657

NB Figures are not strictly comparable due to changes in administrative borders.
1719–1850: figures are for the provinces\territories of Kherson, Tauride, Ekaterinoslav, Don Cossacks, the Caucasus, the Black Sea (later Kuban') Cossacks, Saratov, Astrakhan, and Orenburg, inside borders of 1806.
1897: figures for the provinces\territories of Kherson, Tauride, Ekaterinoslav, Don, Stavropol', Kuban', Terek, Saratov, Samara, Astrakhan, and Orenburg, in their 1897 borders.
1914: figures are for the same provinces and territories as 1897.
Figures for the total population for 1719–1850 are the male population doubled.

Sources: 1719–1850: V. M. Kabuzan, *Izmeneniya v razmeshchenii naseleniya Rossii v XVIII– pervoi polovine XIX v. (Po materialam revizii)* (Moscow, 1971), 59, 63, 67, 107, 111, 115, 155, 159, 163; 1897: N. A. Troinitskii (ed.), *Obshchii svod po imperii rezul'tatov razrabotki dannykh pervoi vseobshchei perepisi naseleniya, proizvedennoi 28 Yanvarya 1897 goda*, 2 vols (Spb, 1905), i. 165–71, 174–7; 1914: B. N. Mironov, *Blagosostoyanie naseleniya i revolyutsiii v imperskoi Rossii: XVIII–nachalo XX veka* (Moscow, 2010), 337.

It is important not to make too sharp a distinction, however, between nomadic pastoralism by the indigenous population and settled, arable farming by the incomers. There was a very long history of arable farming on the steppes. Writing in the fifth century BCE, Herodotus described 'agricultural Scythian tribes' growing grain on the steppes to the north of the Black Sea. The grain was exported via ancient Greek colonies, such as Khersones and Olbia.[56] Arable farming continued for many centuries within a largely pastoral economy. The Venetian merchant Josaphat Barbaro, who visited the Genoese colony of Tana on the delta of the river Don in the mid-fifteenth century, described nomads growing grain, and reaping abundant harvests, on the steppe.[57] Ploughed, arable fields in the Khanate of Crimea were noted in a Russian survey of 1627.[58]

[56] Herodotus, *The Histories*, trans. Aubrey de Selincourt, further revised edn (London, 2003), 246. See also Pavel M. Dolukhanov, 'Alternative Revolutions: Hunter-Gatherers, Farmers and Stock-Breeders in the Northwestern Pontic Area', in Katie Boyle, Colin Renfrew, and Marsha Levine (eds), *Ancient Interactions: East and West in Eurasia* (Cambridge, 2000), 13–24.
[57] Iosafat Barbaro and Ambrodzho Kontarini, *Barbaro i Kontarini o Rossii: k istorii italo-russkikh svyazei v XV v.*, trans. E. Ch. Skrzhinskaya (Leningrad, 1971), 150.
[58] K. N. Serbina (ed.), *Kniga Bol'shomu chertezhu* (Moscow, 1950), 65.

The early Slav settlers were slow to take up arable farming. John Perry, an Englishman hired by Peter the Great to build a canal between the Don and Volga rivers in 1698, wrote that 'by reason of the incursions of the . . . Tatars, the Russes do not plough and sow in these Parts (though the Land is extremely rich), but have every Year Corn brought down to them by the River Wolga'.[59] Livestock husbandry was an important part of the settlers' economy into the nineteenth century. In 1805, the governor of Tauride province noted that the main occupation of Ukrainian settlers was raising livestock. They did not sow grain every year, and were inhibited from doing so by spring droughts.[60] In the late eighteenth century, however, the leaders of expeditions sent across the steppes by the Russian Academy of Sciences noted Ukrainian settlers and German colonists growing grain.[61] The cossacks were very slow to take up grain cultivation, which they considered to be beneath them. It became an important part of their economy, replacing livestock, only in the nineteenth century.[62]

Arable farming spread gradually among the settlers. It took them time to adapt the ways of farming the land they brought with them to the new environment. The traditional Russian horse-drawn wooden plough (*sokha*) could not cut through the matted roots of the steppe grasses and break the sod. In the seventeenth century, Ukrainian settlers brought their heavier, wheeled plough (*plug*) that was pulled by oxen, which was taken up by other settlers. Some adopted the plough (*saban*) used by local Tatars that may have dated back to the ancient Greeks.[63] The settlers found that while some of their crops, such as oats, did not grow well in the new environment, others flourished. Those brought by Ukrainian settlers from the forest-steppe region and Moldavians from the west, such as types of spring wheat and maize, were well adapted to the steppe environment. Settlers also adopted varieties of spring wheat that were already grown locally, in particular girka and arnautka, which became the mainstays of steppe agriculture. Arnautka, which could tolerate drought and winds, was reputed to be the most ancient wheat variety in the region.[64] Thus the settlers, especially in the early decades, drew to some extent on the experience of the

[59] John Perry, *The State of Russia, under the Present Czar* (London, 1716), 88.
[60] RGIA, f.1281, 1804–10, op.11, d.131, l.1.
[61] I. Ya. Gil'denshtedt, 'Dnevnik puteshestviya v Yuzhnuyu Rossiyu akademika S. Peterburgskoi Akademii Nauk Gil'denshtedta v 1773–1774 g.', *Zapiski Imperatorskogo Odesskogo obshchestva istorii i drevnosti*, 11 (1879), 218; I. I. Lepekhin, 'Zapiski Puteshestviya Akademika Lepekhina', *Polnoe sobranie uchenykh puteshestvii po Rossii*, iii (Spb, 1821), 403.
[62] See Pronshtein, *Zemlya Donskaia*, 75–86; Pronshtein (ed.), *Don i stepnoe Predkavkaz'e*, 72–89, 100–26; O'Rourke, *Warriors and Peasants*, 64–9; Barrett, *At the Edge of Empire*, 89–108.
[63] A. Skal'kovskii, *Opyt statisticheskogo opisaniya Novorossiiskogo kraya*, 2 vols (Odessa, 1850–3), ii. 65–6; 'O khlebnoi promyshlennosti v sele Ekaterinovke, Samarskoi gubernii', *SKhiL*, 46 (1853), 148; Deal, *Serf*, 331–3, 395. The classic study is Dm. Zelenin, *Russkaya sokha: ee istoriya i vidy* (Vyatka, 1908).
[64] Andrei Bolotov, 'Primechaniya o khlebopashestve voobshche', *TVEO*, 9 (1768), 45; I. Demol', 'Sel'skoe khozyaistvo v Novorossiiskom krae', *ZhMGI*, 16 (1845), 2nd pagn, 208–15; Skal'kovskii, *Opyt*, 77–88.

indigenous population in the balancing of their activities between raising live-stock and growing grain, the implements they used, and the crops they culti-vated.

There were other factors behind the settlers' decisions over whether to raise livestock or grow grain. From the 1840s, there was a big increase in demand for grain, especially wheat, from abroad. In part this was due to the abolition of the Corn Laws in Britain and reductions in tariffs on imported grain in other European countries. As a result, settlers embarked on a major plough-up of land in New Russia to grow grain for export via Black Sea ports such as Odessa.[65] In 1856, the inspector of agriculture in southern Russia noted that there had been a two- to threefold increase in sowings since the 1840s.[66] Over the same period, the inhabitants of New Russia moved away from raising sheep as they could not compete with the cheaper wool from Australia that began to arrive on the European market. Ploughing up pasture land to sow grain increased further after the abolition of serfdom in 1861 as estate owners and peasants strove to earn greater incomes from their land.[67] The change to arable land in place of pasture took place across the steppe region. In the 1880s, Semen Nomikosov of the Don statistical committee estimated that 90 per cent of the land suitable for farming in the Don region had been ploughed up.[68] Nomadic pastoralism continued to predominate on the more arid steppes, with areas of salty soil, in the far south and south-east of the Don region. By the end of the nineteenth century, however, farmers were ploughing up even this land.[69] Grain cultivation developed rapidly in the North Caucasus over the late nineteenth and early twentieth centuries.[70]

The first generations of settlers practised shifting (*perelozhnaya*), long-fallow (*zalezhnaya*) agriculture. They ploughed up an area of steppe and sowed crops. After a few years, yields declined, so farmers ploughed up new land, and left the previous fields fallow for twenty or thirty years. At any one time, only one-fifth or one-sixth of the land suitable for cultivation was sown with crops. This extensive system of farming, which the settlers also borrowed from the local population, was possible because of the relatively low population densities that lasted into the nineteenth century. Central Russia, where many of the settlers or their forebears came from, was more densely inhabited and the population used more intensive systems of farming, in particular the three-field system. Shifting, long-fallow agriculture remained common throughout the steppe region well into the

---

[65] Patricia Herlihy, *Odessa: A History 1794–1914* (Cambridge, MA, 1986), 101–8; Urry, *None but Saints*, 116.

[66] DAOO, f.1, op.248, 1856, sp.1580, ll.120ob.–121.

[67] Friesen, *Rural Revolutions*, 66–73, 100–2, 170–3.

[68] Semen Nomikosov, *Statisticheskoe opisanie Oblasti voiska Donskogo* (Novocherkassk, 1884), 370–84, 398.

[69] See Nomikosov, *Statisticheskoe opisanie*, 324–7, 379; V. V. Bogachev, *Ocherki geografii Vsevelikogo Voiska Donskogo* (Novocherkassk, 1919), 507–14.

[70] See Shatskii, 'Sel'skoe khoziaistvo'.

nineteenth century. It persisted longest in the less heavily settled, outlying parts. As the population increased and opportunities to market grain grew, farmers made more intensive use of the land. They reduced the fallow period to fifteen, ten, five, or fewer years. In time, in much of the region, shifting, long-fallow agriculture was replaced by various more intensive systems. Some farmers introduced the three-field system.[71] Others devised crop rotations based on their own economic circumstances, including the amount of land they owned, conditions in the domestic and export markets, and the climate and soil of the region. At first, few of the new systems were rational. Peasants, especially those with little land and few draft animals, used the least rational systems. Some farmers used no rotations at all: they cultivated as much land as they could, taking a risk that their crops might fail, and showing no regard for the land, in the hope of making a profit.[72] While the main focus of this book is on grain cultivation, it should be noted that the population grew other crops, including water melons and vines, and continued to keep livestock throughout the period.[73]

Figures can be computed to show changes in land use. The data need to be treated with caution as they are not necessarily comparable, and notions of land use on the steppes were not absolute. The practice Russians adopted from Western Europe of describing land according to its current use, for example 'arable', 'pasture', 'forest', etc., was not appropriate to regions with long-fallow agriculture, since the inhabitants used the same area of land as arable or pasture, or left it fallow at different times.[74] Nevertheless, data computed from contemporary sources can show general trends. (See Table I.2.)

Since the data for Orenburg province include a large area of forested hills in the Urals, I have given two sets of data, with and without Orenburg province. What the figures show is a considerable increase in the area of arable land over the period from around 10 per cent in the early eighteenth century to around or over 50 per cent by the late nineteenth and early twentieth centuries. This reflected the move away from shifting, long-fallow farming, and was achieved at the expense of all other forms of land use. The area of pasture and meadow, that is, steppe or long fallow, declined from 62 to 29 per cent (excluding Orenburg province) over the period. The area of forest fell by well over half to around 5 per cent. And the area of land deemed 'waste' also fell as land that had been considered 'marginal' for arable farming was brought into cultivation. The average figures for the whole region conceal trends within it. By the late nineteenth century, around two-thirds

[71] A. S. Ermolov, *Organizatsiya polevogo khozyaistva: Sistemy zemledeliya i sevooboroty*, 5th edn (Spb, 1914), 67–72, 111–23; Skal'kovskii, *Opyt*, ii. 7–29, 73–4.

[72] 'O khlebnoi promyshlennosti v sele Ekaterinovke', 149; K. Z. Bunitskii, 'Osnovye pravila stepnogo khozyaistva', *ZIOSKhYuR* (1855), 2nd pagn, 326; Sergei Bulatsel', 'Zemledelie v Slavyanoserbskom uezde, Ekaterinoslavskoi gubernii', *TVEO*, 1 (1866), 333–43.

[73] For studies of the rural economy, see the works cited in n.34 above.

[74] Milov, *Velikorusskii pakhar'*, 24.

Table I.2 Land use in the European part of the Steppe region, 1725–1912

1725	Arable	Meadow/Pasture	Forest	Waste
Total	9%	43%	29%	19%
excl Orenburg	12%	62%	12%	13%
1796				
Total	17%	39%	20%	24%
excl Orenburg	22%	57%	8%	18%
1861				
Total	20%	32%	18%	31%
excl Orenburg	27%	40%	7%	24%
1887				
Total	52%	30%	9%	10%
excl Orenburg	57%	29%	5%	9%
1912				
Total	49%			
excl Orenburg	52%			

1725: Data for Ekaterinoslav, Don Cossacks, Saratov, Samara, Simbirsk, Orenburg, and Ufa provinces (in the borders of 1851).
1796, 1861: Data for same as 1725 and Kherson and Tauride provinces.
1887: Data for same as 1861, but excluding Ufa and Simbirsk.
1912: Data for same as 1887.
NB Data not strictly comparable and for illustration of trends only.
Data not available for North Caucasus.

Sources:1725–1887: M. A. Tsvetkov, *Izmeneniya lesistosti evropeiskoi Rossii s kontsa XVII stoletiya po 1914 goda* (Moscow 1957), 93, 111, 114–15, 117; 1912: V. K. Yatsunskii, 'Izmeneniya v razmeshchenie zemledeliya v evropeiskoi Rossii s kontsa XVIII v. do Pervoi Mirovoi voiny', in V. K. Yatsunskii (ed.), *Voprosy istorii sel'skogo khozyaistva krest'yanstva i revolyutsionnogo dvizheniya v Rossii: Sbornik Statei k 75-letiyu Akademika Nikolaya Mikhailovicha Druzhinina* (Moscow, 1961), 126–7.

of the total area of the New Russian provinces of Kherson, Ekaterinoslav, and Tauride had been ploughed up.[75]

COMPARATIVE PERSPECTIVES

The story told in this book can be seen in a wider comparative framework and global perspective. The Russian (and Ukrainian and German) experience on the steppes was part of a broader encounter between farmers, mostly of European

[75] M. A. Tsvetkov, *Izmeneniya lesistosti evropeiskoi Rossii s kontsa XVII stoletiya po 1914 goda* (Moscow, 1957), 93.

origins, and environments around the world. This book seeks to complement environmental histories of European colonialism and other grassland regions, in particular the Great Plains of North America. In his pioneering work *Ecological Imperialism*, Alfred Crosby explored the creation of 'neo-Europes' by migrants from Western Europe in temperate regions, including parts of North and South America and Australasia. The migrants, together with their crops, livestock, and other biota (and supported by their states), successfully exported European-style agriculture to other parts of the world. In the process, they displaced indigenous peoples, their ways of life, and native flora and fauna.[76] Russia's steppes are a possible candidate for a 'neo-Europe' that Crosby did not consider.[77]

Colonists from Western Europe first became aware of their impacts on environments on the Atlantic islands (in particular the Canaries, Madeira, and Cape Verde). The Iberian colonists observed that clearing the native vegetation, especially trees, and introducing crops and livestock, as well as accidently bringing weeds and vermin, was 'degrading' the islands' environments. Deforestation, it seemed, was followed by soil erosion and a change to drier, and more variable, climates. Such impacts were quickly apparent on small islands, but were also observed in European colonies on larger landmasses. The colonists and their governments, who took advice from naturalists and scientists, sought ways to address the impacts they were having on the environments of their colonies. Afforestation played a significant role in the measures that were adopted. The experience of European colonialism in drawing attention to human impact on environments and in inspiring 'environmentalism' was the subject of Richard Grove's seminal book *Green Imperialism*.[78] Grove stimulated further research on the environmental history of colonialism, which has focused largely on Western European colonies. In their environmental history of the British Empire, William Beinart and Lotte Hughes noted in their narrative a 'central tension' between exploitation of the natural resources of empire and concerns expressed by scientists to conserve these resources to ensure their 'efficient use'.[79]

This book offers the steppes of the Russian Empire as a further example of an environment that was changed as a result of European colonialism, albeit as part of a continental rather than an overseas empire. It would be tempting to present

[76] Alfred Crosby, *Ecological Imperialism: The Biological Expansion of Europe, 900–1900* (Cambridge, 1986).

[77] See Moon, 'Peasant Migration', 881–2; David Moon, 'In the Russians' Steppes: The Introduction of Russian Wheat on the Great Plains of the United States of America', *Journal of Global History*, 3 (2008), 211, 223–4.

[78] Richard Grove, *Green Imperialism: Colonial Expansion, Tropical Island Edens and the Origins of Environmentalism, 1600–1860* (Cambridge, 1995).

[79] William Beinart and Lotte Hughes, *Environment and Empire* (Oxford, 2009), 2, 202–3. See also Thomas Dunlap, *Nature and the English Diaspora: Environment and History in the United States, Canada, Australia, and New Zealand* (Cambridge, 1999). For a study of the environmental history of migration that includes the Russian Empire, see John F. Richards, *The Unending Frontier: An Environmental History of the Early Modern World* (Berkeley, CA, 2003).

the steppes as a largely landlocked 'island' that Grove omitted from his study, but it would stretch the analogy too far. It is relevant, however, insofar as the steppe environment proved to be as fragile as those of the Atlantic islands when subjected to European settlement and agriculture. The consequences, or perceived consequences, in particular recurring droughts and increased soil erosion, provoked concern within a few decades of the start of large-scale agricultural settlement of the steppe region. Beinart's and Hughes' tension between exploitation and conservation of natural resources—the fertile soils as well as the limited supplies of woodland and water in the case of the steppe region—also pervades this narrative. Nevertheless, by the turn of the twentieth century, the steppes had become one of the world's main grain producing and exporting regions.[80]

Its chief competitor in the international grain market was the USA, where the Great Plains had a strikingly similar environment and environmental history to Russia's steppes. From the 1860s, Euro-American agricultural settlers (including some Mennonite and German migrants from the steppes) moved onto the plains, displacing the indigenous Native Americans, and ending their mobile way of life based on hunting buffalo. The incoming farmers 'broke the plains' with their sod-busting ploughs, and brought ever larger areas of land into cultivation under grain. The ecological implications of ploughing up semi-arid grasslands were brought to wider attention by the disaster of the 'Dust Bowl' during the drought years of the 1930s. The developments on the Great Plains, however, were a repetition of a similar story that began around a century earlier on the steppes. In Russia, the drought, crop failure, and famine, accompanied by dust storms, in 1891–2 served the same role as the 'Dust Bowl' in focusing attention on the consequences of changing the prevailing form of land use on such grasslands from pasture to arable.[81]

There is a far larger historiography of the Great Plains than the steppes.[82] Historians have debated the causes of the 'Dust Bowl'. Pioneering ecological historian James Malin argued that farmers were capable of adapting to the new environment of the plains. He pointed to evidence for dust storms before the great plough-up of the grasslands.[83] More recently, Geoff Cunfer has argued that

---

[80] B. K. Goodwin and T. J. Grennes, 'Tsarist Russia and the World Wheat Market', *Explorations in Economic History*, 35 (1998), 405–30.

[81] See A. A. Chibilev and S. V. Levykin, 'Tselina, razdelennaya okeanom', *Stepnoi Byulleten'*, 1 (1998), <http://savesteppe.org/ru/archives/5591> (accessed 30 August 2011); A. A. Chibilev and S. V. Levykin, 'Virgin Lands divided by an Ocean: The Fate of Grasslands in the Northern Hemisphere', trans. David Moon, *Nova Acta Leopoldina, Neue Folge* (forthcoming); David Moon, 'The Grasslands of North America and Russia', in J. R. McNeill and Erin Stewart Maudlin (eds), *A Companion to Global Environmental History* (Oxford, 2012), 247–62. Another parallel that merits exploration is the pampas, see Adrián Gustavo Zarrilli, 'Capitalism, Ecology, and Agrarian Expansion in the Pampean Region, 1890–1950', *Environmental History*, 6 (2001), 561–83.

[82] For a recent study, with an annotated bibliography, see James E. Sherow, *The Grasslands of the United States: An Environmental History* (Santa Barbara, CA, 2007).

[83] James C. Malin, 'The Adaptation of the Agricultural System to Sub-Humid Environment', *Agricultural History*, 10/3 (1936), 118–41; James C. Malin, 'Dust Storms, 1850–1900', *Kansas*

the main cause was the extreme drought of the 1930s. He noted that dust storms also took place on land that had not been ploughed up. In a longer-term perspective, he concluded, farmers have adapted to the ecological process of the plains.[84] The prevailing interpretation by the US government in the 1930s, and one which has persisted in the historiography, for example Donald Worster's major study, was that the 'Dust Bowl' was due to careless ploughing up of land that was marginal for arable farming by settlers who were accustomed to farming in different conditions, crucially with more rainfall, in their previous homes.[85] This was the story told in Pare Lorenz's influential documentary film of 1936 entitled *The Plow that Broke the Plains*.[86] The competing interpretations of the environment history of America's grasslands have informed the analysis presented in this book.

SOURCES AND METHODOLOGY

In seeking to understand the parallel, if slightly earlier, story of the environmental history of agricultural settlement on Russia's plains, I have used contemporary primary sources, and have used their words (or rather my translations) to build up a picture of evolving contemporary attitudes, understandings, and debates.[87] Thus in order to give a sense of how outsiders responded to the steppe environment before the start of large-scale agricultural settlement, I have used earlier travellers' accounts, starting with that of Herodotus, as well as subsequent accounts by other foreigners and Russians. Throughout the book, I have tried to find descriptions of the steppe environment and accounts of environmental change for the precise periods I am writing about. This is crucial, since later writers and local inhabitants looking back sometimes ascribed larger areas of forest, fewer droughts, and less soil erosion to earlier periods. Palimpsestov took this to the most extreme lengths with his imaginings of vast forests on the steppes in the past. But he was not the only one. These may have been imaginings, misrecollections, or, indeed, accurate accounts of what the steppes had been like in previous decades and centuries. But by relying on contemporary primary sources, it is possible to offer a perspective on later accounts in which the authors were looking back. For example, as will be seen, writers seeking to explain the

---

Historical Quarterly, 14 (1946), 129–44, 265–96, 391–413; James C. Malin, *The Grasslands of North America* (Lawrence, KS, 1947).

[84] Geoff Cunfer, *On the Great Plains: Agriculture and Environment* (College Station, TX, 2005).

[85] See US Great Plains Committee, *The Future of the Great Plains* (Washington, DC, 1937); Donald Worster, *Dust Bowl: The Southern Plains in the 1930s*, 25th anniversary edition (New York, 2004).

[86] <http://www.archive.org/details/PlowThatBrokethePlains1> (accessed 10 June 2010).

[87] In making extensive use of primary sources, I have drawn on the approach of Eugene Weber, *Peasants into Frenchmen: Modernization of Rural France, 1870–1914* (Stanford, 1976).

prevalence of dust storms in the late nineteenth century with reference to the changes wrought by the population had to deal with descriptions of this precise phenomenon a century earlier, before the wholesale ploughing up of the steppes.

Relying on contemporary primary sources is also important as it reduces the risk of attributing ahistorical attitudes to people in the past. For most of the period I am writing about, many naturalists, scientists, officials, and members of the local population did express concerns about such matters as deforestation, climate change, and soil erosion. In some cases they offered harsh criticism of those they believed to be responsible. But it is important not to assume that they were anticipating present-day environmentalist concerns. Specialists also commented adversely on the survival of wild steppe vegetation, which they saw as evidence for the laziness of the population in not ploughing up the land and growing crops. With the exception of some naturalists, valuing the natural flora and fauna of the steppes for their own sakes developed mostly in the late nineteenth century, as they were fast disappearing.

Contemporary analytical accounts of the steppe environment by naturalists and scientists make up a major source. The Academy of Sciences expeditions of 1768–74, led by the German naturalist Peter Pallas, produced invaluable accounts of their studies and observations of the steppes. The development of science in the Russian Empire over the following decades led to a growing body of research on the steppes by Russian scientists. Particular attention is paid to the work of the pioneering soil scientist Vasilii Dokuchaev and his colleagues in the late nineteenth and early twentieth centuries. These naturalists and scientists sought to understand the steppe environment and the nature and causes of environmental change, including the role of human activity, and over time paid more and more attention to devising ways to overcome the environmental constraints, in particular the shortage of water, on the development of agriculture in the region.

The scientists, who play an important role in this book, are only one part of the story. This book seeks to understand the unfolding scientific study of the steppes in the wider institutional, political, economic, social, and cultural contexts in which the scientists were working. Thus key sources are studies and reports by officials and statisticians on the settlement, economic development, and environmental issues in the region. These were produced or sponsored by agencies of the central government. The most important were the Ministry of State Domains (Agriculture from 1894), which administered state lands and the peasants who lived on them and, increasingly, took charge of agriculture, and the Appanage Department, which managed the estates of the imperial family. In addition, the authorities in the provinces and cossack territories and, from their establishment in 1864, the *zemstva* (elected provincial and district councils) all sponsored important studies. Academic societies, sometimes with official support, promoted and funded statistical and scientific research into the environment, environmental change, and ways to address environmental constraints on agriculture. Among the most important were the Academy of Sciences, the Free Economic Society, the Russian Geographical Society, and agricultural societies, in particular the Southern Russian Agricultural Society based in Odessa.[88] Concerns about the steppe environment and environmental change reached beyond scientific and government circles, and were reflected in works of literature, landscape paintings, and the periodical literature aimed at a wider educated readership. These are referred to periodically in this book in order to locate the issues and debates on the steppe environment in the wider culture of educated Russia.

Members of the region's population—settlers or the descendants of settlers—feature in this story, but most attention will be paid to those who took an interest in the ideas about agriculture and the environment that are at the heart of the book and who, crucially, left written records. For the most part, such sources were produced by some estate owners, foreign colonists, and in the last part of the period by *zemstva* activists. At an early stage in working on this book I decided that to analyse the attitudes of the mass of the peasant population, most of whom were illiterate, to the environment of the steppe region would require other sources and a different methodology. Thus peasants play a less active role in this book than in my earlier work.[89] There is little attention, moreover, to the perspectives of the previous inhabitants of the steppe region: the nomadic pastoralists. This book is self-consciously a history of the 'victors', albeit victors who at times struggled to cope with the environment they had annexed, colonized, settled, ploughed up, and on occasion feared they had 'broken'. The sources indicate, with a few exceptions, a disregard for the local knowledge and expertise of the indigenous population. Detailed consideration of the nomads' perspective on the steppe environment—an extremely important subject that would complement this book—would require a different body of sources, additional linguistic skills, and another methodology.

It is worth pointing out that this book does not seek to offer 'correct answers' based on present-day science to questions about the environment that people in the period I am writing about were trying to understand. Scientists have, of course, continued to engage in important research into the steppe environment, develop sophisticated understandings of that environment, and propose solutions to current environmental problems in the region. They are in dialogue with each other and with policymakers and agricultural interests.[90] Science is constantly evolving. Some of the ideas that are considered in this book and were

---

[88] See below, pp. 46–53.

[89] In my first book, I endeavoured to reconstruct peasant attitudes to the authorities and government policy in a number of areas (including migration, which eventually led me to the topic of this present book). David Moon, *Russian Peasants and Tsarist Legislation on the Eve of Reform: Interaction between Peasants and Officialdom 1825–55* (Basingstoke, 1992).

[90] For a concise discussion of the ecology and geography of the steppes, see Chibilev, *Stepi Severnoi Evrazii*. For current research on steppe science, conservation, and sustainability, see *Stepnoi*

causes of controversy in the period under consideration, for example the role of forests in the climate, are still matters of debate. As an example, there has been much recent discussion over the argument by two Russian physicists that forests serve as a 'biotic pump', attracting moist air from oceans and thus increasing precipitation over forested areas. Their argument reinforces the importance of conserving natural forests as a strategy for water security and climate stabilization. But not all scientists have accepted their findings.[91] Thus the story told here continues to the present day as scientists address and debate key issues. The wider contexts in the Soviet and post-Soviet worlds, however, differ from those of the Russian Empire that preceded them.

The argument of this book thus takes account of evolving understandings of the steppe environment and of the relationship between the human and non-human worlds. In doing so, I have tried to distance myself from the older, environmental-determinist interpretations, and also to move beyond an analysis that focuses mainly on human impact on the environment. The editors of an innovative book on the 'spacial history' of Russia have noted that

the argument for causal determinism today gives way to a more nuanced perspective that seeks to problematize the relationship between society and space as a nexus of interaction and selective engagement, with a strong emphasis on the subjective cognition of the historical actors and groups in question. . . . [T]he natural milieu is itself 'historicized' in the sense that it becomes subject to patterns of selection and manipulation, patterns which vary widely across different social groups, different regions, and different periods.[92]

In recent years, environmental historians have debated whether 'nature' has 'agency' in history; that is, whether the non-human world does not play solely a passive role in the history of its interrelationship with the human world. A recent article has gone so far as to consider the 'complicity of trees' in 'tree

---

Byulleten' online <http://savesteppe.org/ru/sb/> (accessed 29 March 2012). For a wider perspective, see David J. Gibson, *Grasses and Grassland Ecology* (Oxford, 2008).

[91] See V. G. Gorshkov and A. M. Makarieva, 'Biotic Pump of Atmospheric Moisture as Driver of the Hydrological Cycle on Land', *Hydrology and Earth System Sciences*, 11 (2007), 1013–33; V. G. Gorshkov and A. M. Makarieva, 'The Biotic Pump: Condensation, Atmospheric Dynamics and Climate', *International Journal of Water*, 5/4 (2010), 365–85; V. G. Gorshkov, A. M. Makarieva, and B.-L. Li, 'Revisiting Forest Impact on Atmospheric Water Vapor Transport and Precipitation', *Theoretical and Applied Climatology* (2012), pre-publication online, <http://www.bioticregulation.ru/common/pdf/taac-en.pdf > (accessed 7 May 2012). For reactions, see Douglas Sheil and Daniel Murdiyarso, 'How Forests Attract Rain: An Examination of a New Hypothesis', *BioScience*, 59/4 (2009), 341–7; A. G. C. A. Meesters, A. J. Dolman, and L. A. Bruijnzeel, 'Comment on "Biotic Pump of Atmospheric Moisture as Driver of the Hydrological Cycle on Land"', *Hydrology and Earth System Sciences. Discussion*, 6 (2009), 401–16, <www.hydrol-earth-syst-sci-discuss.net/6/401/2009/> (accessed 7 May 2012); 'Seeing the Wood: A Special Report on Forests', *The Economist* (25 September–1 October 2010), 5.

[92] Mark Bassin, Christopher Ely, and Melissa K. Stockdale, 'Introduction—Russian Space', in Mark Bassin, Christopher Ely, and Melissa K. Stockdale (eds), *Space, Place, and Power in Modern Russia: Essays in the New Spatial History* (DeKalb, IL, 2010), 6–7.

theft' in post-socialist Bulgaria.[93] A more modest proposal was made by Linda Nash, who concluded:

perhaps, environmental history should strive not merely to put nature into history, but to put the human mind back in the world. Perhaps our narratives should emphasize that human intentions do not emerge in a vacuum, that ideas often cannot be clearly distinguished from actions, that so-called human agency cannot be separated from the environments in which that agency emerges. It is worth considering how our stories might be different if human beings appeared not as the motor of history but as partners in a conversation with a larger world, both animate and inanimate, about the possibilities of existence.[94]

In line with other recent work on environmental history, this books seeks to understand human history as part of environmental history, and places the inhabitants of the steppe region—even though most were settlers from a different environment—as a part of the environment (or the 'natural world' or 'ecosystems') they lived in.[95] Stefania Barca has put it more eloquently, when describing how her recent book (on an Italian region)

is a reflection on how human history is *also* the history of the environment, for it embodies in particular places and is made of them. The place, with its ecology and culture, will play a huge part in the unfolding of the story.[96]

In order to assist my understanding of the environment and the environmental history of the steppes, to give me a sense of place, and perhaps even to insert myself into this history, I have made a number of field trips to the region (see Preface and Acknowledgements, Epilogue, and Map 3). While recognizing that the environment of the steppes has changed substantially since the period under consideration, basing this book solely on conventional historical research using contemporary sources would be to stage *Hamlet* without the prince. An appreciation of the vegetation, climate, topography, and soil of the steppes can be attained only so far from archives, libraries, and seminar rooms. I have been very conscious, moreover, that I am a native of north-western Europe. For part of the time I was researching this book I lived in Glasgow in the west of Scotland, which receives around 1,000 mm of precipitation a year— about three times more than in much of the steppe region. This undoubtedly influenced my perception of the steppe climate, and not just because I could go outside without my umbrella. I have visited scientific nature reserves (*zapovedniki*), experiment stations, farms, and forestry plantations, and talked to scientists, agronomists,

    [93] Chad Staddon, 'The Complicity of Trees: The Socionatural Field of/for Tree Theft in Bulgaria', *SR*, 68 (2009), 70–94.
    [94] Linda Nash, 'The Agency of Nature or the Nature of Agency?', *Environmental History*, 10 (2005), 67–9.
    [95] See Cunfer, *On the Great Plains*, 6, 232–40; Sherow, *Grasslands*, xiv–vx, 4–5.
    [96] Stefania Barca, *Enclosing Water: Nature and Political Economy in a Mediterranean Valley, 1796–1916* (Cambridge, 2010), 1.

farmers, foresters, and members of the local population (descendants of the settlers and cossacks) in order to deepen my understanding of the region's history, geography, economy, and ecology. I have visited some of the specific locations described in this book. My visits have stimulated further questions which I have then addressed to the sources. I could not have written this book without exploring the region it seeks to understand.

My appreciation of the droughts that afflict the region, to take one example, was greatly enhanced by my presence during a drought and partial crop failure in the spring and summer of 2003. I arrived in Rostov-on-Don at the start of March, still in the depths of winter. Spring began in April, and I experienced a rapid transition from cold to hot weather. With little rain for several weeks, there were serious consequences for the crops. In June, in the company of an agronomist, I walked around a field of wheat near Armavir in Krasnodar region. This is a region with very fertile soil. The wheat should have been flourishing. Instead, it was stunted due to the drought. The agronomist expressed his bitter frustration by remarking that he had visited Britain and could not understand why it was so rich when the land he had seen there was not very fertile. I didn't offer any answers. But I came away with a sense of how much more, indescribably more, frustrating it must have been for the inhabitants of the steppes in the period I was studying when drought and crop failure could and did lead to ruin and famine.

STRUCTURE OF THE BOOK

The main focus of the book is on the period from the early eighteenth to the early twentieth centuries. This allows a detailed analysis of the two centuries from the start of large-scale agricultural settlement of the steppe region until the First World War and demise of the tsarist regime. The book is divided into three parts. The subject of Part I is how people came to understand the steppe environment. Chapter 1 goes back long before the formal start date and considers accounts by outsiders, from Herodotus in ancient times, to Catherine the Great in the late eighteenth century. It emphasizes the otherness of the steppes. Chapter 2 focuses on how naturalists, scientists, and statisticians came to understand the steppe environment from the time of the Academy of Sciences expeditions of the late eighteenth century. The naturalists studied, among other things, the vegetation, climate, relief, and the soil. By the late nineteenth century, scientists such as Dokuchaev began to understand that the different parts of the steppe environment were interconnected, and that this had provided the conditions for the formation of the fertile black earth.

Part II moves on to environmental change. As they studied the environment of the steppes, scientists and others became aware that it was changing. Chapter 3 examines contemporary perceptions of the changes in the vegetation, especially the felling of much of the small areas of woodland, but also the removal of the

Map 3. Locations of author's research and field trips

Adapted from Feliks Shtilmark, *The History of Russian Zapovedniks, 1895–1995*, trans. G. H. Harper (Edinburgh, 2003). Used with the permission of the Russian Nature Press.

steppe grasses. Chapter 4 considers climate change and the vexed question of whether, and if so why, droughts were becoming more frequent. Changes in the land itself—erosion, ground water levels, and soil fertility—are the subjects of Chapter 5. All these changes were detrimental to arable farming on the steppes. At the heart of part two is the question: who, or what, was to blame for environmental change? Were the processes of change 'natural' phenomena, or were the region's inhabitants to blame?

To the extent that contemporaries came to believe that the region's inhabitants were to blame for aspects of environmental change, then some considered that what was to be done was further human intervention. This is the subject of Part III. For a long time, the main focus was on changing the steppe environment by adding what was 'missing': trees and water. Chapter 6 analyses the massive efforts that went into planting trees on the steppes. Artificial irrigation is the subject of Chapter 7. Neither was capable of addressing the environmental constraints on arable farming or of reversing the changes. Attention came to focus on ways of cultivating the land—the fertile black earth—in the environment in which it had formed, rather than trying to change that environment. Thus, agronomy, in particular farming methods that conserved scarce moisture, is the subject of Chapter 8.

The conclusion ties together the argument of the book. It also offers comments on the environmental history of the steppe region in the Soviet and post-Soviet periods, after the formal end date of this book. While many of the issues facing agriculture in the steppe region and some of the solutions proposed resembled those of the previous period,[97] the outcome of the revolution of 1917 greatly altered the wider contexts in which these issues were considered and implemented. The new Soviet regime was aware of the scientific legacy it had inherited, including innovative notions of what we would now term 'conservation' and 'sustainability', but it was committed to change, intervention, and transformation, based on an ethos of conquering nature, and invested vast resources to achieve this.[98]

In the late nineteenth century, the rapid loss of virgin steppe as more and more land was ploughed up so alarmed one estate owner in Tauride province that he set aside an area of unploughed steppe to be conserved. It was still there when I visited the Askaniya Nova *zapovednik* in southern Ukraine in May 2011. As I gazed out over the waves of feather grass and wild flowers on the protected land, I tried to imagine how the far greater expanses of unploughed steppe must have appeared centuries, or millennia, earlier.

---

[97] See Elie, 'Dessicated Steppes'.
[98] For a balanced interpretation, see Stephen Brain, 'Environmental History of the Soviet Union', in J. R. McNeill and Erin Stewart Maudlin (eds), *A Companion to Global Environmental History* (Oxford, 2012), 222–43.

PART I

UNDERSTANDING THE STEPPE ENVIRONMENT

1

The Eyes of Outsiders

HERODOTUS

The first written description of the steppes was produced in the mid-fifth century BCE by Herodotus. He described a region on the frontiers of the world known to the ancient Greeks which he called Scythia. It lay between the rivers Ister (Danube) and Tanais (Don) to the north of the Black Sea. He noted that the whole region was 'treeless', with the exception of an area of woodland to the east of the river Borysthenes (Dnepr) he referred to as 'Hyaea'. Beyond the Tanais, moreover, was 'a stretch of country which runs northward fifteen days' journey from the northern tip of the Sea of Azov, [which] is entirely bare of trees, wild or cultivated'. On the other hand, the grass along the banks of the Borysthenes was 'the most luxuriant in the world'. On the climate of this region, Herodotus commented: 'for eight months a year the cold is intolerable; the ground is frozen iron-hard, so that to turn earth into mud requires not water but fire. The sea freezes over . . . ' The remaining four months of 'summer' were also 'cold'. In the 'summer', moreover, it never stopped raining and there were violent thunderstorms. In contrast to 'all other parts of the world', he intoned, 'no rain worth mentioning falls during the season [winter] when one would most expect it'. Nevertheless, Scythia was 'a rich and well-watered plain, with excellent pasture, and . . . rivers . . . almost as numerous as canals are in Egypt'. The 'level plain' of Scythia, furthermore, had 'good deep soil'. The west and north-west of Scythia were inhabited partly by settled agricultural tribes, who grew grain and other crops for food and export, while most of the remaining inhabitants were nomadic, lived off their livestock, and knew 'nothing of agriculture'.[1]

Commenting in the 1850s on Herodotus' views on the climate, Konstantin Veselovskii (an official of the Ministry of State Domains) noted: 'We must not forget that this was written by a son of the happy Hellenes, of a land of olives and laurel.' He added that ancient Greeks had no conception of cold countries. Veselovskii justified Herodotus' remarks on the seasonality of the rainfall by pointing out that it was the opposite of what he was accustomed to on the shores of the Mediterranean.[2] Echoing Veselovskii, the French structuralist François

---

[1] Herodotus, *The Histories*, trans. Aubrey de Selincourt, further revised edn (London, 2003), 246–9, 255–8.

[2] K. Veselovskii, *O Klimate Rossii* (Spb, 1857), 387.

Hartog argued that Herodotus constructed his writings on Scythians, as nomads without houses, towns, or ploughed fields, as a mirror image of his Greek world of city states.[3] While some critics have argued that Hartog took his interpretation too far,[4] the 'otherness' of Herodotus' Scythia is undeniable. His writings, moreover, have been enormously influential on subsequent attempts to understand the world of the steppes.[5]

OUTSIDERS ON THE STEPPES

Aspects of Herodotus' description—the lack of trees (with the exception of 'Hylaea'), the luxuriant grass, the extremes of the climate, the level plain, the rivers, and the fertile soil—recur in many later accounts of the steppes by 'outsiders'. These accounts can seem superficial and quite subjective, but they do convey the impressions of people from very different environments—generally forested, wetter, and less fertile—when confronted by the steppe world. Implicitly or explicitly, like Herodotus' account, many writers contrasted the steppes with their homelands: they focused on what was different.[6] Before turning to a discussion of how outsiders viewed the steppe environment, some details of the writers and why they were visiting the steppes will provide wider contexts for their accounts.

There are few descriptions of the steppes by travellers from Russia prior to the eighteenth century.[7] Some Russians who did make the journey south in this period and left accounts, such as Metropolitan Pimen who sailed down the Don to Azov and on to Constantinople in 1389, frustratingly wrote little about their reactions to the landscape.[8] A glimpse of how Eastern Slavs in medieval Rus' may

---

[3] François Hartog, *The Mirror of Herodotus: The Representation of the Other in the Writing of History*, trans. Janet Lloyd (Berkeley, CA, 1988).

[4] See, for example, Carolyn Dewald, review of Hartog, *Mirror*, *Classical Philology*, 85 (1990), 217–24.

[5] See, for example, Karl Ernst von Baer and Gr. von Helmersen, 'Vorwort des Herausgebers' to P. von Köppen, 'Ein Bericht an die Commission zur Untersushung der Frage über den Einfluss der Verminderung der Wälder auf die Verminderung des Wassers in der obern Wolga', *Beiträge zur Kenntniss des russischen Reiches und den angränzenden Länder Asiens*, 4 (1841), 181–2; V. Taliev, 'Bednyi Gerodot i drugie "svetil'niki" v rukakh pochvenno-botanicheskoi geografii', *Estestvoznanie i geografiya*, 8 (1905), 28–43. See also Larry Wolff, *Inventing Eastern Europe: The Map of Civilization on the Mind of the Enlightenment* (Stanford, CA, 1994), 11, 287–8; A. A. Chibilev and O. A. Grosheva, *Ocherki po istorii stepevedeniya* (Ekaterinburg, 2004), 14–15.

[6] For discussions of foreign accounts of Russia, which are suggestive in this context, see Charles J. Halperin, 'In the Eye of the Beholder: Two Views of Seventeenth-Century Muscovy', *Russian History*, 24 (1997), 409–23; Wolff, *Inventing Eastern Europe*.

[7] See Willard Sunderland, *Taming the Wild Field: Colonization and Empire on the Russian Steppe* (Ithaca, NY, 2004), 19–21; Sara Dickenson, *Breaking Ground: Travel and National Culture in Russia from Peter I to the Era of Pushkin* (Amsterdam, 2006).

[8] 'Khozhdenie Pimenovo v Tsargrad', *Polnoe Sobranie Russkikh Letopisei*, 11 (Spb, 1897), 95–104. He did mention the wildlife he saw.

have viewed the steppes can be seen in the *Song of Igor's Campaign,* or simply the *'Igor Tal'*. This epic poem from the late twelfth or early thirteenth century described a campaign by Prince Igor of Novgorod-Seversk (in the forest-steppe region in the north of present-day Ukraine) against the Polovstsy (or Kumans), who lived on the steppes to the south-east in the valley of the river Don.[9] Further east, the entire length of the river Volga through the steppes was opened up to Russian and other European travellers by Ivan the Terrible's conquest of Kazan' and Astrakhan' in the 1550s. In 1622–3, on the orders of Tsar Michael Romanov, a Muscovite merchant by the name of Fedot Kotov sailed down the river to Astrakhan', and on to Persia and the Orient. Kotov left an account of his epic voyage.[10] There is another Russian description of the steppes from this period. In 1627, Michael Romanov ordered the compilation of 'The Book of the Great Map'. It is a description of an 'Old Map' of Russia and a new map of the lands to the south, including the Khanate of Crimea. The book contains information about the three main roads along the watersheds between the rivers which the Tatars used for their raids into Russia, as well as the valleys of the major rivers. The book's main concern was not to provide a geographical description, however, but to assist in organizing the defence of Russia's steppe frontier.[11]

There are many descriptions of the steppes by foreign visitors from the Middle Ages onwards.[12] Franciscan friars such as William of Rubruck passed through on missions to the Mongols in the thirteenth century. Embassies and merchants, for example an embassy from Holstein in northern Germany including the scholar Adam Olearius, sailed down the Volga en route to Persia in the 1630s. At the end of the seventeenth century, Peter the Great hired specialists such as John Perry from England and Cornelius Cruys from the Netherlands to build canals and map the region. From the 1760s, colonists from other parts of Europe, in particular German lands, settled in the steppe region in response to invitations

---

[9] *Slovo o polku Igoreve,* ed. Yu. A. Andreev, D. S. Ligachev, L. A. Dmitriev et al. (Leningrad, 1985); *The Song of Igor's Campaign,* transl. Vladimir Nabokov (New York, 1960). On the tale's authenticity, see Simon Franklin, 'The *Igor Tale:* A Bohemian Rhapsody?', *Kritika,* 6 (2005), 833–44.

[10] M. P-ii, 'Khozhdenie na Vostok F. A. Kotova v pervoi chetverti XVII veka', *Izvestiya otdeleniya russkogo yazyka i slovesnosti imperatorskoi akademii nauk,* 12/1 (1907), 67–125; N. M. Petrovskii, 'Novyi spisok puteshestviya F. A. Kotova', *Izvestiya otdeleniya russkogo yazyka i slovesnosti imperatorskoi akademii nauk,* 15/4 (1910), 287–99.

[11] For a modern edition, see K. N. Serbina (ed.), *Kniga Bol'shomu chertezhu* (Moscow, 1950). See also A. I. Agafonov, *Istoriya Donskogo Kraya: XVI-pervaya polovina XIX v. Istoricheskie istochniki i ikh izuchenie* (Rostov-on-Don, 2001), 191–4; Denis J. B. Shaw, 'Mapmaking, Science and State Building in Russia before Peter the Great', *Journal of Historical Geography,* 31 (2005), 416–22; Valerie A. Kivelson, *Cartographies of Tsardom: The Land and its Meanings in Seventeenth-Century Russia* (Ithaca, NY, 2006), 1–5, 18–19, 32.

[12] For a fuller discussion based heavily on accounts by foreign travellers up to the eighteenth century, mostly of vegetation and wildlife: S. V. Kirikov, *Chelovek i priroda stepnoi zony: konet X–serediny XIX v (Evropeiskaya chast' SSSR)* (Moscow, 1983).

from the Russian government. Some left accounts of their reactions to the unfamiliar environment of their new homes. Another visitor to the steppes from the German lands was the former Princess Sophie Friederike Auguste von Anhalt-Zerbst-Dornburg, who came from Stettin on the Baltic coast of Germany. As Empress Catherine the Great of Russia, in 1787 she travelled all the way from St Petersburg to the Crimea to see her recently acquired southern lands, and show them off to an entourage of foreign notables including Habsburg Emperor Joseph II.[13]

THE STEPPE ENVIRONMENT

Outsiders acknowledged that the world they were visiting was different by assigning a word to describe the landscape of the region. Prior to the seventeenth century, the word they used was not 'steppe', but '*pole*' ('field'), or '*dikoe pole*' ('wild field').[14] The first use of the word '*pole*' in this context is in the Russian Primary Chronicle for the year 968, when Prince Svyatoslav 'drove the Pechenegs', who had attacked Kiev, to the '*pole*'.[15] The *Igor Tale* uses the word '*pole*' on many occasions, which is contrasted with the 'Russian land'. In Vladimir Nabokov's translation of the epic poem, in order to convey the sense of an open landscape to his American readers, the English word he used for '*pole*' was 'prairie'.[16] The first recorded use of the word 'steppe' in any language was in around 1600 by another wordsmith, William Shakespeare, in *A Midsummer Night's Dream*. In Act II, Scene I, Titania utters the phrase 'the farthest Steppes of India'. This suggests that Shakespeare thought 'steppes' were to be found far off to the east, if he was not sure precisely where. The word 'steppe', or '*step*' in Russian, became more widespread over the following decades and became attached to a particular sort of landscape. Some etymologists consider that the word originally meant a place, or high plain, where trees had been felled.[17]

It was the lack of trees that struck many outsiders the most about the vegetation on the steppes: they noticed what was not there. Herodotus' comments on the treelessness of the steppes were quoted earlier. Most other visitors who drew attention to this phenomenon were from northern and western

---

[13] Sara Dickinson, 'Russia's First "Orient": Characterizing the Crimea in 1787', *Kritika*, 3 (2002), 3–25; Wolff, *Inventing Eastern Europe*, 126–41.

[14] *Slovar' Russkogo yazyka XI–XVII vv.*, xvi (Moscow, 1990), 204–6. Non-Russian speakers may wish to note that '*pole*' is pronounced with two syllables as 'POL–ye'.

[15] 'Lavrent'evskaya letopis'', *Polnoe Sobranie Russkikh Letopisei*, 1/1 2nd edn (Leningrad, 1926), 66–7.

[16] *The Song of Igor's Campaign*, 49, 86–7.

[17] See V. A. Bushakov and N. E. Drogobich, 'O proiskhozhdenii landshaftnogo termina "step"', in A. A. Chibilev (ed.), *Stepi Severnoi Evrazii: Etalonnye Stepnye Landshafty* (Orenburg, 2003), 112–15; *Slovar' Russkogo yazyka XI–XVII vv.*, xxviii (Moscow, 2008), 55; Willard Sunderland, *Taming the Wild Field: Colonization and Empire on the Russian Steppe* (Ithaca, NY, 2004), 34, n.86, 70–1.

Europe and northern and central Russia: regions where the natural environment was primarily a forested one. Friar William of Rubruck (in Flanders) was struck by the absence of trees as he headed east, all the way to Mongolia, from the Crimea in the 1250s: 'with the sea of Tanais [Azov] to our south and to our north a vast wilderness, which in some places is thirty days' journey in latitude and which contains no forest'. 'North of this country', however, 'lies Russia, which is completely covered in forest.'[18] When Kotov wrote his account of his epic voyage from Russia, down the Volga, and on to Persia in 1622–3, he became the first Russian to use the word 'steppe' ('*step*') in a written work. He used it to describe the open and level land between Samara and Saratov.[19] Further south, between Tsaritsyn and Astrakhan', he noted that 'there were no forests at all'.[20] In the description of the Izyum road south to the Khanate of Crimea in 'The Book of the Great Map' of 1627, the last mention of forests is in the vicinity of the Sosna ('Pine') river, which flows into the Don around fifty miles south of Voronezh. The last part of the road, the 120 *versty* between the Molochnaya river and the Perekop Isthmus (which links the Crimean Peninsula with the mainland), is described as having no rivers or forest. The description of the Donets river, a tributary of the Don, makes no reference to forests south of the area around Belgorod.[21]

The scarcity of trees on the steppes, especially the southern steppes, continued to attract comment from outsiders. In the summer of 1634, Olearius noted at Chernyi Yar (south of Tsaritsyn): 'Here, except on the shore, the right side especially, one sees no more trees, but only dry, baked soil and steppe plants.'[22] In the 1760s, German settlers were allocated land on the left bank of the Volga opposite Saratov. According to a register of free land attached to Catherine's invitation to foreign colonists of 22 July 1763, around 37 per cent of the land was forested.[23] When they arrived, after a long journey from their homeland via St Petersburg, however, the Germans were dismayed by the lack of timber to build their new homes. One lamented: 'We came into the steppe . . . where there wasn't a stick of wood or habitation.'[24] When Catherine herself viewed her new southern lands further west in 1787, she noted with dismay the absence of trees.

---

[18] [William of Rubruck], *The Mission of Friar William of Rubruck: His Journey to the Court of the Great Khan Möngke, 1253–1255*, Works issued by the Hakluyt Society, 2nd ser., 173 (London, 1990) 105–6, 141. Rubruck's account was known to scholars in nineteenth-century Russia. See Baer and Helmersen, 'Vorwort', 180–3; Ya. Veinberg, *Les: Znachenie ego v prirode i mery k ego sokhraneniyu* (Moscow, 1884), 252.

[19] Petrovskii, 'Novyi spisok', 292.

[20] P-ii, 'Khozhdenie', 72.

[21] Serbina, *Kniga bol'shomu chertezhu*, 66–77.

[22] Adam Olearius, *The Travels of Olearius in Seventeenth-Century Russia*, trans. Samuel H. Baron (Stanford, CA, 1967), 321–2.

[23] *PSZ*, 1, xvi. 313–16 (no.11,880, 22 July 1763).

[24] Quoted in Fred C. Koch, *The Volga Germans in Russia and the Americas, from 1763 to the Present* (University Park, PA, 1977), 24.

She quickly added, however, that she had taken a thousand *desyatiny*, and ordered forests to be planted.[25] The treelessness of the steppes, the perceived reasons for this, the alleged consequences, and attempts to do something about it are among the main themes of this book.

The absence of trees on the open steppe may not have been quite so striking, however, to natives of the forest-steppe, who were used to grassland as well as forest. From a reading of the *Igor Tale*, the alterity of the 'Kuman field' in contrast to the Russian land is apparent. But it took a careful analysis of the text by a naturalist, Nikolai Sharleman', to trace Igor's route from the forest-steppe to the open steppe in the valley of the lower Don by taking account of the wildlife mentioned. Oak woodland, significantly, is referred to only in the first part of the tale of the campaign, but the lack of trees is not a matter of comment in the *Tale*.[26]

Visitors came across trees in the few locations in the steppe region where they grew naturally, such as river valleys. Scholars have argued that references to '*lug*' in the *Igor Tale* are not to meadows—the later meaning of the word—but to forests along the flood plains of rivers.[27] Olearius wrote about a stretch of the banks of the Volga 60 *versty* south of Samara: 'Because of the thick dark forest that beautifully covers the shore on both sides, this place is pleasing to the eye.' Further south, near Chernyi Yar, he saw 'lovely trees and bushes' on an island in the middle of river.[28] For some the presence of trees was more practical. In 1699, Norwegian-born Dutchman Cornelius Cruys surveyed the valley of the river Don and its tributaries on the orders of Peter the Great. He paid particular attention to the location of trees that could provide timber for shipbuilding. Not far from the Voronezh shipyards, and also further south, he founds forests containing straight, tall oak, beech, birch, linden, and pine trees, which were ideal. His map of the Don shows trees on both sides of the river downstream from Voronezh, with some gaps on the hilly, right bank, and more gaps along the lower reaches from around Razdorskaya.[29] Peter himself found 'huge oaks

[25] [Catherine the Great], 'Pis'ma Imperatritsy Ekateriny II k Yakovu Aleksandrovichu Bryusu, 1787 goda', *Prilozhenie k Kamer-Fur'erskomu Zhurnalu 1787 goda* (Spb, 1889), 25. See also below, p. 180. I am grateful to Professor Simon Dixon for this reference.

[26] N. V. Sharleman', 'Priroda v "Slovo o polku Igoreve"', in *Slovo o polku Igoreve: Sbornik issledovanii i statei* (Moscow and Leningrad, 1950), 213–15; N. V. Sharleman', 'Zametki naturalista k "Slovu o polku Igoreve"', *Trudy Otdela Drevne-Russkoi Literatury*, 8 (1951), 64. I am grateful to Professors Catherine Evtuhov and Boris Gasparov for these references. Nikolai Vasil'evich Dmitriev Sharleman' (1887–1970) was a Ukrainian biologist and zoologist. See *Entsiklopediya 'Slova o polku Igoreve'*, ed. O. V. Tvorogov (Spb, 1995), <http://feb-web.ru/feb/slovenc/es/> (accessed 10 August 2011).

[27] Sharleman', 'Zametki naturalista', 57.

[28] Olearius, *Travels*, 310, 322.

[29] [Cornelius Cruys/K. Kreis], 'Rozyskaniya o Done, Azovskom more, Voronezhe i Azove', *Otechestvennye zapiski*, 20/54 (1824), 46–7 [written in 1699]; [Cornelius Cruys/K. Kreis], 'O nravakh i obyknoveniyakh Donskikh Kazakov, v kontse XVII veka', *Severnyi arkhiv*, 11 (1824), 286; [Cornelius Cruys/K. Kreis], *Nauwkeurige Afbeelding vande Rivier Don, of Tanais, de Azofsche*

suitable for building sea-going vessels' in the Leont'evskii ravine near the location where the city of Rostov-on-Don was founded in 1749.[30]

John Perry, whom Peter hired in 1698 to build a canal between the Volga and Don, was told by local officials 'that no . . . Timber was any where possible to be found'. He did not believe them and 'went myself into the Woods, not two Days Journey from the Work, where in less than fourteen Days time I found very proper, well grown Timber enough for making [sluice] Gates, and furnishing two Pair of Sluices'.[31] (The 'Woods' were probably those that once surrounded the town of Kamyshin on the Volga below Saratov, near the site where the canal was being built.[32]) Further west, after the Battle of Poltava in 1709, Zaporozhian Cossacks who had sided with King Charles XII of Sweden fled across the river Dnepr and sought refuge in the Khanate of Crimea. They settled on land across the river from the site of the future city of Kherson in the '*urochishche*' called Aleshki.[33] The word '*urochishche*' in this context is likely to indicate a wooded area that stood out from the surrounding steppe.[34] This is the probable location of Herodotus' 'Hylaea' or 'Woodland'.

When they weren't on the lookout for trees, outsiders from the time of Herodotus also noticed the predominant natural vegetation of the steppes: grass. The author of the *Igor Tale* made a number of references to grass, using the term '*kovyl*' (feather grass) for the distinctive type of grass in much of the region. He described its characteristic waving in the wind in the spring as 'swishing'.[35] Visitors such as William of Rubruck, Olearius, and Perry all commented on the richness of the grass and its height—as tall as horses' stomachs according to the last two.[36]

More striking, but not quite so striking as the lack of trees, was the climate. Outsiders' reactions to the weather also reflected what they were used to. In contrast to Herodotus, who commented on the cold winters, visitors from northern climes remarked on the hot summers. Near the start of his trip across

---

Zee of Palus Moeotis, en Pontus Euxinus of Swarte Zee (Amsterdam, 1703?), map 25. See also V. S. Popov, 'Materialy k istorii Voiska Donskogo', *SOVDSK*, 12 (1914), 186–201; A. E. Karimov, *Dokuda topor i sokha khodili: ocherki istorii zemel'nogo i lesnogo kadastra v Rossii XVI–nachala XX veka* (Moscow, 2007), 62–3.

[30] Quoted in A. A. Kirillov, 'Voiskovoi ataman Voiska Donskogo graf Matvei Ivanovich Platov i ego administrativnaya deyatel'nost', *SOVDSK*, 11 (1912), 1–56.

[31] John Perry, *The State of Russia under the Present Czar* (London, 1716), 35–6.

[32] A. Leopol'dov, 'Zamechaniya na stat'yu "Ob osnovnykh prichinakh neurozhaev v Rossii i o sredstvakh otvrashchenya onykh"', *ZhMGI*, 6/5 (1842), 2nd pagn, 12. See also P. A. Warneck, 'The Volga-Don Navigation Canal', *RR*, 13 (1954), 285–91.

[33] Ivan Boltin, *Primechaniya na istoriyu drevnie i nyneshnie Rossii G. Leklerka, sochinennie general maiorom Ivanom Boltinym*, 2 vols (Spb, 1788), i. 375–7.

[34] See V. I. Dal', *Tolkovyi slovar' zhivogo velikorusskogo yazyka*, 2nd edn, 4 vols (reprint, Spb, 1991), iv. 509.

[35] *The Song of Igor's Campaign*, 102–3, 106–7. See also Sharleman', 'Zametki naturalista', 54, 57, 64–7.

[36] [William of Rubruck], *Mission*, 105–6; Olearius, *Travels*, 120; Perry, *State of Russia*, 90.

the steppes in the summer of 1253, William of Rubruck wrote: 'we sat under-neath our wagons . . . for the sake of shade, the heat there being so intense during that season'.[37] When Olearius was on the lower Volga in early September nearly four centuries later, he noted: 'It was hot all the time . . . The Russians told us that it was always hot here at this time of year.'[38] Perry contrasted the 'Extremes of Heat and Cold' in continents with 'Islands that are surrounded by the Sea',[39] drawing attention to the moderating influence of seas on the climate of his native Britain, and its absence in the steppe region. Perry, who came from a Britain in the grips of the 'Little Ice Age', liked the steppe climate. 'The Countrey', he enthused, 'is in the best Climate in the World . . . and pleasant to inhabit.' Perry thought the winters were short: 'Snow . . . usually does not lye above two or three Months in these Parts, the warm Weather immediately afterwards takes place.'[40] The warmth of the spring was apparent to Catherine the Great. On 30 April 1787, she wrote from Kremenchug on the Dnepr to Yakov Bruce, whom she had left in northerly St Petersburg in the depths of winter, that it was as warm as it is 'in our country' in July.[41]

Another feature of the climate that attracted comment by outsiders was the wind. The wind is mentioned a few times in the *Igor Tale*, but sometimes as a metaphor for arrows.[42] More directly, Perry wrote that 'in the Height of Summer, from the latter End of *June* to the Middle of *August*, when the Heat has taken its full Power on the Continent, then an Easterly Wind brings more sultry Hot'.[43]

What is notable by its absence from descriptions of the climate of the steppe region by visitors prior to the mid-eighteenth century is the shortage of rainfall and periodic droughts.[44] This is particularly striking as most came from environ-ments that were not only forested, but also wetter. There are a number of possible explanations why visitors did not note this feature of the climate that was so striking later. Many were travelling, passing through, and so did not stay in one place long enough to get a sense of the rainfall. They did not have rain gauges, which in any case had not yet been invented, and so had no hard data to rely on. Perhaps, and this was suspected by many observers of the climate over the nineteenth century, the rainfall was higher in former times. The most likely explanation, however, is that the visitors were not trying to grow crops on the steppes while on their travels. Nor were most of the population of the regions they passed through. The predominant way of life, nomadic pastoralism, was

---

[37] [William of Rubruck], *Mission*, 108.
[38] Olearius, *Travels*, 319.
[39] Perry, *State of Russia*, 73–6.
[40] Perry, *State of Russia*, 90.
[41] [Catherine the Great], 'Pis'ma', 21.
[42] *The Song of Igor's Campaign*, 51, 103.
[43] Perry, *State of Russia*, 73–6.
[44] See also Kirikov, *Chelovek i priroda*, 23, 31, 71.

well suited to the steppe climate as nomads moved their herds around between seasonal pastures. When outsiders settled on the steppes and tried to grow crops—as the first wave of Germans on the Volga and settlers in New Russia did—then they quickly noticed the shortage and unreliability of the rainfall.[45] Thereafter, the shortage of water and periodic droughts were as prominent in descriptions and analyses of the steppe environment as the paucity of arboreal vegetation.

The steppes, as was immediately apparent to outsiders who were unaccustomed to it, were flat, oppressively and disconcertingly so, seemed to stretch interminably for immense distances to the horizon, and were scarcely interrupted by a tree or shaded by a rain cloud.

William of Rubruck noted that 'all we saw was the sky and the ground and on occasions, to our right, . . . the Sea of Tanais [Azov]'.[46] Kotov, making use of the fairly new word 'steppe', noted that some buildings near Saratov were situated on a 'level place' and surrounded 'on all sides' by steppe. Further south, the steppe was 'all around' Tsaritsyn.[47] When Olearius reached Astrakhan' a decade later, he wasted few words on describing the steppe: 'On the side of the river to the west there is a great, flat, dry steppe extending 70 leagues [over 300 miles] to the Black Sea, and—showing the lack of perception of distance that is all to easy in such landscapes—southward 80 leagues [a serious overestimate] to the Caspian Sea.'[48]

The seeming monotony of much of the steppes was broken by a few features. Many visitors commented on the burial mounds, or *kurgany*. William of Rubruck wrote that 'Coman graves' were 'visible to us two leagues off' as he headed east to the north of the Sea of Azov.[49] They were still there five and a half centuries later, at the start of the nineteenth century, when Mennonite settlers arrived at the Molochnaya river, and saw the same '*kurgane* or *mohilen* (old Scythian graves)' on 'the otherwise flat steppe'.[50] Cruys saw some low, sandy hills,[51] but there were few large hills or mountains other than on the periphery of the steppes. Like many visitors, such as Kotov and Olearius, the 'Book of the Great Map' of 1627 described the 'hilly side' (*nagornaya storona*) and flat, or 'meadow side' (*lugovaya storona*) of the Volga.[52] Otherwise, visitors before the late eighteenth century paid little attention to the ravines and gullies that cut through the steppe and joined onto the river valleys.

[45] See Koch, *Volga Germans*, 39.
[46] [William of Rubruck], *Mission*, 108.
[47] Petrovskii, 'Novyi spisok', 292; P-ii, 'Khozhdenie', 71.
[48] Olearius, *Travels*, 325.
[49] [William of Rubruck], *Mission*, 108. The 'Comans', or 'Kumans' were known in Russian as Polovtsy.
[50] Heinrich Goerz, *The Molotschna Settlement*, trans. A. Reimer and J. B. Toews (Winnipeg, 1993), 7.
[51] Cruys, 'O nravakh', 286.
[52] Serbina, *Kniga bol'shomu chertezhu*, 143; Petrovskii, 'Novyi spisok', 290–1; Olearius, *Travels*, 305, 321.

The steppe environment encountered by outsiders before large-scale agricultural settlement was not untouched by human activity. Some visitors noted the impact of the population, indigenous and settlers, on the land. Perry wrote that Russians and Tartars travelling across the steppe

sometimes by accident, and sometimes on purpose, [set] the . . . dry Grass . . . on fire, and [it] spreads and burns the Countrey with great Violence, which may be seen at a great Distance when the Flames are reflected on the Clouds in a dark Night, and in a Cloud of Smoak in the Day.

He continued that fire did not stop until it reached a river or tall wood, but until then, it ran through tall grass or low brushwood for twenty or forty miles. In the spring, moreover, the Crimean Tatars 'burn[ed] the steppe . . . West of the Don, between [Voronezh and Azov]'.[53]

Most visitors from the time of Herodotus who noted the 'good deep soil' commented on the fertility of much of the steppe region. In the mid-fifteenth century, Josaphat Barbaro noted that the land around Tana (near the Don delta) was so fertile that the local population attained yields of up to 1:100. Harvests were so abundant they sometimes left grain unharvested on the steppe.[54] Olearius attributed the height of the grass to the fertility of the 'black soil'. However, he also noted that downstream from Tsaritsyn to Astrakhan' and beyond to the Caspian Sea (where there were very few trees), 'the country is desolate, sandy, and unsuitable for cultivating grain'.[55] Nevertheless, it was the fertile black earth that attracted most attention. Cruys wrote that the 'land [of the Don Cossack territory] is so rich (*zhirna*), that without manuring the inhabitants receive twice as much for their labours as farmers manage to get in other countries'.[56] More succinctly, while she was visiting the 'beautiful city of Kherson' on the Black Sea coast in 1787, Catherine the Great noted 'where they sow, there is abundance'.[57]

CATHERINE THE GREAT

Catherine was filled with optimism when she saw her new southern lands in the spring of 1787. On 30 April, when she reached Kremenchug on the Dnepr—the administrative centre of her new steppe province of Ekatineroslav ('Catherine's

---

[53] Perry, *State of Russia*, 91–2. English visitors to New England in the early seventeenth century noted that Native Americans made use of fire to shape the landscape to their needs. William Cronon, *Changes in the Land: Indians, Colonists, and the Ecology of New England* (New York, 1983), 49.

[54] Iosafat Barbaro and Ambrodzho Kontarini, *Barbaro i Kontarini o Rossii: k istorii italo-russkikh svyazei v XV v.*, trans. E. Ch. Skrzhinskaya (Leningrad, 1971), 150.

[55] Olearius, *Travels*, 120, 319.

[56] Cruys, 'O nravakh', 286. See also Perry, *State of Russia*, 90.

[57] [Catherine the Great], 'Pis'ma', 24.

glory')—she wrote that 'the air and all things and people changed their appearance and all seemed more lively'. She continued:

The local climate I consider the best in the Empire, here, without exception all fruit trees grow in the open air, I from birth have not seen such pear trees the same height and girth as the largest and broadest oak, the air is most pleasant. *This region is in truth a paradise*; it is a great shame, that the unhappy times and location of the borders before my reign did not allow the use of these advantages . . . *here, without forcing nature, with little care and less expenditure, there is everything one could want.*

A few weeks later, after sampling the more obvious beauties of the mountains and seas on the Crimean Peninsula, she wrote: 'I think that even the steppes will be good in time; the bad and unpeaceful neighbourhood [a reference to Tatar rule] turned them into steppe, in fact these are places of abundance; in ten years people will come here, who will travel from curiosity to see regions of abundance and prosperity.'[58] Catherine was thus presenting an optimistic interpretation of the prospects for the steppe region.[59] If these riches were to be achieved, however, it would require more than superficial impressions and optimistic hopes of outsiders. As Catherine, a student of the Enlightenment, was aware, it would require serious study of the steppe environment.

---

[58] [Catherine the Great], 'Pis'ma', 21, 22, 27. The italicized text indicates where she switched from Russian to French, perhaps better to express her delight to Russified Scot Yakov Bruce.

[59] For discussion of similar views, see David Moon, 'Agriculture and the Environment on the Steppes in the Nineteenth Century', in Nicholas Breyfogle, Abby Schrader, and Willard Sunderland (eds), *Peopling the Russian Periphery: Borderland Colonization in Eurasian History* (Abingdon, 2007), 86–90.

2

The Lens of Science and Statistics

INTRODUCTION

Serious study of the steppe environment began in the reign of Catherine the Great (1762–96). It flourished in the late nineteenth and early twentieth centuries, when Russian scientists produced highly original work.[1] Scientific study of the steppes developed in parallel with the natural sciences and scientific training in the Russian Empire and elsewhere. This chapter is framed by expeditions to the steppes in the second half of the eighteenth and late nineteenth centuries. In 1768–74, the Russian Academy of Sciences dispatched expeditions to the steppe region and beyond led by mostly German or German-educated naturalists under Peter Pallas. Just over a century later, expeditions to the steppes were led by the pioneering soil scientist Vasilii Dokuchaev with the support of the Free Economic Society and the Ministry of State Domains. In contrast to the expeditions of the eighteenth century, Dokuchaev's teams comprised Russian-trained Russian scientists.

In the eighteenth and well into the nineteenth centuries foreign, especially German, scholars and ideas were very prominent in intellectual life in Russia. Over the same period, with the development of secular education in Russia and growing opportunities for Russians to study abroad, the number and significance of Russian scientists grew.[2] In 1768–74, the Academy of Sciences expeditions had applied European learning to an outlying region of the Russian Empire. A little over a century later, Dokuchaev and his colleagues consciously applied science, including theories devised in Russia, to understand Russian conditions in a region that was no longer perceived as outlying.[3] There was a further contrast. The eighteenth-century naturalists were looking for natural resources in remote parts of the empire to exploit; the scientists of the late

---

[1] On the development of steppe science, see A. A. Chibilev and O. A. Grosheva, *Ocherki po istorii stepevedeniya* (Ekaterinburg, 2004).

[2] Ludmilla Schulze, 'The Russification of the St Petersburg Academy of Sciences and Arts in the Eighteenth Century', *The British Journal for the History of Science*, 18 (1985), 305–35.

[3] On the 'Russification' of the steppes, see Willard Sunderland, *Taming the Wild Field: Colonization and Empire on the Russian Steppe* (Ithaca, NY, 2004), 169–74.

nineteenth century were seeking ways of managing the exploitation of those resources—in particular the fertile soil—in ways appropriate to the environment.

The same period saw the development of statistical studies of the natural resources and economy in the Russian Empire. 'Statistics', which was in vogue in official circles, entailed gathering information on many subjects to provide the data the authorities needed to devise policies to support their aims. Statistics emerged from 'cameralism', which was a 'science' of government that developed in seventeenth-century German states with the aim of promoting the 'common good' of the state by mobilizing natural and human resources.[4] Thus during the late eighteenth and nineteenth centuries, the Russian authorities gathered statistics on the steppe region to promote its development, in particular the development of agriculture. The main bodies involved in gathering statistics were the central and provincial authorities, the imperial general staff, and, from the late nineteenth century, the *zemstva*.[5] To varying degrees, statisticians drew on research by naturalists and scientists. They also drew on other sources, including local inhabitants, who provided what may be termed 'local knowledge'. Both scientific and statistical studies had the same objectives: studying the environment and resources of the steppe region in order to promote their exploitation in the interests of the state and its inhabitants, in particular the settler population.

Before turning to an analysis of the steppe environment through the lens of science and statistics, we need to consider the wider contexts of the expeditions by naturalists and scientists, the development of science, and the institutions that supported them.

THE WIDER CONTEXTS

The Academy of Sciences expeditions[6]

The Academy of Sciences expeditions were part of a growing attention to the geography of the expanding Russian Empire. The Academy, which was founded by Peter the Great in 1725, emphasized gathering data and collecting specimens for research, and locating natural resources for exploitation.[7] In 1768–74, with

[4] See Keith Tribe, 'Cameralism and the Science of Government', *Journal of Modern History*, 56 (1984), 263–84.

[5] See Susan Smith-Peter, 'Defining the Russian People: Konstantin Arsen'ev and Russian Statistics before 1861', *History of Science*, 45 (2007), 47–64; David W. Darrow, 'The Politics of Numbers: Zemstvo Land Assessment and the Conceptualization of Russia's Rural Economy', *RR*, 59 (2000), 52–75; David Rich, 'Imperialism, Reform and Strategy: Russian Military Statistics, 1840–1880', *SEER*, 74 (1996), 621–39.

[6] For a fuller discussion, see David Moon, 'The Russian Academy of Sciences Expeditions to the Steppes in the Late-Eighteenth Century', *SEER*, 88 (2010), 204–36.

[7] See V. F. Gnucheva, 'Geograficheskii departament akademii nauk XVIII veka', *Trudy Arkhiva Akademii Nauk SSSR*, 6 (1946), 23–86; Denis J. B. Shaw, 'Geographical Practice and its Significance in Peter the Great's Russia', *Journal of Historical Geography*, 22 (1996), 160–76;

Catherine the Great's encouragement, the Academy sent expeditions that travelled through the steppe region.[8] Their itineraries included the valleys of the rivers Don and Volga, the North Caucasus, the Orenburg region, and the steppes to the north of the Black Sea. The leaders were either foreign or had received all or part of their education abroad, in particular at German universities. Peter Simon Pallas, who was born in Berlin and educated at the universities of Halle, Göttingen, and Leiden, moved to St Petersburg in 1767. He played a leading role in organizing the expeditions.[9] Ivan Ivanovich Lepekhin was the only Russian expedition leader. He was born in St Petersburg, and educated at the Academy of Sciences and Straßburg University.[10] Johann Peter Falck, a Swede, was educated at Uppsala University, before moving to St Petersburg.[11] Samuel Gottlieb Gmelin was German born and educated.[12] Johann Anton Güldenstädt was a Baltic German from Riga in Livonia. He was educated in Riga and Berlin.[13] The expeditions included Russian students and assistants. Vasilii Zuev, who took part in Pallas' expedition, completed his education at Leipzig and Straßburg universities.[14]

The Academy of Sciences gave the leaders detailed instructions that had been prepared with the advice of the Free Economic Society.[15] The expeditions were to investigate, among other things: the nature of the land and water; any uncultivated or unpopulated land that could be used for cultivating grain, hay, or trees; the economic activities of populated places; and the weather. The naturalists were also instructed to collect wildlife and plants.[16] The aims could be summed up as researching the natural resources of the regions they visited and how they might be exploited. The steppe region, with its fertile soil but sparse population, was ripe for development. There were two further expeditions to the steppes in the late eighteenth century. Zuev led an expedition to the newly

Alexander Vucinich, *Science in Russian Culture: A History to 1860* (London, 1965), 46–7, 57–62, 65–74, 82, 90–2, 99–101.

[8] See V. F. Gnucheva, 'Materialy dlya istorii ekspeditsii akademii nauk v XVIII i XX vekakh', *Trudy Arkhiva Akademii Nauk SSSR*, 4 (1940), 1–310; S. A. Kozlov, *Russkii puteshestvennik epokhy Prosveshcheniia* (Spb, 2003).

[9] Folkwart Wendland, *Peter Simon Pallas (1741–1811): Materialien einer Biographie*, 2 vols (Berlin, 1992).

[10] T. A. Lukina, *Ivan Ivanovich Lepekhin* (Moscow and Leningrad, 1965), 8–19.

[11] Fal'k, 'Zapiski Puteshestviia Akademika Fal'ka', *PSUPpR*, vi (Spb, 1824), v–vii.

[12] 'Gmeliny', *ES*, xvi (Spb, 1893), 931.

[13] Iu. Kh. Kopelevich, *Iogann Anton Gil'denshtedt* (Moscow, 1997), 9–12.

[14] M. E. Kabun, 'Akademik Vasilii Zuev i ego "Puteshestvennye zapiski" k kontekste kul'turnoi geografii Severnogo Prichernomor'ya epokhi Prosveshcheniya', in V. F. Zuev, *Puteshestvennye zapiski Vasiliya Zueva ot S. Peterburga do Khersona, v 1781 i 1782 godu*, reprint (Dnepropetrovsk, 2011), vii–xxviii.

[15] N. G. Fradkin, 'Instruktsiya dlya akademicheskikh ekspeditsii 1768–1774 gg.', *Voprosy geografii*, 17 (1950), 213–18; M. I. Sukhomlinov, *Istoriya Rossiiskoi akademii*, 8 vols (Spb, 1874–88), ii. 472–7. I am grateful to Dr Aleksandra Bekasova for these references. On the Free Economic Society, see below, p. 51.

[16] PFA RAN, f.3, op. 35, d.1, ll.2ob.–3.

annexed steppe around Kherson in 1781–2. His instructions were similar to those for the earlier expeditions.[17] Pallas made a second trip to the steppes in 1793–4, travelling down the Volga, across the steppes of the North Caucasus, and on to the Crimean Peninsula. He made detailed observations and noted changes since his earlier visit.[18]

The Academy of Sciences expeditions took place after the start of the agricultural settlement of the steppes. Nevertheless they provide invaluable evidence on the steppe environment in the early stages of that process. The accounts of the expeditions, moreover, marked a very important stage in the evolving scientific understanding of the steppes. The foreign and foreign-educated leaders, however, viewed the steppes very much through the prism of their own backgrounds and experiences. Their writings, therefore, shared the sense of 'otherness' of the outsiders who had cast their eyes on the steppes in previous centuries.

The development of science and scientific education in Russia

Secular and higher education, including scientific education, in Russia developed over the eighteenth and nineteenth centuries. The foundation of Moscow University in 1755 was followed in the early nineteenth century by the establishment (or re-establishment) of universities in Kazan', Khar'kov (on the edge of the steppes), Vilna, Dorpat, and St Petersburg. Dorpat University in Livonia, which educated the sons of Baltic German nobles, became an important centre for natural sciences.[19] The longer established and larger system of Orthodox church schools and seminaries, which educated the sons of the clergy, provided significant numbers of men who went on to serve in the state administration or enter universities and scientific life. The curriculum in seminaries was broadened in the early nineteenth century to cover secular subjects, including natural sciences. Seminary graduates included Dokuchaev and others who feature prominently in this book.[20]

For much of the period between 1815 and 1855—the last part of the reign of Alexander I and that of Nicholas I—the Russian authorities limited teaching and publishing on the natural sciences. For several decades until 1855, moreover, there were restrictions on Russian students studying at foreign universities.[21] Russia was not totally cut off from the wider scientific world between 1815 and

[17] PFA RAN, f.3, op. 37, d.1, ll.2ob.–3; d.5, l.1; Vasilii Zuev, *Puteshestvennye zapiski Vasiliya Zueva ot S. Peterburga do Khersona, v 1781 i 1782 godu* (Spb, 1787), 1.

[18] Gnucheva, 'Materialy dlya istorii ekspeditsii akademii nauk', 126; Wendland, *Peter Simon Pallas*, i. 271–5.

[19] See James T. Flynn, *The University Reform of Tsar Alexander I, 1802–1835* (Washington, DC, 1988).

[20] See Gregory Freeze, *The Parish Clergy in Nineteenth Century Russia: Crisis, Reform and Counter Reform* (Princeton, NJ, 1983), 130.

[21] Vucinich, *Science in Russian Culture: A History to 1860*, 231–6, 248–50, 253–6, 258–63, 343, 366–71, 383.

1855. Some Russian students still studied abroad, and a few foreign scholars visited Russia. In 1829, the German geographer Alexander von Humboldt came on the invitation of Nicholas I to explore the Altai and Ural mountains and the Caspian Sea. The Mining Department invited British geologist Roderick Murchison to visit in 1840–2 to study Russian minerals, in which he included the black earth of the steppes.[22] The accession of Alexander II in 1855 led to a thaw. Russian scientists were freer to study abroad. The relaxation of censorship allowed the translation of works such as Charles Lyell's books on geology and Charles Darwin's on evolution.[23] The Russian intelligentsia did not passively absorb the new theories from abroad, but engaged with them in the contexts of their own concerns.[24] There were renewed periods of repression. The authorities briefly closed St Petersburg University on account of student disturbances in 1861–2. Individual scientists, such as the chemist Aleksandr Nikolaevich Engel'gardt, were repressed for their political activities.[25] In the late 1860s and 1870s, moreover, the Minister of Education downgraded sciences in favour of classics. Nevertheless, the state's need for educated specialists meant that secular, and scientific, education continued to expand.[26]

By the mid-nineteenth century, Russians had successfully challenged the domination of 'Germans' in Russian scientific life. From the 1840s, most new members of the Academy of Sciences were Russian. The 'Russification' of the Academy, learned societies, and all levels of the education system was deliberately accelerated by Count Sergei Uvarov. He served as president of the Academy from 1818 to 1849, Minister of Education from 1833 to 1849, and was the author of Nicholas I's official 'ideology' of 'Orthodoxy, Autocracy, and Nationality'. In the 1850s, a faction of Russians, including 'enlightened bureaucrats' Nicholas and Dmitrii Milyutin, took control of the Geographical Society from the 'Germans', such as the Baltic German Karl Ernst von Baer.[27] Scientists of foreign birth continued, however, to carry out important work in Russia. For example, the geobotanist Franz Joseph Ruprecht, who moved to Russia from Austria in 1839 and was elected to the Academy in 1857, published a significant study of the black earth in 1866 (see below, pp. 63–4, 76).

[22] B. P. Ongirskii, 'Aleksandr Gumbol'dt v Rossii', *Delo*, 10 (1872), 113–42; Murchison, 'Issledovaniya o chernozeme vnytrennikh gubernii Rossii', *ZhMGI*, 8 (1843), 125–35.
[23] Alexander Vucinich, *Science in Russian Culture, 1861–1917* (Stanford, CA, 1970), 56–7, 118.
[24] See, for example, Loren Graham, *Science in Russia and the Soviet Union* (Cambridge, 1993), 56–72.
[25] *Aleksandr Nikolaevich Engelgardt's Letters from the Countryside, 1872–1887*, ed. and trans. C. A. Frierson (New York, 1993). (I have included his patronymic to avoid confusion with Aleksandr Platonovich Engel'gardt, an official, who is referred to later in this book.)
[26] See Allen Sinel, *The Classroom and the Chancellery: State Educational Reform in Russia under Count Dmitry Tolstoi* (Cambridge, MA, 1973).
[27] See S. I. Romanovskii, '"Obrusenie" Rossiiskoi nauki kak natsional'naya problema', *VIET*, 3 (1999), 43–50; Vucinich, *Science in Russian Culture: A History to 1860*, 295, 306–8, 329–30, 356–63, 384.

Agricultural specialists trained in the universities were hired by institutions of the central and provincial governments which sought to apply scientific learning to the development of agriculture throughout the empire, including the steppe region. The Ministry of State Domains was set up in 1837 to administer the state's extensive land holdings and its peasants. It took over this responsibility from a smaller department of the Ministry of Finance. The first Minister of State Domains, Pavel Kiselev, was energetic in applying scientific learning, from Russia and abroad, to promote agriculture. From 1841, the ministry published a monthly journal with articles on agriculture which is an important source for this book.[28] The Appanage Department, which administered the extensive estates of the imperial family, was also active in applying scientific learning to managing its lands.[29] The provincial authorities, the administrations of cossack territories, and from the late nineteenth century the *zemstva* all recruited specialists and sponsored scientific and statistical studies of the natural resources of the steppes and how to utilize them.[30]

A major role in the development of the natural sciences in Russia was played by learned societies, which were set up partly on state and partly on private initiatives.[31] One of the most important was the Free Economic Society, which was established with Catherine's support to promote economic, in particular agricultural, development in 1765.[32] The Russian Geographical Society, founded in 1845, became an important forum for the collection of statistics. There were also specialist societies, such as the St Petersburg Society of Naturalists, and agricultural societies.[33] The Southern Russian Agricultural Society was set up in Odessa on the initiative of Governor General Vorontsov of New Russia

[28] See *IOPDMGI*; A. P. Zablotskii-Desyatovskii, *Graf P. D. Kiselev i ego vremya: materialy dlya istorii imperatorov Aleksandra I Nikolaya I Aleksandra II*, 4 vols (Spb, 1882). The journal was *Zhurnal Ministerstva gosudarstvennykh imushchestv* (*ZhMGI*), which was renamed *Sel'skoe khozyaistvo i lesovodstvo* (*SKhiL*) in 1865.

[29] See *Istoriya udelov za stoletie ikh sushchestvovaniya, 1797–1897*, 3 vols (Spb, 1902).

[30] See G. P. Sazonov, *Obzor deyatel'nosti zemstv po sel'skomu khozyaistvu (1865–1895 gg.)*, 3 vols (Spb, 1896); N. G. Koroleva (ed.), *Zemskoe samoupravlenie v Rossi, 1864–1918*, 2 vols (Moscow, 2005); O. Yu. Elina, *Ot tsarskikh sadov do sovetskikh polei: istoriya sel'sko-khozyaistvennykh opytnykh uchrezhdenii XVIII-20-e gody XX v.*, 2 vols (Moscow, 2008), i. 287–384.

[31] On the wider implications, see Joseph Bradley, *Voluntary Associations in Tsarist Russia: Science, Patriotism, and Civil Society* (Cambridge, MA, 2009).

[32] A. I. Khodnev, *Istoriya Imperatorskogo Vol'nogo ekonomicheskogo obshchestva s 1765 do 1865 goda* (Spb, 1865); Elina, *Ot tsarskikh sadov*, i. 149–59, 241–2. On the readership of its publications, see Colum Leckey, 'Provincial Readers and Agrarian Reform, 1760s–70s: The Case of Sloboda Ukraine', *RR*, 61 (2002), 535–59.

[33] Vucinich, *Science in Russian Culture: A History to 1860*, 349–53; W. Bruce Lincoln, *In the Vanguard of Reform: Russia's Enlightened Bureaucrats, 1825–1861* (DeKalb, IL, 1982), 91–100, 102–3, 122–3; S. A. Kozlov, *Agrarnye traditsii i novatsii v doreformennoi Rossii (tsentral'no-nechernozemnye gubernii)* (Moscow, 2002); S. A. Kozlov, *Agrarnaya ratsionalizatsyia v Tsentralno-Nechernozemnoi Rossii v poreformennyi period (po materialam ekonomicheskoi pechati)* (Moscow, 2008).

in 1828. It promoted the application of scientific agriculture on the steppes and encouraged research into the region's environment.[34]

One of its most active members, who served as secretary for many years from 1853, was Ivan Palimpsestov (1818–1901). Palimpsestov was an example of the cohort of scholars interested in the natural history of the steppes and improved agriculture before the predominance of university-trained scientists later in the century. He came from the clerical estate and was ordained an Orthodox priest. In 1843, after completing his education at the seminary in his native Saratov, he studied at the Gorygoretskaya agricultural school near Mogilev. On graduating, he left the clerical estate, and was promoted up the Table of Ranks. He went on to teach agriculture and sciences. In 1851, he moved to Odessa, in Kherson province, at the other end of the steppe region. There he taught in the seminary, the Richelieu Lycée, and, from its foundation in 1865, the University of New Russia. Palimpsestov broadened his experience during two trips abroad, to France, Germany, Algeria, and other destinations, in 1858 and 1862.[35] His extensive and exhaustive writings, which will be referred to repeatedly in this book, show a man who was passionate about the steppes, committed to developing agriculture in the region, and who had a lively and at times quite original mind.

By the second half of the nineteenth century, Russian universities had educated scientists who superseded men such as Palimpsestov. The majority were Russian-born and largely Russian educated. Most, but not all, spent a period studying at universities in Germany or elsewhere in Europe. In the early twentieth century, some, for example Nikolai Tulaikov, went instead to the USA, as well as visiting Western Europe.[36] From the late nineteenth century, Russian scientists at Russian institutions were engaging in research of international importance. Loren Graham concluded:

The tsarist government gradually came to realize that the promotion of science and technology was in its interest. By the end of the [nineteenth] century, science had become an important part of Russian culture, and in some areas—mathematics, physiological psychology, soil science, animal and plant ecology—Russia was emerging as a leader.[37]

Many Russian scientists were not concerned with science for its own sake, but, along with other members of the intelligentsia, wanted to use science in the

---

[34] See I. Palimpsestov, *Otchet o deistviyakh Imperatorskogo Obshchestva sel'skogo khozyaistva yuzhnoi Rossii* (Odessa, 1855); M. P. Borovskii, *Istoricheskii obzor pyatidesyatiletnei deyatel'nosti Imperatorskogo Obshchestva Sel'skogo Khozyaistva Yuzhnoi Rossii s 1828 po 1878 god* (Odessa, 1878), 3–4.

[35] See I. U. Palimpsestov, *Moi vospominaniya* (Moscow, 1879); 'Ivan Palimpsestov', *ES*, xlviii (Spb, 1897), 631; DAOO, f.22, op.1, 1852, sp. 229 (which contains his 'formulyarnye spiski').

[36] Tulaikov spent 1908–9 at the University of California, Berkeley, and visited Western Europe on his way home. K. P. Tulaikova, *Ot Pakharya do Akademika: Ob Akademike Nikolae Maksimoviche Tulaikove* (Moscow, 1964), 54–69.

[37] Graham, *Science in Russia*, 3.

service of society: they wished to have an impact on the social and economic life of their country.[38]

Russia was emerging as a leader in soil science due to the work of Vasilii Dokuchaev (1846–1903) and his associates. They also carried out pioneering work into other aspects of the steppe environment, and ways to exploit it that would today be termed 'sustainable'. They were motivated by the importance of agriculture in the region, and the need to overcome the problem of recurring droughts. Like Palimpsestov, Dokuchaev came from the clerical estate. He was educated in seminaries in his native Smolensk province in the forest region in western Russia. Unlike Palimpsestov, he decided against the priesthood at an early stage, and in 1867 entered St Petersburg University to study natural sciences. He rose eventually to become professor of mineralogy. In contrast to the normal pattern of training for Russian scientists, Dokuchaev did not spend a period studying abroad, and may not have had much knowledge of Western European languages. Instead, his formative experiences were regular field trips to study the natural environment of his native Russia.[39] A Russian philosopher has recently pointed to other peculiarities in Dokuchaev's education and approach. In his final years at university, he did not apply himself to his studies, preferring 'maps and drinking'. To some extent, moreover, he was an autodidact. No one supervised his graduate work, and he found his own way to a subject of study, and an original methodology for undertaking that study.[40]

Dokuchaev's expeditions

In 1876, in the wake of droughts in the black-earth region in 1873 and 1875, the Free Economic Society commissioned Dokuchaev to lead research into the fertile soil. He put together a team of scientists, including his students Nikolai Sibirtsev and Petr Zemyatchenskii. They embarked on an expedition around the black-earth region, which by Dokuchaev's calculations occupied 80–90 million

[38] See Michael D. Gordin and Karl Hall, 'Introduction: Intelligentsia Science Inside and Outside Russia', in Michael D. Gordin, Karl Hall, and Alexei Kojevnikov (eds), *Intelligentsia Science: The Russian Century, 1860–1960, Osiris*, 2nd ser., 23 (2008), 1–19; Elizabeth A. Hachten, 'In Service to Science and Society: Scientists and the Public in Late-Nineteenth-Century Russia', *Osiris*, 2nd ser., 17 (2002), 171–209.

[39] There are several biographies, some of which verge on hagiography. For a selection, see L. A. Chebotareva, 'Vasilii Vasil'evich Dokuchaev (1846–1903). Biograficheskii ocherk', in V. V. Dokuchaev, *Sochineniya*, 9 vols (Moscow and Leningrad, 1949–61), ix. 49–153; I. Krupenikov and L. Krupenikov, *Vasilii Vasil'evich Dokuchaev* (Moscow, 1950); S. V. Zonn, *Vasilii Vasil'evich Dokuchaev, 1846–1903* (Moscow, 1991). See also V. A. Esakov, 'Dokuchaev, Vasilii Vasil'evich, 1846–1903', in *Dictionary of Scientific Biography*, iv (1971), 143–6. On his early expeditions, see I. Krupenikov and L. Krupenikov, *Puteshestviya i ekspeditsii V. V. Dokuchaeva* (Moscow, 1949), 5–30.

[40] E. S. Kul'pin-Gubaidullin, 'Vasilii Dokuchaev kak predtecha biospherno-kosmicheskogo istorizma: sud'ba uchenogo i sud'by Rossii', *Obshchestvennye nauki i sovremennost'*, 2 (2010), 109–10. I am grateful to Mary Bailes for this reference.

desyatiny, covering the forest-steppe as well as much of the steppe regions. He travelled around 10,000 *versty* in the summers of 1877, 1878, and 1881.[41] Dokuchaev's black-earth expedition covered some of the same ground as the Academy of Sciences expeditions just over a century earlier, but he and his team were able to do so more quickly, travelling by trains and steamers on the Volga.[42] The outcome was the book *The Russian Black Earth* (*Russkii chernozem*): the founding text of the new genetic soil science. Dokuchaev was commissioned by the *zemstva* of Nizhnii Novgorod province, which straddled the forest and forest-steppe regions, and Poltava province, which included steppes, to carry out detailed investigations into the soils to assess the quality of the land for taxation and other purposes.[43]

In the wake of the catastrophic drought, crop failure, and famine of 1891–2, the Forestry Department of the Ministry of State Domains sponsored Doku-chaev to lead a 'special' scientific expedition to the steppes to investigate ways of tackling the problem of droughts. The main focus was to be on forestry and managing water resources.[44] He put together a team of scientists, including Sibirtsev and Zemyatinskii, and younger scientists, such as the forestry specialist Georgii Vysotskii and the botanist Gavriil Tanfil'ev. Dokuchaev set up three field research stations on plots (*uchastki*) of state land of around 5,000 *desyatiny* on carefully selected sites that contained typical features of the steppe environment. He chose plots that were situated on watersheds, that is, far from large rivers, in places with little water that regularly suffered from drought, strong winds, and other 'unfavourable features of steppe nature'. The plots were: Starobel'sk (Derkulinskii) in eastern Khar'kov province, on the watershed between the Donets and Don rivers, which was an example of exposed, open steppe; Khre-novskoi in south-eastern Voronezh province, between the Don and Volga river systems, which included the Kamennaya steppe as well as natural coniferous and broadleaved woodland, and was thus an example of forest-steppe; and Velikii Anadol' to the north of the Sea of Azov in eastern Ekaterinslav province, between the Donets and Dnepr rivers, which contained a forestry plantation on the open steppe.[45] (See Map 4.)

---

[41] V. V. Dokuchaev, 'Russkii chernozem', *Izbrannye sochineniya*, 3 vols (Moscow, 1948–9), i. 25–7; Krupenikov and Krupenikov, *Puteshestviya*, 31–48.

[42] For example, Dokuchaev, 'Russkii chernozem', 52, 146, 163.

[43] Krupenikov and Krupenikov, *Puteshestviya*, 56–82; Catherine Evtuhov, 'The Roots of Dokuchaev's Scientific Contributions: Cadastral Soil Mapping and Agro-Environmental Issues', in B. P. Warkentin (ed.), *Footprints in the Soil: People and Ideas in Soil History* (Amsterdam, 2006), 125–148; Catherine Evtuhov, *Portrait of a Russian Province: Economy, Society, and Civilization in Nineteenth-Century Nizhnii Novgorod* (Pittsburgh, PA, 2011), 25–7, 30–4, 170–2.

[44] For a fuller discussion, see David Moon, 'The Environmental History of the Russian Steppes: Vasilii Dokuchaev and the Harvest Failure of 1891', *Transactions of the Royal Historical Society*, 6th ser., 15 (2005), 149–74.

[45] V. V. Dokuchaev, 'Osobaya ekspeditsiya, snaryazhennaya lesnym departamentom, pod rukovodstvom professora Dokuchaeva', in *Sochineniya*, vi. 118–22. On Velikii Anadol', see also below, pp. 185–6.

Map 4. Dokuchaev's expeditions

Adapted from I. Krupenikov and L. Krupenikov, *Puteshestviya i ekspeditsii V. V. Dokuchaeva* (Moscow 1949).

The research stations contained what Dokuchaev believed to be examples of the 'virgin' steppe environment, of which ever smaller areas were left on account of the wholesale ploughing up of the steppe over the preceding decades. For the purposes of Dokuchaev's research, the areas of 'virgin' nature were subjected to inviolable management to preserve their status: all human activity other than scientific work was banned. The scientists carried out detailed research into the flora and fauna, climate, relief, drainage, geology, and soil of these samples of 'virgin' nature. The results were published in a number of volumes.[46] The

---

[46] *TESLD, Nauchnii otdel*, 4 vols (Spb, 1894–8).

scientists used the data as controls or baselines for assessing the impact of experiments they carried out into different regimes of tree planting and water management. The expedition's scientists were seeking also to learn from 'nature' in devising agricultural methods appropriate to the steppe environment.[47]

THE STEPPE ENVIRONMENT

The studies carried out by naturalists, scientists, and statisticians over the late eighteenth, nineteenth, and early twentieth centuries allow us to trace the emerging understandings of the steppe environment. The following discussion considers the subjects of vegetation, climate, relief, and, finally, the soil.

Vegetation

The Academy of Sciences expeditions approached the steppes from the north. The leaders commented favourably on the wooded areas, that is, a familiar landscape, they passed through. In 1769, Pallas remarked of the countryside along the road from Samara to Orenburg:

fancy can scarce point a prettier district; the most beautiful woods of ash and birch, relieved in turns, with green hills and luxuriant meadows. No country surely deserves cultivation more than along the river Samara, there being plenty of arable land, no want of wood, and great extent of very rich and beautiful meadow.[48]

As they moved further south and south-east, however, they commented negatively on the increasingly treeless environment they encountered. Lepekhin—the only Russian expedition leader—seems particularly to have suffered from the scarcity of trees. En route from Moscow to Simbirsk on the mid-Volga, he recorded one place as mostly steppe where large forests could no longer to be seen. On his way to Stavropol' (on the Volga),[49] 'one could not hope that there would be anything worthy of comment', he despaired, where 'the vast steppes and little-forested areas begin'. At last, near Saratov, they stopped at a monastery in 'a pleasant place, surrounded by fine groves' of trees.[50] In 1839,

---

[47] Dokuchaev, 'Osobaya ekspeditsiya', 122–5.
[48] S. Pallas (*sic*), 'Travels into Siberia and Tatary, Provinces of the Russian Empire', in John Trusler (ed.), *The Habitable World Described, or the Present State of the People in all Parts of the Globe . . .* vols 2–4 (London, 1788–89) ii. 141; see also 60–1, 63, 80, 123–4.
[49] As distinct from Stavropol' in the North Caucasus.
[50] I. I. Lepekhin, 'Zapiski Puteshestviya Akademika Lepekhina', *PSUPpR*, iii (Spb, 1821), 90, 228, 397–8. Other expedition leaders commented on the lack of trees. Fal'k, 'Zapiski', 43, 87; Samuel Georg (*sic*) Gmelin, *Puteshestvie po Rossii dlya issledovaniya trekh tsarstv estestva, perevedena s nemetskogo*, 4 vols in 3 parts (Spb, 1771–85), ii. 344; I. Ya. Gil'denshtedt, 'Dnevnik puteshestviya v Yuzhnuyu Rossiyu akademika S. Peterburgskoi Akademii Nauk Gil'denshtedta v 1773–1774 g.', *Zapiski Imperatorskogo Odesskogo obshchestva istorii i drevnosti*, xi (1879), 207.

Andrei Leopol'dov, a local inhabitant who produced a statistical description of Saratov province, noted that there were 'no forests' on the steppes beyond the Volga. He described the territory that became Samara province in 1851 as 'an immense plain'. 'Looking down on it from hill tops [on the hilly side of the Volga],' he continued, 'one's gaze is lost in the immensity; neither a hillock nor a tree are to be seen.'[51]

All the sources, from the travellers' accounts discussed in Chapter 1 to the scientific and statistical studies considered here, indicate that trees and shrubs were restricted to certain locations in the steppe region: river valleys, ravines, uplands, and areas with sandy soil. Dokuchaev considered the woodland Herodotus called 'Hylaea' to be the 'best example' of trees growing in a river valley on the steppes.[52] Herodotus placed 'Hylaea', which he considered the exception in otherwise treeless Scythia, to the east of the Borysthenes (Dnepr) river.[53] Scholars attempted to locate Hylaea and to estimate its size. In 1803, K. I. Gablits wrote that it had extended from the estuary of the river Dnepr along the coast to the Perekop Isthmus (which links the Crimean Peninsula with the mainland) and then north-west to the Samara river (a tributary of the Dnepr, nowhere near the city of Samara). This was a substantial area of land. He added that at the time he was writing, apart from a few locations along the Dnepr, there was no forest left.[54] In spite of the limited evidence available, speculation on the former extent of Hylaea continued. Some writers argued it had been even larger, reaching the Molochnaya river or even further east. Others were inclined towards a smaller 'Hylaea', located nearer the estuary of the Dnepr and on a large area of sand near the town of Aleshki. In the early twentieth century, Valerii Taliev and Grigorii Vysotskii debated the issue. Taliev speculated that Hylaea may have been larger, while Vysotskii systematically picked holes in the evidence Taliev presented.[55]

The presence of trees in river valleys was noted by the leaders of the Academy of Sciences expeditions. As he made his way downstream between Saratov and Tsaritsyn in 1769, Lepekhin recorded: 'Along the left side towards the Volga dense and tall dark forest is to be seen everywhere, and on the right hand, open

[51] A. Leopol'dov, *Statisticheskoe opisanie Saratovskoi gubernii*, 2 vols (Spb, 1839), i. 12, 14.

[52] V. V. Dokuchaev, 'Nashi Stepi prezhde i teper', in *Sochineniya*, vi, 13–102, 61.

[53] Herodotus, *The Histories*, trans. Aubrey de Selincourt, further revised edn (London, 2003), 243, 246–7.

[54] K. I. Gablits, *Geograficheskie izvestiya sluzhashchie k ob"yasneniyu prezhnego sostoyaniya nyneshnei Tavricheskoi gubernii sobrannye iz raznykh drevnikh i srednikh vremen Pisatelei* (Spb, 1803), 3–4.

[55] V. Taliev, 'Bednyi Gerodot i drugie "svetil'niki" v rukakh pochvenno-botanicheskoi geografii', *Estestvoznanie i geografiya*, 8 (1905), 28–43; G. Vysotskii, 'Iz naibolee drevnikh dokumentov o skifakh, glavnykh rekakh i beslesii stepei yuzhnoi Rossii', *LZh*, 35/2 (1905), 241–4; G. Vysotskii, 'Po povodu zametki g. Talieva', *LZh*, 36/1 (1906), 92–6.

steppe', although in places there were small groups of trees. The 'dense and tall' forest on the left bank was on the flood plain of the river. Along the same stretch in 1793, Pallas also noted trees in sandy soil on the high, right bank.[56] Güldenstädt found plenty of trees as he made his way down the Don in 1769. He noted that both the high west (right) bank and low, sandy east (left) bank of the river were covered in trees, especially oak.[57] Güldenstädt and Pallas noted the existence of 'good' and 'abundant' forest in the Kuma and Terek river valleys, especially along the upper reaches towards the foothills of the Caucasus mountains.[58] In 1781–2, Zuev reported the presence of trees and shrubs near rivers as he travelled across the steppes to Kherson.[59] A study of the rivers in the Don Cossack territory carried out between 1847 and 1853 recorded that there were patches of fairly dense woodland in the Don river valley upstream from Kachalinskaya cossack settlement (the crossing point to the Volga), in the Donets valley, and in the valleys of the Khoper and Medveditsa rivers in the north of the territory. Trees were much sparser further south. The main types of trees in the river valleys were oak, elm, asp, wild apple, willow, and poplar.[60] In southern Samara province, according to *zemstvo* surveys in the 1880s, there were few trees, with the exception of a narrow band, or isolated groves, of broadleaved trees along the left bank, that is, the flood plain, of the river Volga and other rivers.[61]

Studies also noted the presence of trees in ravines and gullies. Back in the 1760s, the lands the government authorized for settlement by foreign colonists on the steppes in the Volga region included areas of woodland, many of which were located in ravines. For example, 'between the course of the Bol'shoi Tarlik river and the Kamyshev ravine, there were ... 2,254 [*desyatiny*] of woodland in the ravine'.[62] Deep, forested ravines to the south of Saratov attracted the attention of Lepekhin, who characteristically was struck by their beauty. Further south, beyond Tsaritsyn, the landscape was 'wholly steppe, and trees were not to be seen anywhere, except in the ravines, which were full of blackthorn, hawthorn, and wild apple trees, which attracted a beautiful species of bird'.[63] The ravines that cut through the steppe between the Don and the Volga were also full of trees.[64] Güldenstädt found 'many very good oaks, linden, apple and pear trees' in

---

[56] Lepekhin, 'Zapiski', 310, 358, 371–3, 402 (quotation); Peter Simon Pallas, *Travels through the Southern Provinces of the Russian Empire, in the Years 1793 and 1794*, 2 vols (London, 1802), i. 67.

[57] Johann Anton Güldenstädt, *Reisen durch Russland und im Caucasischen Gebürge*, 2 vols (Spb, 1787–91), i. 62, 69, 74, 86, 89, 96, 114. See also Gmelin, *Puteshestvie*, i. 200–1; ii. 56; Fal'k, 'Zapiski', 40, 43–4.

[58] Iogann Anton Gil'denshtedt, *Puteshestvie po Kavkazu v 1770–1773 gg.*, trans. T. K. Shafranovskoi (Spb, 2002), 35, 36, 290–1; Peter Simon Pallas, *Puteshestvie po raznym provintsiyam Rossiiskoi Imperii*, 3 vols (Spb, 1773–88), iii. 198. See also Fal'k, 'Zapiski', 88, 95.

[59] Zuev, *Puteshestvennye zapiski*, 226.

[60] GARO, f.46, op.1, d.590, ll.69ob., 130ob., 140, 144ob.–145ob.

[61] *SSSpSG*, i, *Samarskii uezd* (1883), 1st pagn, 3; vii, *Novouzenskii uezd* (1890), 6–7.

[62] *PSZ*, 1, xvi. 313–16 (no. 11,880, 22 July 1763).

[63] Lepekhin, 'Zapiski', 408–11, 465–6, 480. The bird was a type of thrush.

[64] Fal'k, 'Zapiski', 48–50. See also Zuev, *Puteshestvennye zapiski*, 226.

the ravines and gullies in the basin of the upper reaches of the Mius river, near Taganrog.[65] In the early twentieth century, ravines were one of the main locations of trees in the Don region.[66]

The sources also record that trees grew on uplands. Lepekhin visited a German settlement south of Saratov surrounded by forested hills.[67] The foothills of the Caucasus mountains were forested. Güldenstädt noted that: 'On Mashuk [one of the five hills around the site where Pyatigorsk was founded in 1780] . . . there were many forests.'[68] In the mid-1770s, an army officer sent to survey locations for a line of fortresses across the North Caucasus found forests on the foothills and upland areas, including the site where the fortress and later city of Stavropol' was founded in 1777.[69] The Ural mountains were covered with trees. Pallas regularly commented on the wooded hills when he travelled in the area in 1769 and 1770.[70] In the late nineteenth century, substantial areas of natural woodland survived on the boundary of the forest-steppe and steppe regions, such as the broadleaved Shipov forest in south-eastern Voronezh province and the coniferous Buzulukskii bor, where pine trees grew on sandy soil in eastern Samara province. Indeed, locations with sandy soil were among the few places in the steppe region where trees grew naturally.[71]

From the late eighteenth century, naturalists, scientists, and foresters investigated why there were so few trees in the steppe region, and why those that were there were limited to certain locations. Lepekhin recorded that the oak trees he found in a ravine had been attacked by insects that had eaten all their leaves, presenting a 'pitiful sight'.[72] Members of the expeditions also noted a connection between shortage of water and lack of trees. Gmelin wrote that, in contrast to bare steppes with no rivers, trees grew in areas that were supplied with water. Lepekhin noted the presence of trees in ravines that contained springs.[73] The Odessa botanical garden, which was founded in 1820, served as a laboratory for investigating the reasons for the limited extent of forests. Trees were imported from various parts of the world. Some did well initially, but began to die after a few years. The director, Aleksandr Nordman (a native of densely forested Finland), attributed this to the hot summers, winds, droughts, and the alkaline subsoil. The last, he believed, was fatal for trees. He concluded that with the

[65] Gil'denshtedt, 'Dnevnik', 206, 217.

[66] V. V. Bogachev, *Ocherki geografii Vsevelikogo Voiska Donskogo* (Novocherkassk, 1919), 172–3.

[67] Lepekhin, 'Zapiski', 413–14.

[68] Gil'denshtedt, *Puteshestvie*, 286, 293, 307.

[69] Excerpts are quoted in I. V. Bentkovskii, 'O lesakh v predelakh byvshei Kavkazskoi, a nyne Stavropol'skoi gubernii', *Stavropol'skie gubernskie vedomosti* (3 January 1876).

[70] Pallas, 'Travels', iii, for example, 32, 39, 60.

[71] See D. Kravchinskii, 'Istoricheskii i lesovodstvennyi ocherk Shipova lesa, Voronezhskoi gubernii', *LZh*, 17/2 (1887), 189–97; 17/4 (1887), 474–91; G. N. Vysotskii, 'Buzulukskii bor i ego okrestnosti (mezhdu dolinami rek Kineli i Samary)', *LZh*, 39/10 (1909), 1133–78.

[72] Lepekhin, 'Zapiski', 408.

[73] Gmelin, *Puteshestvie*, i. 201; Lepekhin, 'Zapiski', 408. See also Güldenstädt, *Reisen*, 95.

exception of certain areas, such as river valleys, the environment of the New Russian steppes was not suitable for trees.[74] The debate continued. In 1857, Veselovskii stated that the prevailing easterly winds made the soil and air too dry for forests in the steppe region.[75] In the 1890s, Dokuchaev's colleagues Tanfil'ev and Vysotskii returned to the issue of the subsoil. They argued that it was not directly the supply of water, but the soil conditions, that explained the limited extent of trees. Trees were restricted naturally to areas where the salts in the subsoil had been leached out by water. River valleys (obviously), ravines (where rainwater and melted snow, as well as spring water, ran through), and uplands (which had more rainfall) were precisely such areas in the steppe region. To the north of the steppes, in the forest-steppe and forest regions, the higher rainfall had created soil conditions in which trees could thrive.[76]

All these arguments also contributed to the long-running debate about the extent of forests in the region in the past, which began in the late eighteenth century.[77] The prevailing view then and in the early nineteenth century was that much of the steppe region had once been forested. The nomadic pastoralists who had lived in the region for millennia prior to the Russian conquest and settlement, and other inhabitants, were blamed for destroying the forests. In 1793, Pallas noted: 'The steppes are frequently fired, either by the negligence of travellers, or wilfully by the herdsmen [nomads], in order to forward the crops of grass; or . . . out of malice, by Yaik Cossacks who did so to surround Russian troops sent against them.' Such fires endangered crops, dwellings, and forests.[78] Lepekhin complained that Kalmyks in the mid-Volga region were felling trees without any care and had created a shortage.[79] The nomads' livestock, moreover, prevented trees from regenerating by grazing on saplings. The remaining trees suffered from further depletion by the settlers who displaced the nomads (see Chapter 3).

The implication of this argument, which was spelled out by Karl Hermann among others, was that the environment of the steppes, including the soil and the climate, was suitable for trees to grow and flourish, and that the treeless landscape

---

[74] A. Nordman, 'O gorode Odesse v estestvoispytatel'nom otnoshenii', *Listki Imperatorskogo Obshchestva Sel'skogo Khozyaistva Yuzhnoi Rossii*, 4 (1837), 208–10; A. Nordman, 'Opisanie imperatorskogo Odesskogo sada i vzglyad na rastitel'nye i klimatologicheskie otnosheniya okrestnostei g. Odessy', *ZIOSKhYuR*, 6 (1847), 108–11; I. Palimpsestov, *Stepi yuga Rossii byli-li iskoni vekov stepami i vozmozhno-li oblesit'' ikh?*, revised edn (Odessa, 1890), 262.

[75] K. Veselovskii, *O Klimate Rossii* (Spb, 1857), 262, 316, 320.

[76] G. Tanfil'ev, 'Predely lesov na yuge Rossii', *TESLD, Nauchnyi otdel*, 2/1 (1894); G. N. Vysotskii, 'Pochvennye zony Evropeiskoi Rossii v svyazi s solenosnost'yu gruntov i kharakterom lesnoi rastitel'nosti', *Pochvovedenie*, 1/1 (1899), 19–26. See also Chapter 6, this volume.

[77] For a summary, see Ya. Veinberg, *Les: znachenie ego v prirode i mery k ego sokhraneniyu* (Moscow, 1884), 251–4. For a fuller analysis, see N. F. Komarov, 'Etapy i faktory evolyutsii rastitel'nostogo pokrova chernozemnykh stepei', *Zapiski vsesoyuznogo geograficheskogo obshchestva*, new ser., 13 (1951), 7–328.

[78] Pallas, *Travels* i. 114–15.

[79] Lepekhin, 'Zapiski', 257.

had been created by the inhabitants, especially the nomads.[80] Palimpsestov became almost obsessed with the idea that the steppes had once been forested. In a number of publications from the 1850s to the 1890s, he asserted and reasserted this argument, and that humans were responsible for the forests' destruction.[81] He had no real evidence that could stand up to scientific scrutiny at that time, however, and in 1881, an older and perhaps beleaguered Palimpsestov expressed the hope that people who were 'wiser' than him would come along and prove the general existence of forests on the steppes of 'southern Russia'.[82]

Over the mid- and later decades of the nineteenth century, there was a growing consensus that the steppes had never been forested. In the 1840s and 1850s, Karl Ernst von Baer noted that the difficulty in growing trees in the steppe region indicated that the environmental conditions were not suitable. His most interesting argument concerned the absence of squirrels in the forests of the Crimea. This was evidence, he argued, that the steppes to the north had never been forested as squirrels had not been able to cross the grasslands between the Crimea and the forests of central Russia.[83] The development of geobotany and soil science later in the century seemed, at least for the time being, to settle the argument. Ruprecht and Dokuchaev argued that the black earth had evolved under steppe, that is, grassy vegetation, and thus the steppes had been grasslands for a very long time. Dokuchaev dismissed Palimpsestov's work in a devastating review.[84] There was little room in Dokuchaev's ideas for the role of humans in the creation of the steppe environment. He explicitly denied that the past

---

[80] Komarov, 'Etapy', 47–50; [Carl Theodor] Hermann, 'Geschichte und gegenwärtiger Zustand des Forstwesens in Russland', in Heinrich von Storch (ed.), *Russland unter Alexander dem Ersten: Eine historische Zeitschrift*, 9 vols (Spb, 1804–8); 4/11 (1804), 185–203; 5/13 (1805), 47–62; 5/14 (1805), 47–57.

[81] P[alimpsestov], 'Lesovodstvo. Nechto v rode "Vvedeniya" v uroki lesovodstva dlya Novorossiiskogo kraya', *ZIOSKhYuR*, 1 (1852), 15–80; I. Palimpsestov 'Peremenilsya li klimat yuga Rossii?', in I. Palimpsestov (ed.), *Sbornik statei o sel'skom khozyaistve yuga Rossii, izvlechennikh iz Zapisok Imperatorskogo Obshchestva sel'skogo khozyaistva yuzhnoi Rossii s 1830 po 1868 god* (Odessa, 1868), 1–35; Palimpsestov, *Stepi yuga Rossii.*

[82] I. U. Palimpsestov, 'Odin iz otvetov na vopros: 'byli li lesa na yuge Rossii?', *Izvestiya imperatorskogo Obshchestva lyubitelei estestvoznaniya, antropologii i etnografii*, 41/1 (1881), 20–6.

[83] Karl Ernst von Baer and Fr. von Helmerson, 'Vorwort des Herausgebers' to P. von Köppen, 'Ein Bericht an die Commission zur Untersushung der Frage über den Einfluss der Verminderung der Wälder auf die Verminderung des Wassers in der obern Wolga', *Beiträge zur Kenntniss des russischen Reiches und den angränzenden Länder Asiens*, 4 (1841), 165–98; Karl Ernst von Baer, 'Die uralte Waldlosigkeit Steppe', *Beiträge zur Kenntniss des russischen Reiches und den angränzenden Länder Asiens*, 18 (1856), 109–115.

[84] F. Ruprekht, 'Geo-botanicheskie issledovaniya o chernozeme', *Zapiski Imperatorskoi Akademii Nauk*, 10, appendix 6 (1866), 1–131; V. V. Dokuchaev, 'Otzyv o trude Iv. Palimpsestova: 'Stepi yuga Rossii byli-li iskoni vekov stepami i vozmozhno-li oblesit' ikh?', in *Sochineniya*, vi. 239–45 (1st pub. 1895). See also Anastasia A. Fedotova, 'The Origins of the Russian Chernozem Soil (Black Earth): Franz Joseph Ruprecht's "Geo-Botanical Researches into the Chernozem" of 1866', trans. David Moon, *Environment and History*, 16 (2010), 271–94.

inhabitants of the steppes had burnt down the forests that were alleged to have existed.[85] The debate rumbled on into the early twentieth century. Tanfil'ev and Vysotskii skirmished in the periodical press with the botanist Taliev and others.[86]

Naturalists and scientists also paid attention to the main steppe flora: the wild grasses and flowers. Since many of the plants in the region were new to natural history in the eighteenth century, the Academy of Sciences expeditions devoted a lot of effort to cataloguing, drawing, and collecting specimens of the plants they found. The books produced by the expedition leaders contained many very carefully executed illustrations of the plants of the steppes.[87] Pallas became a leading authority on the flora of Russia.[88]

As he made his way south from Simbirsk in the spring of 1769, Lepekhin noted that the steppe was 'greening over' with feather grass (*kovyl'*), 'the young stems of which provide succulent fodder for the grazing herds'.[89] Much further south between the Don and Volga, on his way to Tsaritsyn, Güldenstädt noted that the steppe was covered in feather grass.[90] A traveller's account of Dneprovsk district, Tauride province, written in the late 1830s pointed out that '*kovyl* (*Stipa pennata*)', known as 'tirs' to the Nogai nomads, grew 'in large quantities', and comprised the distinctive feature of the local steppes. Later studies confirmed that feather grass was the predominant type of grass on unploughed, or virgin, land throughout much of the region, from the forest-steppe in the north to the more arid steppe in the south-east. Feather grass is a perennial plant, most species of which reach around half a metre, and some a metre, in height. The leaves provide good fodder for livestock, especially horses. In the late spring, it grows long, silver-grey spikelets, with the appearance of feathers, that blow off in the wind to propagate the grass across the steppe. The spikelets, however, were fatal to sheep if they pierced their skin. While the spikelets are still attached, the grass blows in the wind creating the appearance of waves, giving rise to the character-istic description of the steppes as a sea or ocean of grass.[91]

---

[85] V. V. Dokuchaev, 'Nashi Stepi prezhde i teper', in *Sochineniya*, vi. 67.

[86] For a few examples, see G. Tanfil'ev, 'K voprosu o bezlesii stepei', *Estestvoznanie i geografiya*, 5 (1901), 62–71; V. Taliev, 'Byli nashi stepi vsegda bezlesnymi', *Estestvoznanie i geografiya*, 5 (1902), 33–46; V. Taliev, 'Vopros o proshlom nashikh stepei i pochvovedenie', *LZh*, 35/9 (1905), 1507–30; G. Vysotskii, 'Otvet na "vopros o proshlom nashikh stepei i pochvovedenie" g. Taliev', *LZh*, 35/9 (1905), 1588–90. More recent analysis of fossil pollen has shown that, although for the wrong reasons, Palimpsestov was broadly correct. David Moon, 'Were the Steppes ever Forested? Science, Economic Development, and Identity in the Russian Empire in the 19th Century', in L. Jelecek (eds), *Dealing with Diversity: 2nd International Conference of the European Society for Environmental History: Proceedings* (Prague, 2003), 206–9.

[87] See, for example, Gmelin, *Puteshestvie.*

[88] See Wendland, *Peter Simon Pallas*, i. 415–38, 542–5.

[89] Lepekin, 'Zapiski', 306.

[90] Güldenstädt, *Reisen*, i. 98.

[91] 'Putevye zametki pri ob"ezde dneprovskogo i melitopol'skogo uezdov tavricheskoi gubernii, v 1835 godu', *Liski Imperatorskogo Obshchestva sel'skogo khozyaistva yuzhnoi Rossii*, 3 (1838), 175–6; S. David, 'Kovyl'', *PERSKh*, iv (1901), 324–6.

Wild flowers, herbs, and flowering shrubs brought striking colour to the steppes in the spring. They were carefully studied by the Academy of Sciences expeditions.[92] Lepekhin, who came to appreciate the beauty of the steppe flora, described how the two-coloured iris (*iris biflora*) and anemones covered the steppe with their flowers.[93] Making his way up the Volga in 1773, Pallas noted how 'beautiful broom' grew on the slopes of water-filled, wide ravines, while on the high, dry, hilly steppe on the right bank of the river, where all the grasses dried up in the summer, 'there is one exception a yellow flowering grass that almost alone flowers in the autumn'.[94] On his second trip in 1793, he made a very detailed study of the flora on the left bank of the Volga, noting, among other plants, the wild tulips.[95] Another plant that was characteristic of the steppes, Russian thistle (*perekati-pole, Salsola Kali*), had an unusual way of spreading its seeds: it formed a ball, which broke from the stem and was blown around by the wind, as a 'tumbleweed'.[96]

Several leaders of the Academy of Sciences expeditions noted that different plants grew in different parts of the steppe region. Especially noticeable were the plants that grew on the salty soils in the south-east. Lepekhin listed the 'rare plants', such as the thistle '*tatarnik*', which he found on the steppe near Tsaritsyn on the lower Volga and had not seen in other places.[97] Pallas and Falck paid attention to the 'salt plants', especially saltwort (*solyanka kustovataya, Salicornia Arabica*), which they found near salt lakes east of the Volga. Falck also found such plants on the sandy and salty Kuma steppe in the North Caucasus. He contrasted these plants with what he termed 'ordinary vegetation'.[98] Lepekhin made a study of plants that lived in the salty environment between the Volga and the Yaik/Ural rivers, while Pallas studied plants that thrived in similar conditions in the valley of the latter river.[99]

Over the nineteenth century, botanists began to make closer and more direct connections between types of plants and the environments—in particular the climates and soils—in which they grew. In the 1860s, Ruprecht produced a list of plants he considered to be 'typical' of steppes with black earth. Botanists started to cite species from his list as indicators of this type of soil. Anastasiya Fedotova concluded:

[92] See, for example, Pallas, 'Travels', ii. 124–5.

[93] Lepekhin, 'Zapiski', 306, 486, 495.

[94] [Peter Simon Pallas], 'Puteshestvie po raznym provintsiyam Rossiiskoi Imperii', in V. Alekseev (ed.), *Istoricheskie puteshestviya: izvlecheniya iz memuarov i zapisok inostrannykh i russkikh puteshestvennikov po Volge v XV–XVIII vekakh* (Stalingrad, 1936), 247–9, 257, 259–61.

[95] Pallas, *Travels*, i. 114, 121, 131–8.

[96] G. Tanfil'ev, 'Geografiya rastenii', *PERSKh*, ii (1900), 536.

[97] Lepekhin, 'Zapiski', 472–3.

[98] Pallas, 'Travels', iii. 8, 14; Fal'k, 'Zapiski', 50, 92–3.

[99] Lepekhin, 'Zapiski', 441; [P. S. Pallas], *Nauchnoe nasledie P. S. Pallasa: pis'ma 1768–1771 gg.*, trans. V. I. Osipov and G. I. Fedorova (Spb, 1993), 89. The Yaik river was renamed the Ural river by Catherine the Great in the aftermath of the Pugachev revolt of 1773–4.

It would not be an exaggeration to state that Ruprecht's work marked the start of the development of a scientific conception of steppe as a specific type of landscape with particular flora, vegetation and soil. It can also be considered that the theme of Ruprecht's research—the study of the interdependence between vegetation and soil —anticipated the direction of the work in Russian plant geography over the following decades.[100]

These ideas were further developed by the scientists, such as Tanfil'ev, on Dokuchaev's expedition in the 1890s. They carefully catalogued the plants on the areas of virgin steppe on their field research stations, making distinctions between plants that grew on black earth and on salty soils, and in different parts of the steppe region.[101] A study of the natural history of the steppes in the early twentieth century noted the transition in the main types of plants, as the environmental conditions changed to the east and south-east, from feather grass to *tipchak* (*Festúca valesiáca*) and wormwood (*polyn'*, *Artemisia*).[102]

The appearance of the steppes also changed over the year. Based on observations on the Starobel'sk and Khrenovskoi research stations during Dokuchaev's expedition of the 1890s, Tanfil'ev described the changes, beginning 'with the awakening of life with the spring and ending with the dying down of the steppe prior to the long winter rest'. First to emerge, once the snow had gone, were bright green mosses and the curious, dark green fingers of algae (or cyanobacteria) that covered the black earth between the remains of the previous year's vegetation. In the second half of April, the first spring flowers appeared, including wild tulips, small, purple pasque flowers or prairie crocuses, followed a little later by the larger, white-flowered Tatar bread plant, and the yellow curveseed butterwort, which Tanfil'ev, unscientifically and ungallantly, considered 'plain'. The most luxuriant period for vegetation on the Starobel'sk 'virgin' steppe began at the end of May or in early June, when the early spring plants were followed by many, many more that flowered over the summer months. The predominant plants at this time, when all others retreated into the background, were feather grass and sage. The picture changed again at the end of the summer, when most plants began to wither. Only a few new ones took their place, and areas of bare, cracked soil appeared between clumps of plants, including feather grass that made up the bulk of the vegetation in the autumn. In contrast to the various and changing colours since the spring, however, by the end of autumn only the dried and withered stalks of the steppe grasses and other plants remained. The last plants to appear, unharmed by the start of the frosts, were

---

[100] Fedotova, 'Origins', 284–5. See also Anastasia Fedotova, 'Botanicheskie issledovaniya v Nizhegorodskoi ekspeditsii V. V. Dokuchaeva i izmenenie podkhoda k izucheniyu rastitel'nosti', *Istoriko-Biologicheskie Issledovaniya*, 2/4 (2010), 66–83.

[101] For a summary, see Tanfil'ev, 'Geografiya rastcnii', 552–9.

[102] V. V. Morachevskii (ed.), *Yugo-Vostok Evropeiskoi Rossii (Samarskaya, Saratovskaya, Simbirskaya, Penzenskaya, Voronezhskaya i Tambovskaya gubernii): Obshchaya kharakteristika oblastnogo paiona v estestvenno-istoricheskom i statistiko-ekonomicheskom otnosheniyakh* (Spb, 1911), 19.

the mosses and algae that had been the first to show signs of life in the early spring.[103]

Climate, droughts, and harvest failures

The sharp differences between the seasons were reflected in the itineraries of the Academy of Sciences expeditions. Stops were scheduled each year for the winter. At the end of the first year of his expedition, Pallas stopped for the winter in Simbirsk in late October. On 21 October he crossed the partly frozen Volga with difficulty. By mid-December, the temperature had plummeted to around −27°C. Pallas stayed in Simbirsk until 10 March 1769. The winter lasted longer as he travelled east. His expedition ended for the year when he arrived in Ufa in the southern Urals on 2 October 1769. He did not leave until 10 April 1770.[104] Pallas' expedition travelled across the north and east of the steppe region, where the climate was harsh. The expeditions that travelled across the southern steppes stopped for less than two months in the winter.[105] In a description of the provinces of Astrakhan' and the Caucasus (later renamed Stavropol') prepared for the Free Economic Society in 1809, Rovinskii drew attention to periodic, very cold winters, such as in 1803, when crows froze to death, 'not only on the steppes, but also in the city'. In the winters of 1788 and 1799, the local Kalmyks had lost many of their livestock to the severe cold.[106]

In contrast, summers could be very hot, and the effects of the heat were exacerbated by the wind. Pallas described the heat and winds he encountered at Tsaritsyn in the summer of 1774: 'The hottest and most intolerable of all the summer months is July, when it blows constantly.'[107] Herodotus was not the only visitor to note the 'violent thunderstorms' in the summer. Many centuries later, Güldenstädt recorded thunder and lightning during his time on the lower Don in the summer of 1773.[108] Pallas also noted thunderstorms, with violent hail and rain, in Tsaritsyn in August 1773.[109] In sharp contrast to Herodotus' statement that it never stopped raining in the summer, however, the Academy of Sciences expeditions coincided with a serious drought and heatwave in the Volga basin in 1769. Pallas wrote in Samara at the end of May that, although clouds appeared on the horizon, not a drop of rain had fallen in the whole region

[103] Tanfil'ev, 'Botanikogeograficheskie issledovaniya', 9–12.

[104] Pallas, 'Travels', ii. 87–90, 102, 115; iii. 34; [Pallas], *Nauchnoe nasledie*, 73–4, 94, 118; PFA RAN, f.3, op.30, 1768–72, d.1, ll.2–2ob., 5–6ob.; op.32, d.1, ll.1, 3.

[105] Yu. Kh. Kopelevich, *Iogann Anton Gil'denshtedt* (Moscow, 1997), 32–5; PFA RAN, f.3, op.33, 1768–74, d.1. l.3; op.34, 1768–74, d.1, l.6; Gil'denshtedt, *Puteshestvie*, 35.

[106] [I. V. Rovinskii], *Khozyaistvennoe opisanie Astrakhanskoi i Kavkazskoi gubernii* (Spb, 1809), 60–1.

[107] Pallas, 'Travels', iv. 315.

[108] Gil'denshtedt, 'Dnevnik', 188, 190, 192.

[109] Pallas, 'Travels', iv. 316.

since the start of April.[110] According to Lepekhin, who was also in Samara, all the rural inhabitants were praying for rain after a great drought that spring.[111] The drought continued thoughout the summer of 1769.[112] Rovinskii noted that droughts on the steppes of Astrakhan' and the North Caucasus were a 'burden' on the population. In 1802, for example, there was no rain between 18 June and 16 July, and not only the grain but even the grass on the flood plains withered.[113]

For the farmers who had settled on the steppes, the periodic droughts were a recurring nightmare, causing crop failures and famines. One of the worst years was 1833. The Economic Department of the Ministry of Internal Affairs, which was responsible for famine relief, reported the unfolding disaster. It affected all the southern, and some central, provinces, stretching from the Carpathian mountains in the west to the Caucasus in the south-east. In the autumn of 1832, in many provinces there was a lot of rain, followed by early snow and frosts. This aroused fears for the winter crops that had sprouted. There was no spring at all in southern Russia in 1833. Unusually severe cold and hard frosts persisted in March and April, but were followed directly by heatwaves. There was a total drought that lasted for several months, the effects of which were exacerbated by strong winds. The authorities in the afflicted areas started to report on the limited prospects for the harvest in June. The ataman of the Don Cossacks wrote that the drought had killed off all the crops and the grass. Livestock faced starvation. Reports indicated that all hope had been lost of harvests of winter and spring grain in Ekaterinoslav, Kherson, Tauride, Caucasus, Poltava, Slobodsko-Ukraine (later Khar'kov), Voronezh, and Penza provinces, and some districts of Saratov province. The situation worsened over the summer and autumn, with reports that: 'There was no precedent for such a harvest failure'; 'Now, almost the entire southern region of Russia' has been hit by the 'most fearsome, widespread harvest failure of all products of the plant kingdom.' In some places, peasants lost all their sowings, in others, between a half and three-quarters, and in places the harvest barely returned the seed.[114] Further reports from local inhabitants confirmed the extent of the disaster. K. Engel'ke (a German colonist) in Saratov province wrote: 'In general 1833 was very unfavourable. The very unusual drought lasted from spring to autumn: the failure of grain and grass harvests was complete.'[115] Leopol'dov noted tersely that the summer of 1833 'was an act of God'.[116]

---

[110] [Pallas], *Nauchnoe nasledie*, 79.
[111] Lepekhin, 'Zapiski', 341.
[112] Gmelin, *Puteshestvie*, ii. 30.
[113] [Rovinskii], *Khozyaistvennoe opisanie*, 58, 62.
[114] RGIA, f.1287, op.2, 1833, d.146, ll.229ob.–34, 242–ob., 256, 269, 296ob.
[115] K. Engel'ke, 'Khozyaistvennoe polozhenie Saratovskoi gubernii', *ZhMGI*, 1/2 (1841), 371.
[116] Leopol'dov, *Statisticheskoe opisanie*, i. 118. On the wider consequences of the disaster, see David Moon, *Russian Peasants and Tsarist Legislation on the Eve of Reform, 1825–1855* (Basingstoke, 1992), 41–4.

Droughts caused bad harvests of varying degrees of magnitude affecting parts of the steppe region over the following decades, for example in 1840, 1848, 1855, 1873 (especially bad in Samara province), 1875, 1880, and 1885 (particularly severe in the North Caucasus).[117] The only year comparable to 1833 was 1891. Future Minister of Agriculture Aleksei Ermolov described the course of events. The unusual weather began in 1890. The first half of the summer was very wet. The weather changed sharply in the second half of June to a 'tropical' heatwave, drought, and scorching hot winds from the south-east. As a result, the harvest in 1890 was adversely affected, and in many places sowing the winter crops was delayed until late September or early October. Winter began early. There were hard frosts in late October and early November. When the snow came, strong winds blew it around and, crucially, denuded the fields of snow cover to protect the winter crops and provide melt water when it thawed. In the spring of 1891, consequently, there was little water in the rivers and no floods that usually irrigated the meadows. Nevertheless, there was sufficient moisture to allow the spring crops to be sown as usual, and the winter crops began to recover.

Recovery was temporary, however. In late April and May, the weather swung back and forth between cold snaps with hard frosts and heatwaves with droughts. The young crops could not survive. Trees dried up and died in their dozens. Even weeds expired. The drought continued for much of the summer. Worst affected was the area around Tsaritsyn, where there was no rain for ninety-six days. Large parts of the steppes received no rain for two months. The effects of the drought were exacerbated by scorching winds that dried out the parched topsoil even more, and then blew it around in dust storms. It was no surprise when the harvest failed. In the seventeen worst-affected provinces, the harvest was down by 45 per cent compared with the average for 1883–7. The most badly hit provinces were Orenburg, in the east of the steppe region, where the shortfall was 73 per cent, and Voronezh, on the boundary of the steppe and forest-steppe, where it was 69 per cent. The disaster affected most of southern and south-eastern European Russia. The steppes of southern Ukraine, part of the Don region, and the North Caucasus, however, escaped and had good harvests in 1891.[118] Droughts and crop failures continued to hit parts of the steppe region after 1891, for example in 1898, 1901, 1905–6, and 1908.[119] The failure of the harvest in a largely peasant society had catastrophic results for the population, some of whom died of

---

[117] See A. Kahan, 'Natural Calamities and their Effect on the Food Supply in Russia,' *JGO*, 16 (1968), 353–77; 'Neurozhai na Rusi', *TVEO*, 2/5 (1891), 145–77; A. S. Ermolov, *Nashi neurozhai i prodovol'stvennyi vopros*, 2 vols (Spb, 1909), i. 43–55, 84–9; James Y. Simms, 'The Crop Failure of 1891: Soil Exhaustion, Technological Backwardness, and Russia's "Agrarian Crisis"', *SR*, 41 (1982), 236–50.

[118] [A. S. Ermolov], *Neurozhai i narodnoe bedstvie* (Spb, 1892), 3–34. See also M. N. Raevskii, 'Neurozhai 1891 goda v svyazi s obshchei kharakteristikoi nashei khlebnoi proizvoditel'nosti a takzhe vyvoza khlebov zagranitsu za predydushchie gody', *IRGO*, 28/1 (1892), 1–29.

[119] Ermolov, *Nashi neurozhai*, i. 153–4, 232, 273, 306–31, 571–98.

starvation or disease. The state suffered serious setbacks to its plans for economic development.[120]

Extreme events such as droughts stood out, but scientific study of the climate required data over significant periods of time. Back in 1809, Rovinskii had been frustrated in seeking to make comparisons with the climate in 'remote times' since he was not able to find 'meteorological observations' beyond a few anecdotes. He noted, however, that a local official had started to collect some data.[121] The systematic collection of meteorological data developed slowly in provincial Russia over the nineteenth century, and even more slowly in the steppe region.[122] General data were collected in some places. Vasilii Sukhorukov's description of the Don Cossack territory compiled between 1822 and 1832 contained crude data on temperatures, the number of days with rain and snow, and wind direction (easterlies prevailed).[123] The Southern Russian Agricultural Society organized 'meteorological observations' from 1831 in recognition of their importance for agriculture.[124] Provincial governors and atamans of cossack territories began to collect data. From the early 1840s to the late 1850s, for example, the annual reports of the Don Cossack ataman included data on the highest and lowest temperatures over the year and the number of days on which it snowed or rained, but not the volume of precipitation, in Novocherkassk. The data give an indication of the variability of the steppe climate. Between 1844 and 1856, the date on which the river Don at Novocherkassk was free from ice fluctuated between 14 February and 7 April, and the date on which it was closed to shipping varied from 21 November to 26 December.[125] A few years later, however, the ataman complained to the local statistical committee about discrepancies in the data on the climate it had sent him.[126]

There was a steady increase in the amount, and reliability, of data that were collected on the climate. Regional officials of the Ministry of State Domains and provincial officials gathered information on extreme climatic events that affected

[120] David Moon, *The Russian Peasantry 1600–1930: The World the Peasants Made* (London, 1999), 28–32. Crises were short-term and regional, and interrupted an upward trend in living standards. See B. N. Mironov, *Blagosostoyanie naseleniya i revolyutsiii v imperskoi Rossii: XVIII–nachalo XX veka* (Moscow, 2010); Stephen Wheatcroft, 'Crises and the Condition of the Peasantry in Late Imperial Russia', in Esther Kingston-Mann and Timothy Mixter (eds), *Peasant Economy, Culture, and Politics of European Russia, 1800–1921* (Princeton, NJ, 1991), 128–72.

[121] [Rovinskii], *Khozyaistvennoe opisanie*, 61.

[122] See Veselovskii, *O Klimate Rossii*, x–xii; G. L., 'Meteorologicheskie nablyudeniya', *ES*, xix (1896), 175–9.

[123] [V. D. Sukhorukov], *Statisticheskoe opisanie zemli Donskikh kazakov, sostavlennoe v 1822–1832 godakh* (Novocherkassk, 1891), 46–51.

[124] Borovskii, *Istoricheskii obzor*, 210–1.

[125] GARO, f.46, op.1, d.522 [1844], ll.95ob., 113–ob.; d.531 [1845], l.77, d.563 [1848], ll.25, 31ob., 39; d.571 [1849], l.31; d.583 [1850], ll.43ob.–44; d.594 [1852], l.25ob.; d.603 [1853], l.41ob.; d.612 [1854], l.43; d.621 [1855], l.28ob., 36ob.–37; d.634 [1857], ll.45–ob.; d.630 [1856], ll.39–ob.; f.353, op.1, d.81, ll.1–45.

[126] GARO, f.353, op.1, d.81, ll.102–3ob.

the harvest, in particular droughts. The inspector of agriculture in the southern provinces presented a detailed report on the crop failure of 1855 that contained data on temperature in seven cities, the wind direction, and the duration of the drought, but not the amount of precipitation.[127] To take another example, the governor of Stavropol' province in the North Caucasus reported in 1878 on the frequency of droughts—seven in the previous seventeen years.[128] The General Staff's statistical surveys of provinces in the steppe region tended to be limited to generalities about hot summers, cold winters, winds from the east, and periodic droughts.[129] Such information that was available in the mid-nineteenth century was used by statisticians Konstantin Arsen'ev and Veselovskii to write broader accounts of the climate of Russia's regions. Veselovskii noted that the prevailing winds in the steppe region came from the east, and that this was a major cause of the extremes of temperature and low rainfall.[130]

A leading role in the growth of meteorology in Russia was played by Aleksandr Voeikov (1842–1916). Voeikov entered St Petersburg university in 1860, but when the university was temporarily closed in 1861 he went to Germany, where he was awarded a doctorate by Göttingen University in 1865. On his return to Russia, he became an important member of the Geographical Society and, in 1885, professor of physical geography at St Petersburg University. He was a strong advocate of collecting accurate and comparable meteorological data and of scientific study of the climate. He made his reputation with a book on the climate of Russia in a global context, published in 1884, in which he demonstrated both his erudition and his energy. Like other Russian scientists of this period, Voeikov was interested in practical applications, and was involved in the development of agricultural meteorology as an applied science.[131] On his and others' initiatives, the systematic collection of more reliable meteorological data began in the late nineteenth century. From the 1870s, the Geographical Society and Academy of Sciences took a lead in organizing meteorological observations, including for the first time in Russia the quantity of precipitation. It took a couple of decades, however, to build up a network of meteorological stations with instruments to

---

[127] [D. Strukov], 'O sostoyanii sel'skogo khozyaistva v yuzhnoi Rossii, v 1855 g.', *ZhMGI*, 60 (1856), 2nd pagn, 172–9, 185.

[128] GASK, f.101, op.4, d.732, ll.2–3.

[129] *MDGSR, Khersonskaya guberniya*, comp. A. Shmidt, 2 vols (1863), i. 359–79; *Zemlya voiska donskogo*, comp. N. Krasnov (1863), 156–70. See also *VSORI*, 5/4, *Saratovskaya guberniya*, comp. Beznosikov (1852), 57–61; 11/4, *Ekaterinoslavskaya guberniya*, comp. Drachevskii (1850), 89–93.

[130] K. Arsen'ev, *Statisticheskie ocherki Rossii* (Spb, 1848), 187–202; Veselovskii, *O klimate Rossii*, 234–7, 261–2, 316.

[131] See 'Voeikov', *ES*, xii (Spb, 1892), 830–1; V. V. Pokshishevskii, 'Aleksandr Ivanovich Voeikov i ego raboty o cheloveke i prirode', in A. I. Voeikov, *Vozdeistvie cheloveka na prirodu: izbrannye stat'i*, ed. V. V. Pokshishevskii (Moscow, 1949), 3–39; A. I. Voeikov, *Klimaty zemnogo shara v osobennosti Rossii* (Spb, 1884).

make accurate measurements that covered much of the steppe region.[132] Meteorological stations were set up in specific locations on the field research stations during Dokuchaev's expedition in the 1890s. They collected data on the temperature of the air and soil, air pressure, hours of sunshine, the amount of precipitation, and its distribution over the year, snow cover, the depth of ground water, humidity, the force and direction of the winds, and also, crucially, the evaporation of moisture.[133]

There was also local initiative. In Stavropol' province, a network of meteorological stations was established in 1886 on the proposal of Józef Bentkowski, the secretary of the Provincial Statistical Committee. The spur was the serious drought of 1885. The stations were based on the recommendations of the Academy of Sciences, and advice from the Russian Geographical Society. Local school teachers were entrusted with recording data collected with thermometers and rain and wind gauges purchased in Germany and St Petersburg.[134] In 1904, however, the official yearbook stated that there was a lack of 'correctly organized meteorological observations' of the climate in the province.[135] Meteorological stations were set up in the 1880s in Samara province, which also suffered from regular droughts. By 1891, the Samara provincial *zemstvo* had detailed information on the climate throughout the province to enable it to conduct a serious study of the causes of the catastrophe of that year.[136] In St Petersburg, in 1894, the new Ministry of Agriculture established a Meteorological Bureau to examine the influence of the climate and weather on agriculture, and to determine the best way to combat harmful atmospheric conditions. The Bureau collected data from meteorological stations across Russia, including the steppe region.[137]

Thus by the early twentieth century, sufficient accurate data had been collected to make a fairly detailed description of the steppe climate. From the point of view of agriculture, what mattered was the availability and distribution over the region and over time of heat and moisture. The climate of the steppes was continental, that is, the summers were hot and the winters cold and semi-arid. The climate became more extreme, moreover, to the south and east.

According to data collected in major cities around the beginning of the twentieth century, average temperatures in July were over 20°C throughout the

[132] See G. L., 'Meteorologicheskie nablyudeniya', 175–9; A. V.[oeikov], 'Meteorologicheskaya kommissiya', *ES*, xix (Spb, 1896), 171–2; A. V.[oeikov], 'Meteorologiya' *ES*, xix, 179–81; P. Brounov and V. Gauer, 'Sel'skokhozyaistvennaya meteorologiya', *PERSKh*, viii (1903), 923–42.

[133] See N. Adamov, 'Meteorologicheskie nablyudeniya 1892–1894 godov', *TESLD, Nauchnii otdel*, 3/1 (1894), 1–245; N. Adamov, 'Meteorologicheskie nablyudeniya 1894–1895 godov', *TESLD, Nauchnii otdel*, 3/2 (1898), 1–264.

[134] GASK, f.80, op.1, d.205a (1885–1900). Bentkowski was Polish by origin, hence the spelling of his name, and moved to the North Caucasus while serving in the Russian army in 1834: V. V. Gosdanker, 'Istorik-Kavkazoved I. V. Bentkovskii (1812–1890)', *Materialy po izucheniyu Stavropol'skogo kraya*, xiv (1976), 222–51.

[135] *Pamyatnaya knizhka Stavropol'skoi gubernii na 1904 god* (Stavropol', 1904), 2.

[136] *SSSpSG*, iii, *Buzulukskii uezd* (1885), 5; vii, *Novouzenskii uezd* (1890), 7–11; *Sel'skokhozyaistvennii obzor Samarskoi gubernii za 1891 god*, 2 vols (Samara, 1891).

[137] RGIA, f.382, op.7, l.1 (*sic*). See also, RGIA, f.382, op.7, d.78.

region, and exceeded 25°C in Astrakhan' in the south-east. Mean January temperatures fell from –4°C in Odessa in the west to –16°C in Orenburg in the east. The duration of the seasons and the length of the growing period can be gauged from the number of days a year when the average temperature was above 6°C (the temperature necessary for cereal crops to grow). The growing period varied from 225 days (about 7.5 months) in Odessa to 170 days (about 5.5 months) in Orenburg, and from 210 days in Stavropol' in the south to 180 days in Saratov in the north of the region. The number of days a year when the average temperature was below freezing ranged from 155 (just over 5 months) in Orenburg to 80 (over 2.5 months) in Odessa.

The average amount of precipitation (rain and snow) also varied across the region, but was relatively low everywhere and, critically, varied sharply from year to year. Mean annual precipitation declined from the north-west to the south-east. Voronezh, in the forest-steppe region, received 537 mm. The steppes to the east of the Caspian Sea, in the far south-east, however, had to make do with only 150 mm. More typical of the steppe region as a whole were Samara and Saratov on the Volga, where average yearly precipitation was just under 380 mm. In southern Samara and Saratov provinces, the south of the Don region, and the depression between the Manych and Kuma rivers in the east of the North Caucasus, however, average precipitation was below 300 mm a year. An exception to the pattern of low rainfall was the uplands of the North Caucasus. The Stavropol' hills, for example, had a mean annual rainfall of around 700 mm. The average annual figures for the region concealed striking fluctuations. Over the late nineteenth and early twentieth centuries, the amount of precipitation falling on Voronezh ranged from 263 to 767 mm. Droughts were more frequent, however, in the drier south-east of the region.

There is another reason, besides periodic droughts, why average data do not convey the full picture of the availability of moisture from the atmosphere. The season with the most rainfall was (as Herodotus had noted) the summer. June and July were the wettest months. In the hot summer months (as Herodotus had also recorded), rain tended to fall in torrential downpours, accompanied by thunder, lightning, and hail storms. Large amounts of water could fall in short periods of time. N. Adamov, one of the scientists on Dokuchaev's expedition in the 1890s, reported that on 5 July 1895, 38.3 mm (15.4 inches) of rain fell in 28 minutes on the Khrenovskoi research station in south-eastern Voronezh province. Such downpours, it was noted, were of little use for agriculture as they damaged crops. The rainwater, moreover, tended to run off the surface of the fields, through gullies, and into rivers, rather than soaking down into the soil and replenishing ground water. In addition to rain, an important source of moisture for ground water was snow cover, which scientists paid increasing attention to in the late nineteenth century. The number of days when snow lay on the ground declined from around 140–50 days a year in the north of the region to 120 in the south and east. Severe frosts occurred when there was no snow in the far south-east.

Meteorologists were starting to pay attention to evaporation, which was critical as it reduced the amount of moisture available, and which increased in the hotter and drier south and east of the region.

Evaporation was increased by the wind. The prevailing winds in most of the region in the autumn, winter, and spring blew from the east. In the summer months, moreover, easterly winds were frequent, although westerlies prevailed. Easterly winds, significantly, brought drier air from the centre of the Eurasian continent. In the winter the air from the east was cold, but in other months was hot. The hot, dry winds, known as *sukhovei*, could dry out the land and vegetation very quickly.[138]

Compared with the climate of the lands to the north and north-west, and Central Europe, where most of the migrants to the steppe region came from, the steppe climate was more arid and hotter. Annual precipitation ranged from around 400 to 600 mm in the forest-steppe and forest regions, but the winters there were colder and longer, and the summers cooler and shorter, than in the steppe region, and so less moisture evaporated. In the European part of the Russian Empire, adequate supplies of heat and moisture coincided with fertile soil to create good conditions for arable farming only in the forest-steppe region. The conditions to the north, in the forest, and to the south and south-east on the steppes, approached the margins for growing crops. In both the forest and the steppe regions, moreover, in some places and some years the conditions exceeded those margins. On the steppes the crucial limiting factor was availability of moisture, which meteorologists now measure by subtracting evaporation from precipitation.[139]

Relief

During the Academy of Sciences expeditions, Falck, like so many visitors to the steppes, described the relief of land between the Don and Volga as 'boundless, level, dry, open, and without trees'.[140] Güldenstädt described the landscape in the northern Don Cossack territory as 'boundless, flat steppe'.[141] Over the years of his expedition, however, he became familiar with a variety of landscapes in southern Russia and the North Caucasus with varying degrees of flatness. When in July 1773 he reached the river Manych, which rises halfway between the Black

---

[138] A. Voeikov, 'Klimat Rossii', *PERSKh*, iv (1901), 237–56; Morachevskii, *Yugo-Vostok Evropeiskoi Rossii*, 6–10; Adamov, 'Meteorologicheskie nablyudeniya 1894–1895 godov', 257–64. See also V. P. Semenov (ed.), *Rossiya: Polnoe geograficheskoe opisanie nashego otechestva*, 11 vols (Spb, 1899–1914), v, *Ural i Priural'e*, 64–5, 78–83, 91–3, 105–8; vi, *Srednee i nizhnee Povol'ze i Zavol'zhe*, 50–4, 64–6, 69–86; xiv, *Novorossiya i Krym*, 39, 51–2, 57, 60–4, 72–89.
[139] See Moon, *Russian Peasantry*, 42, 44.
[140] Fal'k, 'Zapiski', 49–50.
[141] Güldenstädt, *Reisen*, i. 50.

and Caspian Seas, he described this part of the steppe quite simply as 'absolutely flat'.[142] This is the location of the present-day Rostov steppe nature reserve that I visited in 2003 and found so flat it seemed two-dimensional. However, the flatness of the steppes was relieved by some features. Like earlier visitors, Pallas and other members of the expeditions described the burial mounds (*kurgany*) they saw on the steppes.[143]

When he arrived on the steppes in the north of the Don Cossack territory, Güldenstädt enquired about the relief of the land between the rivers Khoper and Don as his map seemed to show hills. He was told that it was 'level steppe', but that there were deep valleys and ravines.[144] Thus another distinctive feature of the landscape is created, not by hills rising above the steppe, but by ravines and river valleys cutting through it. Güldenstädt and the other expedition leaders recorded the presence of many ravines and gullies running perpendicular to the Don and Volga.[145] They also noted ravines between river valleys. Crossing the steppe from the Don to the Volga, Güldenstädt came across a ravine 50 *sazheny* (about 350 feet) deep.[146] The leaders of the expeditions sought to explain how the ravines had formed. On his way down the Volga in the spring of 1769, Lepekhin began to note ravines south of Simbirsk. Further downstream, near Samara, he described a deep ravine that got larger as it approached the river. And by the time he reached Saratov, he had worked it out: he wrote that the Saratov ravine had been created by water erosion. He went on to describe the different layers of soil, rock, and clay that had been exposed in the process.[147] Other naturalists concluded that ravines were created by water flowing downhill, across the steppes, and into the rivers. Pallas noted that two steep ravines near Chernyi Yar by the side of the lower Volga had been 'eroded by spring and rain water'. He also described how ravines further up the Volga had developed 'with time', emphasizing the continuous process involved.[148]

A century later, in the 1870s, a young Dokuchaev studied the formation of ravines and river valleys during several summers of fieldwork. He spent time in his native Smolensk province, in Kursk and Voronezh provinces on the northern edge of the steppes, on the lower Dnestr river in Kherson' province, and between Tsaritsyn on the Volga and the Don in the steppes proper. He was familiar with Pallas' work, and carefully critiqued more recent studies of ravines by Russian and foreign scientists.[149] An important influence was the work of the British

---

[142] Gil'denshtedt, *Puteshestvie*, 303.

[143] Pallas, 'Travels', ii. 149–51; [Pallas], 'Puteshestvie', 249.

[144] Güldenstädt, *Reisen*, i. 65–6.

[145] Gil'denshtedt, 'Dnevnik', 202; [Pallas], 'Puteshestvie', 260–1; Fal'k, 'Zapiski', 99, 121.

[146] Güldenstädt, *Reisen*, i. 114. See also Fal'k, 'Zapiski', 50.

[147] Lepekhin, 'Zapiski', 325, 352, 392–3, 401.

[148] [Pallas], 'Puteshestvie', 249, 259–61; [Pallas], *Nauchnoe nasledie*, 72. See also Güldenstädt, *Reisen*, 76; Gil'denshtedt, 'Dnevnik', 184.

[149] V. V. Dokuchaev, 'Ovragi i ikh zhachenie', in *Sochineniya*, i. 103–11 (first published 1877); V. V. Dokuchaev, 'Sposoby obrazovaniya rechnykh dolin Evropeiskoi Rossii', in *Sochineniya*, i. 113–273 (first published in 1878). See also Krupenikov and Krupenikov, *Puteshestviya*, 5–28.

geologist Charles Lyell. He was a proponent of uniformitarianism: the theory that the geological processes that had formed the features on the earth's surface in the past were those that were still in operation in the present. Among the 'causes now in operation' were the climate and running water. Lyell was arguing against the view that the surface of the earth was a result of sudden, catastrophic changes in the past. Lyell's *Principles of Geology* (1830–3) was translated into Russian and published in 1866, which was the edition cited by Dokuchaev.[150]

Dokuchaev thus looked for factors still in operation that could have caused the formation of ravines. He concluded that they started to form when water running down sloping land encountered cracks or indentations, which then gradually increased in size as the sides were eroded by the force of the water. He went on to argue that the various types of ravines were 'nothing other than different stages of the same action of atmospheric precipitation, moreover, ravines are the initial stage of the eroding action of water, gullies—the middle [stage], and rivers—the final [stage]'. Development could, in certain conditions such as low volumes of water, stop at the middle stage, leaving gullies that did not develop into rivers. He argued that ravines developed more forcefully and more quickly in Russia than in Western Europe for a number of reasons: the friable (crumbly) soil with a lower layer of sand; the continental climate; the short but heavy downpours of rain in the summer; the large volumes of meltwater in the spring; the topography; and the treelessness of the steppes. While Dokuchaev was aware that the landscape had been altered by human activity, he stated that ravines had existed for a very long time, before there were people on the earth.[151]

Naturalists and scientists noted that the steppes were affected by wind as well as water erosion. While in Tsaritsyn in the hot summer of 1774, Pallas noted that the winds blew

constantly from the arid step [*sic*] and [the] sea, S.S.E. or E. After this arise the hot winds, which, though they blow irresistibly, so as to sweep off all the dust from the step [*sic*], and carry it through the air, are yet as hot as if they came from a fiery furnace.... During their blowing, sheep often drop down dead, like flies ... This hot, glowing wind is often owing to the burning of the step [*sic*], and is then of longer duration.[152]

Gmelin reported sandstorms in the lower Volga basin in the autumn of 1769 (after the hot, dry summer).[153] The wind also caused sandy soils to drift. Pallas wrote from Yaitsk, on the Yaik/Ural river, in July 1769 that sand was drifting to a depth of over a *sazhen'* (about 7 feet). Pallas' journey along roads of sandy soil at

---

[150] Charl'z Lyaiell', *Osnovnye nachala geologii ili noveishie izmeneniya zemli i ee obitatelei*, trans. Andrei Min, 2 vols (Moscow, 1866), cited by Dokuchaev in 'Ovragi', 107, n.1.
[151] Dokuchaev, 'Ovragi', esp. 104, 109; Dokuchaev, 'Sposoby', esp. 153–73 (quotation 168).
[152] Pallas, 'Travels', iv. 315.
[153] Gmelin, *Puteshestvie*, ii. 58.

the side of the Volga to Astrakhan' in 1770 was hampered by the 'uninterrupted sandy hills, some of which consisted purely of drifting sand'. The horses got stuck and the drifts partly covered buildings.[154] Just over a decade later, Zuev reported the same problem in Kremenchug on the Dnepr. He wrote that there were not enough trees around the town to protect it from sand blown around by the wind. Moreover there was no arable land near the town due to the sand.[155] These accounts by the leaders of the Academy of Sciences expeditions from the late eighteenth century provide important evidence for water and wind erosion before the wholesale plough-up of much of the steppe region. This is important as it serves as a corrective to arguments advanced in the late nineteenth century that emphasized the role of human activity in causing erosion (see Chapter 5).

Soil

Much of the soil in the steppe region, as most visitors noted, was extremely fertile, black-coloured earth. The leaders of the Academy of Sciences expeditions paid particular attention to the black earth. When he reached the steppes near Stavropol' (on the Volga) in 1769, Lepekhin observed that the land was much more fertile than that immediately to the north. He attributed this to the fact that the steppes had not been inhabited for as long, and so 'the land still abounds with the full forces of fertility for growing grain'.[156] Further south, between the Don and Volga, Falck noted areas covered with 'good black earth'.[157] Four years later, in the low foothills of the Caucasus, Güldenstädt wrote that 'everywhere [was] . . . covered with fertile black earth'.[158] Pallas took a particular interest in the soil. In August 1768, as he travelled through the mid-Volga region, he commented on the

rich black soil so common to the Sura, Wolga, and other rivers, which flow from the east into the Wolga. In all these parts, the happy husbandman has no occasion to manure his grounds . . . Here are spots where the soil never fails, but, where it diminishes in richness, there is plenty of ground in the less inhabited part . . . which if turned up, produces the finest arable imaginable.[159]

On his second expedition to the steppes in 1793–4, Pallas again commented on the 'excellent black soil' and 'most fertile soil' in the mid-Volga region and the 'good arable land' in the North Caucasus.[160]

Besides the fertile 'black earth', the accounts of the Academy of Sciences expeditions also noted less fertile soils in parts of the steppe region. Güldenstädt found sandy soil, often in river banks and along roads, in the north of the Don

154 [Pallas], *Nauchnoe nasledie*, 80, 82; [Pallas], 'Puteshestvie', 246.
155 Zuev, *Puteshestvennye zapiski*, 214–15.
156 Lepekhin, 'Zapiski', 230.   157 Fal'k, 'Zapiski', 50.
158 Gil'denshtedt, *Puteshestvie*, 292.
159 Pallas, 'Travels', ii, 43–4. See also Pallas, 'Travels', ii, 63, 79, 80.
160 Pallas, *Travels*, i, 12–13, 33, 317.

Cossack territory.[161] In the same area, Falck described earth consisting largely of sand and salty clay mixed with black earth.[162] Several expedition leaders found more sandy and salty soil in the south and south-east of the steppe region, such as along the lower reaches of the Volga.[163] Pallas reported large areas of salt flats (*solonchaki*) on the steppes adjoining the Yaik/Ural river.[164] Falck found sandy and salty soil on the Kuma steppe in the North Caucasus. He speculated that the area was a dried-up seabed.[165]

Naturalists and scientists paid far more attention, however, to the fertile black earth. They mapped the distribution of this valuable resource and tried to explain its origins.[166] The leaders of the Academy of Sciences expeditions put forward differing theories. Güldenstädt made a connection between the black earth and the grasses that comprised the main vegetation of the steppes.[167] Writing in the 1790s, however, Pallas argued: 'There is not the least doubt that the aforementioned black vegetable stratum of the soil, which is upwards of two feet thick, originated from the forests that formerly covered these regions.' He was in the mid-Volga region when he made this argument. Further south-east, he speculated, like Falck, that the salty soils were evidence of a former sea.[168] Forest and maritime arguments for the origins of the black earth prevailed into the mid-nineteenth century. In the 1860s, however, Ruprecht revived Güldenstädt's view on the role of steppe grasses, not forest vegetation, in the origins of the black earth. He studied samples of black earth under a microscope and identified elements in the organic matter, or humus, as the decomposed remains of steppe grasses, such as feather grass (*kovyl'*), that had built up over many centuries.[169]

Ruprecht's discovery set the stage for Dokuchaev's groundbreaking study of the Russian black earth published in 1883. Dokuchaev's study was based on research conducted on a series of expeditions in the black-earth region since 1876 (see pp. 53–4). While most of his book on the Russian black earth is written in a scholarly manner, in a few places, especially when describing the south-eastern steppes, he let slip the typical attitude of outsiders. Crossing 'the neck of land between the Don and Volga', he remarked upon the

extremely monotonous picture: the locality is flat, waterless, dry, scored in places by shallow gullies, the sides of which reveal only reddy-brown clay, sometimes with

---

[161] Güldenstädt, *Reisen*, i, 50, 77, 85, 95–8.
[162] Fal'k, 'Zapiski', 50.   [163] Gmelin, *Puteshestvie*, ii, 46–60.
[164] [Pallas], *Nauchnoe nasledie*, 89.   [165] Fal'k, 'Zapiski', 92–3.
[166] For an overview of studies of the soil, in Russia and elsewhere, from the eighteenth century to the 1870s, see I. A. Krupenikov, *Istoriya pochvovedeniya ot vremeni ego zarozhdeniya do nashikh dnei* (Moscow, 1981), 99–150.
[167] Güldenstädt, *Reisen*, i. 33–4.
[168] Pallas, *Travels*, i. 33, 78–80.
[169] Ruprecht, 'Geo-botanicheskie issledovaniya'. For a fuller discussion of Ruprecht's work, and research on the black earth over the preceding decades, see Fedotova, 'Origins'.

efflorescences (*vytsvety*) of salt; thin, brownish-grey soil is almost indistinguishable from the ground; the vegetation—sparse feather grass and low sage-brush—hardly covers the steppe, only the countless gopher mounds and artificially planted groups of poplars slightly vary the impression of the traveller.

A little later, while sailing down the Volga from Tsaritsyn to Astrakhan', he could not restrain himself from writing that 'this whole locality gives little material to the soil researcher: everywhere you see ... the same, tiresome, monotonous, reddy-yellow, here loamy, there sandy, salty (*solonchak*) steppes; in July there was almost no vegetation; the soils hardly differed from the ground'. Earlier, he had written of the 'depressing monotony' of the steppes in Novyi Uzen' district in southern Samara province. But he also noted how steppes that appeared 'almost completely bare' could yield harvests up to twenty-five times the amount of seed sown: 'Such is the richness of young virgin soils', he marvelled.[170]

All the time, however bored by the scenery, Dokuchaev and his assistants were meticulously collecting samples of soil, in sections several feet deep, and making painstaking notes of the environment of the locality, including the geology of the parent rock, the vegetation and wildlife, the climate, and relief. After the expedition, the samples were carefully analysed in laboratories. Some of the chemical analysis was conducted at St Petersburg University under the supervision of his colleague Dmitrii Mendeleev. Dokuchaev noted that there were discrepancies in how the term 'black earth' (*chernozem*) was used in the scientific literature. He set out to define what constituted 'black earth' in terms of its mineral and organic (humus) constituents, origin, and colour in order to reach a precise account of its geographical distribution.[171] The analysis of the soil samples collected in different areas varied in thickness (or depth), and in the amounts of humus (organic matter) and water they contained. There was a pattern to the variations, which can be illustrated by considering the samples from one of the routes of the expedition, which ran along a north-west–south-east axis, from Gryazi in Tambov province in the heart of the more humid forest-steppe region, through the north-east of the Don region, to Tsaritsyn on the semi-arid steppe on the lower Volga. From the north-west to the south-east, there was a gradual decrease in the content of organic matter (humus), in the thickness of the soil, and the water content. The colour also changed from darker to lighter. (See Table 2.1 and Map 4.)

A cross-section of the black earth observed on high, level steppe near Filonovo in the north-east of the Don region reveals more of Dokuchaev's method. The soil scientist described three distinct levels, or 'horizons'. The A, or 'soil', horizon was 'dark-grey, loamy, crumbly, black earth, around 2 feet thick', and contained

170 Dokuchaev, 'Russkii chernozem', 310, 331, 333.
171 Dokuchaev, 'Russkii chernozem', 26, 35–45.

Table 2.1 Soil samples collected by Dokuchaev on a route from Gryazi, Tambov province, to Tsaritsyn, Saratov province

Locality	Composition	Position	Thickness	Humus %	Water %
Gryazi, Lipetsk district, Tambov province	Loam	Level arable field	3 ft 7 inches	9.595	6.452
Volkonskaya, Borisoglebsk district, Tambov province	Loam	Level arable field	2 ft 5 inches	9.148	6.363
Filonovo, Khoper district, Don region	Loam	Level steppe	2 ft 3 inches	6.667	3.663
Gorodishche, Tsaritsyn district, Saratov province	Loam	Level pasture	11 inches	2.536	5.127
Tsaritsyn, Saratov province	Loam	Virgin steppe	9–10 inches	0.908	1.081

Source: adapted from Dokuchaev, 'Russkii chernozem', 259.

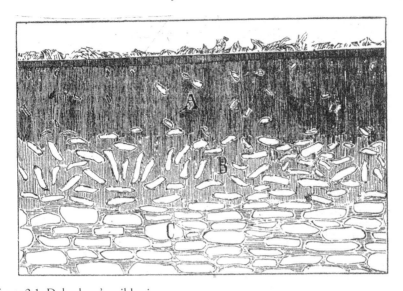

Figure 2.1 Dokuchaev's soil horizons

From V. V. Dokuchaev, *Russkii chernozem: Otchet Imperatorskomu Vol'nomu Ekonomicheskogo Obshchestva* (Spb, 1883).

granite pebbles the size of a nut and a fist. This was the top soil. The B, or 'transition', horizon was 'typical yellowy-brown loess loam with many concretions of $CaCO_3$ [Calcium Carbonate]'. This layer was 15–20 feet thick, and contained siliceous and limestone pebbles, and crystalline gneiss, granite, quartzite, and diorite boulders, up to 1 ft 6 in in diameter. The C horizon, the 'parent rock', was bluish-grey clay. Dokuchaev found soils of similar thickness, humus content, and colour, but not necessarily on the same parent rock, throughout the 'black-earth region', including the samples he collected at Gryazi and Volkonskaya in Tambov province. Dokuchaev categorized all three as 'black earth'. The last two samples collected on this route, however, were significantly different in their thickness and humus content, and were not classified as 'black earth'.[172] (See Fig 2.1.)

Dokuchaev then turned to the question of the origins of the black earth he had defined. It was the great intellectual achievement of Dokuchaev and his fellow scientists to see soils as natural and historical bodies that had a 'special character' and needed to be studied in their own right, not as part of geology. He devised a theory to explain soil formation that took account of the environment in which the soil was situated and which went beyond anything put forward by his predecessors.

[172] Dokuchaev, 'Russkii chernozem', 233, 258–60, 281–8, 317, 322–4, 346–9, 386.

The composition and structure of the parent rock was carefully noted by Dokuchaev and his team. Drawing on previous studies of the geology of Russia, they recorded a wide range of different types of rock—granite, clay, limestone, sandstone, marl, chalk, loam, coal, loess, sandy loams, chalky marls, boulder loess—and different ages: Devonian, Carboniferous, Permian, Triassic, Jurassic, Cretaceous, and Tertiary. Some types of parent rock, for example loess, were more favourable than others for the formation of black earth, but it was clear from the wide variety of geological material found in the C horizons, that is, the lowest layer of the soil samples, that certain types of parent rock were not a prerequisite for the formation of black earth. Loess was not always covered in black earth. In China, for example, it underlay different types of soil. However, parent rocks did influence the thickness and humus content of black earth. The thickest soil was found on sandy loam, and the highest proportions of humus on chalk and limestone.[173] Parent rock, therefore, was only one of Dokuchaev's soil-forming factors.

Dokuchaev followed Ruprecht in assigning great importance to steppe, that is, grassy, vegetation in the formation of black earth. He noted, however, that characteristic 'black-earth vegetation' could be found far to the north of the black-earth region on quite different types of soil. Thus vegetation could be only one of his soil-forming factors. The type of grassy vegetation affected the thickness of the black earth. In the north of the region, where the grasses were perennial with deeper roots, black earth was thicker than on the drier, south-eastern steppes with annual grasses that had shallower root systems. Dokuchaev was adamant that black earth could not form under forests. In parts of the black-earth region, such as south-western Ukraine, where there were more trees and which may have had more forest cover in the past, he argued strongly that forests must have been preceded by grassland for the black earth to form. In forested areas in the black-earth region, such as the large pine forest in Buzuluk district, Samara province, different soils, which were lighter in colour, thinner, and lower in humus content had formed.[174] There was also a role for the wildlife. The rodents, lizards, insects, and worms that burrowed into the soil assisted in aerating it, weathering the parent rock, creating a more uniform distribution of humus, and breaking up the soil into smaller particles. The decaying bodies of wildlife, moreover, contributed to the organic matter in the soil. He disagreed with Charles Darwin, however, who had made a case for a larger role for worms in soil formation.[175]

Dokuchaev argued that the climate was very important in soil formation as it influenced the quality and quantity of vegetation that grew and decayed each year, and the process of decay. The climatic conditions—the length of the

[173] Dokuchaev, 'Russkii chernozem', 163–8, 240–3, 281–8, 325, 382–3, 400.
[174] Dokuchaev, 'Russkii chernozem', 146–7, 232–3, 282–4, 300, 307, 324, 377–80, 382.
[175] Dokuchaev, 'Russkii chernozem', 380–1.

seasons, the amount of heat and precipitation—were most favourable for the development of black earth in the centre of the black-earth region (in the forest-steppe region), which was the location of the best soil. He noted that the orientation of the black-earth region, from south-west to north-east, followed particular isotherms and the distribution of precipitation. The northern boundary of the black-earth region coincided approximately with the isotherms 17–18°C in June and 20°C in July. Parts of Russia with similar climates had different types of soil, however, and so the climate was not sufficient to explain the formation of black earth.[176]

A further factor in the formation of black earth was the relief of the land. The studies seemed to show that black earth formed best on level land, and it continued to form in flat areas, getting thicker, as far as the parent rock, plant and animal organisms, and climatic conditions permitted. Black earth did form on gently sloping land, and was thickest towards the bottom of slopes and in low-lying areas. On uneven terrain, in hilly areas, and on steep slopes, however, black earth tended to be washed away by the action of water, or if it did occur was atypical. Black earth was unlikely to form on the tops of hills and narrow elevated plains since rain water washed away the constituent parts of the black earth, leaching the salts out, and leading to the formation of different types of soils. Dokuchaev's analysis of the soil in the Crimea and Caucasus proved to him that black earth could not form in mountainous regions. The particular topography of river valleys in the steppe region also had an impact on soil formation. The terraces of the low, left banks of rivers were sandy, and had less humus, clay, and calcium carbonate due to the action of the water that had flowed over them in the past and during spring floods each year. In time, black earth formed on older, upper terraces that were further from the flood plains. Black earth was either atypical or absent on hilly right banks for the same reasons as in other hilly areas. Normal black earth was to be found on level steppe 1–10 *versty* from rivers.[177] Thus the monotonous flatness of the steppes, which had bored Dokuchaev, was another crucial factor in the formation of black earth.

The series of soil horizons, or layers, in the soil samples that Dokuchaev identified showed the gradual process of soil formation. The C horizon was the parent rock. The B or transition horizon showed the soil being formed by the action of humus on the parent rock, and the A or soil horizon was the top soil of the 'black earth'.[178] This transformation of parent rock into black earth took place as a consequence of all the above-mentioned soil formation factors over time. Time, therefore, was Dokuchaev's final soil-forming factor. Ruprecht had tried to estimate the age of the black earth. He compared the thickness of the soil on the top of burial mounds (*kurgany*) in Chernigov province, which

[176] Dokuchaev, 'Russkii chernozem', 159–60, 383–5.
[177] Dokuchaev, 'Russkii chernozem' 351, 410–19.
[178] Dokuchaev, 'Russkii chernozem', 258, 283.

were believed to date back to the time of Batu Khan in the mid-thirteenth century, with soil on surrounding, level, unploughed land. The soil on top of the *kurgany* was 6–9 inches thick, while on nearby flat land it was 2–5 feet. Ruprecht therefore calculated that the black earth in the region was between 2,400 and 4,000 years old. Dokuchaev argued against this as soil thickness did not increase in a linear manner and in any case had limits. He further pointed out that the *kurgany* may have been built from black earth.[179] Dokuchaev did not initially try to estimate the age of the black earth. Herodotus' description of the 'good deep soil' and the aspects of his account that match Dokuchaev's soil-forming factors suggested that it had been forming over a long period, and was well under way two and a half millennia earlier, when Herodotus was writing. In 1892, Dokuchaev argued that the black earth had to be a minimum of four to seven thousand years old.[180]

Dokuchaev neatly summarized his theory: soils were 'the result of the extremely complex interaction' of the composition and structure of parent rocks, plant and animal organisms, the local climate, the relief of the locality, and, finally, 'the age of the land'. Soils therefore demanded of their researchers—the soil scientists—continual excursions into different branches of science.[181] He acknowledged that a commonly held view in the black-earth region, which he and earlier scientists had heard from the local population, was that the soil originated from the decay of steppe vegetation, facilitated by the atmosphere, and the amalgamation of the resulting humus with the loamy subsoil. The term '*chernozem*', moreover, was one used by the local population and was made a scientific classification by Dokuchaev.[182]

During his expedition, Dokuchaev paid attention to other types of soil he encountered in parts of the region with environmental conditions different from those necessary for the formation of black earth. In between the areas where the samples of black earth had been collected on the route from Gryazi to Tsaritsyn, Dokuchaev noted areas of sandy soil with trees in the river valleys. In general, he concluded that inside the 'black-earth region' there were areas with different soils, which were characterized by the following features: forests, bogs, hills, river valleys, sands, and saline soils.[183] The last two samples collected on this route, which were less than a foot thick, had a lower humus content, and were lighter in colour, were not classified as 'black earth'. Dokuchaev's assistant noted in his diary that the Tsaritsyn soils seemed to have been 'burned by God'. These were beyond the south-eastern margin of the 'black-earth region'. Dokuchaev noted similar soils, which tended to be chestnut in colour and contained saline soils in

---

[179] Dokuchaev, 'Russkii chernozem', 421–2.
[180] Dokuchaev, 'Nashi stepi', in *Sochineniya*, vi. 85.
[181] Dokuchaev, 'Russkii chernozem', 27.
[182] Dokuchaev, 'Russkii chernozem', 35–40, 367.
[183] Dokuchaev, 'Russkii chernozem', 259–60, 354.

places, in southern Samara province, in belts immediately to the north of the Black, Azov, and Caspian Seas, including the steppe in the north-east Caucasus. These areas were characterized by shortages of water, very hot summers, hot, dry winds, and sparse vegetation, including wormwood and saltwort rather than feather grass. The vegetation dried up completely in the summers and so did not form sufficient organic matter. He speculated that burrowing rodents brought saline subsoils to the surface. Some of these areas he believed were once seabeds. The parent rock in these locations was salty clay and sand that was not usually covered with black earth since the rainfall was not sufficient to leach out the salt to form good soil. These lighter soils in the south-east of the steppe region, where conditions were not right for the formation of black earth, came to be classified as chestnut soils (*kashtanovye pochvy*).[184] (See Fig. 2.2.)

Dokuchaev's theory came in for criticism from his contemporaries, including the meteorologist Aleksandr Voeikov and agronomist and soil scientist Pavel Kostychev. Both argued that he had attached too much importance to the climate. Voeikov even characterized a talk by Dokuchaev to the St Petersburg Society of Naturalists in 1881 as a presentation of his 'climatic theory' on the origins of black earth. Voeikov also argued that Dokuchaev had travelled around the black-earth region too quickly, implying that his research was superficial. Kostychev agreed with Dokuchaev on the importance of grassy vegetation rather than forest in the formation of the black earth, but felt that he had added nothing to Ruprecht's work. He further argued that the influence of the relief of the land was more complex than Dokuchaev allowed.[185] There was some animosity between Kostychev and Dokuchaev. The former, the son of serfs from Tambov province in the black-earth region, resented the decision of the Free Economic Society to ask Dokuchaev, and not him, to lead the research into the black earth.[186] Dokuchaev withstood the criticisms, and his theory and methodology became the basis for the further development of soil science in Russia. His collaborators, in particular Sibirtsev and Konstantin Glinka, developed his ideas and brought them to international attention.[187]

[184] Dokuchaev, 'Russkii chernozem', 161, 259 (quotation), 322–3, 333, 336–8, 340, 344–5, 417–19, 433.

[185] V. V. Dokuchaev, 'O zakonnosti izvestnogo geograficheskogo raspredeleniya nazemno-rastitel'nykh pochv na territorii evropeiskoi Rossii', in *Sochineniya*, ii. 303–16 (first published 1881); A. I. Voeikov, 'Vystuplenie po soobshcheniyu V. V. Dokuchaeva...', *Trudy S.-Peterburgskogo obshchestva estestvoispytatelei*, 12/1 (1881), 83–5; Dokuchaev, 'Otvet na vozrazhdeniya A. I. Voeikov...', in *Sochineniya*, ii. 317–24 (first published 1881); P. A. Kostychev, 'Po voprosu o proiskhozhdenii chernozema', *SKhiL*, 147 (1884), 259–82; Dokuchaev, 'K voprosu o Russkom chernozeme', in *Sochineniya*, ii. 462–99 (first published 1885).

[186] On frosty relations between Dokuchaev and Kostychev, see Kul'pin-Gubaidullin, 'Vasilii Dokuchaev', 103, 105, 111; I. A. Krupenikov, *Pavel Andreevich Kostychev 1845–1895* (Moscow, 1987), 96, 101, 126–34.

[187] See, for example, N. Sibirtsev, *Chernozem v raznykh stranakh* (Warsaw, 1896); K. D. Glinka, *Pochvoobrazovanie, kharakteristika pochvennykh tipov i geografiya pochv* (Spb, 1913); K. D. Glinka,

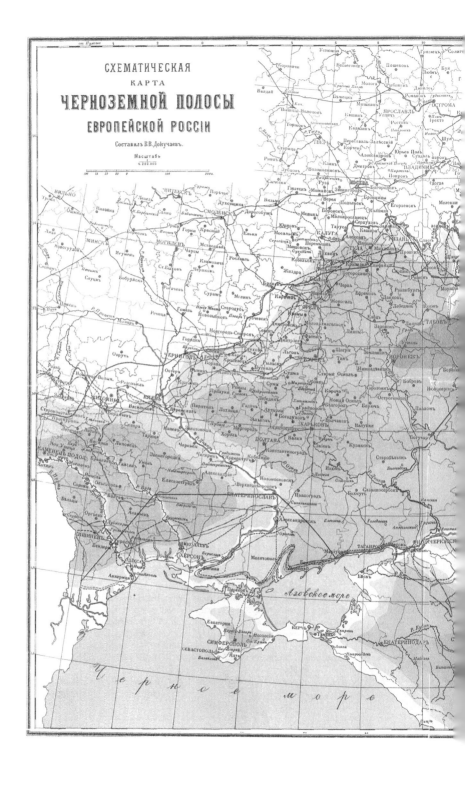

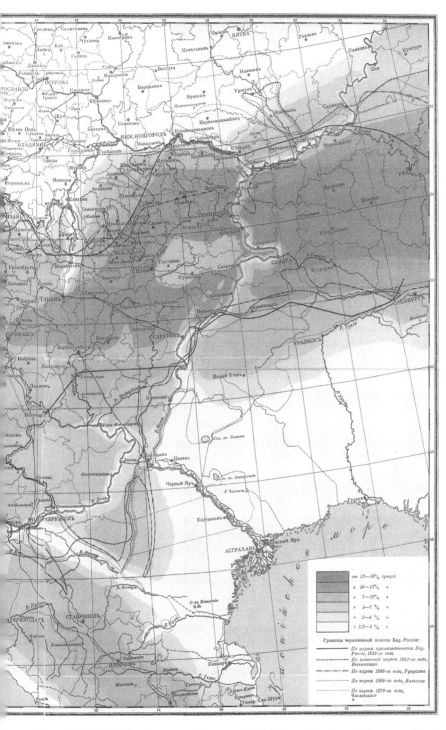

Figure 2.2. Dokuchaev's systematic map of the black-earth region of European Russia

From V. V. Dokuchaev, *Russkii chernozem: Otchet Imperatorskomu Vol'nomu Ekonomicheskogo Obshchestva* (Spb, 1883).

Thus, Dokuchaev argued that the black earth, and other types of soil, formed as a result of a series of 'soil forming factors' (parent rock, vegetation and other living matter, climate, relief, and time). This was the basis of the new, genetic soil science that emphasized that soils formed in the environmental conditions in which they existed. It has been argued that one of the reasons Dokuchaev was able to devise his theory was that the sheer size of the Russian Empire, with such a variety of environments and soil types, provided an ideal laboratory for soil scientists. Another factor was the nature of his education noted earlier. His limited knowledge of Western European languages, lack of a period of study abroad, preferring field trips around Russia, and the extent to which he was self-taught all meant that he disregarded the prevailing approach among European soil scientists. His predecessors and counterparts elsewhere in Europe focused on the characteristics of the parent rock, that is, inorganic matter, not on the wider range of factors that Dokuchaev considered. The approach of European soil scientists led them to recommend the application of inorganic fertilizers. Dokuchaev's conception, in contrast, led him and his followers to think about soils as a part of the wider environment in which they had formed, and so needed to be treated accordingly.[188]

The work of genetic soil scientists revealed the central paradox of the steppe soils: the very fertility that gave such bumper harvests in good years, when the rains came, was largely a consequence of the low rainfall that, in years of drought, led to harvest failures and famine. The low rainfall meant that the minerals that made the soil so fertile had not been leached out, and thus created conditions ideal for the accumulation of organic matter. In 1901, Voeikov summed up the paradox—and indeed the tragedy for farmers who lived on the steppes—when he remarked that the climate of the black-earth region of Russia was 'not so favourable for agriculture' as for the soil.[189]

CONCLUSION

From the mid-eighteenth century, as the process of agricultural settlement of the steppes was under way, naturalists and scientists began to engage in detailed research into the steppe environment. One of several achievements by Russian scientists, in particular Dokuchaev and his collaborators, in the late nineteenth century was to show how the various parts of the steppe environment were

---

Die Typen der Bodenbildung: Ihre Klassifikation und Geographische Verbreitung (Berlin, 1914). see below, pp. 286–7.

[188] See Kul'pin-Gubaidullin, 'Vasilii Dokuchaev', 111 and *passim*.
[189] Voeikov, 'Klimat Rossii', 247.

interconnected. Thus the black earth with its extraordinary fertility had formed in an environment that, to many outsiders, seemed lacking in trees and water. In the 1890s, Russian scientists, including the geobotanist Andrei Krasnov and Dokuchaev, went on to present theories about distinct natural zones, including steppes, that had counterparts around the globe, such as the prairies and Great Plains of North America.[190]

The Russian encounter with the steppes reflected the quite different environment many of the settlers came from. The migrants who moved to the steppes from the eighteenth century came mostly from Russian and Ukrainian lands to the north and north-west as well as from German lands. It is significant that, together with most of the outsiders discussed in Chapter 1 and the naturalists and scientists whose works has been discussed in this chapter, they came from lands where trees and water were not in short supply. It was perhaps difficult for non-natives of the steppes to acquire a genuine liking for the steppe environment. Even scholars such as Lepekhin (from St Petersburg), who took part in the Academy of Sciences expeditions, and also at times Dokuchaev (from Smolensk province) over a century later did not conceal their dislike of the flat, treeless, arid environment.

Over the eighteenth and nineteenth centuries, however, some inhabitants of the Russian Empire came to take a pride in the Russian landscape. Rather than seeing the forests of the northern half and flat steppes of the southern half as inferior, or 'meagre', in comparison with the more dramatic landscapes of the Alps and the Mediterranean, some writers and artists consciously presented a landscape that incorporated the steppe (and rivers and mountains) as well as the forest as beautiful and, above all, as a national space that was 'Russian'.[191] Among the literary figures and painters who showed a new aesthetic appreciation of the flat, treeless steppes were the writers Sergei Aksakov, Nikolai Gogol, Anton Chekhov, and landscape painter Arkhip Kuindzhi. All four, however, were natives of the region. Gogol was born in Poltava province in Ukraine on the edge of the steppes, which he romanticized in some of his writings. He was aware, however, of the irony that he produced most of his writings on the provinces while living in Western Europe.[192] Aksakov was born in Ufa and brought up on his family estate on the Orenburg steppes. He celebrated the life of his

---

[190] A. N. Krasnov, 'Travyanye stepi Severnogo polushairiya', *Izvestiia Obshchestva lyubitelei estestvoznaniya, antropologii i etnografii,* 81/7 (1894), 1–294; V. V. Dokuchaev, 'K ucheniyu o zonakh prirody.' in *Sochineniya,* vi. 398–414 (first published 1899). See also Denis J. B. Shaw and Jonathan D. Oldfield, 'Landscape Science: A Russian Geographical Tradition', *Annals of the Association of American Geographers,* 97 (2007), 111–26.

[191] Sara Dickenson, *Breaking Ground: Travel and National Culture in Russia from Peter I to the Era of Pushkin* (Amsterdam, 2006); Christopher Ely, *This Meagre Nature: Landscape and National Identity in Imperial Russia* (DeKalb, IL, 2002).

[192] Dickenson, *Breaking Ground,* 23, 192–3; Edyta M. Bojanowska, *Nikolai Gogol: Between Ukrainian and Russian Nationalism* (Cambridge, MA, 2007).

grandfather, a pioneer Russian estate owner on the 'boundless steppe' in Catherine's reign, in the first part of his family chronicle published in the 1850s.[193] Chekhov, who portrayed the steppes in several of his writings, including his (rather long) short story *The Steppe* of 1888, was born in Taganrog,[194] and Kuindzhi, who was of Greek descent, was from Mariupol'. Both Taganrog and Mariupol' are on the north coast of the Sea of Azov. It is worth pointing out that Chekhov conveyed, no doubt partly ironically, the tedium of the landscape, and that Kuindzhi added drama to his steppe landscape paintings by making them studies of light, for example his *Red Sunset on the Dnieper* of 1905–8 on display in the Metropolitan Museum in New York. Thus some Russians (and Ukrainians and settlers of foreign origins) were coming to understand, and even like, the steppe environment, and to consider it a part of their homeland, rather than an alien, outlying region. This continued in the twentieth century. Mikhail Sholokhov celebrated the environment of his native Don region in his novels.[195]

All the sources considered in this chapter and in Chapter 1—from Herodotus to Dokuchaev—reveal that while there were common features across the steppe region as a whole, the steppes were neither uniform nor unchanging. There were significant variations inside the region, especially towards the south and east, where the climate was drier and the vegetation and soil different. The grassland environment, moreover, changed over time. It had evolved over the millennia since the end of the last ice age under the influence of a range of factors, including human impact such as the use of fire and grazing of livestock by nomads. The components of the steppe environment that were most important from the perspective of the agricultural settlers, and for the purposes of this book, were the vegetation, the climate, especially precipitation, the relief and drainage, and, perhaps above all, the soil. Any changes in these were very important, especially since conditions in parts of the steppe region were approaching the margins for arable farming.

[193] Sergei Aksakov, *A Russian Gentleman*, trans J. D. Duff (Oxford, 1982). Buguruslan district, where the family's estate was situated, became part of Samara province in 1851.
[194] Anton Chekhov, 'The Steppe', in Anton Chekhov, *The Steppe and Other Stories, 1887–1891*, trans. R. Wilks (London, 2001), 3–101.
[195] For an anthology of writings on the steppe, by natives and non-natives, see A. A. Chibilev (ed.), *Stepnye shedevry* (Orenburg, 2009).

PART II

UNDERSTANDING
ENVIRONMENTAL CHANGE

INTRODUCTION: WHO IS TO BLAME?

Scientists and other specialists in the Russian Empire over the period covered by this book were aware that the steppe environment was changing even as they were studying it. In 1892, the Vasilii Dokuchaev bemoaned the disappearance of unploughed steppe. 'Tomorrow', he wrote, the steppes would have little in common with those of the cossack era.[1] A few years earlier, he had visited Dikan'ka, the former home of the writer Nikolai Gogol', in Poltava province.[2] In the 1830s, in his historical novella *Taras Bulba* about cossacks in sixteenth-century Ukraine, Gogol' had portrayed the grassland at that time as

one green wilderness, whose countless waves were untouched by the plough and trampled on . . . by horses alone, which hid in droves as in a forest. Nature has nothing fairer that these steppes, with their surface like a green-gold ocean, strewn with a million flowers. Posies, lilac, blue and white shimmered in the tall, slim grass; yellow gorse and white clover danced upon the surface.[3]

The sense of a world that was being lost was felt by local inhabitants and officials as well as scientists and writers. As agricultural settlers moved onto the steppes, together with their livestock, ploughs, and crops, over time they displaced the nomadic pastoralists and their herds of animals who had lived on there for millennia. In the process, the settlers fundamentally altered the pattern of land use. Ploughed fields gradually but inexorably replaced pasture. The farmers, their livestock, and crops displaced the previous vegetation, including the wild flowers and ocean of grass Gogol' had described, and wildlife of the region. The

---

[1] V. V. Dokuchaev, 'Nashi stepi prezhde i teper', in *Sochineniya*, 9 vols (Moscow and Leningrad, 1949–61), vi, 57–8.

[2] I. Krupenikov and L. Krupenikov, *Puteshestviya i ekspeditsii V. V. Dokuchaeva* (Moscow, 1949), 74, 77.

[3] N. V. Gogol', *Taras Bul'ba*, trans. E. I. Prokhorov and N. L. Stepanov (Moscow, 1963), 16–18. (The original was first published in 1839.)

author of a *zemstvo* study of Nikolaevsk district in southern Samara province in 1889 wrote that as a result of 'influence of the population', many species of flora and fauna had 'disappeared from the face of the land' since the start of the century.[4] Contemporaries paid most attention to the destruction of the small areas of woodland that existed in river valleys, ravines, and on uplands in the otherwise treeless region. This was a cause of major concern since trees provided the population with the timber and firewood they needed. Deforestation became a cause of greater anxiety over the nineteenth century as there was a growing belief in Russia and elsewhere that forests played an vital role in the environment. In particular, it was believed that forests moderated the climate and provided shelter from the hot, dry winds that blew from the east, thus restricting erosion and assisting in conserving moisture in the soil.

Contemporaries were also worried that the climate was changing, becoming more extreme and, crucially for arable farming, more arid. Many farmers, officials, agricultural specialists, and scientists thought that the periodic droughts were recurring more frequently and with ever greater consequences. They also noticed that the relief of the region was changing due to erosion. Drifting sands, moved by the wind, were inundating productive arable land. Among the most dramatic manifestations were dust storms—similar to those on the southern plains of the USA during the 'Dust bowl' of the 1930s—when dust whipped up by the wind blocked out the sun and valuable top soil was blown away. Contemporaries noted, with growing concern, that the ravines which carved fissures through the steppes were getting larger as water ran through them, washing away fertile black earth. This created a further problem as the soil ended up in the rivers, silting them up. Some scientists further believed that the more rapid drainage of water down enlarged ravines and gullies was causing the water table to fall and the steppes to dry out. Over the nineteenth century, worries were expressed that the black earth itself was losing its fabled fertility and becoming exhausted. Moreover, many contemporaries felt that many if not all the changes in the steppe environment were not random, year-by-year fluctuations, but progressive changes, the pace of which was increasing.

Many of the changes contemporaries were observing involved those features of the steppe environment—the treelessness, shortage of water, but very fertile soil—that marked it out as different from the homelands of the settlers or their forebears and the forest-heartland of the Russian state. The changes were, thus, harmful to the interests of the agricultural settlers, who had moved from regions with plentiful supplies of trees and water to exploit the black earth of the steppes. The changes were also harmful to the interests of the Russian state that had overseen the conquest and settlement of the steppes.

[4] *SSSpSG*, vic, *Nikolaevskii uezd* (1889), 14.

In 1903, Aleksandr Platonovich Engel'gardt looked back to an article on the increasing frequency of bad harvests in the lower-Volga region that had been published a decade earlier. The article was entitled 'Who is to blame?'. The author gave the sweeping answer that to blame were the estate owners. Engel'gardt—who was the governor of Saratov province and had served as deputy minister of state domains—agreed.[5] Who was to blame for the deteriorating conditions was also discussed in 1903 at a meeting in the Ministry of Agriculture involving officials, including the minister Aleksei Ermolov, scientists, and estate owners. They reached a more balanced verdict: the causes of the deterioration in the 'physical conditions of the country' were both 'certain natural forces' and the 'rapacious attitude of man' to the wealth of nature that surrounded him.[6]

Anxieties about human impact on the steppe environment had reached a peak at the time of the catastrophic drought, crop failure, and famine of 1891–2. The crisis provoked an outburst of disquiet among the intelligentsia. Some moved beyond environmental issues to raise questions about the cultural identity of the steppe region. One of the most pessimistic responses was by the philosopher Vladimir Solov'ev. In October 1891, he wrote:

Since the start of the last decade, some writers have persistently pointed out that Russia, with the existing order, or disorder, of its national economy, is threatened with being transformed into an uninhabited desert. Indeed, for whom could it be a secret that the primitive economy, appropriate only in virgin lands, has already exhausted our land; that the black earth is being more and more depleted by ploughing; that at the same time, as a result of the felling of the forests and especially the draining of marshes, the rivers are becoming shallower and permanent repositories of land and atmospheric moisture are being destroyed. This process is being carried out before our very eyes, and in order to see where it will finally lead, there is no need to go beyond the present borders of the Russian Empire: our Turkestan—a desert with a few oases—was once a flourishing, well populated country with one of the main centres of Islamic education.[7]

In 1892, he developed his idea that the 'enemy'—the desert—was 'advancing on us from the East'.[8] Solov'ev had first written on the subject in 1884 and was well aware of the concerns among scientists over human impact on the steppe environment.[9]

---

[5] A. P. Engel'gardt, *Chernozemnaya Rossiya* (Saratov, 1903), 52–3. On Engel'gardt, see V. A. Skripitsyn, *Voistiny chelovek: iz vozpominanii ob Aleksandre Platonoviche Engel'gardt* (Spb, 1903) (I have used his patronymic to avoid confusion with the chemist Aleksandr Nikolaevich Engel'gardt).

[6] 'Sed'maya sessiya sel'skokhozyaistvennogo soveta', *SKhiL*, 211 (1903), 209.

[7] Vladimir Solov'ev, 'Narodnaya beda i obshchestvennaya pomosh'', *Vestnik Evropy*, 10 (1891), 781. Turkestan was the contemporary term for Central Asia.

[8] V. S. Solov'ev, 'Vrag s Vostoka', in *Sochineniia v dvukh tomakh*, ed. A. V. Gulyga and A. F. Losev, 2 vols (Moscow, 1988), ii, 480–92 [1st published July 1892]. For similar views, see N. V. Vereshchagin, 'Po povodu neurozhaya tekushchego goda', *TVEO*, 2/5 (1891), 178–96.

[9] V. S. Solov'ev, 'Evreistvo i Khristianskii vopros', *Pravoslavnoe obozrenie*, 8 (1884), 755–72; 9 (1884), 76–114, 103–7.

In some cases, such as ploughing up virgin steppe and cutting down trees, there was no question who was to blame. In the others, trying to disentangle changes caused or exacerbated by human activity from those that occurred independently of human actions was more difficult. Distinguishing between them still causes debate among environmental scientists.[10] It was harder for inhabitants of the Russian Empire, and elsewhere, over the eighteenth, nineteenth, and early-twentieth centuries to tell anthropogenic from autogenic changes in the environment. Some of the relevant scientific disciplines were still in their infancy. They did not, moreover, have long runs of reliable and comparable data on some parts of the environment, such as the climate, in particular levels of precipitation. These did not prevent a great deal of speculation about who or what was to blame. In many cases this was based on the recollections of 'old timers' (*starozhily*) about changes they had witnessed over their lifetimes. Such recollections were largely dismissed by the new generation of professional scientists, who were part of a wider, international, positivist movement. Current historians of science attach more importance to the memories of the population as examples of 'local knowledge'. They are also evidence for what people at the time thought was happening, which together with how scientists then understood changes in the environment, are important in seeking to understand how contemporaries responded to environmental change.

To some extent, the increasing pace of human impact on the environment was attributed to the abolition of serfdom in 1861, which prompted estate owners and freed serfs to make more intensive use of their land to increase their incomes.[11] Further factors included the growing population that put more pressure on the land. As a result of the largely extensive nature of agricultural development in the Russian Empire, settlers were moving to the east and south-east of the steppe region, bringing marginal land in areas with more arid climates into cultivation, where crops were more susceptible to fluctuations in the climate.[12] Concerns about environmental change, and the role of human activity, predated the mid-nineteenth century. The naturalists who took part in the Academy of Sciences expeditions of 1768–74 identified a number of the issues, such as deforestation, that subsequently provoked greater discussion. Thus, from the late eighteenth century, there was a pessimistic interpretation of the prospects for the development of the steppe region, for which part of the blame was

[10] See, for example, W. B. Meyer, *Human Impact on the Earth* (Cambridge 1996), 201–15.
[11] See M. Borovskii, 'Sposoby vedeniya pravil'nogo khozyaistva v Khersonsoi gubernii', *ZIOSKhYuR*, 2 (1876), 182–97; *Ob okhrane vodnykh bogatstv: Glavnye rezul'taty chetyrekhletnikh trudov ekspeditsii dlya issledovaniya istochnikov i glavneishikh rek Evropeiskoi Rossii [pod rukovodstvom A. Tillo]* (Spb, 1898), 1. See also Nina Sergeevna Tsintsadze, 'Demograficheskie i ekologicheskie aspekty podgotovki i provedeniya krest'yanskoi reformy 1861 goda v otsenkakh sovremennikov', Candidate dissertation, Tambov State University, 2009.
[12] On the cultivation of marginal land in the south-east of the Don region, see RGIA, f.382, op.2, 1894, d.1291; GARO, f.301, op.11, dd.323–4; f.301, op.14, d.342; f.301, op.27, d.89.

attributed to impact of the settlers on the environment. This may be contrasted with the optimistic view presented by Catherine the Great and others, which emphasized the ability of the settlers to transform the steppe environment to suit their designs.[13]

The Russian experience on the steppes can be compared with that of other European states in their overseas colonies. European colonists observed that removing native flora and fauna and transplanting their ways of life, crops, and livestock to other parts of the world was changing the natural conditions. Deforestation, climate change, and soil erosion were recurring themes in the accounts of European colonists as they sought to understand the processes of environmental change they seemed to have set in motion.[14] As Russians analysed the changes that were taking place in the steppe environment, and tried to work out who, or what, was to blame, they drew on the accumulated experiences and learning of scholars from other parts of the world as well as their own research that reflected Russian concerns about the changing environment of Russia's steppes.

Thus, part two of this book analyses perspectives on environmental change in the steppe region through the eyes, and words, of the various interested parties: the local population; the authorities in region and St Petersburg; naturalists and scientists, in particular the growing numbers of university-trained, professional scientists towards the end of the period.

Understanding contemporary perceptions of the changing environment is essential before moving on to the next stage in the story—how Russians tried to deal with the changes that were adversely affecting the development of agriculture on the fertile soil of the steppes—which be considered in Part III of this book.

[13] See David Moon, 'Agriculture and the Environment on the Steppes in the Nineteenth Century', in Nicholas Breyfogle, Abby Schrader, and Willard Sunderland (eds.), *Peopling the Russian Periphery: Borderland Colonization in Eurasian History* (Abingdon, 2007), 81–105.

[14] See Richard H. Grove, *Green Imperialism: Colonial Expansion, Tropical Island Edens, and the Origins of Environmentalism, 1600–1860* (Cambridge, 1995).

3

Vegetation

INTRODUCTION

The change in the vegetation of the steppe region that caused most concern among contemporaries was the destruction of the small areas of woodland that did exist there. While the steppe region was largely devoid of forests, there were trees in certain locations, such as river valleys, ravines, uplands, and areas with sandy soil. From the mid-eighteenth century, local inhabitants, officials, naturalists, and scientists expressed ever greater anxieties about the increasing pace at which the local population was felling these woodlands. Some scientists were moved to express their feelings. In 1858, Vasilii Chernyaev made an impassioned speech at Khar'kov University, where he was professor of botany. He decried the 'senseless' and 'increasing' destruction of the forests of 'Ukraine'. Like many of his contemporaries, he agonized over the consequences of deforestation. These included shortages of timber and firewood for the local population, but also wider, environmental issues, such as the impact on the climate and the soil.[1] One of the reasons why the shortage of trees and subsequent deforestation in the steppe region attracted so much comment was that most who drew attention to them came from northern and central Russia and Ukraine and Central Europe where forests, rather than grassland, were the norm. The rapid destruction of the few trees in the steppe region, therefore, was especially alarming. One of the main reasons for the felling of the woodland in the region, moreover, was that many of the settlers came from, or were the descendants of migrants from, forested environments, who were accustomed to using wood for many of their everyday needs from timber for construction to firewood.

The native vegetation of most of the steppe region, of course, was wild grasses, for example the iconic feather grass (*kovyl'*), and a rich variety of other plants. The ocean of grass that stretched to the horizon in the accounts of earlier travellers gradually and inexorably became confined to ever smaller seas, lakes,

---

[1] V. M. Chernyaev, *O lesakh Ukrainy: rech', proiznesennaya v torzhestvennoi sobranii imperatorskogo khar'kovskogo Universiteta, 1-go sentyabrya 1858 g.* (Moscow, 1858), 47. He used the term 'Ukraine' for the territory between the rivers Dnepr and Don.

and ponds of grass as the settlers ploughed up more and more virgin land. They replaced the native vegetation with cultivated grain, in particular wheat. The settlers grazed their livestock on the remaining grassland. In contrast to the nomadic pastoralists, however, the settlers did not move their livestock around between seasonal pastures, and thus risked over-grazing. The transition from steppe to arable fields occurred at varying rates across the region. It took place earliest and most quickly in the north of the region, which was the first to be settled and ploughed intensively, while the more arid south and south-east retained more of its native vegetation for longer. By the late nineteenth century, however, over half the total area of the steppe region had been brought under the plough. (See Table I.1.)

While almost all contemporaries considered the destruction of woodland to be a negative phenomenon, attitudes to the loss of the steppe grasses were less clear cut. Some, in particular proponents of the expansion of arable farming, saw it as a positive development. In 1856, the inspector of agriculture in southern Russia noted that the big plough up of land since the 1840s had had the beneficial result of destroying feather grass, which was harmful to sheep (the spikelets that grew in the spring could pierce sheep's skin and prove fatal). Thus, the area of safe pasture had increased.[2] Two years later, Krylov, who conducted an official survey of the Don Cossack territory, noted that when he crossed the border from Voronezh province, he was struck 'by the melancholy picture of uncultivated steppes, overgrown with wormwood (*polyn*') and feather grass, while in the neighbouring province, the fields are sown and there are signs of the population's activity everywhere'. Krylov believed that the cossacks needed to develop their agriculture to the same level as the population of other provinces.[3] Conserving the native vegetation that was soon to be scarce was far from minds of these officials.

From the mid-nineteenth century, with the increasing pace of the plough-up of the grasslands, the tone of many comments on the loss of the native vegetation began to change. In a speech at the Richelieu Lycée in Odessa in 1864, Ivan Palimpsestov looked back to the 'luxuriant' grass described by Herodotus. He went on:

However, the steppes of southern Russia in recent times were still covered by rich vegetation. Local old timers say that . . . you could put oxen out to graze, and if it was windy, then you would not be able to find them, because it was possible to locate them only by the waves they made in the grass. Such vegetation extended right to the shores of the Black Sea. More than one old timer related to me that . . . it was possible to get lost in the tall weeds on the top of Zhevakhov hill; that it was necessary only to turn ten *sazheny*

---

[2] DAOO, f.1, op.248, 1856, sp.1580, l.121.
[3] Krylov, 'Ocherk sovremennogo sostoyaniya zemli voiska Donskogo' [1858], in E. I. Dulimov (ed.), *Zemlya v sud'bakh donskikh kazakov: Sobranie istoriko-pravovykh aktov, 1704–1919 gg.* (Rostov-on-Don, 1998), 173.

[70 feet] from the road leading to Odessa in order to hide oneself and one's oxen from thieves, of whom, by the way, there were far fewer in those days. . . .

Palimpsestov continued that 'now' everything that emerged from the ground was eaten by huge herds of livestock, especially sheep, or cut down by scythes. 'Huge areas around our towns, villages, and [alongside] main roads are not covered by any vegetation.' Vast areas of land, moreover, were left fallow after being used to grow grain. 'The extensive fields of . . . grain', he carried on, 'cannot . . . substitute for the previous rich flora of the steppes: after 2–3 months at the time of ripening, they are the colour of a sandy plain, and then become bare of vegetation.'[4]

In 1906, I. Timoshchenkov of the Don statistical committee also described the changes in the plant cover in a critical manner. He listed, for example, the range of wild grasses, flowering herbs, and other plants that once provided an 'inexhaustible supply' of very good fodder for livestock. 'Now', he wrote, 'this has changed out of all recognition', and only poor grasses remained. He attributed the ruin of the pastures and meadows in part to over-grazing. His views need to be treated with caution. Timoshchenkov wrote that in the Second Don district 'in former years' the hills were covered with juniper (*mozhzhevel'nik*), an evergreen shrub, but that 'now' it was rarely to be found as almost all of it had been destroyed to be used as fuel.[5] His notion of the extent of the shrub in the past, however, differs from that of sources from earlier times. In his study of the geographical extent of coniferous trees in European Russia, published in 1885, Fedor Köppen argued that *mozhzhevel'nik* (*Juniperus sabina*) was to be found only in a few 'islands' of southern Russia, including on sand and chalky hills in parts of the Don Cossack region.[6] When Güldenstädt passed through the same area in 1769, he wrote that he came across '*Juniperus sabina*', which he noted was called '*mozhzhevel*'' in Russian, on sandy banks of the river in a radius of 15 *versty* around the cossack settlement of Novogrigorevskaya, but that it was not to be found anywhere else.[7] Timoshchenkov's account of the former extent of the shrub was, therefore, exaggerated. Thus, care needs to be taken in relying on descriptive accounts of environmental change looking back in time from the late nineteenth and early twentieth centuries. Like Palimpsestov, Timoshchenkov drew on the memories of old timers,[8] which may have been tinged with

[4] I. Palimpsestov, 'Peremenilsya li klimat yuga Rossii?', in I. Palimpsestov (ed.), *Sbornik statei o sel'skom khozyaistve yuga Rossii, izvlechennikh iz Zapisok Imperatorskogo Obshchestva sel'skogo khozyaistva yuzhnoi Rossii s 1830 po 1868 god* (Odessa, 1868), 4.

[5] I. Timoshchenkov, 'Vtoroi Donskoi okrug oblasti Voiska Donskogo. Statisticheskoetnograficheskii ocherk', *SOVDSK*, 6 (1906), 95–6, 99, 105.

[6] Fedor Keppen, 'Geograficheskoe rasprostranenie khvoinykh derevev v Evropeiskoi Rossii i na Kavkaze', *Zapiski Imperatorskogo Akademii Nauk*, 50/4 (1885), 456, 478–9.

[7] Johann Anton Güldenstädt, *Reisen durch Russland und im Caucasischen Gebürge*, 2 vols (Spb, 1787–91), i, 98.

[8] Timoshchenkov, 'Vtoroi Donskoi okrug', 105.

nostalgia. Caution needs to be used, therefore, and not just in this case, in interpreting the writings of people looking back in time.

DEFORESTATION[9]

Concerns about deforestation

Concerns about deforestation were raised in the eighteenth century. Early in the century, Peter the Great sought to protect woodland, including woodland in the steppe region, that could provide timber for shipbuilding.[10] In 1766, in the Free Economic Society's journal, Johann Gottlieb Lehmann argued that, following the experience of other European countries, the area of forest in Russia was decreasing 'daily'.[11] The next year, in the same journal, Petr Rychkov wrote of the need to protect forests and increase their area in his native Orenburg province in the east of the steppe region.[12] The leaders of the Academy of Sciences expeditions of 1768–74 also raised the issue. Ivan Lepekhin, a native of forested northern Russia, expressed concern about the 'neglect' of forests. In one village, he noted that the peasants were poor, because they had to buy wood for fuel, implements, and construction.[13] The situation was similar in the 1780s and 1790s when Vasilii Zuev and Peter Pallas made further expeditions across the steppes. Both commented on the wasteful use of timber, the 'unpardonable' destruction of forests, and the existence of towns, such as Belgorod, which were built almost entirely from wood in the midst of a largely treeless environment.[14] In 1793, in an account of his native Ekaterinoslav province, I. I. Veber noted that in past times forests had not been nearly as scarce. He continued 'it is already noticeable that the shortage of this material which is so necessary and essential is

---

[9] An earlier version of this section was published as David Moon, 'The Destruction of Woodland in the Steppe Region, 1760–1914', *Istoriko-biologicheskie issledovaniya/Studies in the History of Biology*, 2/4 (2010), 51–65. In his global history of deforestation, Michael Williams stated 'richly textured detail . . . does not exist for the continental extent of the Russian forest. What happened where and when is largely unknown, and [the] causes are obscure': Michael Williams, *Deforesting the Earth: From Prehistory to Global Crisis* (Chicago, 2003), 285. This section offers part of the Russian story.

[10] See A. E. Karimov, *Dokuda topor i sokha khodili: ocherki istorii zemel'nogo i lesnogo kadastra v Rossii XVI-nachala XX veka* (Moscow, 2007), 58–66.

[11] [J.-G.] Lehmann, 'Mnenie o lesakh', *TVEO*, 3 (1766), 118–19.

[12] P. R[ychkov] 'O sberezhenii i razmnozhenii lesov', *TVEO*, 6 (1767), 84–113. On Rychkov, see Denis J. B. Shaw, 'Utility in Natural History: Some Eighteenth-Century Russian Perspectives of the Living Environment', *Istoriko-biologicheskie issledovaniya/Studies in the History of Biology*, 2/4 (2010), 43–5.

[13] I. I. Lepekhin, 'Zapiski Puteshestviya Akademika Lepekhina', *PSUPpR*, iii (Spb, 1821), 98.

[14] Peter Simon Pallas, *Travels through the Southern Provinces of the Russian Empire, in the Years 1793 and 1794*, 2 vols (London, 1802), i, 14, 34; Vasilii Zuev, *Puteshestvennye zapiski Vasiliya Zueva ot S. Peterburga do Khersona, v 1781 i 1782 godu* (Spb, 1787), 49, 144, 163.

from year to year becoming more painful, and presents a very sad spectacle for future times'.[15]

Over the nineteenth century, the destruction of woodland became a cause of ever growing anxiety among officials, agricultural specialists, naturalists, scientists, and the wider educated public as well as the local population. Studies were produced right across the steppe region documenting the continuing loss of woodland that were, in part, mournful and tinged with nostalgia, and, in part, angry. Some writers may have exaggerated the extent of forest cover on the steppes in the past, however, and therefore overstated the degree of loss of woodland. This may have been due to a shortage of adequate statistics, which was a cause of constant complaint among specialists.[16] In the 1950s, Soviet geographer M. A. Tsvetkov used contemporary data to estimate that the area of woodland in most of the steppe region fell by over a half to around 5 per cent by the late nineteenth century (see Table I.2).[17] The intention here is not to revisit Tsvetkov's figures, but to consider what the destruction of woodland in the steppe region meant to people at the time.

Measuring deforestation

By the early twentieth century, specialists had data on the area of woodland in the steppe region, that covered entire provinces as well as individual settlements, going back over several decades. In his 1906 study of the cossack settlement of Nizhne-Chirskaya in the Second Don district of the Don region, Timoshchenkov reported that between 1853 and the start of the twentieth century the inhabitants had felled around half their forest, reducing it in area from 4,053 *desyatiny* to 2,087 *desyatiny*.[18] A quarter of a century earlier, an official study of forest on cossack lands in the Second Don district as a whole reported that: 'Almost half of the entire forested area . . . has been destroyed in 25 years.' Of 54,492 *desyatiny* of forest in the 1840s, approximately 30,000 were left.[19] Back in 1821, after extensive archival research, Vasilii Sukhorukov, an official attached to the ataman of the Don Cossacks, estimated that the total area of forest in the Don Cossack territory was around 421,000 *desyatiny*, or about 3 per cent of the total area. He was not able find comparable data for earlier periods, and his conclusions on changes over time were of necessity vague

---

[15] I. I. Veber, 'Primechaniya o razlichnykh predmetakh khozyaistva v Ekaterinoslavskom Namestnichestve', *TVEO*, 50 (1795), 179–80.

[16] See Jane Costlow, 'Imaginations of Destruction: The "Forest Question" in Nineteenth-Century Russian Culture', *RR*, 62 (2003), 99.

[17] M. A. Tsvetkov, *Izmenenie lesistosti evropeiskoi Rossii: s kontsa XVII stoletiia po 1914 god* (Moscow, 1957).

[18] I. Timoshchenkov, 'Stanitsa Nizhne-Chirskaya. Statistichesko-etnograficheskii ocherk', *SOVDSK*, 6 (1906), 117–21.

[19] GARO, f.55, op.1, d.1366 [1875], ll.11–12.

all the present forests are only the remnants of those majestic and impenetrable forests that once straddled the banks of the Don, Donets, Khoper, Medveditsa, Buzuluk, Mius, and other rivers. . . . Over the last 50 years, these forests have been . . . destroyed, at times as a result of the needs of the Cossack Host, at times of the wilfulness of the powerful, and finally the inhabitants themselves, chopping them down without any economic calculation, with little attention from the local authorities, have brought [them] to such a state that now very few cossack settlements meet the needs of their inhabitants from their own forest.[20]

Cossacks had lived on the Don, and been felling trees, since the sixteenth century. In parts of the steppe region that had been annexed and settled by migrants from forested regions more recently, it was easier to trace their impact on the local woodland. The territory of Stavropol' province in the North Caucasus was annexed from the Ottoman Empire in 1774. A century later, the secretary of the Provincial Statistical Committee, Józef Bentkowski, compared the extent of woodland in the 1870s and 80s with descriptions from Pallas' expedition of 1768–74 and a military report from the 1770s. Bentkowski also made comparisons with descriptions and data on forest area in I. V. Rovinskii's 'economic description' of the Caucasus and Astrakhan' provinces of 1809. Bentkowski's comparisons indicated many places where forests had disappeared completely in the century since Russian annexation. He presented statistics, moreover, to show that the area of forest within the contemporary borders of Stavropol' province had fallen from around 80,000 *desyatiny* in 1806 to 32,000 *desyatiny* in 1882. In some cases, only place names and memories were left.[21] Three years later, a detailed study of Stavropol' province was carried out by D. L. Ivanov. He was a mining engineer who had been sent by the Ministry of State Domains, on the request of the provincial governor, to investigate whether the eastern part of the province was suitable for settlement. Ivanov's visit, however, coincided with the very serious drought and crop failure of 1885, which greatly coloured his impressions. He wrote that of the luxuriant forests, 'which we know about from historical documents and the testimony of old people', very little was left. 'If we had a modern forestry map with forested lands

---

[20] [V. D. Sukhorukov], *Statisticheskoe opisanie zemli Donskikh kazakov, sostavlennoe v 1822–1832 godakh* (Novocherkassk, 1891), 209–10. On Sukhorukov, see A. I. Agafonov, *Istoriya Donskogo kraya (XVI-pervaya polovina XIX v. Istoricheskie istochniki i ikh izuchenie)* (Rostov-on-Don, 2001), 9–10.

[21] I. V. Bentkovskii, 'O lesakh v predelakh byvshei Kavkazskoi, a nyne Stavropol'skoi gubernii', *Stavropol'skie gubernskie vedomosti* (3 and 10 January 1876); I. V. Bentkovskii, 'Reka Kuma i neobkhodimost' uluchshit' ee ekonomicheskoe znachenie', *Stavropol'skie gubernskie vedomosti*, (3 and 10 July 1882); [I. V. Rovinskii], *Khozyaistvennoe opisanie Astrakhanskoi i Kavkazskoi gubernii* (Spb, 1809), 98–100. See also V. N. Gnilovskoi, 'Lesa Stavropol'skoi vozvyshennosti po istoriko-geograficheskim dannym', *Materialy po izucheniyu Stavropol'skogo kraya*, 12–13 (1971), 109–36; V. N. Gnilovskoi, 'Novye dannye o lesnykh kartakh Stavropol'ya nachala XIX veka', *Materialy po izucheniyu Stavropol'skogo kraya*, 14 (1976), 46–54. I am grateful to Dr Tat'yana Plokhotnyuk for these references.

and their quality accurately marked', he continued, 'then we would be struck by the insignificant and insipid specks of colour amid a denuded huge area....' He cited similar figures to Bentkowski that there were 30,700 *desyatiny* of forest remaining in the province, comprising only half of 1 per cent of the total area. Over the previous eighty years, 46,892 *desyatiny* of forest had been destroyed.[22]

The varied availability and reliability of data on the extent of former forest cover created problems for many nineteenth-century attempts to measure deforestation. Specialists looked back to earlier written sources, only to find that many were qualitative rather than quantitative, and general and subjective, if evocative.[23] A *zemstvo* study of Samara district in the 1880s tried to assess the timing and degree of deforestation by looking back to Adam Olearius's brief description when he sailed down the Volga in the 1630s.[24] Often, however, writers turned to recollections of 'old timers' or local lore.[25] A study of Nikolaevsk district in southern Samara province in 1880 reported that 'according to local legends', the banks of the Bol'shoi Irgiz and other rivers and streams had once been covered by forests of oak, maple, elm, asp, and birch, which had 'refreshed the boundless steppe', but that they had been destroyed by earlier settlers.[26] By the time of a *zemstvo* study of the district in 1889, however, the 'legends' seem to have evolved into 'facts' about the extent of forest cover in the early nineteenth century. The hard data presented on the area of woodland in the district dated back only to 1879, but revealed a decline from 24,954 *desyatiny* to 16,372 *desyatiny* in 1886, which was a little over one half of 1 per cent of the total area.[27]

In some locations it was very obvious that the inhabitants had recently chopped down lots of trees. 'The stumps which are left', Vasilii Chernyaev asserted in his impassioned speech in 1858, 'are evidence for the merciless destruction that has taken place in our memory.'[28] In 1873, an inhabitant of the cossack settlement of Pyatizbyanskaya in the Don region recalled a time not long before when all the gullies in the vicinity had been full of good oak woods, but that they had been cut down to build houses. Only 'individual ... stumps, scattered around the gullies, like watchmen recalling the recent downfall of their

[22] D. L. Ivanov, 'Vliyanie Russkoi kolonizatsii na prirodu Stavropol'skogo kraya', *IRGO*, 22/3 (1886), 238–9. See also 'Mestnaya khronika', *Severnyi Kavkaz* (18 June 1885).
[23] On the range of sources, see D. Strukov, 'O lesakh Novorossiiskogo kraya i Bessarabii', *ZhMGI*, 46 (1853), 1st pagn., 153–83, 209–44.
[24] *SSSpSG*, i, *Samarskii uezd* (1883), 3.
[25] See, for example, I. Palimpsestov, 'Stepi yuga Rossii byli-li iskoni vekov stepami i vozmozhno-li oblesit' ikh?', *LZh*, 12/2 (1882), 134–5.
[26] I. Lishin, *Ocherk Nikolaevskogo uezda (Samarskaya guberniya) v statisticheskom i sel'sko-khozyaistvom otnosheniyakh* (Spb, 1880), 45.
[27] *SSSpSG*, vi, *Nikolaevskii uezd* (1889), 14, 41.
[28] Chernyaev, *O lesakh Ukrainy*, 47.

centuries-old comrades' were left.[29] Even more poignant was a story from a village in Buzuluk district, Samara province recorded in 1885:

In the village of Dalmatovo, out of all the forest that was allotted to it, there is . . . only one birch tree left, which the peasants have deemed protected for ever, so that religious services can be held in its shade.[30]

One tree left was a very long way from Palimpsestov's vision that the steppes as a whole had been forested to a far greater extent in the past (see above pp. 60–2 this volume). In 1850—in his characteristic verbose style that is difficult to convey in translation—he bemoaned the destruction of the forests in his native Saratov province:

Yes, those ancient oaks with great girths which grew in broad bands along both sides of the Medveditsa and Khoper rivers, of which those mighty fellows that have escaped destruction remind us . . . of the might and splendour of the verdure in Saratov province, are no longer with us. Those dense, lofty forests of oak, lime, maple, asp, cherry, elm, pine, and birch, which almost completely covered the basins of the Khoper and Medveditsa [rivers], the remnants of which we now find along ravines and streams flowing into those rivers—and which as small copses are oases of woodland among the bare steppe—are also no longer with us.[31]

Palimpsestov struggled to find sufficient evidence to convince the growing numbers of doubters among scientists in his argument on the former extent of forests in the steppe region. Nevertheless, his was a persistent voice, eccentric and visionary, that drew attention to the harm of destroying woodland.

Identifying the causes of deforestation

Many contemporaries considered who was to blame for the destruction of the scarce woodland in the steppe region. The use of wood for construction attracted comment from at least the time of the Academy of Sciences expeditions of 1768–74. Several expedition leaders noted with surprise that peasant settlers, who were recent arrivals, and cossacks, who had lived in the region for generations, used scarce timber, rather than stone or brick, for construction. Lepekhin commented that that there were no stone buildings in Saratov with the exception of seven churches and two monasteries.[32] At Tsaritsyn, further down the Volga, Falck recorded that the churches and houses were all wooden.[33] Gmelin and Güldenstädt both noted that the Don Cossacks built their houses from wood. It became

---

[29] Letter to *Donskie oblastnye vedomosti* in 1873, quoted in A. Kryukov, 'O stanichnykh lesakh Donskoi oblasti', *SOVDSK*, 10 (1910), 81.

[30] *SSSpSG*, iii, *Buzulukskii uezd* (1885), 39.

[31] I. Palimpsestov, 'Saratovskaya step' v khozyaistvennom otnoshenii', *TVEO*, 4 (1850), 113.

[32] Lepekhin, 'Zapiski', 378.

[33] Fal'k, 'Zapiski Puteshestviia Akademika Fal'ka', *PSUPpR*, vi (Spb, 1824), 128.

apparent to Gmelin, as he travelled down the Don, that there were more trees on the far side of the river, where the nomadic Kalmyks lived, than the cossack side, where there were almost no trees left.[34] Güldenstädt visited Taganrog and the nearby defensive line. All the houses in the port were made from logs and there was, he noted, a shortage of forest in the area. Settlers on the defensive line, moreover, used timber brought from forty *versty* up the river Mius, as all the trees lower down had been felled.[35] The Russian predilection for timber was especially noticeable in areas where Russian settlers and cossacks lived alongside other ethnic groups. Falck noted that on the Terek river in the North Caucasus, the Russians' houses were wooden, while those of other people were made out of *mazanka* (wattle daubed with clay).[36]

The use of timber for construction contributed to the rapid deforestation in the North Caucasus after Russian annexation in 1774. A defensive line was constructed from Mozdok on the river Terek to Azov near the delta of the river Don. Migrants moved in behind the line, built settlements, and cultivated the fertile land. In his 1809 description of the region, Rovinskii recorded: 'The town and village houses are largely build of [local] timber.' The inhabitants carefully selected tall, straight trees, such as poplars, for construction. They also used the forests to provide fuel. Many rural inhabitants, moreover, carted large quantities of firewood to towns for sale.[37] The fortress and later city of Stavropol', founded in 1777 on upland, developed at great cost to the surrounding woodland. A source from 1845 indicated that in the vicinity of the city, where there had once been forests that could provide timber fit for construction, were 'now' only 'shrubs'.[38] Bentkowski later wrote about the '[r]uthless destruction of forests' that had followed the construction of the fortified line, including the fort at Stavropol', and the settlement of land behind the line.[39] Settlers continued to fell trees to provide timber for construction later in the nineteenth century when they moved to more outlying parts of the steppe region, where trees were in very short supply. The author of a *zemstvo* study of the largely treeless Nikolaevsk district in southern Samara province in 1889 noted, accusingly, that the churches in the town of Nikolaevsk and in the villages were all made out of oak.[40]

[34] Samuel Georg Gmelin, *Puteshestvie po Rossii dlya issledovaniya trekh tsarstv estestva, perevedena s nemetskogo*, 4 vols in 3 parts (Spb, 1771–85), i, 244, 265; Güldenstädt, *Reisen*, i, 50, 60.
[35] I. Ya. Gil'denshtedt, 'Dnevnik puteshestviya v Yuzhnuyu Rossiyu akademika S. Peterburgskoi Akademii Nauk Gil'denshtedta v 1773–1774 g.', *Zapiski Imperatorskogo Odesskogo obshchestva istorii i drevnosti*, xi (1879), 212.
[36] Fal'k, 'Zapiski', 66.
[37] [Rovinskii], *Khozyaistvennoe opisanie*, 100–2.
[38] Quoted in [I. F. Shtukenberg], 'Opisanie Stavropol'skoi gubernii s zemleyu Chernomorskikh kazakov', *Statisticheskii trudy Ivan Fedorovicha Shtukenberga*, 2 vols (Spb, 1857–8), i, article 3, 28–9, 35.
[39] Bentkovskii, 'O lesakh'.
[40] *SSSpSG*, vi, *Nikolaevskii uezd* (1889), 14.

Timber was also used to build ships and bridges. In Kherson province, on the north coast of the Black Sea, a study in 1849 reported: 'The first settlers of this region destroyed many forests for the construction of buildings and ships when [the ports of] Kherson and Nikolaev were founded.' The ports had been founded by Grigorii Potemkin, after the annexation of the territory, in 1778 and 1789 respectively. By 1849, the total area of forest in Kherson province was only 120,062 *desyatiny*: a little over 2 per cent of the total area.[41] An investigation in the Don Cossack territory in 1847–53 revealed that new barges were being constructed every year to ship goods down the Donets river. The report recommended that, in order not to deplete the forests, barges should be sent back upstream and reused. The inhabitants of settlements on the Khoper and Medveditsa rivers, moreover, were building new wooden bridges annually, and leaving the old ones to be broken up by the ice and flotsam after the end of navigation each year. The investigator argued it would be better to use ferries to cross the river rather than 'destroy the remnants of the settlements' forest' to build new bridges.[42]

A further use of timber that attracted adverse comment was fences between fields. In 1858, Vasilii Chernyaev had commented that in Western Europe, where he had studied, hedges were used for this purpose.[43] A more important cause of deforestation was clearing land for arable fields, meadows, and pasture.[44] In his account of Ekaterinoslav province in 1793, Veber made a direct connection between the growing population and cultivation of ever more land and the destruction of a large part of the forests.[45] In the mid-1850s, Bauman, the manager of the Ekaterinoslav state farm, described how forests along the Kashlagach river had been felled illegally since 1809. The land had first been used for grazing sheep, which had killed off the remaining trees and shrubs. Later, the land had been ploughed up. In the process, all traces of the former woods had been removed. He speculated that the same process may well have occurred in adjoining parts of the Don Cossack territory.[46] In 1839, Andrei Leopold'ov wrote that the forests in much of Saratov province had been 'ruthlessly destroyed' in some places by grazing livestock, and in others to provide arable land. He noted that some people 'erroneously' thought that arable farming (*zemledelie*) was more profitable than protecting forest.[47] Deforestation to clear land for farming increased over the late nineteenth century as the growing agricultural

---

[41] *VSORI*, 11/1, *Khersonskaya guberniya*, comp. Rogalev, fon Vitte, Pestov (1849), 132–3.
[42] GARO, f.46, op.1, d.590 (1857), ll.49ob.-52, 147.
[43] Chernyaev, *O lesakh Ukrainy*, 47–8.
[44] See Tsvetkov, *Izmenenie*, 83.
[45] Veber, 'Primechaniya', 190.
[46] Bauman, 'Putevye zametki po nekotorym okrugam zemli voiska Donskogo', *ZhMGI*, 60 (1856), 2nd pagn, 22–3, 26–7.
[47] Andrei Leopol'dov, *Statisticheskoe opisanie Saratovskoi gubernii*, 2 vols (Spb, 1839), i, 12–14; ii, 142.

population and their livestock put ever greater pressure on the available land. An official survey of Nikolaevsk district, Samara province, in the 1890s noted that land had been cleared of trees for arable, meadows, and other uses.[48] In 1892, in the Donets district of the Don region, a total of 1,049 *desyatiny* of land—which was designated as forest but no longer had any trees—was leased out for cultivation and grazing.[49] The Stavropol' official yearbook for 1904 noted that the forests in the province had been almost completely destroyed 'in connection with the growth of agriculture and the progressive expansion of the area of tillage'.[50]

One of the ways trees were cleared was by fire. 'Slash-and-burn' farming dated back to the origin of farming in densely forested central Russia in medieval times.[51] On the steppes, the nomads had used fire for millennia to encourage the growth of fresh grass to provide fodder for their livestock.[52] Russian settlers burned the steppe in the belief that the ashes would improve the soil.[53] In the 1760s, Rychkov noted that fires set by the local population to burn stubble in fields and by travellers to keep themselves warm at night could quickly get out control due to the wind. Fire spread so fast that a man on horseback could not escape. On the steppe, moreover, fire could jump and destroy everything, including young forests, in its path.[54] Fires also broke out spontaneously. When the Don Cossack authorities planned to plant trees on the steppe beyond in the Don in the 1840s, they decided to avoid areas where steppe fires spread from Astrakhan' province to the south as they destroyed young trees.[55] The destructive capacity of fire on the steppes was brought home to me when I visited a forestry plantation near Veshenskaya in northern Rostov region in 2003. The foresters told us, with dismay, that trees were being destroyed by fire faster than they could plant them. The plantation contained an entire stand of trees that had been turned to charcoal by fire.

Another way fire contributed to the destruction of woodland was the use of firewood for domestic purposes and, increasingly, in industry and transport. Concerns about the impact of burning firewood on the area of forest were expressed from the mid-eighteenth century. In 1768, correspondents of the Free Economic Society noted that the increase in distilling had caused the destruction of forests in Slobodskaya Ukraine (later Khar'kov province).[56] Later in the eighteenth century, Veber noted that the majority of estate owners

[48] GASO, f.834, op.30, d.7 (1893–99), l.48.
[49] GARO, f.301, op.27, d.89 (1892).
[50] *Pamyatnaya knizhka Stavropol'skoi gubernii na 1904 god* (Stavropol', 1904), 2.
[51] See R. E. F. Smith, *The Origins of Farming in Russia* (Paris, 1959), 51–74.
[52] See Tsvetkov, *Izmenenie*, 36–7.
[53] Gmelin, *Puteshestvie*, i, 134.
[54] R[ychkov], 'O sberezhenii', 96–100.
[55] GARO, f.243, op.1, d.19, ll.1ob.-2. See also p. 183.
[56] 'Prodolzhenie otvetov na ... voprosov o nyneshnem sostoyanii v raznykh guberniyakh i provintsiyakh zemledelii i domostroitel'stva, po Slobodsko-Ukrainskoi gubernii', *TVEO*, 8 (1768), 171.

in Ekaterinoslav province derived a lot of their income from distilling and preparing saltpetre. Both required large amounts of firewood, which was contributing to the destruction of the remaining woodland.[57] Among the causes of the 'rapid destruction of the forests' Vasilii Chernyaev referred to in his speech in 1858 was the use of increasingly scarce timber, rather than substitutes such as peat or pressed dung (*kizyak*), for fuel. A lot of firewood, he continued, was burned in distilleries, sugar refineries, brickworks, and other factories.[58] Vast amounts of firewood were burned by the steamships that first appeared on the Volga in 1821, and increased in numbers over the following decades. By the 1880s, over five hundred steamships carried freight and passengers along the Volga, and burned 80 million *pudy* (over a million tons) of firewood a year. This was the equivalent of 10,000 *desyatiny* of forest. Much, however, came from the forested, northern part of the Volga basin.[59]

The practice of making many domestic items out of wood rather than other materials came in for adverse comment by Vasilii Chernyaev in 1858. He also criticized the Ukrainian custom of decorating houses for Pentecost with young maple trees, which in the city of Khar'kov alone resulted in the destruction of over a hundred thousand of the 'best young trees' every year.[60] Almost a century earlier in the Orenburg region, Rychkov criticized the practice among Russian settlers of continuing the custom they had brought with them from the forest-heartland of making footwear (*lapty*) out of bast (inner bark) from lime trees. He pointed out that other people in the steppe region, including Ukrainians and Bashkirs, made their footwear out of leather, which he argued was stronger, and warmer in winter, than bast.[61]

Contemporaries increasingly remarked on what they saw as the wasteful attitude to woodland among many inhabitants of the steppe region. This was implicit in the accounts of the Academy of Sciences expeditions of 1768–74, but became more explicit in subsequent decades. In 1835, the governor of Orenburg province identified the main causes of the shortage of trees along the Orenburg defensive line. He included the 'disordered felling of trees' and the 'complete inability and lack of desire among the cossacks to take measures that would assist in the conservation and regeneration of forests'.[62] A report compiled in 1863 on the state of forests in the Don Cossack territory noted that woodland was disappearing, not because of the large population, but due to 'incorrect and wasteful use' of forests. Cossacks were felling trees without regard to the instructions from their communities. Some cut several times the amount of timber they were permitted to. In any case, until the late 1860s, regulation was lax. This

---

[57] Veber, 'Primechaniya', 179
[58] Chernyaev, *O lesakh Ukrainy*, 47–8.
[59] Ya. Veinberg, *Les: znachenie ego v prirode i mery k ego sokhraneniyu* (Moscow, 1884), 395–6.
[60] Chernyaev, *O lesakh Ukrainy*, 47–8.
[61] R[ychkov], 'O sberezhenii', 108–11.
[62] RGIA, f.398, op.83, d.129, l.1.

attitude to woodland, it was noted, showed little concern for future generations.[63] The notion of the population felling trees with little regard for their
descendants was repeated in a study of southern Samara province with its largely
peasant population.[64] Some local inhabitants went so far as to deny that there
had once been woods in the vicinity of their settlements. In the mid-1850s,
inhabitants of Mius district in the Don Cossack territory claimed that there had
never been forests nearby, on account of the wind, only shrubs.[65] Illegal felling of
trees took place throughout the steppe region. Some, but only some, of the
culprits were caught and prosecuted.[66]

The sheer waste was conveyed by an official in the Don region in 1875:

unmanaged felling [of cossack forest] each year . . . has gradually destroyed whole areas,
and has now diminished the remaining [forest]. In place of forest with timber fit for
construction and centuries-old oaks only individual relics . . . remain. . . . In many settlements I was a witness to the sad fact that protected [forest] had been felled, the timber lay
in piles on the roads for several years, and in time rotted.[67]

The situation was little changed in 1910, when an article published by the Don
statistical committee described the forests of cossack settlements as 'neglected,
desolate, and uncared for'. The author presented data showing a 34 per cent
decline in the area of such forest in the Don region since the 1870s from 291,902
to 191,462 *desyatiny*. Around one hundred thousand *desyatiny* had 'perished
under the barbaric strikes of the axe'. He gave as reasons for the destruction:
criminal waste of the 'gifts of the creator'; lack of understanding and ignorance;
but also the demands of 'new ways of life', and the 'battle' between arable land
and forest. He cast doubt over the idea that land shortages were to blame,
however, noting that it was better-off cossacks who were felling the forests.[68]

Contemporaries noted that the abolition of serfdom in 1861, and consequent
need for estate owners and peasants to earn more from their land, had led them to
fell more trees to use or for sale, and to clear land for crops.[69] A fictional
impoverished noble family who sold woodland on their estate to the son of a
former serf was immortalized by Anton Chekhov in his play *The Cherry Orchard*,
which was first performed in 1904.[70]

---

[63] GARO, f.55, op.1, d.829 (1863), ll.1–2; d.860 (1867–8), ll.13ob.–18ob.
[64] Lishin, *Ocherk*, 45.
[65] Bauman, 'Putevye', 24.
[66] For examples from the Don Cossack territory and Samara province, see GARO, f.46, op.1, d.497 (1840), l.95; GASO, f.112, op.98, d.5 (1860–67).
[67] GARO, f.55, op.1, d.1366 [1875], ll.10–ob.
[68] Kryukov, 'O stanichnykh lesakh', 79, 85–6.
[69] See Tsvetkov, *Izmenenie*, 30, 48.
[70] A. P. Chekhov, *Polnoe sobranie sochinenii i pisem*, 18 vols (Moscow, 1972–84), xiii, 195–254.

Understanding the consequences of deforestation

The initial reason for concern about deforestation was that the growing settler population needed forest to provide for various basic needs, especially as many came from regions where they were accustomed to using forest products. This was one of Lepekhin's concerns as he travelled through the steppe region in 1768–74. Later writers also noted the impact of deforestation on the region's inhabitants. In the 1820s, Sukhorukov wrote that there was little shipping on the river Don upstream from Kalachinskaya (the crossing point to the Volga), because there was so little timber available in Voronezh province that inhabitants had to import it to make boats.[71] Voronezh province was the location where Peter the Great had built his first fleets, from local timber, for his Azov campaign in 1695–6.[72] In 1835, the governor of Orenburg reported that there was a shortage of timber for construction and that firewood was so expensive that heating had become one of largest items of household expenditure.[73] In the North Caucasus there were serious shortages of wood by the 1840s. Shtukenberg wrote that the local population had insufficient wood for fuel, and so had to burn pressed dung, reeds, and straw. They had to import all wooden implements and utensils, moreover, from central Russia.[74] At around the same time, Captain Petukhov noted that due to the shortage of timber, Russian settlers in the North Caucasus were starting to build their houses from clay mixed with cattle dung and chopped-up straw.[75] Peasant farmers on the steppes in Samara province were experiencing similar shortages by the 1880s. In Samara and Nikolaevsk districts, the *zemstvo* reported that peasants had insufficient forest left to provide them with firewood and timber. They were burning pressed dung and using bricks for building. And, the *zemstvo* noted, the peasants had started to value the remaining forest and protect it more carefully. In Novyi Uzen' district, in southern Samara province, the population imported timber down the Volga by the 1880s.[76]

It was not just the cost of importing timber or the inconvenience of seeking substitutes for people accustomed to using wood for many everyday needs that explained the growing concerns about the destruction of woodland in the steppe region. The idea gradually took hold in Russia, as elsewhere in the world, that forests played a vital role in the environment, and that their destruction could entail serious consequences. In 1793, Veber wrote that the abundant and dense

---

[71] [Sukhorukov], *Statisticheskoe opisanie*, 27.

[72] See E. J. Phillips, *The Founding of Russia's Navy: Peter the Great and the Azov Fleet, 1688–1714* (Westport, CT, 1995), 31–44.

[73] RGIA, f.398, op.83, d.129, l.1ob.

[74] [Shtukenberg], 'Opisanie Stavropol'skoi gubernii s zemleyu Chernomorskikh kazakov', 34–5.

[75] [Capt] Petukhov, 'Opisanie chasti Kavkazskoi oblasti mezhdu rekami Egorlykom, Kalausom i Manychem', *Trudy Stavropol'skoi Uchenoi Arkhivnoi Komissii*, 1 (1911), 2nd pagn, 12. [Compiled in 1843.]

[76] *SSSpSG*, i, *Samarskii uezd* (1883), 30–1; vi, *Nikolaevskii uezd* (1889), 41; vii, *Novouzenskii uezd* (1890), 37–8.

forests that had once existed in Ekaterinoslav province had provided strong resistance to the ruinous force of the easterly and northerly winds in the autumn and spring, had protected the surface of the land and the plants against harsh frosts, had provided shelter from snow drifts and fodder for livestock, and had moderated the extremes of the climate in the winter. 'Now', he remarked, 'in large areas there is not a single tree to be seen.'[77]

The drought, crop failure, and famine, which afflicted much of the steppe region in 1833, focused attention on the environmental consequences of deforestation. At the first meeting of the Russian Forestry Society in February 1833, a paper was read entitled: 'On the pernicious consequences of the devastation of forests.' The author and other Russian specialists at this time cited or translated work by their counterparts elsewhere in Europe, including Alexander von Humboldt and Charles Lyell. Specialists in Russia summarized the experiences of other countries that had destroyed their forests throughout human history and around the globe, from North Africa and Asia Minor in ancient times to Caribbean islands, Peru, and the French Alps more recently. The Russian forestry journal published a series of articles in the 1830s that warned of the harmful consequences of destroying forests: the climate becoming hotter and drier; the loss of shelter against the wind; drifting sands, dust storms, and soil erosion; the land drying up; and the risk that settled and productive land would be transformed into infertile deserts. This was not idle speculation, but reflected very real fears rooted not just in what had happened elsewhere in the world, but contemporary perceptions of what was taking place on the steppes.[78] In 1835, for example, the governor of Orenburg noted that, as a result of the destruction of the forests, 'the very climate has noticeably changed, the fertility of the soil is gradually declining. . . .'[79]

These concerns were repeated by other specialists, for example Vasilii Chernyaev and Palimpsestov, in the 1850s.[80] They were reiterated with ever growing frequency and alarm over the rest of the nineteenth century as Russians continued to draw on their own experience and the work of foreign specialists. Palimpsestov drew heavily on Humboldt's work, later citing his prediction that by destroying forests, humankind would inevitably prepare two great calamities for itself: shortages of water and fuel.[81] The book by the American

---

[77] Veber, 'Primechaniya', 191.

[78] 'Rassuzhdenie o neobkhodimosti okhraneniya vladel'cheskikh lesov ot istrebleniya i o pol'ze pravil'nogo lesnogo khozyaistva', *LZh*, 1 (1833), 51–103; Breitenbakh, 'O pol'ze lesov v prirode', *LZh*, 1 (1835), 383–91; 'O vliyanii lesov i istrebleniya onykh na klimat', *LZh*, 1 (1837), 427–42; 'O vliyanii lesov na klimat, reki i prozyabenie, i vrednykh posledstviyakh ikh istreblenya', *LZh*, 3 (1837), 325–50.

[79] RGIA, f.398, op.83, d.129, ll.1ob.-2.

[80] I. Palimpsestov, 'Saratovskaya step' v khozyaistvennom otnoshenii', *TVEO*, 4 (1850), 111–22; Chernyaev, *O lesakh Ukrainy*, 2.

[81] Palimpsestov, 'Peremenilsya', 2, 4, 5, 6, 11, 16, 20; id., 'Odin iz otvetov na vopros: "byli li lesa na yuge Rossii?"', *Izvestiya imperatorskogo Obshchestva lyubitelei estestvoznaniya, antropologii i etnografii*, 41/1 (1881), 18.

environmentalist George Perkins Marsh, *Man and Nature*, that attached great significance to deforestation, was quickly translated into Russian and published in 1866.[82] In the 1870s, Yakov Ignat'evich Veinberg was commissioned to write a detailed study of 'forests and their significance in nature' by two Moscow natural history societies. Veinberg was a graduate of the Odessa Richelieu Lycée (before Palimpsestov taught there) and Moscow University. He was a teacher, author of popular articles on science, in particular meteorology, and had translated some of Humboldt's writings.[83] Veinberg produced a detailed analysis of the scientific literature, both Russian and foreign, on forests. The results were published as a series of articles, written for a broad, educated readership, in the thick journal *The Russian Herald* (*Russkii Vestnik*) in 1878–9, and as a book in 1884. Veinberg explained how, when he embarked on the study, he had been fully prepared to deny that forests had any wider impact, but that his views had changed as he studied the arguments for and against the significance of forests. He drew conclusions about the serious consequences of deforestation, similar to those presented in the 1830s, and urged the protection of existing woodland and planting new forests. He recognized, moreover, the particular impact of the destruction of woodland in the steppe region.[84]

Anxieties about the devastation of Russia's forests, including woodland in the steppe region, were taken up by the cultural intelligentsia. Jane Costlow has traced how, from the 1860s, 'the forest question' crossed over from specialized to general publications, in particular 'thick journals' such as *The Russian Herald*. It was also reflected in landscape painting. In the background of a painting by Il'ya Repin, *Procession of the Cross in Kursk Province* completed in 1883, is a low hillside covered with the stumps of recently felled oaks. (We know they were oaks as the trees before they were chopped down were included in an earlier version of the painting.) In the foreground, the religious procession is accompanied by an officious mounted policeman. Costlow 'reads' the final, deforested, version of the painting thus: 'When our gaze moves back into the upper plane of the painting, we see both absence (of trees) and the presence (of violent authority).'[85] Kursk province was in the forest-steppe region. The artist was familiar with the region as he was born in Khar'kov province. Anxieties about deforestation and its consequences also found expression in literature. In Anton Chekhov's play *Uncle Vanya* of 1897, the character Dr Astrov makes an impassioned speech

    [82] G. Marsh, *Chelovek i priroda, ili o vliyanii cheloveka na izmenenie fiziko-geografiskikh uslovii prirody*, trans. N. A. Nevedomskii (Spb, 1866).
    [83] See obituary in *Moskovskie vedomosti*, 9–10 (1898), <http://dic.academic.ru/dic.nsf/enc_biography/128393/> (accessed 29 June 2009).
    [84] Veinberg, *Les*, 28–9. See also Ya. Veinberg, 'Les i znachenie ego v prirode', *Russkii vestnik*, 139 (1879), 5–35, 514–52; 141 (1879), 48–75; 142 (1879), 483–517; 143 (1879), 644–73; 144 (1879), 59–78.
    [85] Costlow, 'Imaginations', 102–5.

on the consequences of deforestation.[86] Chekhov knew what he was writing about as he was a native of the steppe region and was familiar with the natural sciences as he trained as a physician at Moscow University.[87]

STEPPE VEGETATION

Regardless of the preoccupation with the loss of woodland, the main change in the vegetation of the steppe region was caused by the conversion of grassland to arable fields. The early generations of settlers encountered an abundance of land that allowed extensive systems of farming, mostly shifting, long-fallow agriculture. Farmers cleared an area of its native grasses and other vegetation, often by burning, ploughed it up, and then sowed grain. Over the following years, they sowed rye, barley, wheat, and other crops in rudimentary rotations. Yields declined from year to year as the soil came to resemble, in Rychkov's words, 'charred logs', and fields became covered in weeds. Since land was plentiful, however, farmers simply ploughed up new fields. The old fields were turned over to pasture or, after a few years, used for mowing hay. Land was left fallow for as many as twenty to thirty years before it was once again ploughed up and sown with crops. At any one time, only one-fifth or one-sixth of the land was under cultivation. Such systems of farming were employed throughout the much of the steppe region into the nineteenth century, persisting for longest in more outlying parts.[88] From the perspective of the native vegetation, shifting, long-fallow agriculture had a very important feature: it allowed the former flora time to return. Land left fallow for many years was gradually reclaimed by the surrounding steppe.

Over the second half of the nineteenth century, estate owners and botanists observed and sought to explain what happened to the vegetation in long-fallow fields. In the mid-1860s, Sergei Bulatsel', who owned an estate in Slavyanoserbsk district, Ekaterinoslav province, described how, in the first years, weeds grew in the fallow field. They were followed by couch grasses (*pirei, Triticum repens*), and then feather grass (*kovyl', Stipa*). Bulatsel' considered the presence of feather grass to be the best indicator of 'old fallow' (*staryi zalezh*').[89] Around the same time, the botanist L. Chernyaev carried out a wider study and produced a more

[86] Chekhov, *Polnoe sobranie sochinenii*, xiii, 72–3.
[87] D. Rayfield, *Anton Chekhov: A Life* (Evanston, IL, 1997).
[88] See A. S. Ermolov, *Organizatsiya polevogo khozyaistva: Sistemy zemledeliya i sevooboroty*, 5th edn (Spb, 1914), 67–72, 111–23; Petr Rychkov, 'Otvety na Ekonomicheskie voprosy, kasayushchiesya do zemledeliya, po raznosti provintsii kratko i po vozmozhnosti iz"yasennye, v razsuzhdenii Orenburgskoi gubernii', *TVEO*, 7 (1767) 121; [Sukhorukov], *Statisticheskoe opisanie*, 199–201; S. Nomikosov, *Statisticheskoe opisanie Oblasti voiska Donskogo* (Novocherkassk, 1884), 370–84, 398; DAOO, f.1, op.248, 1856, sp.1580, ll.55ob.-56.
[89] Sergei Bulatsel', 'Zemledelie v Slavyanoserbskom uezde, Ekaterinoslavskoi gubernii', *TVEO*, 1 (1866), 338.

detailed account of what he termed the 'succession' of plants in the fallow field. In the first stage, couch grasses grew for between seven and ten years. They were followed by another type of grass, koeleria (*tonkonoga*), which also persisted for seven-ten years. Then, after an indefinite number of years, feather grass returned. L. Chernyaev noted that the pattern of succession could vary. Sometimes, as Bulatsel' noted, weeds grew in the fallow field before couch grasses. Couch grasses could also be preceded by vetch, growing as a weed. In cases where various weeds appeared first, there was a greater diversity of plants in the fallow field as the succession unfolded.[90]

In the 1880s, the soil scientist and agronomist Pavel Kostychev studied long-fallow agriculture in southern Samara, Saratov, and Voronezh provinces. His lists of species at various stages in the succession in the fallow fields were longer than L. Chernyaev's. He made a clearer distinction between weeds in the first stage, 'long-fallow (*zalezhnye*) grasses', such as couch grasses, brome (*koster*), and sweet grass (*chapolot*), in the second stage, and what he termed 'steppe grasses', such as koeleria, fescue (*tipchak*), and feather grass in the third stage. The grasses grew back from rootstocks, or rhizomes, that had survived in the ground during the period of cultivation. Kostychev concluded that long-fallow fields recovered their full fertility only when the original character of the steppes, and the native vegetation, returned.[91] Feather grass was the last of the main native species to come back. The time it took varied across the region. In parts of the North Caucasus, it could reappear after only nine–ten years.[92] Elsewhere in the region, however, it took fifteen–twenty years before the iconic feather grass once again covered the fallow field.[93]

Kostychev and other Russians were among a number of scientists working on plant succession at this time. In Nebraska on the Great Plains of the USA, Frederic Clements was investigating the revegetation of old trails. The succession he and other American botanists observed on the Great Plains was similar to that on the steppes, and also included grasses similar to feather grass (*Stipa*) towards the end. In 1916, Clements presented his theory of plant succession as the development of plant populations in harmony with a particular habitat culminating in a stable, climax formation. Clements was familiar with the work Russian scientists, for example Sergei Korzhinskii and Tanfil'ev, from abstracts in German. He referred to Russian work on the invasion of the steppe by oak

---

[90] L. Chernyaev, 'Ocherki o stepnoi rastitel'nosti', *SKhiL*, 88 (1865), 2nd pagn, 46.

[91] P. Kostychev, 'Iz putevykh zametok: Perelozhnye khozyaistva s kratkosrochnymi zalezhami', *SKhiL*, 161 (1889), 2nd pagn, 338. A *zemstvo* study of Nikolaevsk district, Samara province, noted that forty village communities complained about weeds choking the spring grain. *SSSpSG*, vi, *Nikolaevskii uezd* (1889), 43.

[92] A. Filipchenko, 'Sel'skoe khozyaistvo na severnom Kavkaze', *SKhiL*, 182 (1896), 245.

[93] See D. N. Pryanishnikov, *Izbrannye sochineniya*, 3 vols (Moscow, 1965), iii, 112–13; *SSSpSG*, vi, *Nikolaevskii uezd* (1889), 68.

forests in the forest-steppe region, but does not seem to have been familiar with research on the succession of grasses on the steppes.[94]

On the steppes, as long as fields were left fallow for at least fifteen–twenty years—which was the practice into the nineteenth century—then the native vegetation could survive as rootstock underground and return. What happened over the nineteenth century, however, was that farmers cut back the time fields were left fallow. Later, farmers introduced more intensive systems of farming, including the three-field rotation, which in most cases had much shorter fallow periods. Farmers made more intensive use of the land for a number of reasons: population increase; to meet demand for grain on the domestic and international markets; and to make more productive use of the land after the abolition of serfdom.[95] Farmers also introduced new crop rotations to maintain soil fertility and in attempts to cope with the recurring droughts (see Chapter 8).

In Slavyanoserbsk district, Ekaterinoslav province, for example, shifting, long-fallow agriculture was in decline from the 1830s, and was replaced by variety of field systems, which much shorter fallow periods. By 1860s, only a few owners of large estates still used the long-fallow system.[96] There was a regional pattern to the change. Shifting, long-fallow agriculture, and longer fallow periods, persisted into early twentieth century in more outlying, sparsely settled southern and south-eastern areas of the region, such as parts of Samara and Orenburg provinces, the far south and south-east of the Don region, and parts of the North Caucasus. Even where long-fallow agriculture persisted, the fallow period was cut back to fifteen, ten, and fewer years.[97] In Samara district by the early 1880s, for example, the period land was left fallow had been cut from twenty–thirty to a maximum of five–ten years.[98] In Nikolaevsk district in southern Samara province by the late 1880s, farmers who still practised long-fallow farming had reduced the fallow period to fewer than ten–twelve and often only three–four years.[99] Thus, the land was not left fallow for long enough to allow the native steppe vegetation, in particular feather grass, to return.

The intensification of agriculture, with serious consequences for the native steppe vegetation, continued. Steppe farmers gradually introduced the three-field system, which was common in central regions.[100] In Buzuluk district, Samara province, the *zemstvo* reported that by the 1880s long-fallow fields had been

---

[94] Frederic E. Clements, *Plant Succession: An Analysis of the Development of Vegetation* (Washington, DC, 1916), 3–7, 18–32, 214–25, 270–2.

[95] See Ermolov, *Organizatsiya*, 64–85; Leonard Friesen, *Rural Revolutions in Southern Ukraine: Peasants, Nobles, and Colonists, 1774–1905* (Cambridge, MA, 2009), 119–35, 156–8, 170–3.

[96] Bulatsel', 'Zemledelie', 333–43. See also A. Shishkin, 'Sel'skokhozyaistvennyi ocherk Novorossii', *SKhiL*, 113 (1873), 2nd pagn, 277.

[97] Ermolov, *Organizatsiya*, 24–6, 71–80, 123.

[98] *SSSpSG*, i, *Samarskii uezd* (1883), 2nd pagn, 41.

[99] SSSpSG, vi, *Nikolaevskii uezd* (1889), 68.

[100] See A. S. Ermolov, 'Kul'turnye raiony v Rossii i russkie sevooboroty', *SKhiL*, 128 (1878), 2nd pagn, 157–86; A. V. Chayanov, 'Yuzhnaya granitsa preobladaniya trekhpol'noi sistemy

ploughed up and brought into the three-field rotation.[101] In the classic version of the three-field system, fields were left fallow for only one year. Some steppe farmers adapted it to local conditions. Back in 1839, Leopol'dov had noted that some peasants in Saratov province added a fourth field. It was left fallow for fifteen years, allowing the feather grass to return, at which point the land was ploughed up again.[102] In Samara district, after the abolition of serfdom, peasants began to adopt the three-field system. They needed to make more intensive use of their land holdings as the reform had cut their size. They were also motivated by population growth and an increase in rents for additional land. Some also added a fourth field, which was left fallow for longer and used for pasture. But, the maximum length of the fallow period was ten years.[103] In Nikolaevsk district in southern Samara province, peasant communes gradually moved over to the three-field system. By the 1880s, it had been introduced by around a third of communes. Some retained common meadows and pastures, that is, land that was never ploughed, allowing native vegetation to survive, but others integrated pasture land into the rotation and ploughed it up as well.[104] In adjoining Novyi Uzen' district, communes in areas with denser populations moved to more intensive field systems. Land was no longer left fallow for more than seven years.[105] Even these adaptations of the three-field system did not leave the land fallow for long enough for the feather grass to reappear. By the late nineteenth century the feather grass that had once covered vast expanses of steppe was becoming rare.[106]

It was not just growing grain that caused a reduction in the extent and variety of the native vegetation. By the early twentieth century, specialists noted that over-grazing and mowing hay had led to the disappearance of many types of wild flowers and herbs that had once thrived on the steppes. Ploughing, cultivation, grazing, and mowing had also created conditions in which weeds could thrive.[107] A commission established under Lieutenant-General Maslakovets in the late 1890s to investigate the causes of the impoverishment of the Don Cossacks noted, among other factors, that most cossack lands had large areas covered in

polevogo khozyaistva na krest'yanskikh zemlyakh Rossii k nachalu XX veka', *SKhiL*, 233 (1910), 691–710.

[101] *SSSpSG*, iii, *Buzulukskii uezd* (1885), 48–9.

[102] Leopol'dov, *Statisticheskoe opisanie*, i, 117–18.

[103] *SSSpSG*, i, *Samarskii uezd* (1883), 1st pagn, 37–9.

[104] *SSSpSG*, vi, *Nikolaevskii uezd* (1889), 25, 31, 46, 68.

[105] *SSSpSG*, vii, *Novouzenskii uezd* (1890), 42–4.

[106] Compare 'Opisanie Zavol'zhskogo kraya v topograficheskom i agronomicheskom otnosheniyakh', *ZhMGI*, 16 (1845), 2nd pagn, 242; and Lishin, *Ocherk* (1880), 25.

[107] V. V. Morachevskii (ed.), *Yugo-Vostok Evropeiskoi Rossii (Samarskaya, Saratovskaya, Simbirskaya, Penzenskaya, Voronezhskaya i Tambovskaya gubernii): Obshchaya kharakteristika oblastnogo paiona v estestvenno-istoricheskom i statistiko-ekonomicheskom otnosheniyakh* (Spb, 1911), 19.

weeds. He attributed this to 'incorrect cultivation of the soil'.[108] In parts of Samara province in the late nineteenth and early twentieth centuries, peasants needed to plough fields two or three times to bring weeds under control. Weeds competed with grain crops, choking the spring grain as the young shoots struggled to establish themselves.[109] In the more 'natural' succession of types of plants in fields left fallow for long periods of time, it had taken a few years for steppe grasses to supplant the weeds. Under more intensive systems of agriculture, farmers had to find ways to carry out the task previously performed by the native vegetation.

CONCLUSION

Outside scientific circles, where botanists were engaged in serious study of steppe flora, far less attention was paid to the destruction of the native steppe grasses, wild flowers, and herbs than to the loss of woodland. It may have been because the wider consequences of the removal of the native vegetation of the steppes were not as immediately apparent. As was noted at the start of this chapter, moreover, some contemporaries considered ploughing up the steppes, the replacement of wild grasses with cultivated crops, and the removal of the feather grass that was harmful to sheep, to be positive phenomena. Some began to realize, however, that the impact of more intensive systems of arable farming on the native vegetation was rebounding on the cultivation of crops. In 1855, S. Lavrent'ev—an estate manager and member of the Free Economic Society—noted a consequence of the disappearance of shifting, long-fallow farming in the vicinity of Elizavetgrad in Kherson province. Under the old system, various crops were grown for a number of years and then the land was left fallow until it was needed again. The newer systems of farming made more intensive use of the land and fields were no longer left fallow for such long periods. He noted, however, that land needed to be left fallow for at least ten years for it to be good for arable farming again.[110] In the 1880s, Kostychev concluded that fields left fallow recovered their full fertility only when the original character and native vegetation of the steppes returned, which took around fifteen years in most of the region.[111] Thus, a connection was gradually made between the loss of the native vegetation, as land was ploughed up and then the fallow period cut back, and the fertility of the land.

[108] GARO, f.46, op.1, d.3282, l.18.
[109] *SSSpSG*, iii, *Buzulukskii uezd* (1885), 200; *SSSpSG*, vi, *Nikolaevskii uezd* (1889), 43; GASO, f.5, op.11, d.102 (1908–9), l.88ob.
[110] S. Lavrent'ev, 'Polevodstvo v okrestnostyakh Elizavetgrada', *TVEO*, 1/2 (1855), 57–8.
[111] P. Kostychev, 'Iz putevykh zametok', 338.

In the 1880s and 1890s, the scientists Aleksandr Izmail'skii and Vasilii Dokuchaev made a direct connection, between the removal of the native vegetation and the ability of the soil to retain moisture. Dokuchaev's expedition to the steppes in the 1890s engaged in serious study of what they believed to be samples of the native steppe environment, with the native vegetation, in order to devise ways of cultivating the land that best mimicked the steppe environment.[112] Contemporaries came to see that the weeds which were thriving in arable fields after the disappearance of long fallow farming were not just creating more work for farmers and choking crops, but were contributing to the loss of scarce and valuable moisture from the soil through evaporation. In Samara province in the early twentieth century, *zemstvo* agronomists advised local farmers on ways of cultivating the soil between rows of crops fields and rotating crops to keep weeds under control.[113]

Nevertheless, it was the destruction of the woodland in the region that gained the lion's share of attention. It caused anxiety among people—local inhabitants, officials, and scientists—many of whom came from, or were the descendants of people from, forested environments. Over the nineteenth century, however, growing numbers of the settler population were born and brought up in the steppe region. Yet, they were also concerned about the destruction of woodland. Palimpsestov, a native of the steppes, wrote:

[The f]orest is so closely connected with human life that the question of saving and expanding this precious cover on the earth's crust is a national (*narodnyi*) and state question, a question consequently that must be close to the heart of every member of a given national family or given state.[114]

Thus, there was a connection between the growing scientific awareness of deforestation and its consequences and broader cultural sensibilities that seems to have reflected Russia's developing national identity, which was based in part on an appreciation of its landscape.[115]

There were more practical reasons for the concerns over the destruction of woodland in the steppe region. It created shortages of timber and firewood for the population. It was widely believed, moreover, that deforestation had wider, environmental consequences that were making conditions in the region less favourable for agriculture. Woodland, many agricultural specialists and scientists argued, protected the land against erosion, assisted in retaining moisture in the

---

[112] See David Moon, 'The Environmental History of the Russian Steppes: Vasilii Dokuchaev and the Harvest Failure of 1891', *Transactions of the Royal Historical Society*, 6th ser., 15 (2005), 165, 168–9.

[113] GASO, f.5, op.11, d.102 (1908–9), l.98ob.

[114] I. Palimpsestov, 'Stepi yuga Rossii byli-li iskoni vekov stepami i vozmozhno-li oblesit' ikh?', *LZh*, 12/2 (1882), 93.

[115] See Christopher Ely, *This Meagre Nature: Landscape and National Identity in Imperial Russia* (DeKalb, IL, 2002) and see above, pp. 87–8.

soil, and moderated the climate, making it wetter and sheltering the land from the hot, dry winds that blew from the east and south-east. Concerns over the destruction of trees in the steppe region were closely tied up with anxieties over change in the region's semi-arid and variable climate, which even without change already posed problems for the agricultural settlers on the steppes.

4

Climate Change[1]

Agricultural settlers quickly became aware of the main features of the steppe climate: the summers were hot, the winters cold, it was windy, with hot dry winds blowing from the east and south-east, and—most importantly for farmers—there was less rainfall than they had been accustomed to in their previous homelands. The rainfall, moreover, was unreliable. In 1767, Petr Rychkov reported to the Free Economic Society that, on the high steppe in the Orenburg region, there were strong heatwaves and droughts that caused the grass to dry up and burn.[2] The leaders of the Academy of Sciences expeditions of 1768–74 recorded the drought of 1769 in parts of the steppe region (see above, pp. 65–6). Droughts periodically hit the region, with devastating consequences for farmers. In successive years in 1824 and 1825, for example, the Mennonites of Molotschna in Tauride province suffered bad harvests due to drought. It no doubt hurt their pride that they had to seek assistance.[3] Less than a decade later, in 1833, the Mennonites were hit by drought again. By early 1833, Molotschna had received no precipitation for seven months. The elder, Johann Cornies, wrote: 'Not even the oldest people here can remember such weather. The ground is like . . . dry rock, without any moisture.'[4] The drought of 1833, which affected large parts of the steppe region, was one of the worst in the period covered by this book (see above, p. 66). The resulting harvest failure provoked deep discussion in the government on the state of Russian agriculture (see below, p. 243). It also provoked a belief that the climate of the steppe region was changing, for the worse from the perspective of farmers, and that the population was to blame.

---

[1] An earlier version of part of this chapter was published as David Moon, 'The Debate over Climate Change in the Steppe Region in Nineteenth-Century Russia', *RR*, 69 (2010), 251–75.

[2] Petr Rychkov, 'Otvety na Ekonomicheskie voprosy, kasayushchiesya do zemledeliya, po raznosti provintsii kratko i po vozmozhnosti iz"yasennye, v razsuzhdenii Orenburgskoi gubernii', *TVEO*, 7 (1767), 127–8.

[3] DAOO, f.6, op.1, 1824, sp.1774, ll.51–62.

[4] Quoted in John R. Staples, *Cross-Cultural Encounters on the Ukrainian Steppe: Settling the Molochna Basin, 1783–1861* (Toronto, 2003), 89.

In February 1833, at the inaugural meeting of the Russian Forestry Society, a speaker asserted:

In Russia a large part of the surface of the land is level, which requires the protection of forests, and for this reason in some places which have been denuded of them droughts have become more frequent.... The climate of the southern Provinces of Russia has perceptibly changed. On the steppes near the Black Sea, which have been denuded of forests, the climate ... [is] now severe or unbearable from the intense heat, so that these places are incapable not only of supporting human habitation, but even wild animals have abandoned their refuges.[5]

The argument that human action in destroying forests was responsible for climate change, causing greater extremes of temperature, more frequent droughts, and stronger winds was repeated many times over the following decades. For much of the nineteenth century, the argument was asserted most strongly during or in the wake of droughts.

THE CASE FOR PROGRESSIVE, ANTHROPOGENIC CLIMATE CHANGE

Over the middle decades of the nineteenth century, specialists in Russia advanced the case that the climate of the steppe region was undergoing progressive change, and that this was due to deforestation. In 1834, an article in *Forestry Journal* reported that the provinces which had suffered most from the recent drought and harvest failure were those where forests had been depleted. The author deplored the destruction of the forests that he believed had once existed, especially in Tauride province (the former Khanate of Crimea). He noted that the Crimean Tatars said that, since the Russians had arrived [in 1783], the local climate had got colder.[6]

As well as observing the climate of the steppe region, Russian specialists read the works of their counterparts in Western European and North America, where there were similar debates about climate change. Work on the climate of other parts of the world was brought to wider attention in Russia through translations and summaries published in Russian journals. To take just one example, a translation of an article by a German specialist on the influence of forests and their destruction on the climate was published in *Forestry Journal* in 1837. The author asserted that forests influenced temperature, air quality, and wind direction. He was categorical, moreover, that forests increased the quantity of

---

[5] 'Rassuzhdenie o neobkhodimosti okhraneniya vladel'cheskikh lesov ot istrebleniya i o pol'ze pravil'nogo lesnogo khozyaistva', *LZh*, 1 (1833), 72–3.

[6] Andreevskii, 'Zamechaniya o lesovodstve i o neobkhodimosti razvedeniya lesov v yuzhnykh guberniyakh Rossii', *LZh*, 3 (1834), 7–8, 10–11.

moisture in the air, and hence precipitation, through evaporation. He continued that the experiences of several countries had shown that if the area of forest was reduced, it led to a fall in the amount of moisture, and consequently in the quantity of vegetation, and to more heatwaves.[7] In 1854, the journal of the Ministry of State Domains summarized the work of the French scientist Antoine César Becquerel on the influence of deforestation on the climate. Becquerel's study looked back into history and around the world as background to his specific work on France. He concluded that clearing forest reduced the amount of moisture, but whether this was due to reduced rainfall or increased evaporation of rainwater he was not able to say. Deforestation led also, he argued, to increases in the average temperature, made the air drier, and exacerbated the impact of winds.[8] In the mid-1860s, the American environmentalist George Perkins Marsh argued that deforestation could influence local climates, including precipitation.[9]

The views of foreign specialists coincided with those of many, but not all, Russians on the climate in the steppe region in the middle decades of the nineteenth century. In the late 1830s and early 1840s, several statistical studies made similar arguments about the steppe climate. In 1836, V. Passek wrote:

According to the observations of old timers, the climate of Khar'kov province . . . has become more severe, and it is now exposed to more droughts and frosts. It is likely that this change has come about because of the destruction of forests . . . and from the considerable reduction [in the area of forests] in neighbouring Provinces. . . . Such destruction, denuding the surface of the land, exposes it all the more to the wind, which deprives it of a certain amount of moisture.

He continued that deforested land had less attraction for rain clouds, which further contributed to droughts.[10] In his survey of southern Russia for the Ministry of State Domains published in 1841, Andrei Zablotskii-Desyatovskii described how the destruction of forests in southern Chernigov, Poltava, Khar'kov, and Kursk provinces over the previous thirty or forty years had removed protection against the easterly winds which, he stated 'must be the main cause of the disastrous impact of droughts which has been intensifying recently'.[11] Later that year, a more alarming case was made by I. Krestling:

    [7] 'O vliyanii lesov i istrebleniya onykh na klimat', *LZh*, 3 (1837), 427–42. See also 'O vliyanii lesov na klimat, reki i prozyabenie, i vrednykh posledstviyakh ikh istrebleniya', *LZh*, 9 (1837), 325–50.
    [8] [A. C.] Bekkeral', 'Vliyanie istrebleniya lesov na klimat', *ZhMGI*, 52 (1854), 5th pagn, 54–68.
    [9] For the Russian translation, see Georg Marsh, *Chelovek i priroda, ili o vliyanii cheloveka na izmenenie fiziko-geografiskikh uslovii prirody*, trans. N. A. Nevedomskii (Spb, 1866).
    [10] V. Passek, 'Istoriko-statisticheskoe opisanie Khar'kovskoi gubernii 1836 goda', *Materialy dlya statistiki Rossiiskoi Imperii* (Spb, 1839), 140–2.
    [11] A. P. Zablotskii, 'Khozyaistvennye zamechaniya o nekotorykh guberniyakh yuzhnogo kraya Rossii', *ZhMGI*, 1 (1841), 2nd pagn, 12–14.

In former times . . . these steppes, they say, were not so bare: in places forest grew and now old timers assure [us] that around fifty or fewer years ago, the climate was much more moderate. Only to the imprudent destruction of forests can be attributed the severe cold, which is intensifying each winter, the severe storms in the spring, and the extreme heatwaves in the summer that dry out the land even more; deprived of trees, [the land] is becoming infertile, because dry soil does not absorb moisture, and with every year, the rains are becoming rarer.[12]

Ivan Palimpsestov joined the debate in 1850. He made a passionate argument that deforestation had changed the climate of his native Saratov province:

With each year, it is being transformed into a waterless, dry, scorching (*znoinaya*) steppe. With each year, summer heatwaves register higher and higher on the thermometer, and the barometer more and more rarely descends from its heights; each winter the cold is becoming more severe . . . : old timers in Tsaritsyn and Tsarev districts [in the south of the province] still recall that they did not have such hard frosts, nor blizzards, nor deep snows, [and that] livestock grazed all year round on the steppes. Less rain is falling in our province, and the rain that does fall quickly evaporates in the heated up atmosphere . . . '[13]

Palimpsestov said more about the subject in an address to the Richelieu Lycée in Odessa in 1864. He responded to criticisms (see below, p. 127) that some of his evidence was the recollections of old timers by stating that he drew also on meteorological observations over the previous thirty years in Nikolaev and Odessa. But, he skirted over them, and went on to discuss wider issues. His argument was informed by Alexander von Humboldt's *Kosmos*, in which the German geographer had made a case for unity in the complexity of nature.[14] At the heart of Palimpsestov's argument, echoing Humboldt, was that there was a close connection between the atmosphere and the land. Thus changes to the face of the land would cause changes in the climate. Since the onset of large-scale agricultural settlement of the steppes, the former vegetation—wild grasses as well as trees—had been replaced by arable land, pasture, and even land left bare of any vegetation. Palimpsestov asserted that the previous, richer vegetation had reflected more of the sun's rays onto the clouds and had evaporated more moisture into the air. As a result, there had been more rain in the past. The reduction in precipitation, moreover, had led to lower water levels in the rivers and seas, which in turn led to less rainfall. The felling of trees in the region, moreover, had removed a barrier to the hot, dry winds from the east, which made the droughts worse. With a customary rhetorical flourish, Palimpsestov warned his audience:

---

[12] I. Krestling, 'O stepnykh zamechaniyakh v Rossii, *ZhMGI*, 3 (1841), 2nd pagn, 563.

[13] I. Palimpsestov, 'Saratovskaya step' v khozyaistvennom otnoshenii', *TVEO*, 4 (1850), 113.

[14] For references to Humboldt, see I. Palimpsestov, 'Peremenilsya li klimat yuga Rossii? in I. Palimpsestov (ed.), *Sbornik statei o sel'skom khozyaistve yuga Rossii, izvlechennikh iz Zapisok Imperatorskogo Obshchestva sel'skogo khozyaistva yuzhnoi Rossii s 1830 po 1868 god* (Odessa, 1868), 2, 4–6, 11, 16, 20. He cited Aleksandr Fridrikh fon Gumbol'dt, *Kosmos: Opyt fizicheskogo miroopisaniya*, trans. Nikolai Frolov (Spb, 1848).

as the expanses of forest move away from us to the west, south-west, north and north-west, [the] climate will increasingly take on the character of the expanses of steppes in Africa and Asia: the aridity of the air, the unrestrained torrents of . . . winds, especially north-easterlies, the rapid transitions from hot to cold and vice versa, and finally, the severe winter frosts, with their terrible blizzards and snowstorms.[15]

The argument that the climate of the steppe region was changing for the worse was also made in official circles. The Valuev commission, which was set up to investigate the state of agriculture, reported in 1873 that deforestation in the black-earth region was causing the climate to become 'more severe and drier'.[16] In 1878, the governor of Stavropol' province sought permission to protect the remaining forests and plant more trees on account of their beneficial influence on the climate, and the harmful consequences of their destruction. The governor referred to the repeated droughts and crop failures since the 1860s.[17]

Inhabitants of the steppe region noted changes in the climate. In 1879, Achilles Alferaki, who owned an estate near Taganrog, stated that there was plenty of evidence for a deterioration in the climate. It was not just old timers who recalled a different climate in the past: young people had noticed changes in their lifetimes. He gave examples of recent climatic phenomena which he believed to be new: sharp swings from hot to cold weather, and very hot, dry winds that could destroy a field of ripe crops in a couple of days. He wrote that there had been more rain in the past. 'Local inhabitants' did not recall that in the past the land had been cracked so deeply from heatwaves and frosts. He continued that observations of the climate in Odessa, Kherson, and Nikolaev since the 1820s indicated that average temperatures were rising and precipitation was falling. All this he attributed to deforestation.[18]

Writing about his native Don region in 1884, Semen Nomikosov of the Don Statistical Committee pointed out that in 1853 an observer had noted significant changes in the climate in recent years. The changes were of such a magnitude, moreover, that old folk, apparently, did not recognize their homeland. Spring was starting later, winters had got colder, and summer droughts were more frequent. The climate, moreover, had become more changeable. Above all, the region had turned from one rich in water to one where moisture was scarce. Conditions had become worse for arable farming, unfavourable for livestock, even camels, and some wild grasses were dying out. Nomikosov attributed the alleged changes to deforestation. He opened his chapter on climate, however, by

---

[15] Palimpsestov, 'Peremenilsya' (quotation from 25).

[16] [Valuev], *Doklad vysochaishe uchrezhdennoi komissii dlya issledovaniya nyneshnego polozheniya sel'skogo khozyaistva i sel'skoi proizvoditel'nosti v Rossii* (Spb, 1873), 7, 41.

[17] GASK, f.101, op.4, d.732 (1878–1887), ll.1–3, 35ob.–37ob.

[18] A. Alferaki, *O polozhenii sel'skogo khozyaistva v yugo-vostochnom krae* (Spb, 1879), 7–10.

acknowledging that there was no scientific study of the climate of the region based on data collected with meteorological instruments.[19]

In the second half of the nineteenth century, the new generation of Russian scientists paid increasing attention to climate change. In his study of the significance of forests in nature of the late 1870s, Yakov Veinberg included a lengthy discussion of their role in the climate. He considered the work of foreign scientists, including Becquerel and Marsh, which he largely agreed with. He turned to an analysis of the influence of forests, and deforestation, on the climate of Russia, including the steppe region, in which he drew heavily on the work of Russian specialists. He noted that those, such as Palimpsestov, who argued that the climate had changed were also those who argued that the steppes had once been covered by forest. On the other hand, specialists who argued against climate change, for example Konstantin Veselovskii (see below, p. 126), believed that the steppes had always been grasslands. Regardless of the former extent of forest cover on the steppes, Veinberg accepted the overwhelming evidence that there had been substantial deforestation in recent decades. Together with the removal of other steppe vegetation, he argued, this had had a significant impact on rainfall. Without the protective cover of vegetation, the soil heated up to such an extent that it warmed the air, and the rising current of warm air vaporized moisture in the upper layers of the atmosphere that could otherwise have formed droplets of rain. Rain drops that did form, moreover, had to fall through a hotter and drier lower layer of air that caused them to evaporate. This process of evaporation was exacerbated by the hot, dry winds from the south-east, which were no longer blocked by forests. Rain in the steppe region, he further argued, increasingly fell in torrential downpours that quickly drained off the land through ravines.[20]

Thus, the prevailing view that had emerged over the middle decades of the nineteenth century was that the steppe climate was changing for the worse, and that it was a consequence of the destruction of forests. The case was restated in the aftermath of the serious drought of 1891. In a debate over the causes of the drought and crop failure in the Free Economic Society in late 1891, N. A. Khvostov, a estate owner from Orel province in the forest-steppe region, asserted:

I remember in the [18]50s and '60s, warm, light rain at night, and beautiful, warm weather, there were not the choking winds which are common phenomena now. We explain it to ourselves that this change is simply a result of the destruction of forests, which began in the 1860s.

---

[19] Semen Nomikosov, *Statisticheskoe opisanie oblasti voiska Donskogo* (Novocherkassk, 1884), 96–7, 117–51, 199–217.
[20] Ya. Veinberg, *Les: znachenie ego v prirode i mery k ego sokhraneniyu* (Moscow, 1884), 168–208.

He blamed deforestation on the vodka excise reform of 1863, which had made distilling more profitable. This had led to an increase in the number of distilleries, which used timber for their construction, and burned firewood to distil the spirits. Khvostov also blamed the construction of railways. 'According to my personal observations', he concluded, 'our climate has changed; it has become drier.'[21] In the 1850s, however, older timers in Orel province had been just as concerned about climate change, and had also looked back to their younger days, when the climate had been better, before the destruction of the forests, which long predated the 1860s.[22] Khvostov and successive generations of old timers in the forest-steppe region were typical of many inhabitants of the steppes. Throughout the nineteenth century, when they experienced climatic conditions that were unfavourable for agriculture, they thought about whether the heat-waves, droughts, hot and dry easterly winds, and harsh winters had got worse or were recurring more frequently. They also worried about who or what was to responsible, and pointed the finger at deforestation.

In trying to address the issue, however, they came up against the lack of hard data. The problem was summed up in the early twentieth century by Khariton Popov, a local historian on the Don: 'Information on the climate of the lands of the Don Cossacks at the start of the nineteenth century is extremely meagre and does not have . . . a strictly scientific character.'[23] This was also the case for other parts of the steppe region. Thus, until the late nineteenth century, many observers had little choice but to rely on their own recollections of the weather when they were younger, the memories of old timers about the past, and other such largely anecdotal evidence. One problem for proponents of progressive, climate change that relied on such evidence, however, was that old timers could also remember bad weather in the past. A *zemstvo* study of Samara district in 1883 cited old timers' memories of droughts in the past as evidence that they had not become more frequent.[24]

ARGUMENTS AGAINST ANTHROPOGENIC, PROGRESSIVE CLIMATE CHANGE

By the early 1890s, Khvostsov was in a minority in making a case for anthropogenic, progressive climate change. By the turn of the twentieth century, in

[21] 'Besedy v I Otdelenii Imperatorskogo Vol'nogo Ekonomicheskogo Obshchestva po voprosu o prichinakh neurozhaya 1891 goda i merakh protiv povtoreniya podobykh urozhaev v budushchem', *TVEO*, 1 (1892), 110, 121–2.

[22] 'Izmenenie klimata v Orlovskoi gubernii i prichina tomu', *ZhMGI*, 58 (1856), 3rd pagn, 70–6.

[23] GARO, f.55, op.1, d.736, l.13. He referred to [V. D. Sukhorukov], *Statisticheskoe opisanie zemli Donskikh kazakov, sostavlennoe v 1822–1832 godakh* (Novocherkassk, 1891).

[24] *SSSpSG*, i, *Samarskii uezd* (1883), 2nd pagn, 49.

mainstream Russian scientific and official circles, bold arguments that the climate of the steppe region was deteriorating due to deforestation were becoming rare. In his book *Black-Earth Russia* published in 1903—in which he summarized recent studies—Aleksandr Platonovich Engel'gardt did not discuss the climate in terms of deterioration caused by deforestation.[25] There was no discussion of deforestation and progressive climate change in the volumes on the steppe region in the series of geographical descriptions of Russia, edited by the geographer V. P. Semenov-Tyan-Shanskii, which appeared between 1901 and 1910.[26] Since Semenov's volumes presented state-of-the-art discussions of the empire's geography, the absence of discussion of anthropogenic climate change is telling.

Over the middle and later decades of the nineteenth century, arguments had also been put forward that the steppe climate was no different from the past. It was further argued that human activity had not, or indeed could not, affect the climate. Voices of doubt had been raised almost as soon as the issue of climate change was raised. In 1841, K. Engel'ke from Saratov province acknowledged the seriousness of the drought and crop failure of 1833, but described it as 'exceptional'. He continued:

Our old farmers say 'in olden times the years were better, nowadays it is not the same'. By these words they wish to say that in the past the grain grew better, [but] now the air is no longer as healthy, the climate has changed . . .

He agreed that grain had grown better in the past, but did not agree that the climate had deteriorated. On the contrary, he thought that, if anything, it had improved: 'the population of the region is increasing from year to year, dead steppes are being brought to life by settlers and, it seems, droughts do not occur as often as before.'[27]

For those who looked for it, moreover, there was evidence for severe climatic conditions in the steppe region in the past, before the wholesale ploughing up of the land and destruction of woodland. In the mid-1840s, in a survey of Poltava province, N. Arandarenko noted the occurrence of periodic droughts and crop failures, the impact of hot, dry winds from the south-east, and occasional harsh winters. He accepted, to some extent, the view that the destruction of forests along the Vorskla river had made the climate harsher. Nevertheless, he was not convinced that there were big differences between the climate at the time he was writing and in the past. He cited descriptions of severe weather in the seventeenth

[25] A. P. Engel'gardt, *Chernozemnaya Rossiya* (Saratov, 1903), 64–72.
[26] V. P. Semenov (ed.), *Rossiya: Polnoe geograficheskoe opisanie nashego otechestva*, 11 vols (Spb, 1899–1914), vi, *Srednee i nizhnee Povol'ze i Zavol'zhe* (1901), 52–69; xiv, *Novorossiya i Krym* (1910), 49–71.
[27] K. Engel'ke, 'Khozyaistvennoe polozhenie Saratovskoi gubernii', *ZhMGI*, 1 (1841), 2nd pagn, 371–2. This resembles the argument that 'rain follows the plow' on the Great Plains of the USA later in the nineteenth century. W. Kollmorgen and J. Kollmorgen, 'Landscape Meteorology on the Great Plains', *Annals of the Association of American Geographers*, 63 (1973), 434–6.

century from contemporary accounts of military campaigns as evidence that harsh climatic conditions were nothing new.[28]

The General Staff officers who compiled surveys of provinces in the mid-nineteenth century were sceptical about arguments for climate change, and that human activity could affect the climate.[29] In his survey of Khar'kov province in 1850, Captain Mochul'skii denied that the severity of winters was due to the destruction of forests. He pointed out that deforestation had occurred only in 'modern times', while according to old timers and 'history', there were severe winters a hundred years earlier, and also a few centuries before Christ.[30] The latter was clearly a reference to Herodotus' description of cold winters in 'Scythia' (see above, p. 35) 'Old timers' who remembered that the climate had also been bad in the past were cited in the survey of the territory of the Ural Cossacks.[31] Lieutenant-Colonel Shmidt, who compiled the survey of Kherson province of 1863, analysed the climatic observations gathered in Kherson, Nikolaev, and Odessa since the 1820s. The data he presented did not show any progressive trend.[32]

The argument against climate change, and human agency, was made strongly by Konstantin Veselovskii in his book on the climate of Russia published in 1857. The author was well connected. He was head of the statistical section in the Department of Agriculture of the Ministry of State Domains, editor of its journal, permanent secretary of the Academy of Sciences, and a member of the Russian Geographical Society. He was also a native of the steppe region: he was born in Ekaterinoslav province in 1819.[33] He stated that his book was a study of the 'characteristics of the climate of Russia in respect of man and his activities.' He noted the recent growth of observations of the climate in Russia, including parts of the steppe region. He presented data on heat, moisture, and wind, and discussed their impact on agriculture. He argued that the hot and dry climate of the steppes was well suited to growing grain, which was the mainstay of the agricultural settlers. When he discussed moisture, however, he was less sanguine about the prospects for grain cultivation. He acknowledged the relatively low rainfall and frequency of droughts, but pointed out that wheat required less moisture than other grains.[34]

[28] N. A[randarenko], 'Khozyaistvenno-statisticheskii vzglyad na Poltavskuyu guberniyu', *ZhMGI*, 16 (1845), 2nd pagn, 230–3.

[29] See David Moon, 'Agriculture and the Environment on the Steppes in the Nineteenth Century', in Nicholas Breyfogle Abby Schrader, and Willard Sunderland (eds), *Peopling the Russian Periphery: Borderland Colonization in Eurasian History* (Abingdon, 2007), 88–90, 99.

[30] *VSORI*, 12/1, *Khar'kovskaya guberniya*, comp. Mochul'skii (1850), 55.

[31] *MDGSR: Ural'skoe Kazach'e voisko*, comp. A. Ryabinin (Spb, 1866), 156.

[32] *MDGSR: Khersonskaya guberniya*, comp. Shmidt (Spb, 1863), 359–63, 367–8, 376–9, 562–71.

[33] 'Veselovskii', *ES*, vi (1892), 100.

[34] K. Veselovskii, *O Klimate Rossii* (Spb, 1857), vii–ix, 49–52, 332–8.

Veselovskii would have been aware of recent droughts and bad harvests in his native steppe region, since they were reported in the journal he edited.[35] Nevertheless, he argued emphatically that the climate had not changed in historical time. He explained that the climate was a result mostly of global factors, such as the distribution of the continents and oceans, and the position of the earth relative to the sun. He pointed out that the constancy of the prevailing, easterly, winds, which were an important determinant of local climates, demonstrated that the climate had not changed. He believed that the existence or absence of forests were local factors that played little role in influencing the climate. He disagreed with the argument by Becquerel and others that forests influenced rainfall. Instead, he argued, precipitation was caused by the meeting of masses of air of different temperatures and humidities at global, not local, levels. The lack of rainfall in the steppe region, moreover, was not a result of the lack of forests, but the lack of forests was a consequence of the low rainfall, as well as the prevailing winds. He took issue, therefore, with the growing body of opinion that the climate of the steppes was becoming more severe and drier as a result of deforestation. He doubted the evidence—often the recollections of old people—used to support such arguments. He referred specifically to Palimpsestov and Passek in his criticism of writers relying on such recollections. In spite of the growing concerns that human activity was harming the steppe climate, Veselovskii argued that there was not sufficient scientific evidence to prove the case.[36]

A contemporary review of Veselovskii's book by Nikolai Danilevskii was positive, but suggested that the author had paid too little attention to the role of local conditions. Danilevskii wrote that forests deserved more attention, but acknowledged that the idea that they could influence climates was only 'hypothetical'.[37] Krasnov, the author of the General Staff survey of the Don Cossack territory of 1863, drew on Veselovskii's account. He noted that the climate was healthy for people and livestock, and excellent for grain cultivation. He blamed periodic bad harvests on poor farming, not periodic droughts.[38] Veselovskii's account of the climate was influential, and was regularly cited over the following decades, including in volumes in Semenov's series of geographical descriptions of Russia.[39]

[35] See, for example, I. G., 'Khozyaistvennoe obozrenie ekaterinoslavskoi gubernii, za poslednie pyat' let (1847–1851g.)', <i>ZhMGI</i>, 43 (1852), 3rd pagn, 30–5.
[36] Veselovskii, <i>O Klimate</i>, 234–7, 316–20, 385–400.
[37] N. Danilevskii, review of Veselovskii, <i>O Klimate Rossii, VRGO</i>, 25 (1859), 4th pagn, 8, 10.
[38] <i>MDGSR: Zemlya voiska Donskogo</i>, comp. N. Krasnov (Spb, 1863), 161–7, 221–2. Krasnov was inconsistent. Elsewhere he noted briefly that deforestation was making the climate more severe. <i>MDGSR: Zemlya voiska Donskogo</i>, 122, 284.
[39] See, for example, Semenov, <i>Rossiya</i>, xiv, <i>Novorossiya i Krym</i> (1910), 916. See also Engel'gardt, <i>Chernozemnaya Rossiya</i> (1903), 67.

Later in the century, the new generation of Russian scientists wrote about the climate and climate change. The most important was Aleksandr Voeikov, who published a major book in 1884. In contrast to Veselovskii, Voeikov did not consider the climate to be just an external influence on 'man' and 'his' activities, but—echoing Humboldt—as a part of the environment in which vegetation, especially forests, and climate influenced each other. Voeikov discussed how different plants had different requirements for light, heat, and moisture. He considered the climatic requirements for particular crops, for example wheat, and where they could be grown in Russia and elsewhere. In addition, Voeikov analysed the geographical distribution of trees in the context of their require-ments for heat and moisture. He discussed whether the distribution of forests and steppes was due largely or solely to the climate, in particular, the availability of moisture. He argued that land with enough moisture for luxuriant grassy, steppe vegetation also had sufficient for forests. It was the drying winds, he argued, that hindered the growth of forests. Voeikov went on to consider the influence of vegetation on climate. Vegetation, especially forest, he maintained, had a notice-able influence on the heat and humidity of the air in its vicinity by shading the soil, increasing the surface area radiating heat, returning moisture to the air through evaporation of moisture from leaves, and by providing a barrier to the movement of air. He analysed studies by European specialists, such as Becquerel, which showed that forests had a moderating influence on the temperature of the air and soil inside them. In addition, forests increased the humidity of the air and reduced evaporation from the soil. Some French observations, moreover, showed that there was more precipitation over forests than surrounding fields. Forests also weakened the force of the wind. Woodland was particularly important in influencing the climate, Voeikov argued, on the steppes, where the summers were hot and dry as a result of the easterly winds from Central Asia. To emphasize this point, he contrasted the steppes, with their hot and dry summers, with north-western Europe, where the nearby sea and maritime winds caused temperate and wet summers.[40]

Voeikov addressed the issue of climate change over long periods of time and in a global context. He considered whether the study of fossil remains of plants could be used to reconstruct climates in the distant past, but urged caution. With regard to forest cover and climate on the steppes in the past, he accepted that it was 'very possible' that there had been larger areas of forest on the steppes when the local climate had been moister, and thus more suitable for trees. This had been in the distant past, however, and he wrote that the distribution of forest and steppe was a result of a 'long struggle for existence' between trees and grasses, before people had appeared on the scene. Since then, humans had, consciously and unconsciously, made major changes to the vegetation. However, Voeikov

---

[40] A. I. Voeikov, *Klimaty zemnogo shara v osobennosti Rossii* (Spb, 1884), esp. 291–324, 583. On the author, see above, p. 69.

believed that the steppes had been grasslands for a very long time, and that the climate of the steppe region had not undergone major change over the period of human history.[41]

Voeikov took very seriously arguments that forests, and their removal, had an effect on the climate, but always urged caution. He was not fully satisfied with theories that had been put forward, or the data and methodology on which they were based. In 1892, he contrasted contemporary views on the role of forests in the climate. Some people attributed 'all possible benefits to forests' and saw deforestation as a cause of 'all the calamities' which afflicted people. Others, however, denied forests had any influence besides providing shelter from the sun.[42] Voeikov took a carefully balanced view on the wider question of whether human activity had an impact on climate. His view to some extent reconciled the opposing interpretations put forward by Veselovskii and Palimpsestov. In a general essay entitled 'The Influence of Man on Nature' of 1894, Voeikov stated that people could not alter the basic conditions of the climate. On the other hand, they could do quite a lot to change the conditions in the lower layer of air. By planting trees and shrubs, people could weaken the force of the wind, and by chopping them down, they could remove barriers that provided shelter, and by digging ponds and irrigating fields, they could make the air more humid.[43]

A recurring theme in Voeikov's writings on the climate was the need for serious study based on data collected in a scientific manner, which he had done a great deal to promote (see above, pp. 69–70). In a review of a book on the climate of the black-earth region published in 1892, he stated that the book showed once again how little was known about the climate of even the most densely-populated and richest parts of Russia, and how necessary it was to collect new, more accurate, observations of the climate. He continued:

Last year's disaster turned general attention to the need for agricultural meteorological observations. We hope that this interest will not be a flash in the pan, but that we will make the proper observations that are necessary not only in the interests of pure science, but also of practical life, in particular agriculture.[44]

He was utterly scathing about many earlier writings on climate change, in particular those in which arguments were based on the memories of old people.[45]

---

[41] Voeikov, *Klimaty*, 302, 307.

[42] A. Voeikov, 'Po voprosu lesnoi meteorologii,' *Meteorologicheskii vestnik*, 2 (1892), 51. See also A. A. Grigor'ev, 'Rukovodyashchie klimatologicheskie idei A. I. Voeikova', in *Izbrannye sochineniya*, ed. A. A. Grigor'ev, 4 vols (Moscow and Leningrad, 1948–57), i, 13.

[43] A. I. Voeikov, 'Vozdeistvie cheloveka na prirodu', in *Vozdeistvie cheloveka na prirodu: izbrannye stat'i*, ed. V. V. Pokshishevskii (Moscow, 1949), 67–90.

[44] A. Voeikov, review of A. N. Baranovskii, *Glavnye cherty klimata chenozemnykh oblastei Rossii*, *Meteorologicheskii vestnik*, 6 (1892), 246. See also A. Klossovskii, 'Otvety sovremennoi meteorologii na zaprosy prakticheskoi zhizn', *Meteorologicheskii vestnik*, 1 (1891), 5–13; 2 (1891), 53–62.

[45] A. I. Voeikov, 'Kolebanie i izmenenie klimata', *IRGO*, 30/5 (1894), 543–4.

In his contribution to the debate on the causes of the drought and harvest failure in the Free Economic Society in St Petersburg in late 1891, Voeikov pointed out that, although the beginnings of 'agricultural meteorology' had been established in Russia, the volume of data that had been obtained was still very small. Nevertheless, he was prepared to state that the observations being collected were very likely to show that there were not 'large variations in meteorological precipitation'.[46] Other participants in the debate agreed with Voeikov, including fellow scientist Pavel Kostychev and P. S. Ikonnikov, an estate owner from Saratov province.[47] A couple of years later, N. Kravtsov, who farmed in southern Voronezh province, compared the length of the drought of 1891, which lasted from the spring to late autumn, with that only of 1833. He stated that droughts in others years (1862, 1878, 1886, and 1889) had lasted for shorter periods. He did not suggest that the climate was deteriorating, however, but presented the 1891 drought as a rare, but not unique, event.[48]

In the aftermath of the drought and crop failure of 1891, Vasilii Dokuchaev also argued that the climate of the steppe region had not changed in historical time.[49] He had a lot at stake. If the climate had changed significantly, his theory of soil formation was wrong. In his monograph on the Russian black earth of 1883, he had assigned great importance to the climate as one of the factors in the formation of the soil. He had concluded: 'Thus, it is necessary to suppose that for the whole long period of the formation of our black earth, the climate of European Russia remained in *general* the same as it is now.'[50] In 1892, Dokuchaev considered the question of climate change at some length, was prepared to consider change in the deep past, but pointed out that 'more or less accurate data' on the climate of the steppe region had existed only for a few dozen years. 'Therefore', he stated, 'to judge changes in the climate of the south of Russia relying purely on the meteorological method is absolutely impossible.'[51] Dokuchaev's associate Aleksandr Izmail'skii, who carried out extensive fieldwork in the steppe region, also challenged the idea that the climate was changing. He wrote: 'Those meteorological data which we have from Veselovskii hardly give us the right to acknowledge the existence of such a change in the climate.'[52] Izmail'skii and Dokuchaev both argued strongly that it was not the climate that was changing, but the steppe that was drying out (see below, pp. 152–7).

---

[46] 'Besedy', 110.

[47] 'Besedy', 110, 118–19, 124.

[48] N. Kravtsov, 'Po povodu neurozhaev v 1891 i 1892 godakh', *SKhiL*, 172 (1893), 1st pagn, 317–19.

[49] V. V. Dokuchaev, 'Nashi Stepi prezhde i teper', in *Sochineniya*, vi, 81–6.

[50] V. V. Dokuchaev, 'Russkii chernozem', *Izbrannye sochineniya*, 3 vols (Moscow, 1948–9), i, 385. See also above, pp. 80–1.

[51] Dokuchaev, 'Nashi Stepi', 88–9.

[52] A. A. Izmail'skii, 'Kak vysokhla nasha step': Issledovaniya otnositel'no vlazhnosti pochvy i podpochvy, *SKhiL*, 174 (1893), 2nd pagn, 13; see also A. A. Izmail'skii, *Vlazhnost' pochvy i gruntovaya voda v svyazi s rel'efom mestnosti i kul'turnym sostoyaniem poverkhnosti pochvy* (Poltava, 1894), 140, 156.

Thus, even such disastrous conditions as the drought, crop failure, and famine of 1891–2, no longer provoked widespread anxieties among the local population and scientists about climate change and human culpability.

ARGUMENTS FOR AUTOGENIC, CYCLICAL CLIMATE CHANGE

As more scientific observations were made of the climate of the steppe region, and as it was noted that old timers could also recall droughts and harsh weather in the past, discussions of climate change took a new direction. Some observers of the climate began to consider whether there was a cyclical pattern to climate change. Two General Staff officers put forward such ideas. In his survey of Khar'kov province of 1850, Mochul'skii noted that there seemed to be a pattern to the weather: severe winters occurred every ten years and were followed by hot summers.[53] In the survey of Kherson province of 1866, Shmidt reported that local inhabitants had noticed that if the winter was long, constant, and had sufficient snow, then the following spring and summer would have abundant rain and the harvest would be good. This local knowledge was partly confirmed by evidence from the previous forty years. Shmidt noted four years in which mild winters were indeed followed by bad harvests, and five years when cold winters had preceded good harvests. The severe drought of 1833, however, had also been preceded by a cold winter.[54]

Patterns in droughts, and consequent bad harvests, were also noted in Samara province (which was badly affected by both). In his annual report for 1880, the governor wrote that bad harvests caused by droughts and heatwaves were 'periodically recurring'.[55] The *zemstvo* study of Buzuluk district of 1885 reported that 'completely favourable' meteorological conditions for arable farming occurred once in every five to seven years. For example, from 1880 to 1884, there had been a good harvest only once, in 1884.[56] The governor was more specific in his report for 1890:

The closest acquaintance with the conditions in which agriculture in [Samara] province finds itself . . . , shows that poor harvests of grain . . . recur periodically, . . . [there are] a whole series of years with unsatisfactory harvests in succession, . . . ending with a general good harvest.

He had looked back at earlier annual reports, and pointed out that this had happened at the start of the 1870s and 1880s, and was happening again at the

[53] *VSORI*, 12/1, *Khar'kovskaya guberniya*, 55.
[54] *MDGSR: Khersonskaya guberniya*, 376–9.
[55] GASO, f.3, op.167, d.89, [1881], l.6.
[56] *SSSpSG*, iii, *Buzulukskii uezd* (1885), 68.

start of the 1890s.[57] The disaster of 1891, therefore, had not come as a complete surprise to the authorities in Samara.

A number of immediate reactions to the drought and crop failure of 1891 in other parts of Russia also spoke of them as examples of periodic occurrences, rather than evidence for deteriorating climatic conditions. At the annual meeting of the Free Economic Society on 31 October 1891, the agricultural specialist Nicholas Vereshchagin was invited deliver an address on 'the bad harvest' as a last-minute replacement speaker. Hence, his comments have an added degree of immediacy. He spoke about the phenomenon of bad harvests recurring after certain intervals of time, and that this had suggested the idea of the influence of 'more remote, cosmic phenomena such as sun spots'.[58] Future Minister of Agriculture Aleksei Ermolov described the drought of 1891 as 'unusual', and the extent of the crop failure as comparable only with those of 1833 and 1840. It was much more serious, moreover, than 'ordinary droughts', which recurred periodically.[59] The geographer Leonid Vesin published a lengthy article on bad harvests over the long term in Russian history in 1892 in which he speculated on the issue of cyclical climate change.[60]

The terms in which Russian specialists discussed the drought of 1891 demonstrated their familiarity with the contemporary 'preoccupation' among scientists around the world with 'the issue of periodicity of climate' rather than progressive, anthropogenic climate change.[61] A theory of ice ages had been presented by the Swiss-American scientist Louis Agassiz in 1840.[62] The Scottish scientist James Croll published an influential study, *Climate and Time*, in 1875. He argued that the alternate cold and warm periods of the 'Glacial Epoch' were caused by 'the eccentricity of the earth's orbit'.[63] There was much speculation during the nineteenth century, moreover, into the impact of cycles in sun spot activity on the periodic patterns of change in air temperature, rainfall, and river levels (and grain prices, famines, and financial crises). Important research was carried out by the Russian-born German meteorologist Wladimir Köppen. He began his work in St Petersburg in the early 1870s. He argued that there was a inverse relationship between the numbers of sun-spots and the air temperature, and thus cycles of change in both were connected.[64]

---

[57] GASO, f.3, op.233, d.1000, [1891], ll.1–2.

[58] N. V. Vereshchagin, 'Po povodu neurozhaya tekushchego goda', *TVEO*, 2/5 (1891), 182.

[59] [A. S. Ermolov], *Neurozhai i narodnoe bedstvie* (Spb, 1892), 3–4.

[60] L. Vesin, 'Neurozhai v Rossii i ikh glavnye prichiny', *Severnyi vestnik*, 1 (1892), 117–18.

[61] See Nico Stehr and Hans von Storch, 'Eduard Brückner's Ideas—Relevant in His Time and Today', in Eduard Brückner, *The Sources and Consequences of Climate Change and Climate Variability in Historical Times*, ed. Nico Stehr and Hans von Storch (Dordrecht, 2000), 12–15, 20.

[62] Stefan Brönnimann, 'Picturing climate change', *Climate Research*, 22 (2002), 91–2.

[63] James Croll, *Climate and Time in Their Geological Relations*, 2nd edn (Edinburgh, 1885).

[64] See, for example, 'On temperature cycles' [abstract of paper by Dr W. Koppen], *Nature*, 9/219 (1874), 184–5; Henry F. Blanford, 'The paradox of the sun-spot cycle in meteorology', *Nature*, 43/1121 (1891), 583–7; A. B. M., 'Sun-spots and air-temperature', *Nature*, 45/1160 (1892), 271–2.

The work by a foreign scientist on climate change that had, perhaps, the greatest influence on Russian specialists was Eduard Brückner's *Climate Change since 1700*, published in Vienna in 1890. Brückner was German, but had experience in the Russian Empire. He lived in Odessa and the Livonian university city of Dorpat as a child, and was educated in both the Russian Empire and Germany. He worked with Köppen in Hamburg for a while in the late 1880s.[65] Brückner's study of climate change, moreover, drew in part on data from the Russia Empire, including the steppe region. He compared patterns in changing water levels in the Caspian, Black, and Baltic Seas with those of changes in glaciers in the Alps and noted certain similarities. He went on to examine data on rainfall and temperature from around the world over the preceding decades, and the dates of the freezing and thawing of rivers, in particular in the Russian Empire, the dates of grape harvests in France, Germany, and Switzerland, and the frequency of cold winters. Some of his data stretched back over several centuries. Brückner concluded that 'in the course of the past nine centuries our globe has experienced climatic variations with a periodicity of about thirty-five years', during which wet and cool periods alternated with dry and warm. Cycles of thirty-five years did not coincide with the cycles of the sun spots, however, and he rejected the idea of a link between them. He published articles in the press and delivered public lectures, for example at Dorpat University in 1888, as well as presenting his findings to his fellow scientists. He was very interested in the practical implications of his work. He suggested that regions with continental climates, such as Siberia, North America, and Australia, would experience droughts and poor harvests during a dry period that would intensify around the turn of the twentieth century.[66]

Voeikov, who was a voracious reader in several languages as well as a prolific author, assisted in the further dissemination in Russia of international work on 'climate oscillation and change' in an article he published in 1894. He reviewed and engaged with the work of Brückner, Köppen, Croll, Agassiz, and other specialists. He discussed the extent to which the various hypotheses on climate change in historical and geological time fitted what was known of climatic patterns in the Russian Empire. He noted that observations of the climate in south-western Siberia and glaciers in the Caucasus did not fit Brückner's cycles. He concluded:

our knowledge is broadening and improving somewhat, and previous absurd hypotheses are being repudiated and replaced by others, which, although they cannot be considered completely correct theories, at least given the current state of our knowledge can serve as . . . working hypotheses.[67]

---

[65] Stehr and von Storch, 'Eduard Brückner's Ideas', 6.

[66] Stehr and von Storch, 'Eduard Brückner's Ideas', 7–10; Brückner, *Sources and Consequences*, 47–191, 219–42, 255–68.

[67] Voeikov, 'Kolebanie', 543–78 (quotation from 577). Dokuchaev also argued against the applicability of Brückner's theory in Russia. 'Nashi Stepi', 81–6.

Russian specialists continued to suggest some sort of cyclical pattern to the climate, in particular in the occurrence of droughts in the steppe region. As has already been noted, Samara province seems to have been ripe for such observations. The governor wrote in his report for 1897: 'Some farmers who are making observations of the quantity of precipitation have established the fact that droughts in Samara province are unavoidable and their recurrence after certain intervals of time are not accidental and unexpected phenomena.' Thus, after very bad harvests in 1891 and 1892, there had been a series of good years, until another drought and poor harvest in 1897. The biggest fluctuations were in the south of the province.[68] This pattern was confirmed by observations of precipitation over the 1880s and 1890s by E. A. Geints. His data showed that rainfall in the lower Volga basin was lower than the norm in the years 1891–7, when there were four dry years (1891, 1892, 1897, 1898) and four wet.[69] In the second decade of the twentieth century Grigorii Baskin, the chief statistician of the Samara *zemstvo*, studied the recurrence of crop failures. He took account of socio-economic factors as well as climatic, and found waves of 'high' and 'low' harvests in groups of four years, with peaks of 'highs' followed immediately by 'lows'. Thus, the period from 1885 to 1888 with very good harvests preceded the years 1889–92 with poor harvests, and the 'high' in 1901–4 came before the 'low' in 1905–8. His model, moreover, correctly predicted that harvests would start to improve in 1922 after another low period. He disagreed with attempts by other specialists to relate fluctuations in the harvest to Brückner's cycles.[70] In the Don region in the early twentieth century, however, the geologist V. V. Bogachev argued for a correlation between cycles of sun spots, Brückner's cycles, and patterns in the climate.[71] Thus, by the late nineteenth and early twentieth centuries, many Russian specialists, in particular those with experience of the steppe region, considered that droughts recurred periodically for reasons largely beyond human influence.

ARGUMENTS THAT THE WINDS WERE GETTING STRONGER.

The hot, dry winds that blew from the east and south-east (*sukhovei*) were a recurring feature in discussions of the steppe climate. Observers noted that the winds dried out the air and the land. In 1820, Vasilii Lomikovskii, an estate

---

[68] GASO, f.3, op.23, d.1541, [1898], ll.3-ob., 25ob.

[69] See Engel'gardt, *Chernozemnaya Rossiya*, 66.

[70] G. I. Baskin, *Sbornik izbrannykh trudov G. I. Baskin po Samarskoi gubernii*, 6 vols (Samara, 1925), i, 5–11. See also N. S. Belyakova, 'Zemskii statistik Grigorii Ivanovich Baskin (1866–1938)', *Samarskii zemskii sbornik* 1/3 (1999), 14–19.

[71] V. V. Bogachev, *Ocherki geografii Vsevelikogo Voiska Donskogo* (Novocherkassk, 1919), 105–8.

owner in Poltava province, wrote that hot winds blew every year in July and could last for three days or more. Crops dried out and died.[72] While the relationship between forests and the climate as a whole was the subject of much debate, many agreed that the loss of areas of woodland in the steppe region had removed barriers which had sheltered the land from the winds, and thus intensified their impact. As far back as 1807, I. I. Veber wrote from Ekaterinoslav that the destruction of forests in the region had removed barriers to the easterly and northerly winds that blew in the autumn and spring.[73] In the aftermath of the devastating drought and crop failure of 1833, Andreevskii wrote about the role of forests in protecting land from the impact of the wind. He also noted that it was the provinces with least forest that were worst affected.[74] The General Staff surveys of the mid-nineteenth century discussed the impact of the winds. The survey of Kherson province of 1849 noted that the winds were harsher and dried out the land more in the summer in the treeless steppe of the south of the province. The authors remarked on the destruction of forests by settlers. They went on to record the prevailing opinion among the population that: 'one of the main causes of droughts and the scorching impact of the strong winds . . . which have such fatal consequences [as] crop failures is . . . the shortage of forests . . . '.[75] Mochul'skii, who compiled the survey of Khar'kov province of 1850, also noted that winds led to droughts, and dried out the soil, causing bad harvests. He further noted the extent of deforestation in the province, but did not make a connection between the destruction of woodland and the impact of the winds.[76] Palimpsestov did make the connection, arguing that deforestation had opened southern Russia to hot, dry winds from the east, from arid, sandy, parts of Asia. He added that the winds brought droughts with them.[77]

Scientists and other specialists continued to pay close attention to the wind later in the nineteenth century. The importance of forests in acting as windbreaks was noted by Voeikov in 1878. The point was also made in the journal of the Southern Russian Agricultural Society in 1875. The latter published a summary of a book by a German scientist, which stressed that serving as a mechanical barrier to the wind was the main influence of forests on the climate.[78] In the late 1870s, Veinberg analysed the particular harm caused by the hot, dry winds from

[72] V. Ya. Lomikovskii, 'Otvet na zadachu 1820 goda ob unavozhivanii ozimykh polei v yuzhnykh guberniyakh', *TVEO*, 72 (1820), 101.

[73] I. I. Veber, 'Primechaniya o razlichnykh predmetakh khozyaistva v Ekaterinoslavskom Namestnichestve', *TVEO*, 50 (1795), 190.

[74] Andreevskii, 'Zamechaniya', 4–8.

[75] *VSORI*, 11/1, *Khersonskaya guberniya*, comp. Rogalev, fon-Vitte, and Pestov (1849), 12, 71, 132–6.

[76] *VSORI*, 12/1, *Khar'kovskaya guberniya*, 51–3.

[77] I. U. Palimpsestov, 'Odin iz otvetov na vopros: "byli li lesa na yuge Rossii?", *Izvestiya imperatorskogo Obshchestva lyubitelei estestvoznaniya, antropologii i etnografii*, 41/1 (1881), 19.

[78] A. I. Voeikov, 'O vliyanii lesov na klimat', in *Izbrannye sochineniya*, iii, 44, 50, 58 (1st published, 1878); 'Vliyanie lesov na klimat strany', *ZIOSKhYuR*, 2 (1875), 92.

the south-east to crops at the time they were flowering. Damage to crops caused by the winds had become more serious, he noted, due to deforestation:

We have already seen how much, unfortunately, was done to give free access to those winds, by destroying the very forests, which in the not too distant past had protected the southern Russian steppes from the pernicious influence of these winds.

He concluded that 'it was not a shortage of precipitation that caused the frequent and so pernicious droughts in our southern region, but rapid evaporation on account of the dry and hot winds that blow.'[79]

Local studies sponsored by *zemstva* made the same connection between deforestation and the impact of the wind. A study of Novyi Uzen' district in southern Samara province in 1882 noted that the removal of trees from river valleys had left the steppe and soil defenceless against the burning south-easterly winds, which quickly transformed the top soil into dry rock.[80] A study of Samara district the following year noted that two–three days of hot, dry winds from the south-east in the summer were sufficient to dry out most crops and cause them to wilt. 'In olden times', however, 'the deleterious feature of this wind was paralyzed to some extent by the moderating influence of the huge forests and luxuriant meadow vegetation that lay in its path.'[81] Similar remarks were made at this time in surveys of Nikolaevsk and Buzuluk districts in the south and east of Samara province. The author of the latter stated that the 'ruthless destruction of the forests', which caused the influence of the steppe climate to be felt more sharply, was due to recent action by local peasants.[82]

Years of drought, for example 1885 in Stavropol' province, prompted particular attention to the hot, dry winds. Regular reports on the state of the crops over the growing season made by local elders to the provincial administration contained frequent comments on the wind. In the district of Aleksandrovskaya in the south of the province, it was reported from Nogutskaya township on 13 May that a south-easterly wind had been blowing since 10 May, and 'if it continues during the drought, it will harm the flowers on the ears of the rye'. Two weeks later, the elder of the township reported that the grass had grown badly in May due in part to the hot, south-easterly winds. There similar reports elsewhere in the district. At around the same time, elder Rubailov from Severnaya township wrote that strong winds had blown from 11 to 20 May, and that in places the grass and spring grain had died. The elder of Otkazenskaya township reported on 9 June that the winter and spring grain were poor due to drought and 'hot winds'.[83] Winds harmed crops in Novogrigor'evskii district, in the arid north-east of the

[79] Veinberg, *Les*, 243–9, 255 (quotation), 264 (quotation).
[80] I. I. Filipenko, *Vopros obvodneniya stepei: na osnovanii issledovanii proizvedenykh v 1881 godu, po porucheniyu Novouzenskogo zemskogo sobraniya* (Spb, 1882), 15.
[81] *SSSpSG*, i, *Samarskii uezd* (1883), 6.
[82] *SSSpSG*, vi, *Nikolaevskii uezd* (1889), 14; iii, *Buzulukskii uezd* (1885), 68.
[83] GASK, f.101, op.4, d.1502, ll.55, 62, 64, 77.

province which had been badly hit by duststorms whipped up by the wind. On 12 June, elder Bugakov of Blagodarnoe reported that the winter and spring grain were in a poor condition on account of the lack of rain, heatwaves, and strong winds. He did not have any hopes for the harvest.[84] These reports by township elders did not mention the winds as a new phenomenon or one that worse than in the past. D. L. Ivanov, the engineer who conducted a survey of Stavropol' province in 1885, however, wrote about the 'ceaseless easterly winds' in that year and the impact of deforestation in making the climate more extreme.[85]

A particularly dramatic statement on the impact of the easterly winds was made by Vereshchagin in his address (as a last-minute replacement) to the Free Economic Society in October 1891. He considered the causes of the drought and crop failure, and moved on to the consequences of deforestation in exacerbating the impact of the easterly winds: 'we ourselves have greatly assisted the harmful influence of hot, Asiatic winds, but in any case, the proximity to Asia costs us dearly'. He made up for the lack of time he had had to prepare his talk with rhetoric: 'In the deep past we experienced the invasion of [Asia's] savage population, and at the present time we must reckon with the no less destructive violence, which it is sending us—the hot climate, plague, and other disasters.'[86] In the mind of Vereshchagin, therefore, the hot, dry winds from the east were nothing less than the new Mongols. Nikolai was the brother of the artist Vasilii who, together with other intellectuals such as Vladimir Solov'ev, had a distaste for the 'Orient' and feared its malevolent influence.[87]

CONCLUSION

Over the course of the nineteenth century, there was much debate among members of the local population, officials, naturalists, and scientists over the vexed question of whether the climate was changing. The drought and crop failure of 1833, which was one of the worst of the century, prompted considerable anxiety about climate change. It also brought to prominence the argument that the climate was changing for the worse—from the point of view of the settler population—as a result of the destruction of woodland in the region. The argument for anthropogenic, progressive climate change, which was informed by observations in the steppe region and the work of foreign specialists on other parts of the world, was the prevailing view over the middle decades of the nineteenth century. The development of the science of meteorology and the

[84] GASK, f.101, op.4, d.1504 [1885], l.81.

[85] D. L. Ivanov, 'Vliyanie Russkoi kolonizatsii na prirodu Stavropol'skogo kraya', *IRGO*, 22/3 (1886), 236, 252–3.

[86] Vereshchagin, 'Po povodu neurozhaya', 182–3.

[87] See David Schimmelpenninck van der Oye, *Toward the Rising Sun: Russian Ideologies of Empire and the Path to War with Japan* (DeKalb, IL, 2001), 207–8.

start of the collection of more accurate data on the climate in the steppe region undermined this consensus. Scientists argued against the notions that the climate was changing, and that human activity could alter the climate. Some scientists, members of the region's population, and officials began to see cyclical patterns in climatic fluctuations. One area in which most observers agreed was the drying influence of the winds that blew into the steppe region from the east. The destruction of woodland across the region, moreover, had removed barriers to these winds.

5

The Land

INTRODUCTION

The wind, especially the hot, dry *sukhovei* from the east, eroded the soil in the steppe region. The wind blew sand in drifts onto adjoining, fertile land. It whipped up valuable top soil in fearful dust storms that turned day into night. The wind also contributed to erosion in the ravines and gullies, but in this case, water was the more important cause of erosion. Naturalists and scientists initially understood erosion, by wind and water, as mainly natural phenomena. Over the second half of the nineteenth century, however, many specialists came to believe that soil was more likely to be eroded if the native grasses that covered it had been ploughed up and if woodland that provided shelter had been felled. Water erosion created further problems. Water which fell as precipitation drained more rapidly down the enlarged ravines and gullies, and into the rivers, instead of seeping into the soil. As a result, some scientists argued, water tables were falling and the steppes were drying out. This exacerbated the shortages of water in drought years, and increased the likelihood of crop failures. Furthermore, there were growing anxieties that the fertility of the black earth was declining. The most pessimistic observers feared the steppes were turning into a desert. Anxieties about environmental change, and fears that human activity was responsible, were heightened by droughts and crop failures, such as those of 1833 and 1891.

EROSION

Erosion was carrying away the fertile soil that had attracted agricultural settlers to the steppes. This section will focus on three types of erosion: drifting sands; dust storms; and the growth of ravines.

Drifting Sands

Drifting sands (*sypuchie* or *letuchie peski*) blown by the wind were a serious and growing problem for the population of parts of the steppe region over the nineteenth century.[1] It is important to bear in mind in assessing arguments that human action was to blame, that there were areas of such sands before the wholesale destruction of woodland and ploughing up of the steppes. Earlier sources, such as the 'Book of the Great Map' of 1627 and the accounts of the Academy of Sciences expeditions of 1768–74 indicate that there had long been areas of sand, and drifting sand, in the region (see pp. 74–5). In his description of the Caucasus and Astrakhan' provinces of 1809, I.V. Rovinskii described the large extent of sands, including drifting sands. But, he added that many of these 'hillocks of drifting sand' were not blown around as they were held in place by deeply rooted plants.[2] Over the following decades, however, the local population removed such vegetation, allowing the sands to be blown around by the wind. In 1839, Andrei Zablotskii-Desyatovskii, of the Ministry of State Domains, surveyed eight provinces between the rivers Dnepr and Don. He wrote that more and more land was being inundated by drifting sands, and turning into a 'lifeless desert'. He blamed the destruction of the groves of pine trees that typically grew on sandy soil.[3]

Cases from around the steppe region illustrate what was happening, and how contemporaries came to understand the causes. The best example is the vicinity of the town of Aleshki on the left bank of the lower Dnepr in Tauride province. (This is now the Oleshkivs'ki sands in the Kherson region of Ukraine, which I visited in May 2011.) It was part of the Khanate of Crimea before its annexation by the Russian Empire in 1783. At this point, many of the local Tatar population left. Grigorii Potemkin started to resettle the vacated land. In 1784, he sent forty families and allocated each eight *desyatiny* of land, a pair of oxen (i.e. draft animals), one horse, and one cow. The settlers were retired soldiers, cossacks, and foreign colonists from the Balkans. The following year, a further 258 people were moved to Aleshki.[4] The settlers ploughed up the land. In 1786, the harvest was reported to be good.[5] More land near Aleshki was allocated to state peasants in 1802. We have a number of descriptions of the area over the following decades that allow us to trace its transformation into a large and expanding area of drifting sands. By 1831, the state peasants had felled over 5,000 *desyatiny* of forest. As a result, sand blown by the wind had inundated large

[1] Ya. Veinberg, *Les: znachenie ego v prirode i mery k ego sokhraneniyu* (Moscow, 1884), 462–70.
[2] [I. V. Rovinskii], *Khozyaistvennoe opisanie Astrakhanskoi i Kavkazskoi gubernii* (Spb, 1809), 57–8.
[3] A. P. Zablotskii, 'Khozyaistvennye zamechaniya o nekotorykh guberniyakh yuzhnogo kraya Rossii', *ZhMGI*, 1 (1841), 2nd pagn, 48.
[4] F. F. Lashkov, *Knyaz' G. A. Potemkin-Tavricheskii kak deyatel' Kryma: Kratkii ocherk po arkhivnym dannym* (Simferopol', 1890), 8.
[5] 'Raporty V. V. Kakhovskogo G. A. Potemkinu za sentyabr'-noyabr' 1787', *Zapiski Odesskogo Obshchestva istorii i drevnostei*, 10 (1877), 257.

expanses of arable land and meadows. The area suitable for agriculture had fallen from around 59,000 *desyatiny* to just over 38,000 *desyatiny*. It continued to fall as the sand took over. The inhabitants of Chelbasy had to relocate their settlement four times to escape the drifting sand.[6]

In 1837–8, another official from the Ministry of State Domains, Peter Köppen, surveyed Tauride province.[7] He reported that around Aleshki, strong winds were causing sands to accumulate in drifts around buildings, sometimes burying them. Sand was drifting onto meadows and arable fields, turning them into infertile deserts. There were islands of fertile land surrounded by sand dunes, and islands of sand amid fields. The wind formed the sands into long dunes which the locals called '*kuchugury*'. He blamed the local population for this sad picture. In the past, he noted, there had been many more trees. In one area, the local estate owner had felled around 90 *desyatiny* of forest. The local inhabitants added to the problem by grazing tens of thousands of cattle and sheep on the land. The livestock were eating plants, including young shrubs and saplings, that would otherwise bind and cover the sands. Köppen estimated that drifting sands covered an area of 115,000 *desyatiny*.[8] By 1860, another official from the ministry, K. Fromm, reported that drifting sands had spread over around 130,000 *desyatiny*. (Thus, the area inundated had grown by roughly 720 *desyatiny* a year since the end of the 1830s.) Fromm attributed the spread of the sands to the destruction of woodland and the removal of the grass cover by over-grazing. He added that ploughing the land, revealing the sand underneath the thin top soil, was a further cause.[9] While efforts were made to bind the drifting sands by planting shrubs and trees (see below, pp. 195–8), the area covered by sand continued to grow. In 1894, Aleksandr Voeikov estimated that the Aleshki sands occupied around 200,000 *desyatiny*.[10]

Drifting sands were also widespread, and spreading further, in the North Caucasus. D. L. Ivanov, whose survey of Stavropol' province coincided with the serious drought of 1885, described the area around the village of Petrovskoe. The village was situated inside a broad gulley alongside the river Kalaus. It was around 170 metres below the high steppe, and further below a hill named Kutsai. Strong easterly winds blew loose sand from the summit of the hill and the sides of the gulley, which blocked springs, covered the road, inundated vegetable gardens,

[6] Andreevskii, 'Zamechaniya o lesovodstve i o neobkhodimosti razvedeniya lesov v yuzhnykh guberniyakh Rossii', *LZh*, 3 (1834), 8–10.

[7] RGIA. f.383, op.29, 1837–8, d.609, l.1.

[8] [P. I. Kepen], 'Ob Aleshkovskikh letuchikh peskakh', *LZh*, 1 (1841), 401–18.

[9] K. Fromm, 'Ob ukreplenii letuchikh peskov v Dneprovskom uezde Tavricheskoi gubernii', *ZhMGI*, 75 (1860), 3rd pagn, 1–2.

[10] A. I. Voeikov, 'Vozdeistvie cheloveka na prirodu', in *Vozdeistvie cheloveka na prirodu: izbrannye stat'i*, ed. V. V. Pokshishevskii (Moscow, 1949), 50–1. See also RGIA, f.426, op.1, 1894, d.40, ll.300–1.

a nearby farm, and got into the village itself. The cause was clear to Ivanov. 'Around 65 years ago', he wrote, 'the whole gulley was covered by forest, which extended up the sides to the very top.' Just below the summit of the hill was a lake, which was also surrounded by forest. While his source was 'old folks', his account of the previous forest cover is consistent with other information we have on the former extent of woodland in Stavropol' province (see above, p. 100). The scene Ivanov saw in 1885, however, was quite different from how the old folks described it in the past: he saw three sides of the gulley completely denuded of vegetation, revealing thick strata of sand and sandstone, which had eroded to form screes. The trees had also gone from around the lake, which had dried up, as the springs which fed it were blocked by sand. The former lake bed and the summit of the hill were both covered with bare sand. With no trees, there was nothing to prevent the sand from drifting down into the gulley when the wind blew.[11]

A study of the settlement of Beshpagir, also in Stavropol' province, in 1885 revealed that sand had been spread by the wind from the sandy hills that surrounded it onto arable and pasture land. The sand was also burying the settlement. The soil in the area was light, sandy, black earth, and crucially was only 3 *vershki* (5.25 inches) deep in some places: this was a fraction of the depth of the topsoil in much of the black-earth region. The subsoil, as in other parts of the steppe region, was pure sand. Sand covered only 600 *desyatiny* of the surface of the settlement's 13,000 *desyatiny* in 1880, but it was spreading at a rate of 83 *desyatiny* a year. In 1880, the cause was suspected as over-grazing of cattle, but a subsequent investigation in 1885 revealed another cause. According to 'old timers', thirty–forty years earlier, the area 'now' covered by sand had been ploughed up, sown with crops, and had initially given abundant harvests. The peasants, however, had used ploughs intended for deeper soils. Thus, each time they ploughed the land, they brought up more sand to the surface and mixed it with the black earth, making it incapable of resisting the force of the strong, south-easterly winds.[12]

Over-grazing contributed to drifting sands elsewhere in Stavropol' province and the steppe region as a whole.[13] Ivanov made a very important point about this. He contrasted the way the indigenous nomadic people grazed their livestock with the practices of settlers from central Russia. The nomadic pastoralists had moved their herds around on a seasonal basis. Thus, when they moved their

[11] D. L. Ivanov, 'Vliyanie Russkoi kolonizatsii na prirodu Stavropol'skogo kraya', *IRGO*, 22/3 (1886), 243. Petrovskoe is now known as Svetlograd.

[12] GASK, f.101, op.4, d.894 (1880–5), ll.1–3 ob., 18–19. For a similar case in the Don region, see S. S-ov, 'Obsledovanie Donskikh stanits v pochvennom i statistiko-ekonomicheskom otnosheniyakh', *Donskie oblastnye vedomosti* (1 March 1915), 3.

[13] See 'Kade', 'K voprosu o lesorazvedenii v Stavropol'skoi gubernii', *Severnyi Kavkaz* (25 October 1885); 'K ukrepleniyu i obleseniyu ovragov na Donu', *Donskie oblastnye vedomosti* (11 April 1915), 3.

livestock away from one area of pasture, the vegetation growing on the sandy soil had a chance to recover, and to spread, before the nomads returned the following year. The settlers, who displaced them and took over their land, grazed their livestock on the same pasture without respite, and thus the vegetation had no chance to recover. He listed a number of settlements along the Kalaus river, including Beshpagir, where the actions of 'Russian settlers' had helped the sands to spread.[14]

Several causes of drifting sands were identified by a forestry specialist who visited Samara district in 1904. Local people felled woodland that grew on sandy soil, grubbed out the stumps, and then ploughed up the land. In time, the sandy soil drifted onto adjoining land. He noted that a typical sandy area consisted of a relatively small 'source' (*rodnik*) of sand, which spread onto surrounding good soil, thus harming the local economy. He estimated that the area covered by sand had grown by 50 per cent over the previous decade.[15] Other districts of Samara province were also badly affected. In Novyi Uzen' district in the south of the province, sands drifting from the banks of the rivers Volga and Eruslan inundated several villages and their land. The village of Peschanoe (literally 'Sandy') had to be abandoned in 1871 when the sand reached the level of the windows of the village church.[16]

Thus, many contemporaries believed that the growing problem of drifting sands was due to human activity, in particular felling trees, over-grazing livestock, and ploughing land with sandy soils.[17] In 1894, Voeikov wrote that 'there is no doubt' that drifting sands were due to the 'carelessness of man'. He continued that, if left alone by man and his livestock, natural vegetation would grow on sands and keep them in place.[18] The danger was portrayed in near apocalyptic terms in 1903 by Aleksandr Platonovich Engel'gardt:

It is superfluous . . . once again to speak in detail about the significance of the invasion (*nashestvie*) of sand: not to fight it means to prepare a Sahara. Take a look at the sandy steppe in the territory of the *Ural* Cossacks, in *Orenburg* province, in *Astrakhan'* [province] and you will clearly see that this is the invasion of Asia on Europe; you will immediately understand the full horror, the complete danger of it, you will understand how much time we have lost in the struggle and how savagely the enemy has overcome us. . . . It is terrible . . . to say [there are] *millions* of *desyatiny* of land *under sand*. What the sand is doing is well known to the inhabitants of *Kherson, Tauride, Chernigov, Voronezh* and other prov[inces]. The danger is starting to be felt by the inhabitants also of Saratov

---

[14] Ivanov, 'Vliyanie', 249–51.

[15] GASO, f.329, op.1, d.1 (1903), l.18 ob.

[16] *SSSpSG*, vii, *Novouzenskii uezd* (1890), 4.

[17] In addition to the references above, see also V. N. Bogoyavlenskii, 'Ukreplenie i ispol'zovanie letuchikh peskov', in P. N. Sokovnin (ed.), *Nastol'naya kniga russkogo zemledel'tsa*, 2nd edn (Spb, 1914), 692–3; A. Kostyaev, 'Ukreplenie letuchikh peskov', *PERSKh*, x (1907), 122.

[18] Voeikov, 'Vozdeistvie', 50–1.

prov[ince]: in *Kamyshin* and *Tsaritsyn* districts [in the south of the province] vigorously spreading sand has been noted.[19]

Writing in a more measured tone in 1907, V. A. Bertenson estimated that there were about 9 million *desyatiny* of sandy land, around 11 per cent of the area, in eleven provinces of the steppe region. The picture was greatly distorted by Astrakhan' province, which included over half the total. The provinces with the next largest areas of sand were Kherson, Tauride, Ekaterinoslav, Samara, Simbirsk, and Saratov. The Don region and Stavropol' province were also badly affected. Bertenson's estimate included both land with 'small-grained sandy soils', which had a little grass cover, as well as areas already covered by drifting sands. The government estimated in 1907 that the area covered with moving sand was growing by between 1 and 8 per cent a year.[20]

In 1894, Voeikov noted the irony that the vicinity of Aleshki—where drifting sands covered 200,000 *desyatiny* of land—was the location of Herodotus' 'Hylaea': the oasis of woodland on the Scythian steppes.[21]

Dust storms

A recurring phenomenon on the steppes was storms of dust, whipped up by the hot, dry winds from the east and south-east, that damaged agriculture and alarmed the population. The winds picked up large quantities of black earth and other soil from the surface and carried it away in clouds sometimes for considerable distances. The winds could remove the topsoil to a depth of up to an *arshin* (7 inches), sometimes exposing the subsoil. Seeds and crops which had germinated were also blown away. Dust storms were fairly widespread in the south and east of the steppes, but were also reported in the forest-steppe region. They were most common and most serious, however, in Central Asia, from where the *sukhovei* blew dust and sand to the European part of the empire.[22] Dust storms were noted by Peter Pallas around Tsaritsyn in the summer of 1774, however, before the wholesale changes in the vegetation cover over the following decades.[23]

---

[19] A. P. Engel'gardt, *Chernozemnaya Rossiya* (Saratov, 1903), 162. The image of the Sahara was also used by General Maskovets in his report on the Don region. GARO, f.46, op.1, d.3282 [1898], l.18ob. For a similar description, see I. Timoshchenkov, 'Vtoroi Donskoi okrug oblasti Voiska Donskogo. Statistichesko-etnograficheskii ocherk', *SOVDSK*, 6 (1906), 87, 91, 98, 105.

[20] V. A. Bertenson, 'Nepochatyi zemel'nyi fond (ob ispol'zovanii sypuchikh peschanykh pochv)', *SKhiL*, 224 (1907), 136–8. In the Don region, drifting sands occupied half a million of the 15 million *desyatiny*. See A. M. Grekov, 'Nuzhdy Dona v trudakh mestnykh sel'sokhoyaistvennykh komitetov', *SOVDSK*, 5 (1905), 39–40.

[21] Voeikov, 'Vozdeistvie', 50–1.

[22] See E. Geints, 'Pyl'nye buri', *PERSKh*, viii (1903), 50–1; M. Shtal'-Shreder, 'Deistvie vetra na pochvu', *PERSKh*, iii (1900), 174; 'Burya chernozemnaya', *PERSKh*, xii (1912), 165–6.

[23] See above, p. 74.

There were regular reports of dust storms over the nineteenth century, especially during drought years in the late nineteenth century. This may not necessarily be evidence that they were recurring more frequently, since there is a lack of hard data on the preceding period, but dust storms were certainly attracting more attention. Clouds of dust and sand raised into the air by storms in the summer, which turned day into twilight, were reported by Lieutenant Ryabinin in the General Staff survey of the Ural Cossack territory in the mid-1860s.[24] In August 1878, Vasilii Dokuchaev observed dust storms in the Kuban' region of the North Caucasus where he was studying the black earth.[25] The North Caucasus seem to have been particularly badly affected. In July in the drought year of 1885, a resident of Batalpashinsk, in the south-east of the Kuban' region, wrote to a regional newspaper: 'the prolonged drought, . . . has been accompanied by an uncommon heat wave and a fiercely-burning easterly wind, . . . has been blowing continually for weeks, and . . . raising large clouds of dust'.[26]

In the arid north-east of neighbouring Stavropol' province, the elder of the settlement of Kistinskoe, Novogrigor'evskii district, reported: 'from 27 June to . . . 8 July [1885], there was no rain, and every day, fiery, easterly winds with dust from the earth blow, which turn day into dark, impenetrable night'.[27] Kistinskoe had been founded only a decade earlier on former Kalmyk pasture. The new Russian inhabitants came from elsewhere in Stavropol' province and also from central Russia. In 1875, 18 per cent of the settlement's land was described as 'unsuitable' (*neudobnaya*) for agriculture; by 1882, this had increased to almost a third.[28] It is possible that the activities of the settlers, some of whom were unfamiliar with the steppe environment, in farming the former pasture land were making it ever less suitable for agriculture. When hit by drought in 1885, the topsoil blew away, and ruined the harvest. Kistinskoe was one of the settlements worst affected by the crop failure in 1885: the villagers sowed nearly 3,000 *chetverti* of grain, but harvested only 61.[29]

The drought of the early 1890s was accompanied by dust storms. Detailed accounts were produced by the scientists of Dokuchaev's expedition of the 1890s. Petr Zemyatchenskii produced a graphic description in the spring of 1892 at Velikii Anadol' in eastern Ekaterinoslav province:

The dry autumn . . . , the snowless winter and, finally, the dry spring turned the top layer of . . . earth partly into a dry dust, [and] partly into a fine-grained, crumbly, powder,

[24] *MDGSR: Ural'skoe Kazach'e voisko*, comp. A. Ryabinin (Spb, 1866), 156.

[25] I. Krupenikov and L. Krupenikov, *Puteshestviya i ekspeditsii V. V. Dokuchaeva* (Moscow, 1949), 40.

[26] *Severnyi Kavkaz* (26 July 1885). Batalpashinsk is now Cherkessk, the capital of the Republic of Karachaevo-Cherkessiya.

[27] GASK, f.101, op.4, d.1504 (1885), l.96.

[28] GASK, f.146, op.1, d.62 (1875–1877; I. Benkovskii, 'Statistiko-geograficheskii putevoditel' po Stavropol'skoi gubernii', *Stavropol'skie gubernskie vedomosti* (25 Sept. 1882).

[29] *Obzor Stavropol'skoi gubernii za 1885 god* (Stavropol', 1886).

which, with the onset of strong storms in April, lost their hold, and were raised up in whole clouds, concealing the sun's rays and turning day into night. Witnesses unanimously testified that the phenomenon had such a dreadful and frightening character that everyone expected 'the end of the world'.

He continued that it was impossible to go outdoors, trains were halted by drifts of earth, crops were killed by the blows of the dust, and seeds that were starting to germinate were blown from one place to another and perished. Huge areas were left without any vegetation at all, not even weeds.[30]

One of his colleagues, N. Adamov, recorded the impact of a *sukhovei* at the Starobel'sk field research station in eastern Khar'kov province, on 20 July 1892:

From the morning a strong, violent, easterly wind began to blow, which at times raised a significant amount of dust from the road; the air became dry, far off there was a haze in the air, which foreshadowed an abrupt change. By midday . . . the entire horizon was covered with a very fine dust; the sun, which until then had been shining brightly, was obscured as if by a light cloud; all that could be seen was a red blotch (*pyatno*). Although the shutters were closed, it was impossible to sit down in the house: besides the stuffy heat, we swallowed a mass of dust, which had penetrated through narrow cracks in the doors and windows etc. The house trembled under the force of the strong wind, and from all sides broken branches of Russian thistle, 'tumbleweed' etc. were driven along. On the steppe, at times nothing was visible for more than 10 *sazheny* [about 70 feet]. This was a genuine *blizzard*, but, instead of snow, a fine dust of black earth and chalk was flying, rising up high into the air. All living things hid, [and] kept quiet, as if in anticipation of something even terrible . . . This burning snowstorm (*buran*) left behind very large drifts of dust, black earth, and sand; in places the fields were stripped bare, and the grain was seriously scorched.

In the spring of 1894, in the same location, a *sukhovei* and dust storm were accompanied by rain, which fell as black mud. The third field research station of Dokuchaev's expedition, at Khrenovskoi in south-eastern Voronezh province, did not escape. In the summer of 1894, a storm was observed during which a dense column of dust and black earth was raised in the air to a height of up to seven hundred feet. The column changed colour, moreover, from a dull, dirty red to absolutely black as it passed from an area covered with sand to one where the soil was black earth.[31]

These accounts are strikingly similar to descriptions of dust storms in Oklahoma and elsewhere on the Great Plains in the 1930s.[32] As in the USA, moreover, scientists investigated the causes, and asked whether the settlers who had moved onto the grasslands over the previous decades, many of whom came

[30] P. Zemyatchenskii, 'Velikoanadol'skii uchastok', *TESLD, Nauchnii otdel*, 1/3 (1894), 15, 17.

[31] N. Adamov, 'Meteorologicheskie nablyudeniya 1892–1894 godov', *TESLD, Nauchnii otdel*, 3/1 (1894), 235–42.

[32] See Timothy Egan, *The Worst Hard Time: The Untold Story of Those Who Survived the Great American Dust Bowl* (Boston, 2006).

from regions with different environmental conditions, had caused or contributed to this alarming deeply phenomenon.

It was not difficult for Russian scientists to elucidate the underlying causes. Dust storms occurred during periods of prolonged drought when easterly winds brought dry and scorching air from Central Asia. These winds could reach considerable speeds, and the force was sufficient to blow small particles of soil into the air in clouds. The hot, dry air in the *sukhovei* also dried out the surface of the land, making it more susceptible to wind erosion. Experiments showed that evaporation of moisture from the soil was greatest if the layer of topsoil was thin. Further, smaller particles of soil dried out faster than larger particles, and were also more likely to be eroded. Friable, or crumbly, soil also dried out quickly.[33] All these conditions existed in the south-east of the steppe region.

Russian scientists also investigated whether human impact—in particular removing the former steppe vegetation, including woodland, and ploughing up the land—had exacerbated the natural causes of dust storms. In 1886, an agronomist from the University of New Russia in Odessa, A. Bychikhin, embarked on a five-year study 'of the influence of the wind on the soil' in Berdyansk district, Tauride province.[34] His study showed that soils on virgin land or fields that had been left fallow for long periods had a granular (*zernistyi*) structure. This structure was destroyed by ploughing, making the soil more likely to form powder or dust, which was more prone to be dried out and blown away by the wind. The increase in the cultivation of grain over the two–three decades that preceded his study, Bychikhin argued, had intensified this process. He acknowledged that soil had been eroded by the wind in earlier periods, but argued that it had been on a much smaller scale in the past.[35]

The scientists of Dokuchaev's expedition supplemented Bychikhin's study. Grigorii Vysotskii pointed out that dust storms, 'which were so terrible in southern Russia', tended to occur more frequently in the early spring, when the arable fields were still bare, before they were covered by crops. Bare land without vegetation was smooth and did not impede the force of the wind. On the other hand, vegetation—crops, grass, shrubs, and trees—increased the roughness of the surface of the land, increasing the 'coefficient of friction' against the air, thus slowing the wind, and reducing its erosive capacity. Storms came to a halt, and deposited their clouds of dust, when they came up against woodland, hedges, or sometimes fields of densely sown crops. Trees in particular slowed the force of wind and reduced erosion. Deforestation, by implication, increased wind erosion.[36] The practice of 'black fallow' (keeping fallow fields clear of vegetation)

---

[33] See Geints, 'Pyl'nye buri'; 'Burya chernozemnaya'; Shtal'-Shreder, 'Deistvie vetra na pochvu'.
[34] A. Bychikhin, 'O vliyanii vetrov na pochvu', *TVEO*, 6 (1892), 312–90.
[35] Bychikhin, 'O vliyanii'.
[36] G. Vysotskii, 'Materialy po izucheniyu chernykh bur v stepyakh Rossii', *TESLD, Sbornyi otdel*, 1 (1894), 1–16.

employed by some farmers (see below, pp. 263–8), had the disadvantage of leaving land exposed and vulnerable to wind erosion if left unprotected.[37]

When reporting the dust storms in the early 1890s, Adamov noted Pallas' observations of the same phenomenon a century earlier. He argued that the impact of winds was much greater in 1890s, as the wind encountered no barriers to slow or impede it, just endless ploughed fields.[38] Over the nineteenth century, therefore, Russians came to believe that human impact had greatly exacerbated a natural phenomenon that predated the massive expansion of arable farming, and was harmful to steppe agriculture. In 1894, Voeikov concluded that the 'influence of man' on dust storms was 'great', and that 'land, once covered by rich steppe and partly also forest vegetation' was coming to resemble the dry uplands of Central Asia, where dust storms were common.[39]

Ravines

In addition to the wind that caused dust storms and drifting sands, the relief and drainage of the steppe region were also shaped by water erosion. The ravines and gullies that cut through the steppes and joined onto river valleys were a feature of the relief that had long attracted comment from visitors and scientists.[40] During the Academy of Sciences expeditions of 1768–74, Pallas and his colleagues concluded that they were formed by the erosive action of water from springs and rain running downhill across the steppe towards the rivers. In the 1870s, Dokuchaev concluded that the formation of ravines was a natural process that had taken place over an extended period of time, which long predated appearance of humans on the steppes (see above, p. 74). Dokuchaev also noted that Charles Lyell had pointed to the impact of recent forest clearance on the formation of a gulley in Georgia in the USA, implying that human action was also a factor.[41]

In the forest-steppe and steppe regions of the Russian Empire, over the second half of the nineteenth century, it became increasingly apparent that ravines were growing in size, sometimes with alarming rapidity. The authorities, estate owners, agricultural specialists, and scientists were concerned for a number of reasons. As ravines and gullies expanded, they eroded land from the adjoining fields, reducing the area available for cultivation. Fertile soil was washed away into ravines and gullies. D. L. Ivanov noted these and other consequences in his

---

[37] See 'Burya chernozemnaya', 166.

[38] Adamov, 'Meteorologicheskie nablyudeniya 1892–1894 godov', 235.

[39] Voeikov, 'Vozdeistvie', 52.

[40] See, for example, E. E. Kern, *Ovragi, ikh zakreplenie, oblesenie i zapruzhivanie*, 5th edn (Spb, 1913), 1.

[41] V. V. Dokuchaev, 'Sposoby obrazovaniya rechnykh dolin Evropeiskoi Rossii', in *Sochineniya*, 9 vols (Moscow and Leningrad, 1949–61), i, 163. See also Barbara A. Kennedy, 'Charles Lyell and "Modern changes of the Earth": the Milledgeville Gully', *Geomorphology*, 40/1–2 (2001), 91–8.

study of Stavropol' province of 1885. He added that many inhabitants thought that the formation of new ravines dated back to the start of the 1870s.[42] The drought of 1891 spurred the Ministry of State Domains to commission further studies. Specialists such as Eduard Kern paid far more attention to the role of human activity than earlier research. They came to see Dokuchaev's explanation of the formation of ravines as preconditions rather than causes.[43] Dokuchaev renewed his interest in ravines during his expedition of the 1890s. One of the participants, N. Adamov, looked back to Pallas' description of the steppes, and noted that 'ravines were rarer' when 'our steppe was still clothed with luxuriant vegetation' and 'arable land did not occupy such a large area.'[44]

Aleksandr Platonovich Engel'gardt summarized the results of recent studies in 1903. He described how ravines were expanded by the action of running water in the spring caused by the thaw, and in the summer during torrential downpours. The water rushed through ravines, eroding their sides, and causing new branches to form. Engel'gardt argued that there were two types of ravines: active and dead. The sides of the former were bare of vegetation, and were 'harmful', because they were growing as running water eroded the exposed soil. The latter were full of vegetation, including trees and shrubs, which protected the soil from erosion. 'It is not difficult', he wrote, 'to resurrect [dead ravines], which people do without understanding the danger.' People cleared the trees, shrubs, and other vegetation in 'dead' ravines. They then ploughed up the land, thus reactivating the ravines as the soil was exposed, broken up, and left vulnerable to erosion. Ploughing was particularly conducive to erosion if, as was frequently the practice, land was ploughed down the slope (rather than along the line of the contours).[45]

Studies provided evidence for the speed at which ravines were growing. In many cases, small fissures between 2 and 5 feet wide developed into ravines from 20 to 40 feet across and several hundred feet long over twenty to thirty years. To emphasize the extent of the problem, Engel'gardt wrote 'ravines can carry out their marauding raid (*razboinichii nabeg*) on landownership not once, but *several* times a year', 'stealing the land itself from its owner.'[46] His use of the word 'raid' suggests an allusion to the nomads, who had raided Russia from the steppes into the eighteenth century, and had raided the settlements of the first waves of settlers. Making a link between the previous inhabitants, who were hostile to the incoming settlers, and the environmental problems facing steppe agriculture was a recurring theme in writing on the steppes in this period.

---

[42] Ivanov, 'Vliyanie', p. 240.

[43] Kern, *Ovragi*, 5 edns (Moscow, 1892, 1894, 1897, Spb, 1903, 1913). See also V. Masal'skii, *Ovragi chernozemnoi polosy Rossii* (Spb, 1897)119; S. Kizenkov, 'Ovragi i ikh ukreplenie', *PERSKh*, vi (1902), 98–113; 'Sed'maya sessiya sel'skokhozyaistvennogo soveta', *SKhiL*, 211 (1903), 209–46.

[44] N. Adamov, 'Meteorologicheskie nablyudeniya 1894–1895 godov', *TESLD, Nauchnii otdel*, 3/2 (1898), 259–63; N. Adamov, 'Meteorologicheskie nablyudeniya 1892–1894 godov', 235.

[45] See Engel'gardt, *Chernozemnaya Rossiya*, 108–11, 142.

[46] Engel'gardt, *Chernozemnaya Rossiya*, 108.

By the end of the nineteenth century, ravines were 'especially strongly developed' in Saratov, Kherson', and Ekaterinoslav provinces, as well as other parts of the steppe region. Kherson' province, one specialist wrote, was 'notable for the abundance of ravines and gullies, which are reaching huge proportions'. In the Don region, ravines along the banks of the Don, Aksai, Khoper, and other rivers had expanded 'with the increase in the population and ploughing up of the land, and also as a consequence of the destruction of vegetation and grazing livestock on the sides of gullies'. In Samara province, ravines of previously unknown proportions were developing, and dozens of *desyatiny* of land were being eroded. In Aksakovka (the home of the Aksakov family) in Buguruslan district in eastern Samara province, a ravine two *versty* (1.5 miles) long and 20 *sazheny* (140 feet) wide had appeared. Telling evidence for the role of human activity in the growth of ravines came from Stavropol' province. In one location, the inhabitants had felled the trees and grubbed out the stumps from an area of around 35 *desyatiny*. They then ploughed up the land. But, after sixty years, the land was no longer suitable for farming, because it had become fissured with ravines.[47]

Ravines were even more widespread and expanding faster in the forest-steppe region. This is evidence for the role of human activity, because the forest-steppe was more densely populated and had been settled and ploughed up for longer than the steppe region. There were also natural reasons why the growth of ravines was more serious in the forest-steppe region. The region received more rainfall than the steppes, and therefore was at greater risk of water erosion. The undulating relief of much of the forest-steppe was more conducive to water erosion. Parts of the steppe region, for example Novyi Uzen' district in Samara province and Dneprovsk district in Tauride province, were simply too flat for ravines to form: water erosion required a slope for the water to run down.[48]

In 1894, Voeikov assigned the main role in the formation, not just expansion, of ravines in the steppe region to human, not natural, causes:

As far as I am aware neither on primordial steppe, nor in forest, do new ravines form, ... erosion takes place only in permanent water courses, at the expense of their bottoms and sides. However, when man converts forest or steppe into fields, then their previous stability disappears, and erosion ... takes place on a large scale.

He described the action of frosts, heat waves, spring melt water, and summer downpours on soil that had been had been denuded of vegetation by human activity, and how a 'small fissure' could develop into a 'genuine ravine.'[49] Voeikov was thus contradicting the argument by Dokuchaev in the 1870s and

[47] Engel'gardt, *Chernozemnaya Rossiya*, 116–21.

[48] V. P. Semenov (ed.), *Rossiya: Polnoe geograficheskoe opisanie nashego otechestva*, 11 vols (Spb, 1899–914), xiv, *Novorossiya i Krym* (1910), 56; I. Stebelsky, 'Agriculture and Soil Erosion in the European Forest-Steppe', in James H. Bater and R. A. French (eds), *Studies in Russian Historical Geography*, 2 vols (London, 1983), i, 45, 48–9.

[49] Voeikov, 'Vozdeistvie', 45, 48–9.

the conclusions of the Academy of Sciences expeditions a century earlier that ravines formed due to natural forces. Voeikov was also taking further the subsequent argument that human activity exacerbated the natural causes. In asserting that human action was the main cause of the formation, as well as growth, of ravines, however, Voeikov was reflecting the growing anxiety about environmental change, and the role of humans in causing it, in the aftermath of the disaster of 1891–2. The argument for the primacy of human activity in the formation and expansion of ravines was taken up by other writers. In 1899, A. Kostyaev, an official of the Ministry of Agriculture, argued that the formation of ravines, like drifting sands, was due above all to the 'imprudent economic activity of humans' in destroying trees, shrubs, and other vegetation that grew in them. He argued that ravines which formed as a result of climatic, geological, and other factors were 'much rarer'.[50] In the early twentieth century, officials and inhabitants in the Don region pointed to destruction of forests and intensified ploughing up of the land as the main causes of the growing and increasingly harmful development of ravines.[51]

Not all agreed that human activity played such an important role. In 1897, during a discussion of an influential study of ravines by Eduard Kern in the Scientific Committee of the Ministry of Agriculture, one member objected to Kern's statement that the growth of ravines was due to the 'almost complete ploughing up of our steppes', and that they had ploughed up 'more than they should have been'.[52] At a meeting in 1903, the ministry's 'Agricultural Council' took a more balanced view on the relative roles of natural factors and 'incautious' ploughing and felling of trees in the growth of ravines.[53] In 1902, the agricultural specialist S. Kizenkov also put forward a balanced argument, but one which assigned great importance to human action:

In the presence of conditions which are favourable for the formation of a ravine, for one to emerge it is sometimes sufficient only for [there to be] some accidental cause facilitating the erosion of the surface of the soil, such as a ploughed furrow in the direction of the slope of the land, a rut in a road, a path from driving livestock, a ditch, a rut, a fissure formed in a cold, snowless winter, felling forest, [or] grubbing out stumps, and such like. Once the initial ravine (*promoina*) has formed, then its further deepening, widening, and lengthening will depend on the interaction of the conditions for ravine-formation [sufficient precipitation, slope, and the composition of the soil and sub-soil].[54]

Thus, by the turn of the twentieth century, scientists and agricultural specialists were assigning an ever greater role to human activity, in particular in clearing

[50] A. Kostyaev, 'Bor'ba s ovragami', *SKhiL*, 194 (1899), 75.
[51] Grekov, 'Nuzhdy Dona', 38–9; A. Kryukov, 'O stanichnykh lesakh Donskoi oblasti', *SOVDSK*, 10 (1910), 79–99; p. 80.
[52] RGIA, f.382, op.2, 1897, d.1828, ll.10ob.
[53] 'Sed'maya sessiya', 209–10, 226–33.
[54] Kizenkov, 'Ovragi', 105.

woodland and ploughing up the land, in the origins and expansion of the ravines that cut through the steppes and took away valuable black earth.

THE DRYING OUT OF THE STEPPES

The soil that was washed away through the expanding ravines and gullies ended up in the rivers that flowed through the steppe region. This caused growing concerns about rivers silting up, and speculation that the volume of water in the steppe rivers was declining. Characteristically, the finger of blame was pointed at deforestation.[55] Many contemporaries also believed that the amount of water in the ground was falling. Over the mid- and late nineteenth century, scientists, agricultural specialists, and inhabitants of the steppe region returned to this issue regularly. They developed a view that the removal of much of the woodland in the region and the ploughing up of ever larger areas of virgin land were causing the steppes to dry out, exacerbating the impact of recurring droughts as crops could not draw on reserves of moisture in the ground.

The serious drought and crop failure of 1833 drew attention to ground water. The German-born director of the Forestry Institute in St Petersburg asserted that trees assisted soil in holding water, and by implication their removal caused the land to dry out.[56] In 1842, an estate owner in the steppe region wrote to the Ministry of State Domains that the shortage of ground water was one of the reasons why droughts had caused more frequent bad harvests in recent years. (He referred to the 'terrible drought of 1833'.) In his opinion, the shortage of ground water was due to natural causes as well as 'neglect' of forests and lack of attention to conservation of water in rivers and lakes.[57] Ivan Palimpsestov also believed the steppes were drying out. Rainfall, he wrote in 1850, was flowing rapidly in streams away from fields that were bare of vegetation. He had been speaking to 'old timers' as well as relying on his own observations.[58] In his annual report for 1856 (a drought year), the inspector of agriculture in southern Russia considered a related point. He wrote that the denser steppe vegetation in the past, that is, before the wholesale ploughing up of the land, had protected it by reducing evaporation of water which fell as precipitation. This, in turn, had ensured that

[55] See, for example, A. I. Voeikov, 'Izmeneniya urovnya Volgi i Kaspiiskogo morya i vliyanie vyrubki lesov', *IRGO*, 7/1 (1871), 56–64; F. Ignat'ev, 'Otchego meleyut reki?', *Russkii vestnik*, 175 (1885), 204–42; *Ob okhrane vodnykh bogatstv: Glavnye rezul'taty chetyrekhletnikh trudov ekspeditsii dlya issledovaniya istochnikov i glavneishikh rek Evropeiskoi Rossii pod rukovodstvom A. Tillo* (Spb, 1898). See also Marina Loskutova, ' "Vliyanie lesov na obmeleniya rek est' tol'ko nedokazannaya ipoteza": prikladnaya nauka i gosudarstvennaya politika po upravleniyu prirodnymi resursami v Rossiiskoi imperii vtoroi chetverti XIX v', *Istoriko-biologicheskie issledovaniya*, 4/1 (2012), 9–32.

[56] Breitenbakh, 'O pol'ze lesov v prirode', *LZh*, 1 (1835), 38–9.

[57] 'Ob osnovnykh prichinakh neurozhaev v Rossii i o sredstvakh otvrashchenya onykh', *ZhMGI*, 4 (1842), 2nd pagn, 130–1.

[58] Palimpsestov, 'Saratovskaya step'', 112.

the wild steppe vegetation received the water it needed, and which therefore rarely suffered from droughts. Old timers, he added, confirmed this. He further noted that trees sheltered the land and reduced evaporation of water. His conclusion was stark: the Russian population that had settled on the southern steppes, with their customary forms of agriculture that they had brought with them from central Russia, would not be able to conserve moisture in the land.[59]

More sustained arguments that the steppes were drying out were developed in the second half of the nineteenth century. S. A. Zabludskii, an estate owner and member of the Free Economic Society, argued in 1870 that as long as the steppe had been covered by unploughed sod, it had protected the moisture that had accumulated deep in the soil from the drying effect of the wind and the hot sun. Thus, even in years when there was a shortage of rainfall in the summer, there was sufficient water in the soil for the grasses and other vegetation that covered the steppe. Water also accumulated in the soil under marshes, river valleys, and ravines that were covered with shrubs and dense forest. But, the local population had changed all this by felling trees and ploughing up more and more land. The steppes were, therefore, drying out and abundant harvests were a thing of past.[60]

In his study of Stavropol' province in 1885, Ivanov amplified the growing view of what was happening. He made a clear connection, moreover, between the drying out of the land and the processes of erosion he and other scientists had studied:

Rain, which had previously soaked into soil bound together by vegetation, [and] snow, which had gradually melted among brushwood, have now begun to gather in torrents and run off rapidly down the slopes, cutting through the upper layers of the earth, forming ravines . . ., [and] producing wild floods that take away the mass of the water in a short time to the lower steppes. With every year the proportion of moisture remaining in the soil is falling at the expense of waters running off across the surface . . .[61]

In the same year, a *zemstvo* study of Buzuluk district, Samara province, noted that 'virgin soil' held moisture better than land that had been ploughed up. With the growth in the area of cultivated land, the ploughing up of the feather-grass steppe, and the felling of the remnants of the woodland, moreover, the land was starting to lose its 'underground moisture'.[62]

By this time, the issue was the subject of scientific study involving detailed, controlled observations over time by Aleksandr Izmail'skii (1851–1914). He was an example of the new generation of scientists in Russia who were engaged in research into changes in the steppe environment for the practical benefit of the

[59] DAOO, fond 1, opis' 248, 1856, sp.1580, ll.113–15.
[60] S. A. Zabudskii, 'O zasukhakh na yuge i o sredstvakh k sokhraneniyu i uvelicheniyu syrosti v nashikh stepyakh', *TVEO*, 1 (1870), 10–11. A similar argument was made in a *zemstvo* study of Buzuluk district, Samara province. *SSSpSG*, iii, *Buzulukskii uezd* (1885), 199–200.
[61] Ivanov, 'Vliyanie', 240.
[62] *SSSpSG*, 3, *Buzulukskii uezd* (1885), 199–200.

region's farmers. A native of northern Saratov province, in the forest-steppe region, Izmail'skii was educated at the Petrovskaya Agricultural Academy in Moscow. In 1879, he moved to Kherson province, where he taught agriculture and managed the farm attached to the *zemstvo* agricultural school. He carried out research over a number of years into the accumulation and conservation of moisture in the soil.[63] Izmail'skii pointed out that relying on theories derived from research that had been carried out into soil moisture in Western Europe, which some Russian specialists continued to do, was hardly relevant to the particular soil and climatic conditions in the steppe region.[64]

It was apparent to Izmail'skii that the soil on the school farm was altered by ploughing and the removal of the previous vegetation. He measured the moisture content of the soil in different locations at various depths and at different times of the year. He compared the results from unploughed land, pasture, land sown with cultivated fodder grass, black fallow (fallow land kept bare of vegetation), and land sown with crops. He found examples of unploughed land with the original 'luxuriant vegetation that had once covered the steppes' on the steep sides of gullies. He supplemented his research with the memories of old timers (he cited Palimpsestov), who recalled that in the past, the soil got moister as they dug down, whereas 'now' the reverse was the case. When digging wells, in the past they had had to dig only 2–3 *sazheny* (14–21 feet) to find fresh water, but 'now' it was necessary to dig down 15–20 *sazheny* (105–140 feet), at which depth the water was likely to be salty. Izmail'skii argued:

The former virgin steppe, the gigantic vegetation of which we can now gauge only from legends, was undoubtedly able to make use of all the water falling as precipitation, completely without regard to the form of the precipitation [i.e. snow, light rain, torrential downpours].

On the other hand:

Steppe which has been ploughed up is not able to use the entire quantity of precipitation, and in the event of a shortfall of the moisture it needs each year, [it] uses the reserve of moisture in the soil which is left from previous years. As this reserve is exhausted, the vegetation covering the soil becomes more and more dependent on the quantity and form of atmospheric precipitation.

Cultivated land, moreover, lost more moisture through evaporation. Land which had been over-grazed by livestock was affected in similar ways. Using land for crops or pasture 'could fundamentally alter the relationship of the soil to

---

[63] P. D., 'Aleksandr Alekseevich Izmail'skii (Nekrolog)', *SKhiL*, 246 (1914), 519–20.

[64] A. Izmail'skii, 'Vlazhnost' pochvy v svyazi s kul'turnym ee sostoyaniem. (Issledovaniya, proizvedennye v khersonskoi gubernii), *SKhiL*, 140 (1882), 1st pagn, 135–6. Work by the German scientist Ewald Wollny on moisture retention had been published in Russian. G. Vol'nii, 'Vliyanie obrabotki, udobreniya, ukatyvaniya i rastitel'nosti na isparenie i soderzhanie vlagi v pochve', *ZIOSKhYuR*, 1 (1881), 1–12.

moisture'. He argued that former steppe vegetation—wild grasses—must have been at least as important as forests in retaining moisture in the soil.[65]

Izmail'skii continued his research on the black-earth steppe of Poltava district, on the northern edge of the steppes. In 1883, he accepted a position as manager of the large Peschano-Balyasnovskoe estate. He also became an active member of the Poltava agricultural society. He set up a meteorological station and laboratory on the estate, and devised a special borer to collect samples of soil from different depths.[66] Between 1886 and 1893, he conducted further observations and experiments, gathering data on the climate (especially the amount and form of precipitation and temperature), crop growth, the proportion of moisture in the soil at various levels in land under different uses, and the level of ground water, which he measured in wells. Thus, he had far more, and more accurate, data than for his earlier study. Izmail'skii published the results of his research in 1893 in a brochure aimed at a wider readership, especially farmers, entitled 'How Did Our Steppe Dry Out?', and in a longer scientific monograph on soil moisture and ground water the following year.

Izmail'skii believed that his more extensive research had confirmed his earlier findings. The amount of moisture in soil depended almost as much on the form and structure of the surface of the soil as the amount of precipitation. With the same level of precipitation, land cultivated in one way could have plenty of moisture, while land cultivated in another could dry out. For moisture in the soil to increase, it was necessary to have conditions that hindered the flow of precipitation from the surface of the land, assisted the penetration of water, and protected the surface from evaporation. The more favourable the conditions, the closer ground water would be to the surface.

The present-day steppe—he noted—has the least favourable conditions for the accumulation of moisture in the soil. It would be more accurate to say that in the present-day steppe, all conditions have come together in the manner most favourable for it to dry out.

He attributed this to the removal of the former steppe vegetation by farmers to cultivate the land and graze their livestock:

It is obvious, that steppe totally covered by impassable feather grass, and in places by extensive thickets of . . . [shrubs], had a completely different relationship with the precipitation falling from the atmosphere, *in whatever form this precipitation took*, than today's steppes. Torrential downpours, which are damaging to today's steppes, in former times not only did not harm it, but on the contrary, enriched their soil with moisture to a significant depth.

The removal of the former vegetation and ploughing up the steppes, moreover, had contributed to the growth of ravines, which drained the melt waters away in

[65] Izmail'skii, 'Vlazhnost' pochvy', 137, 146–7, 156 (quotations).
[66] P. D., 'Aleksandr Alekseevich Izmail'skii', 521–4.

a short time, causing higher spring floods. The relief of the land also had an effect on the level of ground water. Measurements in wells had shown that the level of ground water was deeper, and the volume of water lower, in areas that were bisected by ravines than in areas with larger expanses of flat land. Ground water levels were lowest near the sides of ravines. Thus, Izmail'skii's research showed that the steppe, which had been denuded of its former, luxuriant vegetation, ploughed up, and was bisected by ravines that were expanding at an alarming rate, was drying out.[67]

Dokuchaev presented similar findings in 1892. Unploughed soils and land covered by native steppe grasses, together with larger areas of woodland, were better able to retain and absorb moisture from melted snow and rain. Ploughed soil and cultivated or mown land, on the contrary, was more liable to lose moisture through evaporation and run off. Ploughing and cultivation, moreover, exacerbated soil erosion and development of ravines. These, in turn, further increased the drainage of water that would otherwise have been absorbed into the land. The consequence of all these was that ground water levels were falling and the steppes were gradually drying out. This drying out of the land made crops more vulnerable to the periodic droughts. For Dokuchaev, therefore, the crop failure of 1891 was explained by the drying out of the land.[68]

The reason for the similarity between Izmail'skii's and Dokuchaev's work was that the two scientists had become acquainted in 1888. They corresponded regularly, shared their research findings, and influenced each other's work. Dokuchaev praised Izmail'skii's monograph on soil moisture: 'You have the honour to be the first *scientifically* to look into the *life* of ground waters.' He singled out the connection he made between ground water levels and the relief of the land.[69] Izmail'skii's findings echoed the significance Dokuchaev had attributed to relief in the formation of the black earth. During Dokuchaev's expedition of the 1890s, his teams of scientists continued Izmail'skii's work, investigating whether there was a connection between the levels of precipitation and ground water.[70] Izmail'skii and Dokuchaev agreed on another matter: they both denied

[67] A. A. Izmail'skii, *Kak vysokhla nasha step': (Predvaritel'noe soobshchenie o rezul'tatakh issledovanii vlazhnosti pochvy v Poltavskoi gubernii 1886–93 gg.)* (Poltava, 1893); also published in *SKhiL*, 173 (1893), 2nd pagn, 267–89; 174 (1893), 2nd pagn, 1–27 (quotations from 12, 14); A. A. Izmail'skii, *Vlazhnost' pochvy i gruntovaya voda v svyazi s rel'efom mestnosti i kul'turnym sostoyaniem poverkhnosti pochvy* (Poltava, 1894). The connection between ground water levels and the relief of the land had been suspected earlier. See, for example, *MDGSR: Khersonskaya guberniya*, comp. Shmidt (Spb, 1863), 230.

[68] Dokuchaev, 'Nashi Stepi prezhde i teper'', in *Sochineniya*, vi, 57–61, 83–9.

[69] 'Iz perepiski s A. A. Izmail'skim (1888–1900)', in V. V. Dokuchaev, *Sochineniya*, viii (1961), 270–1, 284, 287, 297–9, 306–7, 310–12, 316, 319 (quotation).

[70] K. Glinka, N. Sibirtsev, and P. Ototskii, 'Khrenovskii uchastok', *TESLD, Nauchnii otdel*, 1/1 (1894), 15–17, 33–6, 103–6; I. Vydrin and N. Sibirtsev, 'Starobel'skii uchastok', *TESLD, Nauchnii otdel*, 1/2 (1894), 52–9; N. Adamov, 'Meteorologicheskie nablyudeniya 1892–1894 godov', 144–55.

that the climate in the steppe region was changing, and insisted that the drying out of the steppes was sufficient explanation for the recurring harvest failures in drought years.[71]

Such arguments became part of the discussions of the cause of the drought and harvest failure of 1891. In the debate in the Free Economic Society in late 1891, A. E. Filipenko argued that ploughing up the steppes had changed the soil, making it drier and less able to retain moisture, which drained away rapidly through gullies. He added that water tables were falling.[72] A few months later, future Minister of Agriculture Aleksei Ermolov lamented that after two years of drought, the land was drying out, not only on the surface, but underneath (*v glubine*). Almost everywhere, the level of ground water had fallen significantly, and springs and wells were drying up. He concluded: 'the water has gone away, and conditions of a most threatening character have arisen for Russian agriculture inside the borders of our once very rich black-earth region'.[73]

Izmail'skii's and Dokuchaev's conclusions about the drying out of the steppe came to be accepted by many Russian specialists.[74] Later in the 1890s, moreover, the expedition led by Lieutenant-General Aleksei Tillo to study the sources of major rivers in European Russia confirmed the significance of ravines in lowering ground water levels.[75] The conclusions entered official discourse. In the Don region at the turn of the twentieth century, the administration considered falling ground water levels caused by deforestation and the growth of ravines to be reasons for establishing artificial irrigation on cossack land.[76] At a session of the agricultural council of the Ministry of Agriculture in 1903, it was stated emphatically:

The growth of ravines, which has intensified in the last half century under the influence of careless ploughing of the steppes . . . [and] the felling of young trees and shrubs on the tops and sides of . . . gullies . . . without doubt is the . . . most important *cause of the lowering of the level of ground waters*, which serve as a reserve reservoir and natural corrective to the aridity of the climate . . .[77]

[71] Izmail'skii, 'Kak, vysokhla nasha step"', 13; Izmail'skii, 'Vlazhnost' pochvy', 140, 156; Dokuchaev, 'Nashi Stepi', 88–9.

[72] 'Besedy v I Otdelenii Imperatorskogo Vol'nogo Ekonomicheskogo Obshchestva po voprosu o prichinakh neurozhaya 1891 goda i merakh protiv povtoreniya podobykh urozhaev v budushchem', *TVEO*, 1 (1892), 118–19.

[73] [A. S. Ermolov], *Neurozhai i narodnoe bedstvie* (Spb, 1892), 10–1.

[74] See Engel'gardt, *Chernozemnaya Rossiya*, 107–9, 127; P. Ototskii, 'Gruntovye vody', *PERSKh*, ii (1900), 902–7; I. Kolesnikov, 'Prichiny zakhvata khlebov v yugo-vostochnoi Rossii, *SKhiL*, 245 (1914), 69; V. V. Bogachev, *Ocherki geografii Vsevelikogo Voiska Donskogo*, 123.

[75] *Ob okhrane vodnykh bogatstv*, 49.

[76] GARO, f.301, op.11, d.176 (1899–1900), ll.16–17.

[77] 'Sed'maya sessiya', 225–6.

SOIL EXHAUSTION

Over the nineteenth century, growing numbers of farmers, officials, agricultural specialists, and scientists came to believe that the legendary black earth was becoming less fertile. The leaders of the Academy of Sciences expeditions of 1768–74 had extolled the productivity of the steppe soils. Pallas, however, had anticipated that the black earth in the mid-Volga region would become exhausted as the population grew and cultivated grain in ever larger areas.[78] A few decades later, the disastrous drought and harvest failure of 1833 prompted concerns about soil exhaustion in the north of the steppe region. The chairman of the Committee for the Improvement of Agriculture set up to investigate the causes argued:

The system of fallowing without manuring, which is very typical of those places where there is an abundance of fertile land has, however, a certain consequence, which has been demonstrated by experience, that over the course of centuries soil that has been cultivated frequently and neglected gradually becomes exhausted, and is liable to frequent harvest failures.

With the significant increase in the population, he continued, the land could not provide sufficient food. This was already evident in Ukraine and in Slobodsko-Ukraine (later Khar'kov) province.[79]

Over the following decades, commentators returned time and again to soil exhaustion. In 1839, Andrei Leopol'dov noted that when the steppes on the far side of the Volga in Saratov province (the location of Samara province founded in 1851) were first ploughed up and sown with crops, the harvests were good for two or three years. But, from the fourth year, the land started to get old and exhausted, and gave lower harvests, even when the 'air' was 'favourable'. He wrote that farmers overcame the problem by using crop rotations incorporating long fallow for fifteen years. Land farmed in this way was fertile and did not need to be fertilized.[80] According to Ivan Shtukenberg writing in the 1850s, large areas of uncultivated land on the trans-Volga steppes were rented out, and sown with 'good varieties of wheat'. After ten-twelve years, however, the land was so exhausted that it was left fallow for ten years.[81] Already in 1850, however, Palimpsestov wrote that as the process of settlement of the trans-Volga steppes continued, farmers were no longer leaving land fallow for long periods to recover

---

[78] [Pallas], *Nauchnoe nasledie*, 42.

[79] RGIA, f.398, op.83, 1831–8, d.4, l.16 (quotation).

[80] Andrei Leopol'dov, *Statisticheskoe opisanie Saratovskoi gubernii*, 2 vols (Spb, 1839), i, 29, 117–18. See also K. Engel'ke, 'Khozyaistvennoe polozhenie Saratovskoi gubernii', *ZhMGI*, 1 (1841), 2nd pagn, 372.

[81] [I. F. Shtukenberg], *Statisticheskii trudy Ivan Fedorovicha Shtukenberga*, 2 vols (Spb, 1857–8), i, article 15, 'Opisanie Samarskoi gubernii', 6, 10.

its fertility. He asked rhetorically what the steppes could expect in the future, when the soil was exhausted, and would need artificial irrigation and fertilizer.[82]

Palimpsestov's concerns seemed to become reality over the following decades as the growing agricultural population made more intensive use of the land. In 1880, in the wake of a bad harvest, I. Lishin wrote in a study of Nikolaevsk district in southern Samara province:

> Many farmers are already finding that everything which can be taken from the soil has been taken. It is possible that this opinion is not mistaken . . . for those lands, with little rest, have been constantly sown with the same type of grain [wheat].

He continued that this 'rapacious farming . . . has been practised without care and without the slightest thought for the future'. In attributing blame for these damaging practices, he exonerated the local peasants, who 'knew how to plough', and pointed instead to leaseholders who took on thousands of *desyatiny* of land and did not plough it properly. The fertility of the soil was such that they could get away with this in good years and still get good harvests. They were exploiting the land, however, to the extent that it was gradually losing its productivity.[83] A *zemstvo* study of Samara district in 1883 did blame peasants for farming the land without fallow periods or crop rotation so that it 'became weaker and exhausted'. These were peasants who had taken the small, but free, 'beggars' allotments' when serfdom was abolished in 1861. They had too little land to use crop rotations or allow their meagre fields time to 'rest'.[84] In Buzuluk district in the east of province, the *zemstvo* reported that due to population increase and the loss of peasant land due to the 'cut offs' after 1861, peasants were increasing the area of arable land in place of pasture. In addition, they were incorporating land previously left fallow for three–five years in the three-field rotation, where it was left fallow for only one year. As a consequence: 'Land, receiving neither rest nor fertilizer, which is becoming exhausted by uninterrupted sowing of the same cereal crops has got tired, has become weak from old age.' Moreover, crop yields were falling and bad harvests recurring more frequently.[85]

Even land that was left fallow for long periods seemed to be losing its fertility. In his annual report for 1890, the governor of Samara wrote that long-fallow land, which had been able to bear droughts without serious consequences in the past, was no longer able to do so on account of the 'exhaustion of the productivity of the soil'.[86] In the debates in the Free Economic Society at the end of 1891, Ikonnikov, an estate owner in Saratov province, argued that the effect of

---

[82] I. Palimpsestov, 'Saratovskaya step' v khozyaistvennom otnoshenii', *TVEO*, 4 (1850), 114.

[83] I. Lishin, *Ocherk Nikolaevskogo uezda (Samarskaya guberniya) v statisticheskom i sel'sko-khozyaistvom otnosheniyakh* (Spb, 1880), 24–5, 37–9, 63.

[84] *SSSpSG*, i, *Samarskii uezd* (1883), 1st pagn, 39. 'Beggars' allotments' were common in Samara province. David Moon, *The Abolition of Serfdom in Russia 1762–1907* (Harlow, 2001), 101.

[85] *SSSpSG*, iii, *Buzulukskii uezd* (1885), 48–9, 199.

[86] GASO, f.3, op.233, d.1000 (1891), l.1ob.

droughts was stronger than in the past, probably because the soil had become poorer with nutrients and humus that was capable of retaining moisture.[87] The problem continued in the early twentieth century. The Peasant Land Bank was concerned to prevent the 'rapacious exploitation' of its land by leaseholders, some of whom had been ignoring regulations on crop rotations and fallowing, and thus exhausting the land.[88]

On the Don there were debates about whether the soil was becoming exhausted due to the simple farming techniques of many local farmers, who paid little attention to systematic fallowing or use of fertilizers. The careless techniques of commercial farmers who leased Cossack Host reserve land for short terms, and thus had no stake in it, were blamed for exhausting the soil in the General Staff survey of 1863.[89] Writing in the 1880s, however, Semen Nomikosov refuted the notion that the soil in the Don region was becoming exhausted, albeit with the exception of peasant allotment land. He pointed to the continued use of long-fallow agriculture, under which no more than a fifth of the arable land was sown with grain in any one year, as evidence for an a priori argument that the soil could not be exhausted.[90] The proportion of the arable land that was cultivated in any one year, however, was changing. In 1894–5, the authorities on the Don received permission from the Ministry of Agriculture to increase the proportion of the land they leased out that could be cultivated to one third, in spite of concerns that this could lead to soil exhaustion.[91] The Maslakovets Commission on measures to raise productivity of Don Cossack land in late 1890s considered the question of soil exhaustion. K. A. Kartushin described how in the past, 'land, which from the time of Noah had accumulated productive forces' had given high yields even to unskilful farmers. Land that had been farmed almost every year, however, was no longer so productive, and in some places was already 'used up'.[92] In A. M. Grekov's assessment of the needs of agriculture on the Don in 1905, he stated that land which had been cultivated for too long without rest or being used for pasture was becoming 'ploughed out' (*vypakhany*) to the extent that in dry years, harvests did not return the amount of grain sown.[93]

Russian scientists tried to understand what was happening to the fertility of the black earth. By the mid-nineteenth century, many were familiar with the theory of the German chemist Justus von Liebig that soil fertility was due to

[87] 'Besedy', 124.
[88] GASO, f.149, op.1, d.296, ll.46–ob., 65–9ob. See also f.149, op.9, d.84, ll.18ob.–19ob.; f.5, op.11, d.102 (1909), l.27ob.
[89] *MDGSR: Zemlya voiska donskogo*, N. Krasnov (comp.) (Spb, 1863), 40.
[90] Semen Nomikosov, *Statisticheskoe opisanie oblasti voiska Donskogo* (Novocherkassk, 1884), 210.
[91] RGIA, f.382, op.2, 1894, d.1291, ll.5–8.
[92] GARO, f.46, op.1, d.3282 (1898), l.1.
[93] Grekov, 'Nuzhdy Dona', 37.

mineral nutrients, in particular carbon and nitrogen, which became exhausted through cultivation and needed to be returned by applying mineral fertilizer. His book *Organic Chemistry in its Application to Agriculture and Physiology*, published in 1840, was translated into Russian and published by the Ministry of State Domains in 1842. It had great influence on Russian agricultural science. Olga Elina has argued that Liebig's work enjoyed a peak of popularity in Russia in the 1860s and 1870s, when there was a wave of interest in the sciences and the abolition of serfdom brought problems in agriculture to prominence.[94] Liebig's theory was regularly discussed in leading Russian periodicals.[95]

The agronomist Aleksandr Shishkin, who was educated in Moscow, St Petersburg, and abroad in Europe in the 1860s, was influenced by Liebig's theory. At a congress of farmers in Moscow in 1896, he reported his findings on whether Russia was 'threatened by soil exhaustion'. He concluded that on farms in the steppe region which had exploited reserves of 'virgin soil', if no more than one-fifth of the total area was cultivated each year, then yields had remained stable. If the proportion sown with grain every year was increased to a quarter or a third, however, then crop yields fell very quickly. He attributed this to the exhaustion of the 'reserve of soil wealth' which had accumulated naturally.[96] By the end of the nineteenth century a number of Russian scientists believed that the fertility of soil in fields where grain was sown regularly without manuring was declining as mineral nutrients were used up. Only mineral fertilizers could restore fertility.[97]

Other scientists, including Izmail'skii (see above, pp. 153–6) and Pavel Kostychev (see above, p. 112), had an alternative explanation for declining yields. They were especially interested in land in the steppe region that had been brought into cultivation for the first time or was returned to cultivation after a period of long fallow. They argued that the loss of soil fertility after several years of grain cultivation was progressive, but temporary. The soil was losing not mineral nutrients, but its structure that enabled it to hold the moisture that crops needed.[98] In the late 1880s and 1890s, Kostychev investigated the soil in long-fallow fields in parts of the steppe region. He concluded that crop yields on virgin steppe declined after a few years on account not just of the loss of soil structure, but also the growth of weeds which followed the removal of the wild vegetation.

[94] Justus Liebig, *Organic Chemistry in its Application to Agriculture and Physiology* (London, 1840). On the Russian translation and its reception, see Ol'ga Elina, *Ot tsarskikh sadov do sovetskikh polei: istoriya sel'sko-khozyaistvennykh opytnykh uchrezhdenii XVIII-20-e gody XX v.*, 2 vols (Moscow, 2008), i, 198–201.

[95] See, for example, A. Lyudogovskii, 'Ob istoshchenii i statiistike plodorodiya pochvy, po predstavleniyam sovremennoi teorii zemledeliya', *TVEO*, 2 (1864), 467–82; '(Okonchanie)', 3 (1864), 1–27.

[96] 'Letopis' sel'skogo khoyaistva', *SKhiL*, 181 (1896), 459–60. On Shishkin, see *ES*, 79 (1903), 607.

[97] S. K. Bogushevskii, *Neurozhai i istoshchenie zemel': Issledovanie po voprosu o prichinakh istoshcheniya plodorodiya pochv* (Yur'ev, 1900), 203–4.

[98] Bogushevskii, *Neurozhai*, 204.

In order for the soil to regain its structure, and hence fertility, it needed to be left fallow for fifteen–twenty years to allow the original vegetation to return.[99]

As in other areas of debate about environmental change, there was significant disagreement over whether the soil was indeed becoming exhausted. Arguments on both sides assigned a role to human activities. There was a third line of argument, however, that blamed 'nature', not people. Some scientists argued that the soil was not becoming exhausted, but that the crucial factor in the productivity of the land was the availability of moisture that crops needed. This was critical in years of drought, and explained why the size of the harvest varied so sharply between regions that had been hit by drought and those that had not. The case for the pre-eminence of drought, rather than soil exhaustion, as the main cause of the harvest failure in 1891 was made by many contributors to the debate in the Free Economic Society in late 1891.[100] It was also made by American economic historian James Y. Simms who attacked the notion that there was a crisis in Russian agriculture in this period.[101] Thus, in this interpretation, it was the climate not the soil that was the crucial factor.

DESERTIFICATION

Taken together, the various anxieties about environmental change in the steppe region–including deforestation, climate change, soil erosion, and soil exhaustion—developed into an even greater worry that the entire steppe region in the European part of the Russian Empire was turning into a desert. This was the concern expressed by Vladimir Solov'ev in the immediate aftermath of the drought of 1891 quoted in the introduction to this part of this book. Such fears were often expressed in years of drought. In 1885, the official responsible for administering 'nomadic peoples' in eastern Stavropol' province reported:

On account of the intense heat wave in ... April, the easterly winds which blew constantly, and the complete lack of rain, the pasture on the steppe occupied by the ... Nogai is in a very poor condition. The grass has dried up to such an extent that huge areas are devoid of any vegetation and have turned into a desert. I have not seen anything like this in the spring months ...; even along the Kuma river the fodder is very poor and there is little water in the river. If it does not rain and new grass does not grow, then the [nomads]

---

[99] P. Kostychev, 'Iz putevykh zametok: Perelozhnye khozyaistva s kratkosrochnymi zalezhami', *SKhiL*, 161 (1889), 2nd pagn, 337–52. He repeated his argument in the Free Economic Society in late 1891. 'Besedy', 110–12; and in *O bor'be s zasukhoi v chernozemnoi oblasti posredstvom obrabotki polei i nakopleniya na nikh snega* (Spb, 1893), 76–8; I. A. Krupenikov, *Pavel Andreevich Kostychev* (Moscow, 1987), 154–6. See also above, pp. 111–13.

[100] 'Besedy', *passim*; Bogushevskii, *Neurozhai i istoshchenie zemel'*, 204–14.

[101] James Y. Simms, The Crop Failure of 1891: Soil Exhaustion, Technological Backwardness, and Russia's "Agrarian Crisis", *SR*, 41 (1982), 236–50.

will have to move onto cossack land, on which the pasture is very good and in abundance.[102]

The fear of desertification had been expressed earlier in the century, after the serious drought and crop failure of 1833. A forestry specialist expressed the view that with the destruction of forests, soil lost its fertility, and land became depopulated, like the deserts of Africa and Asia, which he stated had once been fertile and populated.[103]

Fears of desertification and the malign influence of 'Asia' were also expressed in years where the rains and harvest had not failed. In 1879, Achilles Alferaki, an estate owner from Taganrog, wrote:

The Central Asian steppe is advancing, slowly but surely, towards us and is threatening finally to devour the fertile plains of southern Russia. Where there was once the rich and abundant Little Russian 'steppe', a steppe which has been burnt by the sun with all its horrors is establishing itself: lack of fertility, lack of water, [and conditions that are] harmful to raising livestock. . . . We have done nothing and are doing nothing in order to stop its advance; on the contrary, we are opening the gates wide by destroying all barriers that are in its way.[104]

Like many others, Alferaki was attributing the threat of desertification to deforestation. Palimpsestov had similar fears that deforestation could cause the climate of the steppes to become like that of parts of Africa and Asia. He was concerned not just about the consequences for agriculture, but also the cultural identity of the steppes, which, he asserted, were 'our blood inheritance', that had been 'returned to us' by Catherine the Great.[105] The views of such writers as these implied that forests and fertile steppes were somehow 'Russian' or 'European', while arid land was 'Asiatic'. If the fears of desertification were realized, moreover, the agricultural settlement of the region by Russians, Ukrainians, and foreign colonists would fail. The steppes would become a 'desert' in both senses of the word. The meaning of the Russian word '*pustynya*', in a similar manner to the English word 'desert', changed over the late nineteenth and early twentieth centuries from an uninhabited place, a region empty of people, to a region with little water and sparse vegetation.[106] In the view of the more pessimistic

---

[102] GASK, f.101, op.4, d.1510 [1885], l.38. It eventually rained on 30 May. GASK, f.101, op.4, d.1510 [1885], l.73. See also *Obzor Stavropol'skoi gubernii za 1885 god* (Stavropol', 1886), 2.

[103] Breitenbakh, 'O pol'ze lesov', 385.

[104] A. Alferaki, *O polozhenii sel'skogo khozyaistva v yugo-vostochnom krae* (Spb, 1879, 15).

[105] I. Palimpsestov, *Stepi iuga Rossii byli-li iskoni vekov stepami i vozmozhno-li oblesit' ikh?*, revised edn (Odessa, 1890), 264.

[106] See *Slovar' russkogo yazyka XI-XVII vv.*, xxi, ed. G. A. Bogatova (Moscow, 1995), 60; *Tolkovyi slovar' zhivogo velikorusskogo yazyka*, comp. Vladimir Dal', 4 vols (Moscow, 1955), iii, 542; *Entsiklopedicheskii slovar'*, 7th edn, 34 (Moscow: Granat, n.d.), 104; *Slovar' sovremennogo russkogo literaturnogo yazyka*, 17 vols (Moscow, 1950–65), xi, 60. See also Willard Sunderland, *Taming the Wild Field: Colonization and Empire on the Russian Steppe* (Ithaca, NY, 2004), 70–1, 206.

observers, especially at times of drought and crop failure, therefore, the steppes were facing a shortage of water, vegetation, and people.

CONCLUSION TO PART II

Anxieties about the changing environment were greatest during or in the aftermath of the catastrophic droughts and crop failures that hit the region, in particular those of 1833 and 1891, but also in other years. The recurring disasters prompted discussion about what was happening, or seemed to be happening, to the steppe environment among scientists, agricultural specialists, the authorities in the region and in St Petersburg, and members of the local population. At the heart of their concerns were the prospects for arable farming on the fertile, but drought-prone, land. The more alarmed people became, the more attention they paid to seeking to understand environment change in the region.

Contemporaries were concerned about changes that were directly and evidently caused by human actions, and those that may have been 'natural' or an indirect consequence of the activities of the population. The former included removing much of the steppe vegetation, in particular the small areas of woodland that had sheltered the land from the easterly winds and the wild grasses whose roots had bound the soil. Over time, many scientists and other specialists came to believe that, to varying degrees, human activity in changing the vegetation cover was a direct or indirect cause of climate change, soil erosion, falling levels of ground water, soil exhaustion, and ultimately the transformation of parts of the region into desert. Russian scientists were well aware of developments in science abroad, but also made original contributions to science, and made major strides in disentangling aspects of environmental change that were caused by human activity from those that were not. The long debate over whether the climate was changing and, if so, whether people were to blame, serves a good example. By end of the nineteenth century, many scientists and others, in Russia and elsewhere, believed climate change to be cyclical and caused by autogenic, rather than progressive and anthropogenic.

Scientists and others sometimes betrayed their anger at what they saw as the careless actions of the population as well as offering dispassionate analysis. Shtukenberg commented on the Black Sea Cossack territory (later part of the Kuban' region) in the North Caucasus: 'Nature here gives everything to man, but he himself does nothing! Beautiful oak forests have been laid to waste . . . '.[107] I. M. Krasnoperov, the author of a *zemstvo* study of Novyi Uzen' district in southern Samara province in 1890, wrote:

---

[107] [Shtukenberg], *Statisticheskii trudy*, i, article 3, 'Opisanie Stavropol'skoi gubernii s zemleyu Chernomorskikh kazakov', 39.

Undoubtedly, man by his rapacious management, by his reckless attitude to nature and its . . . riches has intensified even more the effect of the destructive, elemental forces of nature. Everywhere, steppe has yielded to fields. Axe and plough have terribly altered the flora and fauna of the region. The ploughing up of the soil has had a huge impact on the hydrology . . .'[108]

Ivanov made a more subtle point in his devastating account of the impact of Russian colonization on nature in the North Caucasus. He noted that the settlers had moved mostly from central Russia, from where they had brought their attitudes and practices. Thus, they made wasteful use of water, which was plentiful where they came from, but scarce in the steppe region. The settlers grazed their livestock on sandy soil without respite, denuding it of vegetation, and leaving it open to wind erosion. In contrast, the indigenous, nomadic peoples had not pastured their herds in one place for long, and so the vegetation had been able to grow back. The settlers had destroyed the forests, which were abundant where they came from, but in short supply in the steppe region. They had ploughed up and cultivated excessive amounts of land, and ignored local agricultural practices. The speed of agricultural settlement, moreover, had exacerbated the problems, and weakened the land. The balance with nature had been violated, with serious consequences, making the 'struggle with nature' harder with each year. Fathers had sought to enrich themselves at the expense of the natural resources, with fatal consequences for their children and grandchildren. Ivanov was aware how negative his conclusions were, and acknowledged that they had been coloured by the fact that his visit to the region had coincided with the drought of 1885.[109]

Deciding who was to blame for environmental change was not the only concern. K. A. Kartushin, a member of the Maslakovets commission in the Don region in the late 1890s, considered changes in cossack farming over time and concluded: 'Besides economic parallels between former times and the present, I could also pursue climatic [ones]. But, enough: recollections about the past will not help. It is necessary to think what is to be done. . . .'[110]

---

[108] *SSSpSG*, vii, *Novouzenskii uezd* (1890), 11.
[109] Ivanov, 'Vliyanie', 249–54.
[110] GARO, f.46, op.1, 3282 (1898), l.1ob.

PART III

COMBATING THE STEPPE ENVIRONMENT?

INTRODUCTION: WHAT IS TO BE DONE?

In his study of the Don region of 1884, Semen Nomikosov was aware that human activity was having an impact on the environment, but firmly believed that the solution was more human intervention with the aim of 'subjugating' nature.[1] If human action could cause or contribute to changes that made conditions in the steppe region less favourable for arable farming, then what was to be done was further action to halt or reverse the changed. Human intervention, many specialists hoped, could also assist in overcoming the perennial problem of the shortage of water in the region. Writing in the journal of the Southern Russian Agricultural Society in 1877, K. Gorskii argued:

The steppe is destined by nature to be steppe and it will stubbornly resist all measures which aim to change its character. The reasons for this resistance are the geographical position of the steppe in relation to the air currents, the surrounding landmasses and waters, their topography, geological structure, and the characteristics of the soils. From these arise all the difficulties in afforesting and irrigating the steppe. It stands to reason that the obstacles presented by nature, given the present reserves of human experience and knowledge, with colossal mechanical resources, cannot be considered insurmountable.[2]

What Gorskii and other specialists wanted to do was to change the steppe environment.

They were expressing similar notions of 'conquering nature' to their counterparts elsewhere in this period, and anticipating the colossal schemes of the twentieth century, in the Soviet Union and other parts of the world, to use science and engineering to transform nature to human designs.[3]

---

[1] Semen Nomikosov, *Statisticheskoe opisanie oblasti voiska Donskogo* (Novocherkassk, 1884), 215.

[2] K. Gorskii, 'K voprosu ob oroshenii polei v yuzhnoi Rossii', *ZIOSKhYuR*, 3 (1877), 19.

[3] David Blackbourn, *The Conquest of Nature: Water, Landscape, and the Making of Modern Germany* (New York, 2006); Paul R. Josephson, *Industrialized Nature: Brute Force Technology and the Transformation of the Natural World* (Washington, DC, 2002).

Gorskii also argued that overcoming the natural obstacles to grain cultivation on the steppes required a 'close familiarity with their distinct nature'.[4] Indeed, acquiring a 'close familiarity' with the nature of the steppes had been the aim of naturalists and scientists since the Academy of Sciences expeditions of 1768–74. The growing numbers of university-trained Russian specialists and scientists carried on this work. Thus, by the second half of the nineteenth century, anxieties about environmental change and natural barriers to the development of agriculture on the steppes were to some extent matched by a sense that, armed with knowledge derived from experimental science, people could regulate and control nature for their own purposes.

As we have seen, many Russians contrasted the abundance of forests and water in northern and central Russia with the shortage of both in the steppe region. From this perspective, the solution to the environmental 'obstacles' to farming on the steppes was simple: plant more trees and irrigate the fields.[5] Trees were to be planted in the belief that forests would moderate the climate and provide shelter from the drying effects of the winds. Artificial irrigation was to provide water directly to the fields. A recurring word in the extensive literature on dealing with the barriers posed by the steppe environment was '*bor'ba*', the Russian word for 'struggle' or 'combat'. The term '*bor'ba s zasukhami*', which can translated as either 'the struggle with droughts' or 'combating droughts', was repeated time and again as Russians sought to deploy trees and irrigation ditches in their efforts to fight against droughts by changing the steppe environment. There was a third approach to addressing the barriers to arable farming in the steppe environment: agronomy, in particular, techniques of cultivating the soil to conserve the scarce moisture. The three approaches—tree planting, irrigation, and agronomy—were not mutually exclusive. Many plans advocated the use of all three. Vasilii Dokuchaev was one of several specialists who proposed a combined plan in the aftermath of the drought and crop failure of 1891.[6] Other specialists were more focused. Pavel Kostychev advocated cultivation techniques and accumulating snow to provide melt water in the spring to combat droughts.[7]

There was also a fourth way of dealing with the consequences of the recurring droughts and crop failures: providing insurance by building up reserves of grain and

    [4] Gorskii, 'K voprosu', 19.
    [5] See, for example, A. Zabudskii, 'O zasukhakh na yuge i o sredstvakh k sokhraneniyu i uvelicheniyu syrosti v nashikh stepyakh', *TVEO*, 1 (1870), 8–23; S. Lavrent'ev, 'Po voprosu ob ustranenii stepnykh zasukh', *TVEO*, 3 (1875), 436–43; I. A. Lishin, *K voprosu obvodneniya i obleseniya stepnoi polosy Samarskoi gubernii* (Moscow, 1892); Nomikosov, *Statisticheskoe opisanie*, 215.
    [6] V. V. Dokuchaev, 'Nashi stepi prezhde i teper', *Sochineniya*, 9 vols (Moscow and Leningrad, 1949–61), vi, 87–96, 112–18. See also P. Barakov, *O vozmozhnykh merakh bor'by s zasukhami* (Odessa, 1892); [A. S. Ermolov], *Neurozhai i narodnoe bedstvie* (Spb, 1892); *Trudy Imperatorskogo Moskovskogo obshchestva Sel'skogo Khozyaistva*, 30 (1892), review in *SKhiL*, 172 (1892), 61–6.
    [7] P. Kostychev, *O bor'be s zasukhoi v chernozemnoi oblasti postredstvom obrabotki polei i nakopleniya na nikh snega* (Spb, 1893). See also I. A. Krupenikov, *Pavel Andreevich Kostychev 1845–1895* (Moscow, 1987), 152–9.

funds to dispense as aid in times of dearth. Indeed, the Russian authorities invested considerable resources in providing relief and organising public works during serious crises.[8] Attention in the next three chapters, however, will focus on the 'environmental' approaches of planting trees, artificial irrigation, and agronomy.

Key players in the 'struggle with droughts' and other environmental barriers to the development of agriculture on the steppes included foreign colonists, especially the Mennonites, and improving estate owners. An important role in advising them was played by agricultural societies, in particular the Free Economic Society, the Forestry Society, and the Southern Russian Agricultural Society. The government in St Petersburg reorganized its ministries in part in response to problems in the steppe region. One of the reasons for the establishment of the Ministry of State Domains in 1837 was the state of agriculture exposed by the drought and harvest failure of 1833. The similar events in 1891, moreover, were factors in the reorganisation of the ministry as the Ministry of Agriculture in 1894.[9]

In years of drought, provincial governors, atamans of cossack territories, and, from the late nineteenth century, *zemstva* pressed the government for assistance. They repeatedly requested support for afforestation and irrigation, which they saw as the best means to avert future disasters. In 1891, for example, the *zemstva* of the badly hit provinces of Samara and Saratov sought support for public works to plant trees and set up irrigation systems.[10] In his report for the previous year, which he submitted to St Petersburg in October 1891, the governor of Samara reported another poor harvest caused by lack of rainfall and heat waves. He continued that repeated bad harvests were undermining the economic well-being of the population, and could make agriculture impossible. The main solutions he advocated were planting trees and providing water by artificial irrigation. Tsar Alexander III was sufficiently impressed to note 'This is a serious issue' in the margin of the report. The tsar's note prompted action: the matter was sent to the Minister of State Domains.[11] This seems to have set in motion the process that culminated in government funding for Dokuchaev's scientific expedition to the steppes in the 1890s. The work conducted by the expedition is a very important example of experimentation into ways of overcoming the barriers to agricultural development on the steppes on the basis of scientific research into the environment (see above, pp. 53–5).

[8] See A. S. Ermolov, *Nashi neurozhai i prodovol'stvennyi vopros*, 2 vols (Spb, 1909). As Richard G. Robbins has shown, the tsarist government's reputation for neglecting famine relief is undeserved. *Famine in Russia, 1891–1892: The Imperial Government Responds to a Crisis* (New York, 1975).

[9] O. Yu. Elina, *Ot tsarskikh sadov do sovetskikh polei: istoriya sel'sko-khozyaistvennykh opytnykh uchrezhdenii XVIII-20-e gody XX v.*, 2 vols (Moscow, 2008), ii, 256–7.

[10] RGIA, f.426, op.1, 1894, d.55, ll.8–10, 52–7; I. A. Lishin, *Prilozhenie k zapiske kommissii po obvodneniyu i obleseniyu stepnoi polosy Samarskoi gubernii* (Samara, 1891).

[11] GASO, f.3, op.233, 1890, d.1000, ll.1–ob., 2ob.–3ob.; RGIA, f.1284, op.233, 1891, d.195, l.1; f.387, op.28, 1892, d.1023, ll.5–6; f.426, op.1, 1894, d.55, l.38.

In her study of the development of agricultural experimentation in Russia, Olga Elina assessed the relative roles of monarchical, private, public, and state initiative over time. She traced the origins back to herbal gardens established by monasteries, grand dukes and tsars, in central Russia over the twelfth to seventeenth centuries. In the seventeenth century, Tsar Alexis set up a model farm at Izmailovo outside Moscow. This was where his son, Peter, first became acquainted with agronomy, which he went on to promote. Over the eighteenth and nineteenth centuries, as the centre of gravity of Russian settlement and agriculture moved south, increasing attention was paid to cultivating the fertile soil of the steppes. The eighteenth century was the heyday of aristocrats as patrons of botany. This period also saw the start of experiments with crops and farming techniques by improving estate owners, such as Andrei Bolotov on his estate near Tula in the forest-steppe region. The foundations were laid for agricultural education towards the end of the eighteenth century. Institutions of research and higher education, together with agricultural societies, gradually assumed the initiative in promoting agronomy and experimental work. The *zemstva* took an interest in agronomy from the end of the 1880s. It was only at the end of the nineteenth century and in the early twentieth century, Elina argued, that the central government became the main driving force in organizing agronomy and research. One of the spurs was the disaster of 1891–2. The last decades of the tsarist regime saw a considerable expansion in the numbers of agricultural experiment stations, including some in the steppe region.[12] The Appanage Department, for example, founded a research station at Bezenchuk, in Samara province, in 1903.[13] The results of its research were applied by the Peasant Land Bank, which took over the Appanage Department's estates in 1908, when it put the land in order before selling it on to peasants.[14]

Elina emphasized the international context in which agronomy and experimentation developed in Russia. From the seventeenth century, estate owners and specialists absorbed influences from Western Europe. At the end of the nineteenth century, however, the authorities drew heavily on the experience of American agricultural experiment stations in setting up a network in Russia.[15] The Ministry of State Domains was keen to participate in an exchange of scientific literature proposed by the American government in 1867.[16] Over the nineteenth century, however, Russian agricultural sciences for the steppe region increasingly drew on practical experience and experimentation in the region. From the mid-nineteenth century, in particular, the research was carried out by

---

[12] Elina, *Ot tsarskikh sadov*.

[13] I. Klingen and Ya. Zhukov, 'Udel'naya oblastnaya sel'kokhozyaistvennaya opytnaya stantsiya', *SKhiL*, 225 (1907), 179–207.

[14] GASO, f.149, op.9, d.84; N. A. Ustina, *Krest'yanskii pozemel'nyi bank v srednem povolzh'e (1885–1917 gg.)* (Samara, 2003).

[15] Elina, *Ot tsarskikh sadov*, ii, 65–71. See also PFA RAN, f.184, op.1, d.138.

[16] RGIA, f.382, op.1, 1867, d.48.

Russian scientists who had received at least their initial training in Russian institutions (see above, pp. 49–53). In the process of devising ways of developing arable farming in the steppe environment, Russian agricultural specialists and scientists, such as Dokuchaev and Kostychev, came to realize that the European, in particular German, agricultural and forestry sciences Russians had been relying on were not the most appropriate for what they were trying to do. In their place, Russian agricultural specialists and scientists devised new agricultural and forestry approaches that were appropriate to the steppe environment.[17]

A key issue in developing new approaches for the steppes was research funding. Funds were usually tight in the Russian Empire, especially in the wake of wars. In the 1830s, Finance Minister Kankrin succeeded in balancing the budget, but was stringent in decisions on spending, including spending to address the drought and harvest failure of 1833.[18] There were similar constraints on spending in the 1890s, after the worst consequences of the disaster of 1891–2 had been mitigated. In the late nineteenth century, successive finance ministers assigned priority to industrial and commercial development over agriculture. This was very much the view of Sergei Witte, who served as finance minister from 1892 to 1903. He considered an economy based chiefly on agriculture to be 'backward'. His policy on agriculture was directed at supporting 'profitable estate landholding, agricultural and agronomical science, and general primary education' as the 'pathways' to 'real improvement.' He was sceptical about allocating too much money to agriculture in general and the 'combating droughts' in particular. At the start of his term as minister, in 1892, he vetoed a proposal to allocate large sums of money to public works to combat the threat of drought by planting trees and setting up irrigation systems. He wrote pithily 'with such energetic decisions about the allocation of revenues, the treasury would be deprived of both them and of bountiful harvests'.[19] As we shall see, however, the government allocated significant sums to research into tree planting and irrigation in the first half of the 1890s. But, it advanced smaller sums, in loans, to estate owners and peasant communities for 'melioration', or improvements, in the late 1890s and early twentieth century.[20]

Thus, the main methods advocated to combat the vagaries of, and changes in, the steppe environment were planting trees, artificial irrigation, and agronomy. Planting trees and irrigation were perhaps natural responses by people—settlers, officials of the local and central authorities, and scientists—who for the most part

---

[17] Stephen Brain, *Song of the Forest: Russian Forestry and Stalinist Environmentalism, 1905–1953* (Pittsburgh, PA, 2011), 37–8.

[18] W. M. Pintner, *Russian Economic Policy under Nicholas I* (Ithaca, NY, 1967).

[19] Francis W. Wcislo, *Tales of Imperial Russia: The Life and Times of Sergei Witte, 1849–1915* (Oxford, 2011), 111–12, 141, 154. See also V. S. Dyakin, *Den'gi dlya sel'skogo khozyaistva, 1892–1914: agrarnyi kredit v ekonomicheskoi politike tsarizma* (Spb, 1997).

[20] Z. S. Katsenelenbaum, 'Meliorativnyi kredit v Rossii i ego blizhaishiya zadachi', *SKhiL*, 234 (1910), 479–505.

came from, or were the descendants of migrants from, regions where forests and water were in abundance. The aim was to change the steppe environment, by planting more trees and supplying more water, to make conditions closer to those they were accustomed to elsewhere. The agronomical approach was different. Rather than combating the steppe environment by trying to change it, the aim was to devise ways of working the land that conserved the scarce moisture so that crops could grow. Advocates of the agronomical approach, therefore, accepted the wider environmental conditions in the steppe region, in particular the shortage of water. They sought to make most effective and sustainable use of the very fertile soil that, as Dokuchaev showed in the late nineteenth century, had evolved in precisely those conditions. Earlier efforts to 'combat' the steppe environment, however, focused on planting trees.

6

Planting Trees

INTRODUCTION

Planting trees was the opposite of what had been happening since the start of large-scale agricultural settlement of the steppe region in the eighteenth century. The growing settler population felled much of the small areas of woodland that grew in certain locations in the region. The land was thus exposed to the elements: the winds from the east and south-east that dried out the soil and blew it away in dust storms; the erosive action of downpours of rain in the summer and melt water in the spring that rushed through ravines and gullies; and the blistering summer sun. Some contemporaries made a connection between the destruction of woodland and the frequent recurrence of droughts. From at least the 1830s, prompted by the catastrophic drought and harvest failure of 1833, arguments were advanced in Russia that planting trees would make the climate more moderate, and wetter, and protect against erosion, amongst other advantages. These arguments were based on the work of geographers such as Alexander von Humboldt and other foreign specialists, which in turn was based on experience in Europe and Europe's overseas colonies. Thus, in Russia, in seeking to 'combat' the vicissitudes of the steppe environment and changes that seemed to be making it less favourable for arable farming, some settlers, officials, specialists, and scientists advocated conservation of the remaining woodland and, above all, planting trees.

There was more to it than that. Advocates of planting trees on the steppe region were seeking—sometimes perhaps subconsciously—to recreate the forested environment many of them or their forebears had come from and that played a large role in Russian culture and identity. Like settlers in some of Europe's colonies around the globe, migrants to the steppes did not just transplant themselves to their new homes. They tried to replicate their familiar way of life. In most cases, this meant arable farming and using forest products, such as timber and firewood, for many everyday needs. To achieve this, some settlers and the Russian authorities also wanted to recreate on the steppes the forested Russia (or Germany) they were accustomed to. The scientists who advised them drew heavily on foreign, in particular German, forestry science.

The Russian 'Code on Forests' of 1802 required the Forestry Department of the new Ministry of Finance to establish forestry schools.[1] Right from the start, Russian forestry education was dominated by Germans and the theory and practice of German forestry. Long into the nineteenth century, the directors and instructors in the St Petersburg Forestry Institute were mainly Germans, as were most of the students in the early years.[2] The emphasis on Western European, in particular German, forestry continued after the Forestry Department was transplanted to the new Ministry of State Domains in 1837.[3] Into the twentieth century, aspiring Russian foresters usually spent a year or two studying in Germany.[4] Nevertheless, from at least the 1840s, doubts were raised about the relevance of German forestry to Russia. In 1841, Baron Wrangel (a Russian official from a prominent Baltic German family) noted that measures to improve forestry, including planting and regenerating forests, had not succeeded in Russia because the German foresters who managed the Russian forests did so according to the principles of German forestry, which were not appropriate to the climate and conditions of Russia.[5] German forestry was even less appropriate in the steppe region.

Steppe forestry was informed by the debates over the past extent of forest cover in the region, and whether the environmental conditions were suitable for trees. Men such as Ivan Palimpsestov believed the steppes had once been forested, and that the previous inhabitants had destroyed the trees. From this perspective, planting trees was re-forestation, and would not present great difficulties as the steppe environment was, apparently, well suited to them. On the other hand, some specialists, including Vasilii Dokuchaev and his colleagues, believed that, except for particular locations in the region, the steppes had always been grasslands on account of environmental conditions that were not suitable for trees. Planting trees on the steppes, from this perspective, was afforestation, and would entail considerable research and experimentation to achieve (see above, pp. 60–2).

The numbers of trained Russian foresters who could carry out such work grew over the nineteenth century. Even though their training was based on a German-inspired syllabus, they applied and adapted German forestry to Russian conditions. By the early twentieth century, Grigorii Morozov, who had worked with Dokuchaev, was strongly urging the development of Russian forestry for Russian forests.[6] In the steppe region, the development of forestry appropriate

---

[1] *PSZ*, 1, xxvii, 350–6 (no.20,506, 11 November 1802), 352–3.

[2] Stephen Brain, *Song of the Forest: Russian Forestry and Stalinist Environmentalism, 1905–1953* (Pittsburgh, PA, 2011), 12–17.

[3] A. E. Karimov, *Dokuda topor i sokha khodili: ocherki istorii zemel'nogo i lesnogo kadastra v Rossii XVI-nachala XX veka* (Moscow, 2007), 128–9.

[4] Brain, *Song of the Forest*, 16.

[5] V. Vrangel', 'Lesnoe zakonodatel'stvo v Rossii', *ZhMGI*, 3 (1841), 2nd pagn, 140–1.

[6] Brain, *Song of the Forest*, 8–10, 31–3, 39–40, 86–7.

to the local conditions was greatly aided by the establishment of forestry plantations by the Ministry of State Domains in the 1840s. The most important was at Velikii Anadol' in eastern Ekaterinoslav province. The plantations built on the achievements of some earlier efforts to grow trees on the steppes, for example by Mennonite colonists. The foresters in the plantations also learned from the many attempts that had failed. Later in the century, trained foresters, such as Nestor Genko, a Baltic German who worked for the Appanage Department,[7] and Grigorii Vysotskii, a colleague of Dokuchaev's,[8] applied their learning to conditions on the steppes, and reached differing conclusions. Genko believed that large-scale afforestation was possible. Vysotskii was more sceptical, and argued that smaller-scale tree planting for more specific purposes, such as combating erosion, was all that could be achieved in the steppe environment.

There was much attention to protection of woodland in the steppe region. The Code on Forests of 1802 contained provisions on conservation.[9] Provisions to protect cossack forests were included in the statute for the Don Cossack territory of 1835.[10] In 1839, the Ministry of State Domains established a 'corps of foresters', staffed by graduates of the Forestry Institute, whose duties included forest protection.[11] In 1888, the government issued a new Statute on Safeguarding Forests for the whole of the European part of the empire.[12] Nevertheless, the continued destruction of woodland in the steppe region showed the limitations of the measures that aimed to protect it (see above, pp. 98–111). Many contemporaries felt the best remedy for the shortage and declining areas of woodland was to plant more trees. In the late 1870s, Yakov Veinberg called for planting trees, in particular in the steppe region, which for centuries had been 'condemned to treelessness and droughts'. He continued:

If . . . the human hand in some cases acts counter to nature, paralyzes its forces and scorns its gifts, then fortunately there is no doubt that this same hand can assist nature, can change in the favourable sense the physical conditions, and in certain cases completely alter them.[13]

---

[7] V. T. Sobichevskii, 'Pamyati Nestora Karlovicha Genko', *LZh*, 1 (1904), 1–6.

[8] 'Georgii Nikolaevich Vysotskii i ego trudy (avtobiografiya)', in *Izbrannye sochineniya*, 2 vols (Moscow, 1962), i, 11–32.

[9] *PSZ*, 1, xxvii, 350–6 (no.20,506, 11 November 1802).

[10] *PSZ*, 2, x (no.8163, 26 May 1835), 77, art.36, 78, art.46, 88, arts 209–17.

[11] *Stoletie uchrezhdeniya lesnogo departamenta, 1798–1898* (Spb, 1898), 83–8, 103–5.

[12] *PSZ*, 3, viii, 148–56 (no.5120, 4 April 1888); Brian Bonhomme, *Forests, Peasants, and Revolutionaries: Forest Conservation and Organization in Soviet Russia, 1917–1929* (Boulder, CO, 2005), 22–6.

[13] Ya. Veinberg, *Les: znachenie ego v prirode i mery k ego sokhraneniyu* (Moscow, 1884), 545.

THE BENEFITS OF FORESTS

Veinberg was referring to the belief that became widespread in Russia and elsewhere in the world during the eighteenth and nineteenth centuries that forests bestowed a range of benefits on the environment, and on people who lived forested regions. The environmental benefits of forests mirrored the problems thought to ensue from their destruction. In Russia, the benefits were first raised by members of the Free Economic Society from its foundation in 1765 and the leaders of the Academy of Sciences expeditions of 1768–74. The perceived benefits of forests informed government policy in Russia. Not all specialists agreed in the virtues of forests, however, and doubts grew during the nineteenth century. Nevertheless, discussions of the value of forests in Russia were more intense, and their advantages more strongly advocated, at times of droughts, crop failures, and dust storms. In the wake of the serious drought of 1833, the Russian *Forestry Journal* published a number of articles on the benefits of forests. Breitenbach, the German-born director of the Forestry Institute in St Petersburg, asserted that 'nature' had provided forests in order to supply people with timber for fuel, building materials, and other uses. In addition, forests existed to calm the weather, attract clouds, and serve as windbreaks.[14]

The Mennonites of Molotschna in Tauride province believed in the advantages of trees as a result both of their practical experience and reading the specialist literature. In 1830, the Guardianship Committee which supervised foreign settlers in Russia set up a forestry society under the enterprising Johann Cornies. Under his leadership, the society collected a library of books on forestry in German and Russian.[15] At first, the Mennonites planted trees in low-lying areas. By the early 1840s, however, Cornies and others were convinced that it would also be possible to plant trees on the bare, high steppes, where they would 'improve the air, [and] serve as shelter for grain fields from cold and hot winds'.[16] They further believed that trees would increase the fertility of their land by

---

[14] Breitenbakh, 'O pol'ze lesov v prirode', *LZh*, 1 (1835), 383–91. See also Ledebur, 'O razvedenii lesov po beregam Chernogo morya dlya preduprezhdeniya zasukh', *LZh*, 2 (1834), 173–7; 'O vliyanii lesov i istrebleniya onykh na klimat', *LZh*, 1 (1837), 427–42; 'O vliyanii lesov na klimat, reki i prozyabenie, i vrednykh posledstviyakh ikh istreblenya', *LZh*, 3 (1837), 325–50. Such arguments were repeated many, many times. See, for example, V. M. Chernyaev, *O lesakh Ukrainy: rech', proiznesennaya v torzhestvennoi sobranii imperatorskogo khar'kovskogo Universiteta, 1-go sentyabrya 1858 g.* (Moscow, 1858), 42–7.

[15] John R. Staples, *Cross-Cultural Encounters on the Ukrainian Steppe: Settling the Molochna Basin, 1783–1861* (Toronto, 2003), 114–16; James Urry, *None but Saints: The Transformation of Mennonite Life in Russia, 1789–1889* (Winnipeg, 1989), 108, 112–13.

[16] I. Kornis, 'O sostoyanii khozyaistva v Molochanskikh Menonistskikh koloniyakh v 1842 g.', *ZhMGI*, 8 (1843), 2nd pagn, 70–1.

attracting rain and moisture from the atmosphere, and by protecting the soil from heat waves, storms, and the cold.[17]

The Southern Russian Agricultural Society based in Odessa strongly promoted the benefits of forests. In 1846, its vice president extolled the need for forests in the steppe region. He asserted that they supplied moisture to the dry soil, produced water sources, provided natural barriers against the hot winds, supplied firewood, material for construction, and also altered the climate for the benefit of arable farming.[18] Two years later, Dmitrii Osten-Saken invited estate owners in New Russia to cultivate forests. He argued: 'In our region [which is] blessed with an abundance of rich soil, only one thing is lacking, forests to make the climate wetter and to obstruct the force of the wind. Then this region would have all advantages.'[19] One of the greatest enthusiasts for the advantages of planting trees on the steppes was Palimpsestov. In 1852, shortly after he moved to Odessa, he wrote a lengthy article arguing that in a forested New Russia, the uncertainty of agriculture would be reduced as the climate would be more moderate and, crucially, there would be more rainfall.[20]

The Ministry of State Domains also promoted tree planting because of the practical and environmental benefits that were believed to ensue.[21] In 1865, the ministry proposed sending a scientific expedition to the steppes of Tauride province, which had recently been vacated by their Tatar population, to prepare the land for Slav settlers. The proposal argued the need to conserve existing trees and plant more trees on the mountains in the Crimean peninsula in order to attract rain from the sea. Smaller-scale tree planting on the steppes to the north was advocated to provide shade to protect the moisture in the soil, springs, and streams from the heat of the sun. The proposal also noted, however, that there was disagreement over the benefits of forests.[22]

The belief in the benefits of forests persisted. Over the course of the second half of the nineteenth and early twentieth centuries, scientists continued to put forward arguments for the environmental significance of trees. They were based on detailed research, in Russia and abroad, and the growing practical experience of steppe forestry. A case for the benefits of afforestation of the steppe region was made by Veinberg in the late 1870s. He presented a detailed discussion of the current state of knowledge, among both Russian and foreign specialists, for example Humboldt, George Perkins Marsh, and contemporary French and

---

[17] I. Kornis, 'O sostoyanii khozyaistva v Molochanskikh Menonistskikh koloniyakh v 1843 g.', *ZhMGI*, 11 (1844), 2nd pagn, 136–7.

[18] M. P. Borovskii, *Istoricheskii obzor pyatidesyatiletnei deyatel'nosti Imperatorskogo Obshchestva Sel'skogo Khozyaistva Yuzhnoi Rossii s 1828 po 1878 god* (Odessa, 1878), 113.

[19] Dmitrii Osten-Saken, 'Priglashenie vladel'tsev imenii Novorossiiskogo kraya k edinodushnomu sposobstvovaniyu velikomu delu razvedeniya lesov', *ZIOSKhYuR*, 1 (1848), 33.

[20] P[alimpsestov], "Lesovodstvo. Nechto v rode 'Vvedeniya' v uroki lesovodstva dlya Novorossiiskogo kraya", *ZIOSKhYuR*, 1 (1852), 15–16.

[21] *Stoletie uchrezhdeniya lesnogo departamenta, 1798–1898* (Spb, 1898), 142.

[22] RGIA, f.426, op.1, d.40, ll.3, 7–ob., 12–25.

German scientists. While he noted contrary arguments, Veinberg argued that forests moderated the climate, attracted precipitation, reduced evaporation, retained snow melt water, served as barriers against the wind, protected soil from the forces of erosion, conserved moisture in the soil, maintained water levels in rivers, and reduced the incidence of floods.[23] He emphasized that forests played a particularly valuable role in the steppe region where there was little woodland. In his view, the regular and harmful droughts were caused not by a shortage of precipitation, but by the rapid evaporation of the rain that did fall as a result of the hot, dry winds on land left unsheltered by trees.[24]

Another case for the importance of trees was made by Aleksandr Voeikov in the 1870s and 1880s. He maintained that forests could have a moderating impact on the climate in their vicinity, which was particularly important in southern Russia. He emphasized the significance of forests in offering protection from the drying effects of the easterly winds.[25] In the mid-1880s, he reviewed his earlier conclusions in the light of the latest research. He stated that there was more evidence that vegetation had an influence on precipitation. He cited data from a number of studies, for example on the estate of Belokolodezskoe, Volchansk district, Khar'kov province, during the years 1883 to 1891. One group of rain gauges was located near copses of trees and ponds, another in open fields. From April to September, the average precipitation was 15.6 per cent higher near trees and ponds than on open land. Voeikov speculated that if relatively small copses could give such results, then larger areas of dense woodland could have a greater impact. He also noted, however, that not all scientists accepted the findings of such studies.[26]

Arguments for planting trees were made forcefully during and in the aftermath of droughts and crop failures. In Stavropol' province in the drought year of 1885, D. L. Ivanov (the author of a devastating account of the impact of Russian colonization on province's environment) advocated planting trees 'on as large a scale as possible'. He cited such potential benefits as preventing erosion, assisting in the accumulation of moisture in the soil, and moderating the climate.[27] A number of articles advocating afforestation to prevent a repetition of the drought appeared in the provincial press.[28] The governor of Stavropol' included

[23] Veinberg, *Les*, 30–167.

[24] Veinberg, *Les*, 241–66, esp. 264.

[25] A. I. Voeikov, *Klimaty zemnogo shara v osobennosti Rossii* (Spb, 1884), esp. 291–324, 583; A. I. Voeikov, 'O vliyanii lesov na klimat', in *Izbrannye sochineniya*, ed. A. A. Grigor'ev, 4 vols (Moscow and Leningrad, 1948–57), iii, 42–58 (first published in 1878).

[26] A. I. Voeikov, 'Vozdeistvie cheloveka na prirodu', *Vozdeistvie cheloveka na prirodu: izbrannye stat'i*, ed. V. V. Pokshishevskii (Moscow, 1949), 80–1 (first published in 1894).

[27] D. L. Ivanov, 'Vliyanie Russkoi kolonizatsii na prirodu Stavropol'skogo kraya', *IRGO*, 22/3 (1886), 253.

[28] See, for example, B. Karpov, 'Zametka o neobkhodimosti razvedeniya lesa v Stavropol'skoi gubernii', *Severnyi Kavkaz* (15 March 1885); 'Stavropol, 24 iyunya', *Severnyi Kavkaz* (25 June

arguments for afforestation in his annual report for 1885.[29] In Samara province in 1890, following 'unsatisfactory harvests of grain and grass', the governor urged that planting trees (and irrigation) be made compulsory for the rural population as ways of overcoming the consequences of droughts and heat waves.[30] The catastrophic drought, crop failure, and famine of 1891–2 prompted further calls for afforestation of the steppes amongst other measures. At a meeting of the Southern Russian Agricultural Society in 1892, P. Barakov, an agronomist at the University of New Russia in Odessa, advocated tree planting on the grounds that forested regions of Russia had escaped the disaster.[31] The future Minister of Agriculture, Aleksei Ermolov, advocated protection of remaining forests, reforestation of locations where there had once been trees, and afforestation of other areas.[32] Dokuchaev drew up a detailed plan that included planting trees in particular locations in the steppe region.[33]

It is a measure of the lasting importance attached to the benefits of trees by government officials that they were repeated in 1903 by the governor of Saratov, Aleksandr Platonovich Engel'gardt:

the importance of arboreal vegetation and its influence with respect to agriculture are enormous. . . . I am concerned exclusively with its role as a mighty helper in the . . . the struggle with droughts, as a preserver of moisture in the soil, and protector of agricultural land from various problems caused by the climatic conditions.

He defended the benefits of forests against 'some scholars' who considered the matter to be 'debateable, [and] still little researched'.[34]

PLANTING TREES IN THE STEPPE REGION TO THE MID-NINETEENTH CENTURY

Practical experience of planting trees on the steppes dated back to the turn of the eighteenth century. The urge to do so consumed even emperors and empresses. Peter the Great is reputed to have sown acorns near his new port of Taganrog on

1885); 'Stavropol, 15 iyulya', *Severnyi Kavkaz* (16 July 1885); 'Obshchepoleznye svedeniya', *Stavropol'skie gubernskie vedomosti* (18 January 1886), 1.

[29] GASK, f.101, op.4, d.732, 1878–87, ll.34–9ob. He was repeating arguments that had been made in 1878. GASK, f.101, op.4, d.732, 1878–87, l.3.

[30] GASO, f.3, op.233, d.1000, 1891, ll.1, 2ob.–3.

[31] He expanded his proposals into a short book. P. Barakov, *O vozmozhnykh merakh bor'by s zasukhami* (Odessa, 1892).

[32] [A. S. Ermolov], *Neurozhai i narodnoe bedstvie* (Spb, 1892), 44–54, 74–5.

[33] See V. V. Dokuchaev, 'Nashi Stepi prezhde i teper'', *Sochineniya*, 9 vols (Moscow and Leningrad, 1949–61), vi, 87–96.

[34] A. P. Engel'gardt, *Chernozemnaya Rossiya* (Saratov, 1903), 75–101 (quotation 77). The argument that forests attract rainfall has been revived recently by two Russian scientists. See above, p. 27.

the Sea of Azov in 1696.[35] Catherine the Great ordered trees to be planted on state land near Kherson on her tour of her new southern domains in 1787.[36] The Free Economic Society took an interest in tree planting. It published an essay in 1801 that explained how trees could be planted on the steppes as if it were quite straightforward.[37] It was not. While it was one matter to plant trees, it was quite another to ensure that they survived. In the late eighteenth century, settlers in the steppe region were finding out quite how difficult it was.[38] In the 1830s and 1840s, Aleksandr Nordman, the Finnish director the Odessa botanical garden, found that the trees that had been planted were starting to die off. He concluded that the environment of most of the steppe region was not suitable for trees on account of the climate and alkaline subsoils.[39] Not everyone agreed. When August von Haxthausen visited the steppes, including Odessa, in 1843, he concluded that the conditions were suitable for trees. He was persuaded by the success of some German and Mennonite colonists in New Russia.[40] Writing many decades later, the forestry scientist Grigorii Vysotskii attributed the start of steppe forestry in 'southern Russia' not to Peter or Catherine but to the German colonists.[41]

By the time of Haxthausen's visit to Molotschna in 1843, the Mennonites had accumulated a great deal of experience in planting trees. The Russian government required foreign colonists to plant trees on the land it granted them. The regulations of 1800 stated that they were to sow seeds of fast-growing trees that were suitable to the soil—such as alder, aspen, poplar and willow—in well-ploughed land.[42] From 1830, the Mennonite forestry society under Cornies enforced the colonists' obligation to plant trees on half a *desyatina* per family, provided them with seeds and saplings, and advised them on the best ways to cultivate them in the local conditions.[43] Peter Köppen, an official of the new

---

[35] N. Sredinskii, 'Kratkii istoricheskii ocherk lesorazvedeniya v yuzhno-russkihk stepyakh', *LZh*, 17 (1887), 741.

[36] A. V. Khrapovitskii, *Zhurnal Vysochaishogo puteshestviya ee Velichestva Gosudarnyni Ekateriny II samoderzhavitsy vserossiiskoi v Poludennye Strany Rossii v 1787 godu* (Moscow, 1787), 71; *PSZ*, 1, xxii, 859–60 (no.16,548, 10 June 1787).

[37] Levshin, 'O zaselenii stepei', *TVEO*, 53 (1801), 216–24.

[38] Vasilii Zuev, *Puteshestvennye zapiski Vasiliya Zueva ot S. Peterburga do Khersona, v 1781 i 1782 godu* (Spb, 1787), 226.

[39] A. Nordman, 'O gorode Odesse v estestvoispytatel'nom otnoshenii', *Listki Imperatorskogo Obshchestva Sel'skogo-Khozyaistva Yuzhnoi Rossii*, 4 (1837), 208–10; Nordman, 'Opisanie imperatorskogo Odesskogo sada i vzglyad na rastitel'nye i klimatologicheskie otnosheniya okrestnostei g. Odessy', *ZIOSKhYuR*, 6 (1847), 108–11. See also above, pp. 59–60.

[40] August von Haxthausen, *The Russian Empire: Its People, Institutions and Resources*, 2 vols, trans. Robert Farie (London, 1856) ii, 69–75; August Freiherrn von Haxthausen, *Studien über die innern Zustände, das Volksleben und insbesondere die ländlichen Einrichtungen Russlands*, 3 vols (Hannover, 1847–52) i, 456. (The German original has more detail on the colonists.)

[41] G. N. Vysotskii, 'Stepnoe lesorazvedenie', *PERSKh*, ix (1905), 445.

[42] *PSZ*, 1, xxvi, 635–49 (no.19,873, 16 May 1800), art.70.

[43] Staples, *Cross-Cultural Encounters*, 73–4, 114–8. Cornies's authoritarian manner provoked opposition among Mennonites at the time and mixed assessments among historians. See

Ministry of State Domains who visited Molotschna in 1837, noted: 'Visitors to the colony will look at the forestry plantations which are making progress on the steppes with a feeling of special satisfaction and well being before the forces of nature, which generously repay the labour of man.' He singled out Cornies's model plantation for praise. Köppen attributed the Mennonites' success to careful preparation of the land, which they ploughed several times to a depth of ¾ *arshin* (around 21 inches). The trees they planted most frequently were elm, ash, and maple, and also poplar and black locust. In addition, they had managed to grow some coniferous trees.[44] Cornies reported, with characteristic attention to detail, that by 1848, the colony had planted a total of 636,579 trees, with a further 752,248 in nurseries.[45] Not all foreign colonists were as successful. Vysotskii later noted that in spite of the efforts of some German colonists, who prepared the land well, watered the saplings, and kept the land free from weeds, many trees dried up and died after two or three years.[46]

The government achieved some success in promoting tree planting on its military settlements in the steppe region. Count Arakcheev, who set up the settlements, got the idea from Russian estate owners in the region. In 1817, he visited the estate of Prishib, Slobodsko-Ukraine (later Khar'kov) province, where Ivan Danilevskii had planted pine trees on sandy soil. Arakcheev was impressed. He ordered military settlers in southern Slobodsko-Ukraine and Kherson provinces to plant trees. By the time the military settlements were abolished in 1858, they contained thousands of *desyatiny* of forested land, which were then designated state forestry plantations. Among them was the Chernyi Les plantation in Kherson province.[47]

Another estate owner who engaged in forestry was Viktor Skarzhinskii. He claimed towards the end of his life that he vowed to plant trees on his estate after he dreamt about a forested paradise on his return home from the military campaign of 1813, in which he visited parks in Poland. Whatever his motive, he worked hard over the following decades to plant around 400 *desyatiny* with trees, both broad-leaved and coniferous, in the inhospitable environment of Kherson province. He learned from experience what types of trees grew best in particular areas and how best to cultivate them. He supplied saplings to the military settlements and the Odessa Botanical Garden.[48] Further north, in

H. L. Dyck, 'Russian servitor and Mennonite Hero: Light and Shadow in Images of Johann Cornies', *Journal of Mennonite Studies*, 2 (1984), 9–28.

[44] RGIA, f.383, op.29, 1837–8, d.609, ll.39–41, 66ob. See also Urry, *None but Saints*, 118.

[45] 'O sostoyanii raznykh otraslei sel'skogo khozyaistva v yuzhnoi Rossii v 1848 godu', *ZIOSKhYuR*, 11 (1848), 708. See also Kornis, 'O sostoyanii khozyaistva v Molochanskikh Menonistskikh koloniyakh v 1842 g.', 70–2; Urry, *None but Saints*, 113.

[46] Vysotskii, 'Stepnoe lesorazvedenie', 445.

[47] Sredinskii, 'Kratkii', 741–2, 744. See also Tsvetkov, *Izmenenie*, 46.

[48] Sredinskii, 'Kratkii', 741, 744–5; D. Strukov, 'O lesakh Novorossiiskogo kraya i Bessarabii', *ZhMGI*, 46 (1853), 1st pagn, 224–5.

Novosil' district, Tula province, in the forest-steppe region, the Shatilov noble family hired the German-born Franz Meyer as forest manager on their estate of Mokhovoe. Between 1821 and 1860, he planted trees on around 130 *desyatiny*. His motives were initially aesthetic, to create a park landscape, but as he accumulated experience, he planted trees on land unsuitable for cultivating crops, such as in gullies, ravines, and along the sides of roads, to provide timber and fire wood.[49]

The Southern Russian Agricultural Society actively promoted planting trees. In 1830, it established a nursery on its farm near Odessa, which supplied saplings to the population. Experiments were carried out on the farm into acclimatizing trees and shrubs from other regions, and to work out the most appropriate species and the best ways to grow them. They paid particular attention to ensuring that young trees survived the droughts that killed many saplings. The society's journal published articles on the results of the experiments and the experiences of members such as Skarzhinskii on their estates. The society awarded prizes to local inhabitants for achievements in tree planting. The first prizes, which ranged from 100 to 5,000 silver roubles, were made in 1834. Among the recipients were owners and foreign colonists. In 1850, the society offered prizes of 3,000 roubles for establishing plantations covering 500 *desyatiny*, and lower prizes, presumably aimed at peasants, for smaller plantations. There were no entrants. Discussions of other ways to encourage tree planting, including direct subsidies, were generally inconclusive. In a survey of the activities of the society over its first fifty years in 1878, M. Borovskii concluded 'it has to be said that, in reality, the measures to encourage [tree planting] did not fully lead to the desired results.'[50] None of this deterred Palimpsestov. He was confident that the soil and the climate of the region were suited to trees, but did note that they had been more suitable in the past, when he believed the steppes had been forested.[51]

Attempts to plant trees on the steppes of the Don Cossack territory in the 1830s–50s provided further evidence for the difficulties. The statute on the administration of the territory of 1835 ordered cossack settlements to plant trees to supply their needs. Throughout the 1840s, the ataman requested resources for tree planting and reported the numbers of saplings planted. For example, up to 4 million saplings had been planted by 1840, and a further

[49] Frants Khristianovich Meier, 'Stepnoe lesovodstvo', *TVEO*, 3 (1860), 385–430; 4 (1860), 16–47.

[50] Borovskii, *Istoricheskii Obzor*, 7, 110–31 (quotation 120), appendix, 3, 61–6; 'Pravila dlya polucheniya premii za nasazhdenie lesnykh derev'ev v Novorossiiskom krae', *ZIOSKhYuR*, 3 (1848), 139–42.

[51] P[alimpsestov], "Lesovodstvo. Nechto v rode 'Vvedeniya' v uroki lesovodstva dlya Novorossiiskogo kraya", *ZIOSKhYuR*, 1 (1852), 17, 29–37.

half a million in 1849 alone.[52] Like some other attempts to cultivate trees on the steppes, and in contrast to the accomplishments of the Mennonites and a few estate owners, the cossacks' efforts were not successful. In many cases, the saplings' roots were saturated by spring floods of rivers, causing them to die, or they dried up, withered, and perished during droughts, or they simply did not grow in soils that were unsuitable.[53]

In 1842, the Ministry of War instructed forester Baibakov of the Military Settlement in Khar'kov province to prepare a plan to plant broad-leaved trees on the steppes beyond the river Don in the south of the Don Cossack territory. Ominously, this was an area where there were no trees growing naturally. (It was still fairly treeless when I travelled through the area in 2003.) The areas Baibakov proposed for planting excluded land where the saplings might be damaged by livestock belonging to the Kalmyks or cossacks, and land prone to steppe fires. Baibakov gave detailed instructions on how to prepare the soil to ensure moisture penetrated to the saplings' roots. He stressed the need to protect young shoots from heat and cold. He considered the most appropriate species to be oak, elm, maple, ash, lime, and willow.[54] The cossack official who supervised test plantings of willows in 1842–3 reported, however, that the experiment 'confirmed the absolute impossibility of introducing copses of trees' on this land. The young trees had grown satisfactorily in the spring of 1843, but had been badly damaged by a summer drought, and the survivors had been destroyed by an unusually dry and windy summer in 1844.[55]

Nevertheless, the experiment continued. Baibakov visited the Don most years in the late 1840s, but to little avail. The results were the same every year: either the seeds did not germinate, or once the seedlings were transplanted on to the steppe, they withered and died. In a few places oak seedlings grew to 2 or 3 *vershki* (3.5–5.25 inches), but only those protected from the intense heat by high grass survived. Heat waves destroyed the rest. In April 1850, the cossack official Markov pointed to the unsuitability of the land and climate, especially the scorching easterly winds. More specifically, he added that the locations chosen and the species of trees selected were unsuitable. A further factor was the lack of attention to local knowledge of the climate and soil. Markov recommended detailed studies of the soil in forested areas in the region as a guide to selecting suitable locations and the most appropriate types of trees.[56] The conditions in

[52] GARO, f.46, op.1, d.531 (1846), ll.62ob.–63; d.497 (1841), l.12; d.522 (1845), ll.70ob.–73; d.571 (1850), l.30ob.

[53] GARO f.46, op.1, d.522 (1845), ll.70ob.–73; d.531 (1846), ll.62ob.–63; d.571 (1850), l.30 ob.; d.594 (1853), l.16ob.; d.612 (1855), l.30.

[54] GARO, f.243, op.1, d.19, ll.1–18, 21ob.; f.301, op.14, d.7, 1849–52, ll.13–25, 143.

[55] GARO, f.301, op.14, d.10, 1850, ll.1–ob., 12–ob., 16–20, 105, 186; f.46, op.1, d.531, 61ob.–62.

[56] GARO, f.301, op.14, d.7, 1849–1852, ll.143–54; f.46, op.1, d.563, ll.24ob.–25; d.571, ll.31–ob.

the late 1840s were unusually severe, however. In 1849, the ataman reported that the droughts and hard frosts had also killed older, established, trees.[57]

The experiments continued on four plantations beyond the Don in the early 1850s. At Ol'ginskaya, on the road to Stavropol', there was some success in planting trees by the river Kagal'nika. There were problems on the other plantations. Young saplings were damaged by hares and cattle. Others suffered as the land dried out after it had been ploughed in the spring, and from lack of attention as those in charge did not have the necessary experience and training. Nevertheless, in 1854, the Don Cossack authorities ordered more seed from the state forestry plantation at Velikii Anadol' in Ekaterinoslav province.[58] The contacts with Velikii Anadol' continued. In 1863, the authorities on the Don sent forester Berezovskii to Velikii Anadol' to study 'steppe forestry'. He reported that the foresters there sought to overcome the lack of moisture, long droughts, and the characteristics of the soil by paying special attention to preparing the land. They ploughed the soil deeply to remove weeds and assist in the retention of scarce moisture. Berezovskii produced a new plan for afforestation of the trans-Don steppes, but it was rejected by the Minister of War, who had finally had enough. He ordered the Don Cossacks to plan trees on existing woodlots.[59] A plan to plant trees on the Kalmyk steppe in Astrakhan' province to the south at around the same also failed and was abandoned. The soil and climate were unsuitable, and the Kalmyks had no interest in planting trees on land they had traditionally burned to provide fresh grass for their livestock.[60]

Another section of the population who were unaccustomed, and reluctant, to plant trees were the Russian and Ukrainian peasants. Most were migrants to the steppes, or the descendants of migrants, from central and northern Russia and Ukraine, where there was more, or much more, woodland than on the steppes. In their new homes they continued to use wood for many everyday purposes, as they or their forebears were accustomed to do. Thus, they readily felled trees in the steppe region, often without due regard to their scarcity. On the other hand, they were not keen to emulate their Mennonite or German neighbours or a few enterprising estate owners in planting trees. The amount of work involved and the limited chances of success undoubtedly deterred them. Crucially, peasants had less land and fewer resources and privileges than the foreign colonists and estate owners. A further disincentive was that peasants did not hold their land in hereditary tenure and so could not be certain they would retain land on which

---

[57] GARO, f.46, op.1, d.571, ll.31–ob.
[58] GARO, f.301, op.14, d.22, 1852–60, ll.24–32, 89–94.
[59] GARO, f.301, op.27, d.2, 1860–7, ll.121–33, 136–44ob., 161–4ob., 169–82ob., 186–20, 270–1ob. See also A. A. Pushkarenko, 'Prirodookhrannaya deyatel'nost' v Oblasti Voiska Donskogo vo vtoroi polovine XIX-nachale XX vv.', Candidate dissertation, Rostov State University, 2000, 72–5.
[60] A. Bitnyi, 'O popytkakh lesnogo upravleniya k obleseniyu stepei', *ZhMGI*, 84 (1863), 2nd pagn, 274–81.

they had expended the effort to nurture trees. This was remedied by a decree of 14 September 1828, which granted state peasants who planted orchards, vines, and forest trees in New Russia hereditary tenure of the land. The authorities offered state peasants exemptions from taxes, monetary rewards, and silver medals for success in planting trees.[61] In 1843, the Forestry Department of the Ministry of State Domains ordered trees to be planted in provinces with few forests.[62] By the early 1860s, the ministry's journal reported that state peasants in fifteen provinces of the steppe and forest-steppe regions had planted over 5½ million saplings and 2½ million fruit trees. But, this was nowhere near sufficient for the population's needs. The author blamed the peasants: 'In general, our peasant does not acknowledge the urgent need for cultivating forests, even in places with no forests; he is too occupied with the present to think about the future.' The author contrasted the peasants' failure with the success of foreign colonists and the state forestry plantations, such as at Velikii Anadol'.[63] A few years earlier, an article published by the Southern Russian Agricultural Society noted that local inhabitants allegedly claimed that since God hadn't planted trees on the steppes, then people were not capable of doing so.[64]

TOWARDS MORE SCIENTIFIC STEPPE FORESTRY

Eager to overcome such attitudes, the authorities in St Petersburg set up forestry plantations in the steppe region to carry out research. The most important was the Velikii Anadol' plantation. It was founded in 1843 by the Ministry of State Domains on 2,800 *desyatiny* of state land in Aleksandrovsk district (from 1874 Mariupol' district), in eastern Ekaterinoslav province. A forestry school was attached to the plantation. Minister Pavel Kiselev gave the plantation ambitious aims: to carry out experiments in planting trees on the steppes to work out the most reliable methods and the most suitable species; to acclimatize trees and shrubs to the conditions on the steppes; to encourage the local population to plant trees; to prove that it was possible to cultivate trees on the high steppes as well as low-lying areas; to show that Russians as well as Germans could cultivate trees on the steppes; and, reflecting the perceived benefits of forests, to improve the climate of the steppe region by large-scale afforestation.

The location selected to achieve all these goals was inauspicious. There was very little natural woodland in eastern Ekaterinoslav province as the conditions were unfavourable. The climate was sharply continental, with a short spring and

[61] *PSZ*, 2, iii, 829–30 (no.2280, 14 September 1828); *PSZ*, 2, iv, 102–3 (no.2661, 7 February 1829).
[62] *IOPDMGI*, i, 175.
[63] Bitnyi, 'O popytkakh', 285–90.
[64] A. Zherebko, 'Koe-shto o glubokoi obrabotke zemli', *ZOSKhYuR* (1856), 41–6.

rapid transition from winter cold to summer heat. The winter weather was changeable. There were late frosts in the spring. And, summer heatwaves were relentless, and accompanied by hot, dry, easterly winds. Much of the rainfall evaporated or drained away without seeping into the ground. The soil at Velikii Anadol' was clayey, heavy, black earth, to a depth of 6–10 *vershki* (10.5–17.5 inches), and the subsoil was hard clay in places mixed with lime. There were also patches of saline soil. The land was high steppe, situated 17 *sazheni* (120 feet) above the water in the nearby Kashlagach river. In addition, the land was covered with weeds, and there were insects that attacked trees. Yet the choice of such a location was deliberate. Kiselev ordered that the plantation be established in the worst possible conditions: if trees could be grown on this land, then they could be grown anywhere in the steppe region.

The task of trying to make them grow was given to Viktor von Graff. Born in the Russian Empire of German descent, Graff was a graduate of the Forestry Institute in St Petersburg. At Velikii Anadol', he had to cope not just with the environmental conditions but also with the hostility of the local state peasants who were compelled to work for him. Some were concerned that if the endeavour succeeded, then all the peasants in the area would be forced to plant trees. With great difficulty, Graff managed to mobilize his labour force, get the weeds cleared, the ground prepared, and work out ways to grow trees in the inhospitable conditions. He chose to plant quick-growing trees, such as willow and poplar, near peasants' houses so that they could see the results. During the twenty-three years he worked at Velikii Anadol', Graff established 131 *desyatiny* of artificial forest. He used, according to one estimate, 11,520 days' labour a year. From 1855, the plantation made saplings available to the local population at low prices. With the advantage of Graff's experience, his successor, Lyudvik Bark, increased the forested area by over 1,000 *desyatiny*. He had to do so with more economical use of labour, moreover, since the state peasant reform of 1866 deprived him of free labour. Veinberg concluded that the experience of the first few decades of the Velikii Anadol' plantation indicated that it was the initial period that was the most difficult.[65]

In 1845, another state forestry plantation in the steppe region was established, near Melitopol' in Berdyansk district, Tauride province, under the Mennonite Cornies. Cornies drew on his experience in Molotschna, where the land was carefully prepared before sowing seeds and saplings, to lay the foundations for a successful plantation. The Berdyansk plantation achieved particular success in growing oak trees as well as pine. In contrast to Velikii Anadol', the conditions were fairly favourable, and a significant area of land was forested with little cost or

[65] Veinberg, *Les*, 551–9; Bitnyi, 'O popytkakh', 284–7; N. G. Rachinskii, 'O stepnom drevovozrashchenii v Novorossiiskom krae po povodu preobrazovaniya Veliko-Anadolskogo lesnichestva', *ZOSKhYuR* (1865), 426–38.

effort.[66] During the 1860s–70s, state forestry plantations were established throughout the steppe region. In the 1870s, the Ministry of State Domains worked out a plan for the gradual afforestation of the steppes, both to provide for the needs of the local population for timber and fuel, and for the environmental benefits that were believed to ensue. By 1887, the total area of the state forestry plantations had reached 6,528 ¾ *desyatiny*. This was a tiny part of the entire region, but a big step forward. The ministry managed to cut the costs of planting a *desyatina* of trees in half.[67] The state forestry plantations, which were staffed by trained foresters, made an important contribution to the development of scientific steppe forestry in the Russian Empire.[68]

Forestry scientists investigated the specific conditions that inhibited the natural growth of trees in the region. They considered whether it was the shortage of water that hindered tree growth. Veinberg argued that the problem was not a shortage of rainfall, but that the water which did fall as precipitation ran off the land, through gullies, rather than sinking into the ground. Only forests, he argued, would prevent the moisture from the atmosphere draining away and help it penetrate into the subsoil. Veinberg went on to quote from an article by Voeikov, published in 1878, in which he disagreed with the common argument that droughts were the cause of the lack of trees in southern Russia. The existence of areas of natural woodland in the steppe region and examples of successful cultivation of trees in the Velikii Anadol' plantation, along the Mo-lochnaya river, Tauride province (where the Mennonites had grown trees), and on the Makhovoe estate, Tula province (where Meyer carried out his pioneering work) all gave lie to the belief that there was not sufficient moisture in the steppe region for trees. The only areas of 'European Russia' where the amount of rainfall and snow was insufficient for trees to grow without artificial irrigation, according to Voeikov, were the steppes to the east of the Caspian Sea and parts of the Crimean peninsula, that is, relatively small or outlying parts of the region.[69]

Forestry scientists paid a great deal of attention to the soil, in particular the subsoil, which Nordman had considered to be fatal for trees in the Odessa botanical garden in the 1840s (see above, p. 59). Research by scientists, such as Gavriil Tanfil'ev and Vysotskii, members of Dokuchaev's expedition of the 1890s, showed that the key issue was the alkalinity of the subsoil, which most broad-leaved trees could not tolerate. The subsoil was alkaline, because there was not sufficient precipitation to leach out the salts. The ground water, moreover, was saline. Tanfil'ev observed that in the Velikii Anadol' forestry plantation, artificially planted trees started to die after thirty-five–forty years. This was due,

[66] RGIA, f.426, op.1, 1894, d.40, ll.302–5; Bitnyi, 'O popytkakh', 283–4; P. Sivitskii, 'Lesorazvedenie v Berdyanskom lesnichestve', *SKhiL*, 136 (1881), 1st pagn, 133–58.

[67] *Stoletie uchrezhdeniya lesnogo departamenta, 1798–1898* (Spb, 1898), 153; *IOPDMGI*, i, 176–8; GARO, f.46, op.1, d.1347, l.508.

[68] Vysotskii, 'Stepnoe lesorazvedenie', 445.

[69] Veinberg, *Les*, 545–51. The article he cited was Voeikov, 'O vliyanii lesov na klimat'.

he believed, to their roots penetrating the alkaline subsoil. For Tanfil'ev it was the alkalinity of the soil that determined the boundary between forest and steppe in Russia.[70] Further obstacles to tree growth, especially young trees, were the wind, sharp fluctuations in the temperature over twenty-four-hour periods as well as over the year, and insects (especially in mono-culture plantations), as well as the risk of fire and damage by grazing animals.[71]

Vysotskii divided soils in the steppe region into three types from point of view of forestry. The first was land that had once been forested but where the trees had been felled: this was most suitable. The second was land that had not been forested but was suitable for tree growth, because there was sufficient moisture—from precipitation, snow melt water, and spring floods—to leach out the salts that were harmful to trees from the soil. Such locations included gullies and ravines, slopes, flood plains, sandy areas, and also higher land on watersheds—locations where trees grew naturally in the steppe region. It was possible, with care and attention, to grow trees artificially in such locations. The last type was land that was unsuitable for trees due to aridity and the salinity of the soil. Planting trees on such land was not very reliable and sometimes hopeless. Vysotskii argued that foresters also needed to pay attention to the local climate, in particular heat and precipitation, and to the relief and geology of locations. If trees were planted in unsuitable places, and required constant attention, then natural regeneration could not be expected.[72]

Forestry scientists devised ways of cultivating trees that increased the chances of success. In the early nineteenth century, foreign colonists and others dug large holes in the ground and planted saplings in the way fruit trees were planted in orchards. This was time-consuming and expensive. Over time, and especially after the peasant reforms of the 1860s removed the free labour that the state and serf owners had enjoyed, more efficient methods were developed. Seeds, which had been soaked in advance, were sown in beds in nurseries. Small seedlings were then planted out in rows about a *sazhen* (7 feet) apart. Experience at Velikii Anadol' and elsewhere demonstrated the importance of preparing the soil and keeping it clear of weeds. The best way to do this was to grow crops on the land where the seedlings were to be planted out, and then plough it to a depth of 4–5 *vershki* (7–8.75 inches). If the soil was moist, then seedlings could be planted out in the autumn. Otherwise, it was better to wait until the spring. Most species grew better if they were planted in nurseries and then transplanted. Oaks,

[70] G. Tanfil'ev, 'Predely lesov na yuge Rossii', *TESLD, Nauchnyi otdel*, 2/1 (1894), 28–73; G. Tanfil'ev, 'Botanikogeograficheskie issledovaniya v stepnoi polose', *TESLD, Nauchnyi otdel*, 2/2 (1894), i–ii; G. N. Vysotskii, 'Pochvennye zony Evropeiskoi Rossii v svyazi s solenosnost'yu gruntov i kharakterom lesnoi rastitel'nosti', *Pochvevedenie*, 1/1 (1899), 19–26.
[71] See Veinberg, *Les*, 545; Vysotskii, 'Stepnoe lesorazvedenie', 447–8; I. Shevyrev, 'Vrednye nasekomye yuzhnykh stepnykh lesnichestv v 1889 g.', *SKhiL*, 164 (1890), 1st pagn, 183–208, 273–97; 165 (1890), 1–30, 195–223; 166 (1890), 23–52.
[72] Vysotskii, 'Stepnoe lesorazvedenie', 444, 447–81. See also Tanfil'ev, 'Predely', 115–45.

however, could sometimes be grown successfully from acorns sown in the places where they were to grow. Young trees needed protection against drought, weeds, and also pests, such as insects and burrowing rodents. One autumn in Velikii Anadol', 8 kilograms of roots of oak saplings and 280 acorns were found in the burrow of one mole, which had stored them for the winter. If the mole ate as much over the rest of the year, it was calculated that it had destroyed or damaged 10,000 saplings. Young trees with damaged root systems were more likely to dry out and die.[73]

Oak was the most reliable and valuable of all species of local trees on the black-earth steppes.[74] (In June 2003, I saw large oak trees hundreds of years old on the steppes near Veshenskaya in northern Rostov region.) Around the turn of the twentieth century, Vysotskii recommended that the species which grew best were those that grew naturally in those conditions. Foresters also planted introduced species. Tanfil'ev recommended taking seeds from introduced species that were already growing on the steppes as they had demonstrated they could grow in the conditions. Two introduced species were especially prominent: honey locust (*gledichiya*) and black locust (*belaya akatsiya, Robinia pseudoacacia*). Both were imported from North America, where the latter grew on the prairies and Great Plains in conditions analogous to the steppes.[75] On sandy soil throughout the steppe region, foresters planted coniferous trees, in particular pine, with success.[76]

In the early nineteenth century, it was common to plant just one species. Over time, experience showed that the best results were obtained from planting trees in specific combinations of fast and slow growing species. For example, slow-growing oak grew best if it was planted with elm, which grew more quickly, and maple and ash, which were in between. Oak surrounded by elm and ash grew straighter and more directly upwards, with fewer branches lower down, and developed a straighter trunk. By the 1880s, foresters had developed combinations that worked well. They planted rows of trees alternating with species of elm, for example: elm—Oak—elm—Ash—elm—Maple—elm—Oak—elm—Ash—elm—Maple, etc. The rows were five feet apart and the saplings placed two feet from each other in the rows. The elms were temporary. They were included as they grew quickly and their branches spread densely covering the planted area, thereby cutting the cost of weeding the soil between the rows. After a few years, when the fast-growing elms started to choke and block the light from the slower-growing trees, their branches were cut back.

[73] Vysotskii, 'Stepnoe lesorazvedenie', 448–51, 463–4.

[74] Vysotskii, 'Stepnoe lesorazvedenie', 453.

[75] Vysotskii, 'Stepnoe lesorazvedenie', 444, 451, 468–9, 484–6; Tanfil'ev, 'Predely lesov', 120–1, 144.

[76] See F. Keppen, 'Neskol'ko slov o razvedenii lesov v stepyakh Tavricheskoi gubernii', *ZhMGI*, 84 (1863), 2nd pagn, 6–8.

Some foresters, such as Graff at Velikii Anadol', experimented with combinations of shrubs among the trees. He planted Siberian pea tree (*zheltaya akatsiya, Caragana arborescens*) and Tatar maple (*tatarskii klen, Acer tataricum*] around the trees. In time, they formed a dense undergrowth that protected the soil, kept grassy vegetation under control, and filled spaces left by trees that had not survived. The shrubs produced valuable raw material for wickerwork and fuel, and were sturdy. But, they did not prove sufficiently able to cope with shade and did not adequately protect soil from grass, so the experiment was stopped. In the 1890s, steppe foresters, for example Fedor Tikhonov on the Don forestry plantation, began to devise new types of planting combinations of different species of trees, fast and slow-growing, and shrubs to provide shade. Some foresters planted a second tier of shrubs, such as hedge/field maple (*polevoi klen, Acer campestre*), hornbeam (*grab, Carpinus*), and linden (*lipa*), among the trees to provide shade and keep grass and weed growth down. This became known as the 'Don type' of planting.[77]

In parts of the region, foresters took advantage of these new methods that had been developed on the plantations. In the Don region, serious efforts to plant trees resumed in 1872 after the failures of the 1830s–1850s. Cultivating trees on land that belonged to the Cossack Host was concentrated in the plantations in Mius district in the west of the Don region and near the cossack capital of Novocherkassk. This time, with the development of the new methods, the plantings were successful. Broad-leaved trees were planted on the steppes and coniferous trees on sandy soil. Between 1871 and 1890, the area of forest on land belonging to the Cossack Host increased from 21,967 to 24,418 *desyatiny*.[78] A decade later, the ataman reported that the area of the host forests had increased to 29,534 *desyatiny*.[79] By 1916, host forests covered an area of 36,799 *desyatiny*, of which 12,651 *desyatiny* had been planted artificially since 1872.[80] The figures for the total area take account of the area of forest that was felled, and also the area regenerated naturally each year, all of which were carefully reported (if not always accurately measured).[81]

Not all plans for tree planting in the region received such support or achieved so much. In the late 1870s and 1880s, the governor of Stavropol' was less successful in obtaining support and funding from higher authorities for planting the trees he considered so urgent in his province.[82] Plans for afforestation in southern Samara province were slow to develop, in spite of the shortage of timber

---

[77] Vysotskii, 'Stepnoe lesorazvedenie', 451–7. See also N. T. Mirov, 'Two Centuries of Afforestation and Shelterbelt Planting on the Russian Steppes', *Journal of Forestry*, 33 (1935), 971–3.

[78] GARO, f.46, op.1, d.3164, 1889, l.83; d.1051, l.24ob.; d.860, ll.6–8ob.

[79] GARO, f.46, op.1, d.3276, 1901, ll.100–ob.

[80] GARO, f.46, op.1, d.3510, 1916, ll.93, 91.

[81] For a fuller discussion, see Pushkarenko, 'Prirodookhrannaya deyatel'nost'', 76–84.

[82] GASK, f.101, op.4, d.732, 1878–87, ll.6, 40, 42–74ob., 79–ob.

and firewood, and the recurring droughts.[83] Some plans that were implemented, moreover, continued to fail. In 1872, the Appanage Department embarked on afforestation in various locations in the steppe region. In 1896, Genko described the results as a 'complete fiasco'. The land designated for tree planting included areas with salty soil that were unsuitable, and the soil was not prepared properly. By 1885, only 18.1 *desyatiny* of woodland out of 116 *desyatiny* that had been planted on Appanage Department land in Samara and Stavropol' provinces had survived.[84]

THE BENEFITS OF AFFORESTATION REVISITED

The mixed results of all these efforts to plant trees on the steppes, in particular the limited achievements in large-scale afforestation, paralleled doubts that persisted about the environmental benefits of forests. Some concerns were practical. Writing in 1876, the agronomist Aleksandr Shishkin had no doubt that forests would 'improve' the climate of the steppe region, but pointed out that that they would have to wait too long for the improvement to materialize.[85] There were also sceptics who questioned whether there would ever be any benefits. Veinberg, who was originally a forest-sceptic, noted that back in the 1840s, Karl Ernst von Baer had strongly questioned whether forests influenced the climate.[86] A more trenchant case against the notion that planting trees could help in the 'combating droughts' was made by the agronomist Pavel Kostychev in 1876. He did so in the influential journal *Notes of the Fatherland* (*Otechestvennye zapiski*). His target was a book written by the German botanist Matthias Jakob Schleiden, *Tree and Forest* (*Für Baum Und Wald*), which had been recently published in Russian translation. Schleiden asserted that in some parts of Europe, deforestation had led to reduced rainfall, with adverse consequences for crops, and that planting trees could remedy the situation. Kostychev was not convinced:

It has not been proved that forest can have any influence outside the area it occupies, and if there is such influence, then it is too insignificant to have any effect on the local climate. Therefore, to spend money on planting forests with the aim only of improving the climate, would [be] . . . in vain.

Kostychev called for a discussion to challenge the entrenched view that forests had a beneficial impact on the climate. This was all the more necessary, he

[83] See I. Lishin, *Ocherk Nikolaevskogo uezda (Samarskaya guberniya) v statisticheskom i sel'sko-khozyaistvom otnosheniyakh* (Spb, 1880), 45–6, 51–61.

[84] N. K. Genko, *Razvedenie lesa i ustroistvo vodosbornykh plotin na udel'nykh stepyakh* (Spb, 1896), 13–15.

[85] A. Shishkin, *K voprosu ob umen'shenii vrednogo deistviya zasukh na rastitel'nost'* (Spb, 1876), 167.

[86] Veinberg, *Les*, 18. On his change of mind, see Veinberg, *Les*, 28–9.

believed, since arguments had been made in defence of forests that made appeals to readers' patriotism (i.e. reflecting the importance of forests in Russian culture and identity).[87]

Voeikov became more sceptical about the alleged benefits of trees towards the end of the nineteenth century. In 1892, he concluded that opinions had long been sharply divided due to the lack of quantitative and comparative data.[88] In the mid-1890s, however, the scientists involved in Dokuchaev's expedition carried out controlled experiments into the influence of trees on the environment in several locations, including Velikii Anadol'. The results suggested that forests reduced the force of the wind and made the air more humid. Their observations further indicated that precipitation was higher over areas of forest than steppe. Forests, moreover, assisted in the accumulation of moisture in the upper layer of soil by reducing evaporation. Forests also retained snow, which then melted more slowly, allowing the melt water to seep into the soil and replenish the ground water below. The expedition's scientists planted trees in specific locations, including on water sheds, in belts on exposed places on the steppe, and in ravines and gullies.[89] A few years later, however, Vysotskii (who took part in the experiments) suggested that the explanation for higher levels of precipitation over forest than steppe at Velikii Anadol' may have been that the meteorological station did not measure all the precipitation, especially snow, that fell.[90] Moreover, Gifford Pinchot, the chief of the US Bureau of Forestry who visited Velikii Anadol' in 1902, noted that there was no difference between precipitation inside or outside the forest.[91]

The argument that forests helped raise levels of ground water was also questioned. P. V. Ototskii carried out research at the Chernyi Les plantation in Kherson province and the Shipov forest in southern Voronezh province. He concluded that ground water levels were lower under forest than the surrounding steppe. A French specialist at l'École forestière de Nancy initially expressed surprise, but then duplicated Ototskii's results. He found that the drying influence of forests was strongest under old forests and, crucially for the steppe

---

[87] P. A. Kostychev, 'Sposobstvuet li razvedenie lesov unichtozheniyu zasukh?', *Otechestvennye zapiski*, 225/3 (1876), 2nd pagn, 1–33 (quotation 32); Matthias Jakob Schleiden, *Für Baum und Wald* (Leipzig, 1870); M. I. Shleiden, *Derevo i les*, trans. A. Rudzkii (Spb, 1873).

[88] A. Voeikov, 'Po voprosu lesnoi meteorologii,' *Meteorologicheskii vestnik*, 2 (1892), 51. See also A. A. Grigor'ev, 'Rukovodyashchie klimatologicheskie idei A. I. Voeikova', in *Izbrannye sochineniya*, i, 13.

[89] See N. Adamov, 'Meteorologicheskie nablyudeniya 1892–1894 godov', *TESLD, Nauchnii otdel*, 3/1 (1894), 1–245; G. Vysotskii, 'Programma issledovanii i opytov v Velikoanadol'skom lesnichestve', *TESLD, Otdel prakticheskikh rabot*, 1/1 (1894), 31–9; 'Obshchii proekt opytnykh rabot ekspeditsii', V. V. Dokuchaev, *Sochineniya*, vi, 149–53.

[90] G. Vysotskii, 'Biologicheskie, pochvennye i fenologicheskie nablyudeniya i issledovaniya v Veliko-Anadole', *Pochvovedenie*, 5/1 (1903), 78.

[91] Library of Congress, Manuscript Division, Gifford Pinchot Papers, Box 715, File: 'Notes taken by Mr Pinchot on his trip through Russia and Siberia', folio 92.

region, in drier climates. The findings of his research were published in the Russian soil science journal.[92]

The results experiments such as these led to more cautious assessments of what was possible and could be expected from planting trees on the steppes. Writing in 1905, Vysotskii reviewed the changing views. In the 1840s, foresters had aimed to 'improve' the steppe climate by planting large numbers of trees. This had turned out to be utopian. But, even though they did not 'improve' the climate, the resulting woodland was profitable as it provided timber that would otherwise have had to be transported to the region at great cost. This benefit proved short-lived, however, since the development of railways, coal mining, and changes in construction techniques increased the supply and reduced the demand for forest products in the steppe region, which caused prices to fall sharply. The benefits also proved short-lived, since the 'splendid young forests' that foresters had taken such pride in the 1870s and 1880s were already starting to die without producing naturally regenerating woodland. Vysotskii concluded that steppe afforestation was important only when production of timber was combined with planting trees to combat erosion.[93]

By the late nineteenth century, even Palimpsestov seemed to be losing hope, although his doubts were more practical than theoretical. At the end of the 1880s, he estimated that in order to have a substantial impact on the climate of New Russia, one-quarter of the total area—around 4½ million *desyatiny*—would need to be covered by forest.[94] This was around ten times the existing area of forest. He was in no doubt that such a large area of forest would 'improve' the climate of the region to such an extent that it would be unrecognizable. He looked back to a time when he believed the valleys of the Dnepr, Don, and Volga rivers had been covered by 'mighty forests' that blocked the dry and cold winds from Central Asia. He also believed that there had been huge forests to the north and west of the steppe region that had moderated the flow of cold air from the north and increased the inflow of water vapour from the south. Palimpsestov acknowledged that to 're-create' forests on such scales would be very expensive. It would also come up against property rights as it would entail requiring estate owners to plant trees or compulsory purchase of private land.[95] Palimpsestov was not a man to give up, and at the very least, he urged planting trees along watersheds between rivers and in gullies from south to north as defence against the easterly and north-easterly winds. On a smaller scale, he also believed that planting hedges around fields would provide shelter from winds that dried out

[92] E. Anri (E. Henry), 'Lesa pavnin i gruntovye vody', *Pochvovedenie*, 5/1 (1903), 1–30.

[93] Vysotskii, 'Stepnoe lesorazvedenie', 445–6, 493.

[94] Veinberg cited a figure of 20–25% for the 'correct proportion of the area of forest' proposed by the Russian forester Karl Arnol'd. Veinberg, *Les*, 550–1.

[95] On the issue of property rights with regard to irrigation, see below, pp. 207–8, 213–16.

the soil, and increase the amount of moisture in the ground, in particular by retaining snow.[96]

The conclusions of the specialists who were casting doubt on the wider benefits of forests chimed with the experiences of *zemstva* in trying to encourage the rural population to plant trees. At the end of the 1880s, the Odessa district *zemstvo* was concerned that its attempts to promote afforestation had had few results. In some settlements, on the instructions of the village elders, the population had planted trees along the streets. People could see the advantages, and the *zemstvo* had encouraged it by supplying cheap saplings. But, planting forests was quite a different matter. The *zemstvo* found it almost impossible to prompt the population to plant even small areas of forest. In any case, small forests scattered around the district would not do much good. The *zemstvo* decided to plant trees as a windbreak along the main road, which ran from the south-east to the north-west. Every estate owner and rural community was to plant a certain number of saplings each year.[97] The *zemstva* in Samara province also tried hard to encourage tree planting. In 1912, the district *zemstva* announced that they were giving out seedlings free of charge. They instructed that they be planted on sands, in ravines, and also around schools, hospitals, churches, cemeteries, farmsteads, squares, and along roads. The *zemstva* also promoted local tree-planting festivals.[98] Thus, *zemstva* were trying to encourage tree planting on a more limited scale and for more specific purposes.

PLANTING TREES FOR MORE SPECIFIC PURPOSES

By the late nineteenth century, therefore, the hopes that large-scale tree planting would change the climate of the region had largely disappeared. Instead, trees were being planted, and in significant numbers, but for more particular reasons. The governor of Saratov province, Aleksandr Platonovich Engel'gardt, strongly advocated afforestation in his dealings with the government in St Petersburg and the provincial *zemstvo*. He argued that forests would bind drifting sands, shelter fields against the wind, retain melt water when the snow thawed in the spring, and protect ravines against further erosion.[99] Kostychev noted, moreover, that areas such as drifting sands and the sides of ravines and gullies were appropriate for tree planting as they were not suitable for agriculture.[100] By the end of the

[96] I. Palimpsestov, *Stepi yuga Rossii byli-li iskoni vekov stepami i vozmozhno-li oblesit' ikh?*, revised edn (Odessa, 1890), 259–61.

[97] *Odesskoe uezdnoe zemskoe sobranie XXVI ocherednoi sessii* (Odessa, 1890), review in *SKhiL*, 181 (1891), 2nd pagn, 18–19.

[98] GASO, f.149, op.1, d.296, ll.161ob.–2.

[99] Engel'gardt, *Chernozemnaya Rossiya*, appendices, iii–xiii.

[100] P. Kostychev, *O bor'be s zasukhoi v chernozemnoi oblasti postredstvom obrabotki polei i nakopleniya na nikh snega* (Spb, 1893), 22–3.

nineteenth century, these purposes became the main reasons why trees were planted in the steppe region.

Binding drifting sands

Millions of *desyatiny* of land, in the steppe region (and other parts of Russia), were covered by sands, and the sands were blowing onto to adjoining land, including arable fields, causing great concern during the nineteenth century. Specialists believed the problem was worsened, or indeed caused, by felling woodland that grew on sandy soil, over-grazing livestock, and careless cultivation (see above, pp. 139–44). Specialists in Russia looked to experience elsewhere in Europe for ways of holding back the drifting sands. In 1768, Erik Laxmann, a Finnish naturalist and member of the Russian Academy of Sciences, had described drifting sands he had seen along the Selenga river in eastern Siberia. He noted that the Swedish naturalist Carl Linnaeus had advocated the use of certain type of plants to prevent sands from spreading.[101] Most areas of drifting sands in northern and western Europe, however, were along coasts and in climatic conditions quite different from the steppes.[102] In the Russian Empire, a number of methods were tried to bind sands. There were attempts to legislate to protect trees and shrubs growing on sand, and to prevent over-grazing. Manure was applied to sandy soil, and fences built to hold back the sand. But the main method was to plant shrubs and trees.[103] In 1804, Danilevskii planted pine trees on drifting sands on his estate in Khar'kov province.[104] In the early 1830s, in Voronezh province, 700 *desyatiny* of sands were bound by shrubs planted by Herr Freyreiß, the provincial forester.[105]

Shrubs and trees were also planted to bind the large area of drifting sands on the left bank of the Dnepr near Aleshki in Dneprovsk district, Tauride province. This is the likely location of the woodland Herodotus called 'Hylaea'. It had suffered greatly from deforestation, over-grazing, and ploughing the thin top soil since the area came under Russian rule in 1783. By the early 1830s, the sands were spreading rapidly, threatening nearby agricultural land and settlements (see above, pp. 140–1). In 1834, Finance Minister Kankrin assigned 5,000 roubles to bind the sands on a large area of state land. The new Ministry of State Domains increased the scale of the work later in the 1830s.[106] Following the example of

[101] Laksman, 'Novye nekotorye sposoby k uderzhaniyu nanosnogo i letuchego pesku', *TVEO*, 8 (1768), 60–6. See also *ES*, xxxiii (1896), 267.

[102] See DAOO, f.22, op.1, 1837, sp.343, ll.5–ob., 20–5; S. Yu. Rauner, 'Ukreplenie i oblesenie letuchikh peskov v zapadnoi Evrope', *ZRGO po obshchei geografii*, 18/3 (1888), 1–22.

[103] A. Rudzkii, 'Letuchie peski', *PERSKh*, v (1901), 2–9.

[104] Sredinskii, 'Kratkii', 741–2.

[105] RGIA, f.398, op.83, 1834, d.11. See also N. I. Rubtsov, *Kratkaya istoriya stepnogo i zashchitnogo lesonasazhdeniya* (Leningrad, 1970), 15.

[106] K. Fromm, 'Ob ukreplenii letuchikh peskov v Dneprovskom uezde Tavricheskoi gubernii', *ZhMGI*, 75 (1860), 3rd pagn, 5; *IOPDMGI*, i, 180–1.

forester Freyreiß, a shrub known as sharp-leaved willow (*shelyuga* or *krasnaya iva, Salix acutifolia*)—which grew wild on sand in the area—was planted. A forestry official supervised local state peasants in planting the shrubs in the autumn and spring. They ploughed the land to a depth of no less than ¾ *arshin* (21 inches) in preparation for planting rows of cuttings three *sazheny* (21 feet) apart. The rows were orientated from north to south to protect the sands from the easterly winds. The shrubs were pruned after three or four years to provide material for fencing. The sharp-leaved willow reached maturity after seven years. At that point, it started to dry out, but the roots continued to bind the sand for a further twelve to fifteen years. The author of a study found the plantations of sharp-leaved willow to be pleasing to the eye with their straight rows and fresh green colour, which he contrasted with the grey, lifeless steppe in dry summers, and yellow, infertile sand.

After three or four years, the shrubs made the sands more stable, and grassy plants started to grow among them, thus completing the process of binding the sands. Strict measures were taken to keep livestock off the newly bound sands. Because sharp-leaved willow lived for only a few years, experiments were conducted in planting other shrubs and trees. In the early years, most—including oak, maple, ash, lime, birch, and alder—did not grow well. Some success was achieved with elm and pine. But, the tree that was most successful was black poplar (*osokor'*, *Populus nigra*)—a native species—which was planted in a similar manner to sharp-leaved willow. By 1860s, black poplars planted in the 1840s were four *sazheny* (nearly 30 feet) high, around 5–6 *vershki* (9–10 inches) in diameter, and had formed 'forests'. The initial plantings were mostly near large settlements. In 1858, the ministry extended the plantings to include larger areas of drifting sands. Different species of trees, including pine (both Scots, *obyknovennaya*, and Crimean, *krymskaya*), oak, birch, and black locust, were planted on land that had already been bound. The saplings came from new nurseries staffed by graduates of the Velikii Anadol' and Berdyansk plantation schools.[107]

By 1860, around 7,000 *desyatiny* of sand in the vicinity of Aleshki had been planted with sharp-leaved willow and black poplar. By 1887, this had increased to 11,000 *desyatiny*. But, the total area of sand in Dneprovsk district was 139,000 *desyatiny*, over half of which was state land. In 1903, the Forestry Department planned further large-scale plantings of sharp-leaved willow on the 'huge areas of drifting sands' in the district.[108] Despite all the work since 1834, therefore, the area was a still a long way from returning to the 'woodland' described by Herodotus.

---

[107] Fromm, 'Ob ukreplenii', 4–18; [P. I. Kepen], 'Ob Aleshkovskikh letuchikh peskakh', *LZh*, 1 (1841), 401–18; F. Keppen, 'Neskol'ko slov o razvedenii lesov v stepyakh Tavricheskoi gubernii', *ZhMGI*, 84 (1863), 2nd pagn, 13; RGIA, f.426, op.1, 1894, d.40, ll.301–2. See also A. Kostyaev, 'Ukreplenie letuchikh peskov', *PERSKh*, x (1907), 122–41.

[108] Fromm, 'Ob ukreplenii', 5; *IOPDFMGI*, i, 180–1; RGIA, f.387, op.9, 1903, d.45773, ll.42, 52, 65–ob.

Binding drifting sands by planting shrubs and then trees was taking place elsewhere in the steppe region. In the mid-1840s, the Forestry Department of the Ministry of State Domains advised Mennonite colonies, including Molotschna, to prevent their land being inundated by sands by following the model of the plantings on the Aleshki sands.[109] Further east in the early 1840s, Baibakov (the forester who proposed the ill-fated scheme to plant trees on the trans-Don steppes), put forward a plan to bind drifting sands in the Don Cossack territory.[110] From 1872, shrubs and trees were planted each year on sandy soil in the Don region as part of the systematic policy of afforestation. In the late nineteenth and early twentieth century, thousands of *desyatiny* of sandy land was planted in the Don region.[111] In Stavropol' province, the provincial administration took an active interest in preventing sands from drifting. In the 1880s, for example, the governor ordered two investigations into the causes of sands inundating the land around Beshpagir in Stavropol' district. The first in 1880 recommended banning cattle from grazing on the slopes of the sandy hills, and planting fast-growing types of grasses and trees. A more thorough study in 1885 advocated planting the entire area of the sandy hills with sharp-leaved willow and black poplar.[112] Binding drifting sands started late in Samara province. Lishin had advocated planting willow on sands along the Volga in 1892.[113] In 1904, the Forestry Department sent a specialist to help the Samara district *zemstvo* organize the work. An area of around 1,150–1,200 *desyatiny* of drifting sands was identified. Less than two *desyatiny* had already been planted. By 1908, a total of 186.74 *desyatiny* had been bound by shrubs. In 1909–10, trees (pine, birch, and also oak) were planted on around 80 *desyatiny* that had been anchored by the shrubs.[114]

[109] DAOO, f. 6, op.5, 1842, sp.21, ll.1, 7–8ob., 12–ob.; d.24, ll.4–ob., 6–ob., 35, 67–ob.; Keppen, 'Neskol'ko slov', 14.

[110] GARO, f.301, op.14, d.7, 1849–52, ll.40–2; GARO, f.243, op.1, d.19, ll.4–ob., 18–21ob.

[111] GARO, f.46, op.1, d.3241, 1896, l.9ob.; d.3248, 1898, l.45; d.3276, 1901, l.100 ob.; op.1, d.3338, 1901, l.11; d.3338, 1902, l.56; d.3338, 1903, l.102; d.3338, 1904, l.133; d.3338, 1905, l.180; d.3440, 1906, ll.10–11; d.3440, 1908, ll.54ob.–55ob.; d.3440, 1909, ll.99–ob.; d.3534, ll.10; d.3510, 1911, l.51; d.3534, ll.10–ob., 92ob.–93ob.; d.5723, l.6; 3510, 1911, ll.51–ob.; d.3534, ll.92ob; d.5723, l.101ob.; *Pamyatnaya knizhka oblasti voiska Donskogo na 1915 god* (Novocherkassk, 1915), 19–20; A. M. Grekov, 'Nuzhdy Dona v trudakh mestnykh sel'skokhoyaistvennykh komitetov', *SOVDSK*, 5 (1905), 39–40; 'O raskhodakh na 1915 god iz voiskovogo zemel'nogo kapitala po ukrepleniyu peskov na Donu', *Donskie oblastnye vedomosti* (12 March 1915), 3.

[112] GASK, f.101, op.4, d.894 (1880–5), ll.3ob.–4, 19ob.–20. See also f.101, op.4, d.732, 1878–87, l.39ob.; Kade, 'K voprosu o lesorazvedenii v Stavropol'skoi gubernii', *Severnyi Kavkaz* (25 October 1885); N. N. Bakeev, 'Ekonomicheskie osobennosti rasprostraneniya peschanok i mery bor'by s nimi v usloviyakh vostochnogo Predkavkaz'ya', *Materialy po izucheniyu Stavropol'skogo kraya*, 5 (1953), 59–99. See also above, p. 142.

[113] I. A. Lishin, *K voprosu obvodneniya i obleseniya stepnoi polosy Samarskoi gubernii* (Moscow, 1892), 27.

[114] GASO, f.329, op.1, d.15, ll.160–2; GASO, f.329, op.1, d.1, 1903, ll.18–20. See also f.149, op.9, d.84, l.92 ob.

The Forestry Department promoted such work throughout the steppe region. Between 1898 and 1907, it extended 1.2 million roubles in credit to *zemstva*, estate owners, and peasant communes for this purpose. By 1904, 50,000 *desyatiny* of sand had been bound in fourteen provinces. In the spring of 1906, 221 peasant communes took part in planting shrubs on drifting sands, and in the autumn of that year, 341 communes were involved. The area planted had increased to 60,000 *desyatiny* by 1907, and work continued in subsequent years.[115] A further 1,000–2,000 *desyatiny* were bound each year, but the area of land newly inundated by drifting sands each year amounted to tens or hundreds of thousands of *desyatiny*. Ermolov wrote that all attempts to deal with drifting sands were just 'drops in the sea'.[116]

Shelterbelts (zashchitnye polosy)

A further hindrance to agriculture on the steppes were the winds that blew from the east and south-east, in particular the hot *sukhovei*, that dried out the soil and vegetation, and on occasions whipped up dust storms. It is likely that the idea of planting trees to provide shelter from the wind went back to the early settlers. Foreign colonists in Tauride and Ekaterinoslav provinces planted belts of trees around their settlements.[117] In January 1841, I. Isnar (probably a foreign colonist) read a paper to the Southern Russian Agricultural Society in Odessa 'on improving the steppes of southern Russia'. Noting that the longer he studied the soil and climate of the steppes, the more he became convinced that the main obstacle to agriculture was the 'cold and drying winds', he proposed planting trees around fields to provide 'strong protection' from the winds, the sun, and also to retain snow that would otherwise be blown away.[118] In Molotschna, under Cornies' leadership, the Mennonites planted trees to protect their fields from storms. After his death in 1848, one of his obituaries noted that these plantations would be the 'best memorial' to this man.[119] It became more common later in the century to advocate the advantages of forests in providing shelter. Voeikov emphasized the importance of forests in sheltering land from the wind, reducing evaporation, and retaining snow.[120] Veinberg enumerated the advantages for wheat sown in fields adjoining forests: it grew more slowly and luxuriantly, the ears were larger, and was better protected against drying out and

[115] RGIA, f.387, op.28, 1901, d.2464; GASO, f.329, op.1, d.1, 1903, l.20; Z. S. Katsenelenbaum, 'Melioratsii i meliorativnyi kredit', *PERSKh*, xii (1912), 708. See also RGIA, f.387, op.13, 1907, d.55805, ll.1–16ob.; op.28, 1901, d.2464, ll.74–5, 156–60.

[116] V. A. Bertenson, 'Nepochatyi zemel'nyi fond (ob ispol'zovanii sypuchikh peschanykh pochv)', *SKhiL*, 224 (February 1907), 141. (Bertenson quoted Ermolov.) See also Z. S. Katsenelenbaum, 'Melioratsii i meliorativnyi kredit', 706.

[117] Vysotskii, 'Stepnoe lesorazvedenie', 446.

[118] I. Isnar, 'Ob uluchshenii stepei poludennoi Rossii', *ZhMGI*, 6 (1842), 3rd pagn, 608–10.

[119] Gavel', 'Iogann Kornis' [nekrolog], *ZIOSKhYuR* (1848), 792–3. See also DAOO, f.1, op.248, 1856, sp.1580, ll.124ob.–125.

[120] Voeikov, 'O vliyanii lesov na klimat'.

disease than wheat in unprotected fields.[121] At the same time, Achilles Alferaki, who owned an estate near Taganrog, argued that forests would pose a barrier to dry winds from Asia.[122]

The results in practice, however, were not as clear cut. In the late 1870s, A. A. de Karrier began an experiment with shelterbelts on his estate of Kameno-vatka, Elizavetgrad district, Kherson province, with the aim of creating more favourable conditions for agriculture. To this end, he wanted to increase the moisture content of the soil, which many specialists believed trees could provide. He divided his estate into squares and planted parallel rows of mixed species of trees, in particular, black locust, ash, and birch. The belts were 15 *sazheny* (105 feet) wide and between 110 and 125 *sazheny* (770–875 feet) apart. The Southern Russian Agricultural Society followed the experiment. In the summer of 1892, it sent A. A. Bychikhin to investigate. Incomplete observations showed that the shelterbelts had reduced the force of the wind and increased moisture in the soil. The increase in crop yields that resulted, moreover, had repaid the cost of planting and maintaining the shelterbelts. Significantly, the estate was spared the impact of the drought of 1891 that caused crops to fail elsewhere in Kherson province.[123] The claim that the belts of trees at Kamenovatka had increased soil moisture was soon questioned. A study by P. V. Ototskii, commissioned by the Free Economic Society, found Bychikhin's findings to be tendentious. Ototskii concluded that the trees had had no impact on ground water, and that the 'steppe remained as dry as it had been before the start of the plantings'.[124] Yu. A. Leman visited the estate in 1902 and reported that, since 1892, average crop yields on the estate were similar to the surrounding district. He noted, however, that the shelterbelts did assist in retaining snow, thus providing moisture when it melted, and protected crops from storms.[125] Other studies showed that shelterbelts had some benefits in particular circumstances. On the estate of Novo-Petrovka in Kherson district, the owner planted shelterbelts 17–20 *sazheny* (119–140 feet) wide. He planted longer belts, up to 290 *sazheny* (2030 feet) from north to south, and belts a little over half that length from east to west. Crop yields were significantly higher in fields protected by shelterbelts than exposed fields. Higher yields were especially noticeable in fields sown with winter grain with belts along the eastern side. This was due mainly to the accumulation of snow blown in by the easterly winds.[126]

---

[121] Veinberg, *Les*, 244, 318–33.

[122] Arkhilles Alferaki, *O polozhenii sel'skogo khozyaistva v yugo-vostochnom krae* (Spb, 1879), 12.

[123] A. A. Bychikhin, *Znachenie zashchitnykh nasazhdenii dlya stepnoi polosy* (Odessa, 1893), reviewed in *SKhiL*, 173 (1893), 3rd pagn, 160–3.

[124] P. V. Ototskii, 'O vliyanii lesov na gruntovye vody', *Pochvovedenie*, 2/3 (1900), 180–9; E. Anri, 'Lesa', 1–30.

[125] Yu. A. Leman, 'O zashchitnykh lesnykh posadkakh v stepyakh Novorossii', *ZIOSKhYuR* (1902), 28–33.

[126] *Nasazhdenie zashchitnykh opushek v imenii 'Novo-Petrovka' khersonskoi gub. i uezda* (Odessa, 1896), review in *SKhiL*, 189 (1898), 229–30.

In the late 1880s and early 1890s, under Genko's management, the Appanage Department planted large shelterbelts of trees on its land throughout the steppe region. The main plantings were carried out in Stavropol' and Samara provinces, and in a belt extending from Saratov province towards Orenburg. Genko selected land on watersheds, in part because the soil was less likely to be alkaline and thus suitable for trees. He orientated the belts from the south-west to the north-east, as far as the relief permitted. He also planted belts from north to south and west to east with the aim of blocking the dry winds that blew in from the south-east in the summer. Using the 'Don type' of combining trees and shrubs (see above, p. 190), Genko oversaw the planting of very large belts between 200 and 300 *sazheny* (1400 to 2100 feet) wide and up to 10 or even 20 *versty* in length. He reported the success of his plantings at a congress in St Petersburg in 1902.[127]

The Dokuchaev expedition of the 1890s was established to research ways to use forestry to avert repetitions of the disaster of 1891–2. The expedition's scientists paid particular attention to shelterbelts, and measured their effects at the Velikii Anadol' plantation and other locations.[128] Vysotskii reported the results. The sheltering influence of the belts on crops was limited to a strip 70–100 *sazheny* (490–700 feet) wide leeward of a belt of woodland 8–10 *sazheny* (56–70 feet) high. If the shelterbelt was taller or denser, that is, better able to block the wind, then the influence extended to 190 *sazheny* (1330 feet). Measurements at Velikii Anadol' in May 1895 demonstrated the impact of shelterbelts. The wind speed on the open steppe was 7.3 metres a second, but inside a dense, fifteen-year-old stand of elm and ash, it was only 0.16–0.53 metres a second. In spring, in locations sheltered from the easterly wind and shaded from the sun, vegetation usually developed more successfully—it was denser, bushier, taller, and fresher—than on land outside the sheltering effect of the belts.

The effects of shelterbelts on crops were not all positive. Vysotskii also noted that if sheltered crops grew better in the spring, in some cases they used up more moisture from the soil and created a shortage later in the growing season. This could result in lower crop yields than in unsheltered fields. He further reported that shelterbelts could increase the risk of morning frosts. Shelterbelts, moreover, could cause greater evaporation from the soil, and the roots of the trees could dry out the land, especially the subsoil, for a few metres from the edges of the belts. Thus, the precise local conditions and micro-climates were important in determining the size of the harvest in sheltered fields. Furthermore, shelterbelts were

---

[127] Genko, *Razvedenie lesa*, 17–27; 'Protokol soedinennogo zasedaniya sektsii lesovodstva i sel'skogo khozyaistva 16 dekabrya vecherom', in *Trudy 2-ogo s'ezda deyatelei po sel'skokhozyaistvennomu opytnomu delu v S. Peterburge s 14 po 20 dekabrya 1902 goda*, 2 parts (Spb, 1905), ii, 1st pagn, 187–9.

[128] *Otchet po lesnomu upravleniyu ministerstva zemledeliya i gosudarstvennykh imushchestv za 1893 god* (Spb 1894), review in *SKhiL*, 177 (1894), 3rd pagn, 60.

most effective in protecting fields during dust storms. Vysotskii concluded that outside sandy areas, 'one should not get carried away by the idea of protecting fields on all sides by borders of trees or by belts of trees and shrubs'.[129]

Shelterbelts served another purpose: retaining snow in the winter by preventing it from blowing away so that the melt water seeped into the ground in the spring. Experience showed that 'snow-retention belts' (*snegosborno-zashchitnye polosy*) were most effective if they were dense, wide, and tall. Belts of trees and shrubs between 30 and 70 *sazheny* (210 to 490 feet) wide retained all the snow inside them, and also accumulated snow in drifts from the windward side. They had the beneficial effect of increasing the irrigation of the land underneath them, leaching salts out of the soil, thus making it more suitable for trees. The best way to achieve the desired results was to plant rows of shrubs on the windward southern and eastern sides of fields to block the winds. The belts needed to be sufficiently tall that the trees would not be buried by the snow, which could then blow away. Thus, to be effective, belts needed to have time to mature. The belts planted by the Appanage Department, which were large and located on higher land on watersheds, proved to be effective, but younger belts were less so.[130] Kostychev, who doubted the efficacy of planting trees on the steppe for other purposes, cited studies carried out at Velikii Anadol' that showed the value of tree plantations in retaining snow not just in the forested area, but also in adjoining fields. In the drought year of 1891, fields next to woodland gave higher yields of crops than those in exposed locations.[131]

In spite of the reservations expressed by some specialists, planting belts of trees to shelter fields from the wind and assist in accumulating snow was catching on in the steppe region. In 1892, for example, F. K. Tremlin, an estate owner in Donets district of the Don region, read a paper to the Don agricultural society on his plan to plant 'parallel walls' of trees on his estate.[132] From the mid-1890s, tree planting in Tauride and Ekaterinoslav provinces changed its character as more attention was paid to shelterbelts.[133] In 1905, the Don Statistical Committee called for a special state expedition to plan tree planting to protect the region from dry, south-easterly winds.[134] After 1906, the Forestry Department provided aid for planting shelterbelts to peasants who had separated their land under the Stolypin reforms. In 1914, for example, grants of between 15 and 60 roubles were given to twenty-seven peasants in Nikolaevsk district in southern

---

[129] Vysotskii, 'Stepnoe lesorazvedenie', 493–5.
[130] Vysotskii, 'Stepnoe lesorazvedenie', 494–9; S. Rauner, 'Lesnye snegosbornye polosy v stepyakh yuga evropeiskoi Rossii', *SKhiL*, 217 (1905), 645–57.
[131] Kostychev, *O bor'be*, 18–27.
[132] *Otchet o deyatel'nosti donskogo obshchestva sel'skogo khozyaistva za 1892 god*, review in *SKhiL*, 173 (1893), 13–14.
[133] *Stoletie uchrezhdeniya lesnogo departamenta, 1798–1898* (Spb, 1898), 191.
[134] Grekov, 'Nuzhdy Dona', 38.

Samara province to plant broadleaved trees to act as windbreaks and collect snow.[135]

While most shelterbelt planting was on quite modest scales, some people invested huge hopes in them, and proposed great plans to transform nature. In the 1890s, a member of the Simbirsk *zemstvo*, I. V. Mikhailov, suggested they seek government assistance to plant shelterbelts down both banks of the river Volga, all the way from Samara to Tsaritsyn', and both banks of the Ural river from Orsk to the Caspian Sea. (The total distance was well over a thousand miles.) The cost should not seem great, he asserted, since in the very near future the fate of eleven provinces would depend on it.[136] This idea was revived in the late 1940s when the great hopes that had been invested in tree planting a century earlier were revived and conquering nature was the order of the day (see below, pp. 292–3).

Reinforcing ravines to prevent expansion

Trees were also planted to reinforce ravines to prevent them expanding. The erosive action of water running through them carried away valuable soil, and water that would otherwise have seeped into the land was draining away. In the later part of the nineteenth century, there was a growing consensus among specialists that the expansion in the number and size of ravines in the steppe region was due in large part to human activity. A major cause was felling the trees that grew naturally in ravines and served to bind the soil (see Chapter 5). By the end of the nineteenth century, specialists were advocating measures to stop ravines expanding. Some were based on experience elsewhere in Europe, as well as in Russia. Among the measures recommended was planting trees. Trees were planted on land above ravines to reduce the flow of water, which caused erosion, into them. For the same reason, trees, in particular willows, were planted on the slopes down the sides of ravines. The most important technique for preventing the expansion of ravines, however, was to build dams at the bottom to hold back the water, forming ponds in the ravines, rather than torrents rushing through them, eroding the soil.[137]

The work was expensive and required a lot of labour. Public works set up in 1892 to offer relief to victims of the previous year's crop failure included the reinforcement and afforestation of ravines. *Zemstva* throughout the regions most affected by the growth of ravines took an interest in organizing measures to stop

[135] GASO, f.332, op.1, d.1, ll.1–4ob., 7–10, 18, 58.

[136] See Engel'gardt, *Chernozemnaya Rossiya*, 98.

[137] See E. E. Kern, *Ovragi, ikh zakreplenie, oblesenie i zapruzhivanie*, 5th edn (Moscow, 1892, 1894, 1897, Spb, 1903, 1913). (The 3rd edition was approved by the Ministry of Agriculture for use in its educational establishments. RGIA, f.382, op.2, 1897, d.1828, ll.8–12ob.); V. Masal'skii, *Ovragi chernozemnoi polosy Rossii, ikh rasprostranenie, razvitie i deyatel'nost'* (Spb, 1897), 221–51.

them expanding.[138] In the 1890s, the Kherson provincial *zemstvo*, for example, repeatedly discussed making work to reinforce ravines compulsory for the local population. The *zemstvo* revived the issue in 1899, when torrential downpours after a dry summer washed parched soil into ravines that grew at an alarming rate. *Zemstvo* official P. A. Zelenskii spoke of the need to 'restore the natural balance' by reinforcing ravines. On the *zemstvo*'s request, the Ministry of Agriculture sent a specialist to study ravines in the province and drew up a plan to reinforce them.[139] Similar measures were taken across the steppe region by *zemstva*, the Peasant Land Bank, the Appanage Department, and the Don Cossack authorities.[140]

In some cases, the local authorities received assistance, technical and financial, from the government in St Petersburg. The Forestry Department carried out work to reinforce and plant trees in ravines in provinces throughout the steppe and forest-steppe regions from 1901 to 1917. The total expenditure rose to over 81,000 roubles in 1909, and in excess of 425,000 roubles in 1911 and 1912. The higher figures for these last two years was due to extra expenditure on public works to provide relief after harvest failures. Total expenditure by the ministry on such work over the years 1908 to 1915 came to nearly 2 million roubles.[141] The importance of such work was not left unquestioned. In 1912, a leading specialist argued that investing money to reinforce ravines did not increase the value of estates where such work was carried out, nor did the income from the estates rise.[142]

Reinforcing ravines by damming them and planting trees around them served another purpose: the dammed ravines made ideal reservoirs for storing water for the population and their livestock. In some circumstances, moreover, the water was also used for irrigation (see Chapter 7).[143]

CONCLUSION

When Gifford Pinchot visited Russia in 1902, and saw forestry plantations on the steppes, he noted that trees were planted in the region purely for preventing erosion: controlling drifting sands, sheltering land from the wind, and preventing the expansion of ravines. His Russian hosts advised him that the main barrier to the growth of trees in the steppe region was the alkalinity of the soil. Pinchot was

---

[138] Kern, *Ovragi*, 4th edn, 107–28.
[139] RGIA, f.426, op.1, 1900, d.310, ll.2–3, 13–14.
[140] See, for example, RGIA 426 1 1903 495, l.1–ob.; GASO, f.149, op.1, d.296; f.43, op.8, d.466; d.999; Grekov, 'Nuzhdy Dona', 38–9; 'K ukrepleniyu i obleseniyu ovragov na Donu', *Donskie oblastnye vedomosti* (11 April 1915), 3.
[141] RGIA, f.387, op.28, 1901, d.2464, ll.2–11, 13ob., 22–7.
[142] Katsenelenbaum, 'Melioratsii i meliorativnyi kredit', 706.
[143] Kern, *Ovragi*, 4th edn, 82–106.

not convinced, but did note that the plantations he saw 'appear to be doing superbly', 'except those on alkaline soil'.[144] Thus, by the early twentieth century, most tree planting in the steppe region was restricted to areas with sandy soil and in ravines, where they grew naturally. Shelterbelt planting on the steppes, where they did not, required the new techniques that had been developed over many decades of trial and error and experiment.

Right from the early years of Russian settlement of the steppes, there had been differing views on the possibility and potential benefits of planting trees. Some of the most vociferous advocates were largely armchair foresters. Palimpsestov, who maintained for a long time his confidence in the possibility of nurturing forests on the steppes, saw advantages beyond environmental ones. He asserted that their benefits were also spiritual and nationalist. In some of his writings he implied that planting trees on the steppes would give the region a 'Russian' identity after millennia of domination by nomadic peoples, whom, he asserted, had destroyed the forests that he believed had once covered the steppes.[145]

At a more prosaic level, in 1902, two men with considerable practical experience of steppe forestry, Vysotskii and Genko, debated the issues at a congress in St Petersburg. Vysotskii asserted that the idea of making the climate wetter by afforestation came up against the insurmountable barrier of the shortage of water and the resulting alkalinity of the soil. These made large-scale growth of healthy and sustainable forests impossible. He went on to question the favourable influence of forests on crop yields. He concluded that forests could grow successfully in the steppe region only in hilly areas, on the flood plains of rivers, on sandy soil, and on watersheds (i.e. the locations in which they grew naturally).[146] Genko objected strongly. He cited the successful plantings of forests by the Appanage Department in the steppe region that he had superintended since 1885 (see above, p. 200). He pointed out that fewer than 1 per cent of the trees had dried up and died. He suggested that Vysotskii's conclusions applied only to the dry steppe, such as the vicinity of Velikii Anadol'. Vysotskii countered by referring Genko to the scientific literature, which he claimed his opponent was insufficiently familiar with. He added that great significance could not be ascribed to the Appanage Department's plantings as they were 'no older than twelve–thirteen years, that is, they have not yet reached the critical age when the shortage of water on the steppe starts to have its fatal influence'.[147] After

[144] Pinchot Papers, Box 715, File: 'Notes taken by Mr Pinchot on his trip through Russia and Siberia', folios 43–4, 49, 58.

[145] P[alimpsestov], 'Lesovodstvo', 79–80; [1] P[alimpsestov], 'Les-progress', *ZIOSKhYuR* (1858), 60; I. U. Palimpsestov, 'Odin iz otvetov na vopros: "byli li lesa na yuge Rossii?"', *Izvestiya imperatorskogo obshchestva lyubitelei estestvoznaniya, antropologii i etnografii*, 41/1 (1881), 17.

[146] G. N. Vysotskii, 'O stimulakh, prepyatstviyak i problemakh razvedeniya lesa v stepyakh Rossii', *Trudy 2-ogo s"ezda deyatelei po sel'skokhozyaistvennomu opytnomu delu v S. Peterburge s 14 po 20 dekabrya 1902 goda*, 2 parts (Spb, 1902–5), i, 305, 330, 333–4.

[147] 'Protokol soedinennogo zasedaniya', 186–90, 194–5.

Genko's death in 1904, the Appanage Department commissioned Vysotskii to produce a study of conditions for planting trees on its land in Samara province. His study drew attention to the presence of suitable, forest soils in the north of the province, but also to chestnut soils, with areas of alkaline soil, in the south that were not suitable for trees.[148]

Several decades earlier, in 1844, A. Strudza, an estate owner in New Russia, wrote to the Southern Russian Agricultural Society bemoaning the 'lack of forests and lack of water' in 'our region', which had otherwise been so generously endowed by nature. Like so many of his contemporaries, he saw the solution as planting trees 'we need to apply ourselves to cultivating forests everywhere, so that in time our commercial cities and flowering villages will not once again turn into the camps of steppe nomads, and our trace disappear from the land of the living!'[149] M. Shcherbinin replied that to defeat the 'two cruel scourges' of lack of trees and water, planting trees would not be sufficient. He urged his fellow inhabitants of New Russia to engage 'indefatigably' in making better use of the water in the rivers, springs, and from melted snow to irrigate the land. He concluded: 'Let us unite our energies to introduce an irrigation system in the New Russian region; then our steppe economy will be completely transformed . . . and the . . . region will rank with the most fertile countries in the world.'[150] Thus, the doubts about both the possibility and potential benefits of large-scale tree planting on the steppes turned attention to artificial irrigation.

---

[148] G. N. Vysotskii, *O lesorastitel'nykh usloviyakh raiona Samarskogo Udel'nogo Okruga: Pochvenno-botaniko-lesovodstvennyi ocherk*, 2 vols (Spb, 1909).

[149] A. Strudza, 'Pis'mo novorossiiskogo pomeshchika', *ZIOSKhYuR* (1844), 127–34.

[150] M. Shcherbinin, 'Oroshenie polei', *ZIOSKhYuR* (1844), 5–19.

7

Irrigation

INTRODUCTION

Enormous efforts were expended during the nineteenth century to provide the water needed by the growing settler population and expanding agricultural economy in the steppe region. The settlers needed water for themselves and their livestock, vegetable gardens, fruit trees in orchards, grass in meadows, and crops in the fields. They obtained water from wells and springs, streams and rivers, and specially constructed ponds and reservoirs. The main concern of this chapter is artificial irrigation (*irrigatsiya* or *oroshenie*) to supply water to meadows and arable fields. There were a number of ways to do this. Land was flooded once a year, in the early spring, with water from melting snow that had been retained behind low earthworks. This was called flood irrigation (*limannoe oroshenie*). It was generally used to provide water for meadows. More complicated and expensive was channelling water from reservoirs to fields. This was called channel irrigation (*pravil'noe oroshenie*). It was used to supply water to fields regularly, when the crops needed it, during the growing season. Water was collected by damming rivers, ravines, and gullies to retain water that flowed through them and to accumulate water from rainfall and melted snow.[1]

Providing water for people, livestock, vegetables, fruit trees, and low-lying meadows on the flood plains of rivers proved rather easier than supplying water for crops in fields, not least because the latter were often on the high steppes. Nevertheless, proposals were made, plans drawn up, and experiments conducted into the best ways to irrigate arable land. During the second half of the nineteenth century, plans for more extensive systems were put forward by individuals, private companies, estate owners, agricultural societies, and the authorities in St Petersburg and the steppe region. Russians looked back to the riverine civilizations of ancient Egypt and Mesopotamia, as well as China, and to more recent experience in Europe and Europe's overseas colonies, such as India. They also drew attention to Central Asia and Transcaucasia, where, before they had been annexed by the Russian Empire, the populations had used artificial irrigation. The implication was that Russia needed to learn from experience of irrigation

---

[1] See S. Kizenkov, 'Oroshenie', *PERSKh*, iv (1902), 414–68; A. T., 'Oroshenie', *ES*, xliii (1897), 181–5; A. P. Engel'gardt, *Chernozemnaya Rossiya* (Saratov, 1903), 152–60.

elsewhere if it was to develop agriculture on its semi-arid steppes.[2] In the Russian Empire, as in the British Empire in India, proposals for irrigation were often spurred by droughts and food shortages.[3]

A few advocates of artificial irrigation thought that it would be straightforward, and needed only funding from the government.[4] Most proposals for irrigating arable land, however, either remained on paper or did not get far beyond the experimental stage as artificial irrigation came up against a number of problems. One was legal. Under Russian law dating back to Catherine the Great, private property included the rivers that passed through it, lakes, ponds, and springs and the water in them. According to laws that went back to the code of 1649, moreover, owners of land adjoining rivers had the right to demand that none of their land was flooded by ponds created by landowners on the other side of the rivers. They could also demand that dams should not be built across rivers onto their land without their permission. The aim of these restrictions was to prevent landowners from disrupting watermills belonging to their neighbours.[5] These laws were enacted when the estates of most land owners were situated in central and northern Russia, where water was readily available. In the steppe region, where water was in short supply, such laws were not appropriate. D. L. Ivanov, who surveyed Stavropol' province in 1885, gave an example of the problem created by Russian water law: the absence of downstream water rights. The owners of the estate of Maslov Kut treated all the water in the Kuma river that flowed through their land as their property, as the law allowed them. They diverted two-thirds of the water from the river to power their water mills, thus depriving the inhabitants of the more arid steppe downstream of much needed water.[6]

In contrast, in Central Asia before Russian conquest, 'as in other desert societies', water belonged to everyone, and landowners were guaranteed 'the right to an equitable share of water required for the land's cultivation.'[7] In

---

[2] See, for example, 'O sistemakh orosheniya polei v Khive, Persii i Egipte', *ZhMGI*, 3 (1841), 2nd pagn, 397–437; [Mikhail Vasil'ev Eriks], *Zapiska o vvedenii v Rossii iskustvennogo orosheniya polei i lugov* (Spb, 1868), 37–49 (The pamphlet can be found in GARO, f.46, op.1, d.780, ll.70–100 ob.); A. I. Voeikov, 'Iskusstvennoe oroshenie i ego primenenie na Kavkaze i v Srednei Azii', *Russkii vestnik*, 10 (1884), 569–99.

[3] See, for example 'Stavropol, 15 iyulya', *Severnyi Kavkaz* (16 July 1885); P. Barakov, *O vozmozhnykh merakh bor'by s zasukhami* (Odessa, 1892), 22–33; William Beinart and Lotte Hughes, *Environment and Empire* (Oxford, 2009), 136.

[4] See, for example, a proposal by a civil engineer in 1892. RGIA, f.398, op.75, d.22, ll.61–64ob.

[5] *Svod Zakonov Rossiiskoi Imperii*, 3rd edn, 15 vols (Spb, 1857), x, 73–4, art. 387, 81, art.424, 85, art.442; *PSZ*, 1, i, 52 (no.1, 29 January 1649), art.238. See also Ekaterina Pravilova, 'Les *res publicae* russes. Discours sur la propriété publique à la fin de l'empire', *Annales Histoire Sciences Sociales*, 69/3 (2009), 579–609.

[6] D. L. Ivanov, 'Vliyanie Russkoi kolonizatsii na prirodu Stavropol'skogo kraya', *IRGO*, 22/3 (1886), 249.

[7] Muriel Joffe, 'Autocracy, Capitalism and Empire: The Politics of Irrigation', *RR*, 54 (1995), 381.

1838, an official of the Ministry of State Domains had identified the need to determine the mutual legal rights of estate owners in southern Russia to water flowing across their land.[8] A further change in the law was needed to permit estate owners to build dams and dig channels to carry water for irrigation that encroached, as they almost inevitably would, on the property of other land-owners. Changing the law to facilitate irrigation proved to be a long process.[9]

It was easier to change the law, however, than to increase the amount of water available or alter the topography of much of the steppe region. The rivers in the region—a potential source of water for irrigation—did not contain sufficient water at the times it was needed. Water levels were highest in the spring, when they were fed by melted snow, but fell over the following weeks. Some rivers dried up altogether in the summer. Due to the flatness of the terrain, the gradient of most steppe rivers was inadequate to allow water to be channelled by gravity to irrigate surrounding land. Many rivers, moreover, flowed through deep valleys, far below the fields on the high steppes above them. Nor was precipitation able to provide the necessary water. The amount of water that fell as snow in the winter or rain in other seasons was generally lower than in central and northern Russia. More importantly, the distribution of precipitation over the year was not ideal for grain cultivation. There was less precipitation in winter, which could be stored up for the early spring when germinating crops needed it, than at other times of the year. Torrential downpours in the summer drained away quickly through ravines, gullies, and rivers, and the volume of precipitation varied sharply from year to year. In drought years crops dried up and died. And, the summer heat and drying winds from the east caused some of the water that was available to evaporate. Another potential source of water was in the ground. In the steppe region, however, levels of ground water were lowest in the aftermath of droughts when it was most needed.[10] Many specialists, moreover, believed the volume of water was declining during the course of the nineteenth century due to changes in the climate and the land (see above, pp. 119–24, 152–7).[11]

In 1876, the agronomist Aleksandr Shishkin argued that it was too difficult and expensive to irrigate the steppes as the water would have to be transported too far and raised too high from the river valleys onto the high steppes. In any case, there was not sufficient water in the rivers and streams to meet the needs of agriculture. He concluded that irrigation was practicable for only small areas.[12] The topographical argument against the practicality of irrigation had

[8] *Proekt pravil ob osushenii i oroshenii zemel'* (Spb, 1870), i, v.

[9] *IOPDMGI*, iv/i, 240–6.

[10] See S. Kizenkov, 'Istochniki vody dlya orosheniya', *PERSKh*, iii (1900), 1179–89; P. Ototskii, 'Gruntovye vody', *PERSKh*, ii (1900), 903; S. Rauner, 'Lesnye snegosbornye polosy v stepyakh yuga evropeiskoi Rossii', *SKhiL*, 217 (1905), 645–7.

[11] I. Klimenko, 'K obvodneniyu Novorossiiskikh stepei', *ZIOSKhYuR* (1879), 2nd pagn, 161–4.

[12] A. Shishkin, *K voprosu ob umen'shenii vrednogo deistviya zasukh na rastitel'nost'* (Spb, 1876), 167.

been made in 1853 by A. Skal'kovskii, who considered supplying water to arable fields to be 'impossible'. The argument was strongly restated by M. N. Gersevanov in 1890.[13] Nevertheless, recurring droughts in the steppe region prompted repeated calls for government support for irrigation. At the heart of this chapter is the 'Expedition for Irrigation (*oroshenie*) in the South of Russia and the Caucasus' led by General Zhilinskii which was launched in 1880 after the droughts of the 1870s. The expedition revealed both the possibilities and problems entailed in this solution to the environmental constraints on agriculture in the steppe region.

In essence, efforts to provide water in the steppe region by artificial irrigation, like the tree planting discussed in the previous chapter, were attempts to make the semi-arid steppes more like the moister, and forested, regions of central and northern Russia and central Europe, which were the homelands of most of the settlers or their forebears, and many of those who administered them or studied the region.

IRRIGATION TO THE MID-NINETEENTH CENTURY

From the early days of agricultural settlement of the steppe region, the population provided themselves with water and irrigated small areas of land. The leaders of the Academy of Sciences expeditions of 1768–74 noted some examples. Samuel Gmelin described how the German settlers at Sarepta on the lower Volga transported water from a spring to their settlement for their vegetable gardens and domestic use through a wooden pipe.[14] Settlers near Taganrog constructed a dam across a wide gulley. Johann Güldenstädt noted with evident approval that it served two purposes: it retained water for use and carried the road across the gulley.[15] As he travelled across the high steppe south-west from Poltava towards Kremenchug in August 1787, Vasilli Zuev recorded how the population had dug wells in almost every field to provide water for livestock and, in times of drought, the water melons they cultivated. Water was to be found between two and three *sazheny* (14–21 feet) down. Zuev was very impressed by the wind pumps some settlers had built to bring

---

[13] A. Skal'kovskii, *Opyt statisticheskogo opisaniya Novorossiiskogo kraya*, 2 vols (Odessa, 1850–3), ii, 52; M. N. Gersevanov, 'Ob obvodnenii yuzhnoi stepnoi polosy Rossii', *Zapiski imperatorskogo russkogo tekhnicheskogo obshchestva*, 1 (1891), 1st pagn, 1–30.

[14] Samuel Georg Gmelin, *Puteshestvie po Rossii dlya issledovaniya trekh tsarstv estestva, perevedena s nemetskogo*, 4 vols in 3 parts (Spb, 1771–85), ii, 30.

[15] I. Ya. Gil'denshtedt, 'Dnevnik puteshestviya v Yuzhnuyu Rossiyu akademika S. Peterburgskoi Akademii Nauk Gil'denshtedta v 1773–1774 g.', *Zapiski Imperatorskogo Odesskogo obshchestva istorii i drevnosti*, 11 (1879), 210.

the water to the surface. He recommended that they be used in other flat areas that were short of water.[16]

In the first half of the nineteenth century, some inhabitants of the steppe region irrigated their land. The Mennonites of Molotschna in Tauride province started to irrigate their meadows in 1835, after the drought of 1833. Their land was almost completely flat and there were few streams. Spring floods from the rivers did not reach all the land that needed irrigation. So, the Mennonites built earthen dams across the rivers to collect water from melted snow, and then released it over larger areas. The newly irrigated meadows yielded more than twice as much hay as before. By 1842, they had built forty-six dams, at a cost of between 50 and 150 silver roubles each, which irrigated 1,384 *desyatiny* of meadows.[17] The Mennonites' efforts to irrigate part of their land were rather unusual in this period. A survey by the Ministry of State Domains in 1843 revealed that there was little artificial irrigation in the Russian Empire outside 'Asiatic' parts, such as Transcaucasia. Some irrigation was noted in Astrakhan', Saratov, and Tauride provinces, where it was used mostly in orchards, vineyards, and low-lying meadows.[18] Another reason for the limited use of irrigation, besides the obstacles noted earlier, may have been suspicion. In the 1850s, some estate owners in Saratov province believed that irrigating crops would lead to good straw, but poor grain.[19] At the same time, a specialist noted that irrigation would be of little use in Kherson province as he knew of no system that could provide sufficient water to benefit the plants before it evaporated in the heat.[20]

There was more extensive use of irrigation in the North Caucasus. There are two possible reasons for this. First, the hilly topography suited irrigation and, second, there were large quantities of water available in the rivers that flowed down from the Caucasus mountains. Thus, water from the rivers could readily be diverted by channels using gravity to irrigate land that was downstream. In much of the steppe region, in marked contrast, the population faced the problem of raising water from river valleys onto the high steppe. The cossacks who lived along the Terek river had been digging irrigation channels since at least the eighteenth century. Indeed, it was so easy to irrigate land that they caused floods and turned dry land into swamps. By digging irrigation channels too steeply, moreover, they caused erosion. Not deterred, in the 1850s, ataman Eristov had three long canals dug to carry water from tributaries of the Terek deep into the steppe.[21]

---

[16] Vasilii Zuev, *Puteshestvennye zapiski Vasiliya Zueva ot S. Peterburga do Khersona, v 1781 i 1782 godu* (Spb, 1787), 206.

[17] I. Kornis, 'Ob oroshenii lugov v molochanskikh koloniyakh', *ZhMGI*, 6 (1842), 2nd pagn, 260–3.

[18] 'O iskustvennom oroshenii zemel'', *ZhMGI*, 9 (1843), 2nd pagn, 254–6.

[19] *VSORI*, 5/4, *Saratovskaya gub.*, comp. Beznosikov (1852), 99.

[20] O. Komstadius, 'O prichinakh neurozhaev v khersonskoi gubernii', *TVEO*, 3/7 (1852), 5–6.

[21] Thomas M. Barrett, *At the Edge of Empire: The Terek Cossacks and the North Caucasus Frontier, 1700–1860* (Boulder, CO, 1999), 69–73; Ivanov, 'Vliyanie Russkoi kolonizatsii', 246–9.

In spite of the practical problems in other parts of the steppe region, the shortage of water left settlers with little choice but to find ways to accumulate it by artificial means. The population of southern Samara province suffered particularly from shortage of water. In the late 1850s, settlers in the province received permission from the Ministry of State Domains to build a dam to store water near their village.[22] A later *zemstvo* survey of Novyi Uzen' district in southern Samara province noted that agricultural settlement of the waterless steppe would have been impossible unless the inhabitants had obtained water artificially. Peasants had dug wells, built dams to hold snow melt water, and constructed hundreds of ponds.[23] Until the second half of the nineteenth century, however, most attempts to irrigate land in the steppe region outside the North Caucasus were small scale and local.

PLANS FOR LARGER-SCALE IRRIGATION FROM THE MID-NINETEENTH CENTURY

Grandiose plans

From the mid-nineteenth century, there were growing numbers of proposals for artificial irrigation on a larger scale. Some were on a vast scale, anticipating the gargantuan hydro-engineering projects of the twentieth century. In 1848, in the wake of the drought and harvest failure of that year, the Free Economic Society received a plan from a Saratov estate owner called Safonov. He proposed constructing a navigable canal across the steppe to the east from the river Volga from Pokrovskaya to Lake El'ton, on to the river Akhtuba (which flows parallel to the lower Volga), and thence east to Gur'ev, on the mouth of Ural river. The canal would serve to transport salt from Lake El'ton to markets, and also provide water to irrigate a number of settlements that Safonov proposed to establish along its length. He noted that huge expanses of steppe in the region were left empty because there was no fresh water. With irrigation, however, several million *desyatiny* would become productive. He estimated that his scheme would cost four million roubles. It was considered by the Free Economic Society, the Main Administration for Transport, and the Ministry of State Domains, but all rejected it on grounds of cost, the lack of technical personnel, and viability.[24]

A decade later, there was discussion of linking the Sea of Azov (and therefore the Black Sea) with the Caspian Sea by a canal joining the Manych' and Kuma rivers. The aim was to promote settlement and agriculture on the low-lying

[22] GASO, f.112, op.47, 1859–65, d.10.

[23] *SSSpSG*, VII, *Novouzenskii uezd* (1890), 5.

[24] RGIA, f.91, 1848, op.1, d.331, ll.14–67ob. The Free Economic Society took little interest in irrigation. For a rare example, see 'Ob oroshenii ili irrigatsii', *TVEO*, 3/3 (1851), 1–12.

steppe in the region. An investigation in the summer of 1860, however, showed the idea to be unfeasible. The area was not suitable for agriculture as the water and soil were too salty. There was not sufficient water in the rivers outside the spring for a canal. And, there was little water at all in the summer, when the local Kalmyk nomads took their herds to other pastures. Advocates of the proposal to link the seas had reported vast expanses of water in the Manych' basin, but the investigation dismissed these as mirages.[25]

A rather larger mirage appeared on the other side of the world in 1876. An American engineer, Henry C. Spalding, put forward an ambitious scheme to link the Black and Caspian Seas. He noted that the Caspian was gradually becoming shallower as a result of alluvium deposited by the Volga and Ural rivers. In time, these processes would 'convert this sea into a great marsh, and the lands into barren and desert regions'. The 'requisite supply of water' to reverse the process could be found, he noted, in the Black Sea. Since the Caspian Sea was 15 metres below the level of the Black Sea, he proposed digging a cutting to allow water to flow from one to the other. Another channel linking the rivers Don and Volga, letting water flow from the Don into the Caspian rather than the Black Sea, would speed up the process. Spalding calculated that in about twenty-five years the Caspian Sea would rise to the level of the Black Sea. The area of the Caspian would increase by just under half 'from 493,000 square kilometres to about 700,000'. As a result, he asserted, the rainfall in the region would also increase by about a half. This higher rainfall would wash out the salts from the soil of the Caspian steppes, making it more fertile. 'Such a great triumph of a nation over Nature would be by far the greatest conquest in the annals of human material progress,' he concluded.[26] Spalding's scheme was reported in the journal of the Ministry of State Domains. The journal also reported that the experience of the Suez Canal (which had opened in 1869) had confirmed Spalding's reasoning: French scientists had noted that the increase in the amount of water in the lakes connected by the canal had led to higher rainfall. Spalding's scheme was on an even larger scale, however, and the journal pointed out that the huge expense would make it unrealizable for the present generation.[27]

While languishing in exile in Siberia in 1881, Sergei Yuzhakov—a philology graduate from Odessa—went further. In a letter to the newspaper *Russkie vedomosti*, he proposed taking water by canal from the Black Sea to increase the area of the Caspian Sea to two and a half times its size. This would avert the 'degradation of the climate of our steppes'. Instead, the climate of the entire black-earth region would be completely changed, making it moister and more moderate.

[25] K. Kostenkov, N. Bardot-de-Marni, and N. Kryzhin, 'Ocherk vostochnogo i zapadnogo Manycha', *ZhMGI*, 76 (1861), 2nd pagn, 82–107.
[26] Henry C. Spalding, 'The Black Sea and the Caspian', *Van Nostrand's Eclectic Engineering Magazine*, 15/92 (1876), 122–7.
[27] A. A. P., 'Svoevremmenost' orosheniya v stepyakh', *SKhiL*, 122 (1876), 2nd pagn, 323–6.

He recognized that there would be costs. Some cities, including Astrakhan', and many rural settlements would need to be relocated. Around 160,000 nomads would have to be moved to new lands 'somewhere in the interior of Asia'. He believed the costs were outweighed by the benefits, and concluded that 'the game was manifestly worth the candle'.[28] Achilles Alferaki, who owned an estate near the Sea of Azov, was less inclined to gamble. He wrote that they could not even dream of such schemes being implemented. He argued that irrigation was too expensive for the population, and that the state should take responsibility. Indeed, he stated that if farmers in the steppe region were to be able to compete with their counterparts in America and Australia in the world grain market, then the Russian government would need to support them.[29] The government in St Petersburg did not undertake serious efforts in support of irrigation until the 1880s. In the meantime, initiative was left to companies, estate owners, and agricultural societies.

Private companies and the issue of water law

In 1866, a group of estate owners founded a company to promote irrigation in the Don Cossack territory. They stressed the potential benefits in letters to prominent figures in St Petersburg. The company emphasized the advantages nature had bestowed on the region: fertile soil, abundance of land, a favourable climate, and rich vegetation. Thus, the territory could have a brilliant future, and the steppe region as a whole could become the bread basket of Russia and Europe. The chief impediment was the shortage of water and regular droughts. The company requested land where they could, at their own expense, set up artificial irrigation. They hoped that other estate owners would follow suit. Their requests were referred back to the ataman of the Don Cossacks, who investigated their feasibility. He consulted the deputy of the nobility in Mius district, who supported the plan, but noted that it was experimental as artificial irrigation of arable fields had not yet been introduced in south-eastern Russia. If it were successful, however, it could bring about a 'revolution in agriculture in the southern belt of Russia' and the entire Russian economy. He doubted the scheme could be undertaken without government assistance, but noted that governments elsewhere in the world funded irrigation. The ataman was not prepared to take responsibility, however, and sent the case back to St Petersburg. There is no further record in the regional archives in Rostov-on-Don, and it seems the company's request was turned down.[30]

[28] S. Yuzhakov, *K voprosu o zemledel'cheskoi budushchnosti russkoi chernozemnoi polosy (Iz Russkikh Vedomostei za 1881 g.)* (Moscow, 1881), 28–38. On Yuzhakov, see *ES*, xli (1894), 287–8. Discussions on linking the Sea of Azov and the Caspian Sea continued. A. I. Voeikov, 'O vodnykh putyakh Rossii', in *Vozdeistvie cheloveka na prirodu: izbrannye stat'i*, ed., V. V. Pokshishevskii (Moscow, 1949), 218–21.

[29] A. Alferaki, *O polozhenii sel'skogo khozyaistva v yugo-vostochnom krae* (Spb, 1879), 16–20.

[30] GARO, f.46, op.1, d.780, ll.2–9, 10–ob., 16–21, 31, 33–5ob., 42–51ob., 54–ob., 62–ob.

One member of the company was very persistent. Mikhail Eriks, a native of the Baltic provinces,[31] was a hydraulic engineer. He had had worked for the Ministry State Domains in Tauride province in the steppe region.[32] In 1862, he had tried to secure support, and loans, from the Southern Russian Agricultural Society to build a pipeline from the river Dnepr to Odessa to irrigate the steppes. The society turned him down for practical reasons.[33] Undeterred, in a pamphlet published in 1868, Eriks contrasted the productivity of agriculture in Russia with Central and Western Europe. He went on to draw attention to the differences between the northern half of Russia, where the soil was becoming exhausted, and the black-earth region in the south, where harvests were also declining in spite of the fertility of the soil. 'It has . . . been noted for a long time', he wrote, 'that the climate of southern and south-eastern . . . Russia is getting drier . . . . and . . . bad harvests recurring more . . . frequently.' Stressing the importance of agriculture to Russian national wealth, and the potential for increasing grain exports from the steppes, Eriks urged artificial irrigation 'to protect the soil from the ruinous influence of the climate, from the shortage of rainfall, . . . from winds and drought.' Citing examples from the ancient world as well as the modern, Eriks urged the Russian government and private individuals to combine their efforts to promote irrigation on the steppes.[34] Eriks was involved in several companies that promoted irrigation. His plans, however, provoked scepticism as to their feasibility, on practical and financial grounds.[35]

Eriks's efforts were also frustrated by the legal barrier to large-scale irrigation: building dams and digging irrigation channels would encroach on the property rights of other landowners. In 1867, one of Eriks's companies petitioned the Ministry of State Domains to grant it all unoccupied state land in New Russia, which the company would then irrigate. It also asked to be granted the land—to be alienated from other landowners—that it needed to set up irrigation schemes. Eriks's company suggested a solution to the legal barrier by referring to the laws that allowed railway companies to buy land by compulsory purchase. Eriks's company withdrew its request in order to revise it, but the legal question was raised again over the following years.[36] In 1872, a group headed by a man named Rothschild petitioned the Ministry of Internal Affairs for permission to establish a joint-stock company 'to introduce irrigation in the south of Russia'. In

[31] Eriks was one of several people from the Baltic provinces who was interested in irrigating the steppes. Grain from the steppes was shipped up the Volga and, eventually, exported from Baltic ports, and there was some use of irrigation the Baltic region. N. F. Tagirova, 'Volzhskii khleb na Rossiiskom rynke nachala XX v.', *Samarskii zemskii sbornik*, 1/5 (2001), 35–40; *IOPDMGI*, iv/i, 234.
[32] GARO, f.46, op.1, d.780, l.96.
[33] DAOO, f. 22, op.1, 1862, sp.396, ll.15–23.
[34] [Eriks], *Zapiska*, 12, 17, 18, 21, 33, 37–49.
[35] A. S., 'Pamyati minuvshego goda. Po povodu goloda v Samarskoi gubernii', *TVEO*, 1 (1874), 5–7.
[36] RGIA, f.382, op.1, 1867, d.56, ll.1–ob., 5–6.

particular, they requested the right to alienate the land belonging to other landowners they needed. The government authorized them to carry out preliminary investigations at their own expense. The following year, the company was joined by Egor Langner, a merchant from the Baltic port of Reval' (now Tallinn in Estonia). He invested significant sums in the venture, and persisted in seeking official ratification of a charter for the company. The government did not ratify it, however, as there was no law to allow the transport of water across the property of other landowners.[37]

The government recognized the importance of the legal barrier. The State Council had set up a commission under Prince Obolenskii to prepare a draft statute on compulsory alienation of private land by companies in return for compensation. The commission consulted the Ministry of Transport. Indeed, compensation for land subject to compulsory purchase to build railways was the overriding concern of the law issued on 19 May 1887. All cases, however, required individual decrees by the tsar.[38] The government still did not ratify Langner's charter, because he was also seeking protection from competition. Langner tried again in 1891. He argued that irrigating the steppes would prevent future harvest failures and bans on grain exports, such as happened in 1891. Langner dropped the request for protection against competition and, finally, on 30 August 1896, the Imperial Russian Senate ratified a revised charter for the company. It could set up irrigation schemes, but only on the conditions that: the owners of all the land affected agreed; that the work did not entail transporting water across land belonging to other owners; and water would not be taken from waterways designated for navigation. Nevertheless, the company was authorized to acquire the land it needed. After all Langner's efforts, however, he struggled to raise the capital he needed.[39]

The legal barriers also frustrated the scientist Vasilii Dokuchaev, who investigated ways of regulating rivers and irrigating land during his expedition of the 1890s. In 1892, he requested permission from the Ministry of State Domains to review the laws on water rights and ownership of river banks. The ministry felt he was exceeding his remit.[40] Nevertheless, the ministry agreed with Dokuchaev in principle and, in 1895, argued that water laws needed revision.[41] Two years later, a government commission to review irrigation of state land in southern Russia noted the absence of laws to allow water to be brought from further afield.[42] In 1898, the expedition set up under General A. I. Tillo to study the sources of the main rivers in European Russia concluded that much research remained to be

[37] RGIA, f.426, op.1, 1894, d.58, ll.4, 7–8.
[38] RGIA, f.426, op.1, 1894, d.58, ll.11–12; *PSZ*, 3, vii/i, 239–44 (no.4470, 19 May 1887).
[39] RGIA, f.426, op.1, 1894, d.58, ll.3–7ob., 12–13, 20–45ob., 80, 84–98, 104, 107–116ob., 142–53ob.
[40] RGIA, f.426, op.1, 1891, d.30, ll.52 ob., 56.
[41] *Kratkii ocherk orositel'nogo dela v Rossii* (Spb, 1895), review in *SKhiL*, 182 (1896), 226–7.
[42] PFA RAN, f.184, op.1, d.119, l.11.

done before a general water law could drawn up. It recommended a lawyer be added to the staff of a future expedition.[43] In 1902, the government finally enacted legislation that allowed irrigation work that infringed on the property of other landowners in the European part of the empire. Crucially, the new laws laid down a procedure to allow landowners to build irrigation channels across other owners' land, without the agreement of the latter, but in return for payment and in carefully defined circumstances. The government did not, however, legislate for downstream water rights.[44] Ekaterina Pravilova has pointed out that the government paid more attention to reforming water laws in the Caucasus and Central Asia.[45] It was in these parts of the empire, as will be seen, that the government decided to prioritize irrigation.

Estate owners

Until the legal barrier was removed, among the few people who could set up larger-scale irrigation were the owners of substantial estates. Large estate owners, moreover, were more likely to have the financial means. An example is Countess Elena Shuvalova, who owned the estate of 'Shikany' which covered 54,000 *desyatiny* in Saratov and Samara provinces. In 1884, she hired Morits Roland to manage the estate. Roland had studied agriculture in his native Baltic region, and had experience of managing estates in central Russia and Poltava province. Among his innovations on Shuvalova's estate was irrigation. He introduced irrigation on the estate's land in Vol'skii district, Saratov province. He experimented by irrigating vegetable gardens, but quickly moved to arable fields and meadows. Roland dammed the river Bagalei to create two ponds. These, together with two springs, supplied water which was transported by channels and ditches to the land to be irrigated. He claimed that his use of siphons—to raise water—was an innovation in Russia. A model of his work was awarded a gold medal at the Saratov agricultural exhibition in 1889. By 1893, he had irrigated 726½ *desyatiny* of arable fields, 253 *desyatiny* of meadows and 24 *desyatiny* of vegetable gardens. The total cost was 10,495 roubles 50 kopecks, or 13 roubles 51 kopecks a *desyatina*. The average yields of grain on the irrigated land during the years 1890–3 were over twice those on unirrigated land. The biggest difference, not surprisingly, came in the drought year of 1891, when the yields from irrigated land were around four times higher.[46] Other private estates where larger-scale irrigation was set up in the late nineteenth century included the Zherebtsov estate in the Don region, where 1,200 *desyatiny* were irrigated

[43] *Ob okhrane vodnykh bogatstv: Glavnye rezul'taty chetyrekhletnikh trudov ekspeditsii dlya issledovaniya istochnikov i glavneishikh rek Evropeiskoi Rossii pod rukovodstvom A. Tillo* (Spb, 1898), 4–5.
[44] *PSZ*, 3, xxii/i, 366–72 (no.21491, 20 May 1902); 540–2 (no.21582, 3 June 1902).
[45] Pravilova, 'Les *res publicae* russes'.
[46] RGIA, f.426, op.1, 1894, d.74.

with water from melted snow at a cost of 72 roubles per *desyatina*.[47] Irrigation of fields was possible, therefore, but very expensive, and far beyond the means of many estate owners and most village communities in the steppe region.

Agricultural societies

Irrigation was considered by agricultural societies. From the 1840s, the Southern Russian Agricultural Society published some articles and pamphlets arguing for irrigation that were based on practical experience of local estate owners. They explained how to accumulate water in gullies by building dams, and how to use the water to irrigate fields and meadows.[48] Among the authors was Ivan Palimpsestov, who admitted in 1855 that the shortage of water was the 'first defect of this rich region', which would cost 'huge sums' of money to overcome.[49] The society took some interest in irrigation in the 1870s. It proposed an essay competition on irrigating fields in southern Russia.[50] The society's journal discussed irrigation as a way to increase income from the land in the aftermath of the abolition of serfdom in 1861.[51] In 1876, moreover, it began experiments with irrigation on its farm with funds from the Ministry of State Domains.[52] The results were mixed, and the society's interest in irrigation did not last. Between 1830 and 1894, the society's journal published around forty articles on water supply, only a minority of which dealt with irrigating fields. Over the same period, however, it published 120 articles on forestry.[53] At the end of an article on irrigation (which was spelled wrongly in the title), Palimpsestov reminded his readers that his real passion was forestry.[54]

[47] K. Verner, 'Melioratsii', *PERSKh*, v (1901), 616–18.

[48] See, for example, M. Shcherbinin, 'Oroshenie polei', *ZIOSKhYuR*, 3 (1844), 5–19; V. Skarzhinskii, 'Voprosy i otvety na zaprudy v stepnykh mestakh Novorossiiskogo kraya, *ZIOSKhYuR*, 9 (1852), 427–52; I. Palimpsestov, *Ob ustroistve vodokhranilishch v stepyakh yuga Rossii* (Odessa, 1867).

[49] I. Palimpsestov, *Otchet o deistviyakh Imperatorskogo Obshchestva sel'skogo khozyaistva yuzhnoi Rossii* (Odessa, 1855), 286–7.

[50] DAOO, f.22, op.1, 1862, sp.396, ll.8–10.

[51] M. Borovskii, 'Sposoby vvedeniya pravil'nogo khozyaistva v Khersonsoi gubernii', *ZIOSKhYuR*, (1876), 186. See also K. Gorskii, 'K voprosu ob oroshenii polei v yuzhnoi Rossii', *ZIOSKhYuR* (1877), 2nd pagn, 19–38; M. V. Neruchev, 'Popytki ustroistva orosheniya v Khersonskoi gubernii', *ZIOSKhYuR* (1879), 2nd pagn, 678–83.

[52] M. P. Borovskii, *Istoricheskii obzor pyatidesyatiletnei deyatel'nosti Imperatorskogo Obshchestva Sel'skogo Khozyaistva Yuzhnoi Rossii s 1828 po 1878 god* (Odessa, 1878), 209–10.

[53] A. S. Borinevich, *Sistematicheskii ukazatel' statei, zametok, protokolov, otchetov i proch. pomeshchennykh v 'Listakh' i 'Zapisak' Imperatorskogo Obshchestva Sel'skogo Khozyaistva Yuzhnoi Rossii s 1830 po 1894 g.* (Odessa, 1895), 21–2, 45–9.

[54] I. Palimpsestov, 'Iskustvennoe ovodnenie [*sic*] lugov v Novorossiskom krae', *ZIOSKhYuR*, (1854), 2nd pagn, 24–32.

Central and provincial authorities

From the mid-nineteenth century, the central and provincial authorities paid increasing attention to irrigation. In 1842, the Ministry of State Domains held a competition to identify the best and cheapest ways to obtain water in the steppe region.[55] Baron A. K. Bode, who taught at the Forestry and Surveying Institute, advocated damming gullies to create ponds to collect melt water in the spring and rain water in the summer. He recommended planting trees around the ponds to reduce evaporation in the summer and to retain snow blown across the steppe in the winter.[56] Another writer noted that irrigation elsewhere in Europe saved crops from drought. Citing the experience of the Mennonites in Tauride province, he stated that irrigating the steppe region was not as difficult and expensive as might be thought. He advocated using water from steppe rivers and making ponds to store water.[57] This article provoked a response from I. Gulak, a local estate owner, who pointed to the unsuitable topography of the region for using water from rivers to irrigate the land up on the high steppes. He argued that the only way to raise water to that level was by digging artesian wells.[58] At around the same time, the ministry sent three engineers abroad to learn how to bore artesian wells. On their return, two were sent to the steppe region. The ministry sent another engineer to the Crimean Peninsula in 1848 to investigate irrigating fields. But this was the total of the ministry's activity on irrigation until the 1860s.[59]

The Ministry of State Domains resumed its interest in the wake of the Crimean War, when many Tatars left Tauride province for Ottoman lands. They left behind 12,700 *desyatiny* of land, which was acquired by the ministry. In 1859–61, it resettled 18,000 state peasants from ten provinces, including Voronezh, Kursk, Khar'kov, Chernigov and Poltava in the forest-steppe region, on the land vacated by the Tatars.[60] The ministry set out to help the migrants establish themselves in the unfamiliar environment. In June 1865, an official reported that 'nature and the climate present . . . such great impediments that only continued and persistent struggle against them is possible'. The first problem, he noted, was to supply the settlers with the water that was essential for agriculture.[61] The ministry sent an expedition headed by Rear Admiral Glazenap to Tauride province in 1866, with a budget of 14,000 roubles.[62] Its staff included

---

[55] *IOPDMGI*, iv/i, 61–2, 65.

[56] A. Bode, 'O dobyvanii vody v stepnykh mestakh yuzhnoi i yugo-vostochnoi chasti Evropeiskoi Rossii', *ZhMGI*, 9 (1843), 4th pagn, 141–5. See also Karimov, *Dokuda*, 147.

[57] 'O iskustvennom oroshenii zemel'', *ZhMGI*, 9 (1843), 2nd pagn, 240–57.

[58] I. Gulak, 'O iskusstvennom oroshenii polei Novorossiiskogo kraya', *ZhMGI*, 10 (1844), 2nd pagn, 160–4.

[59] *IOPDMGI*, iv/i, 234.

[60] *IOPDMGI*, ii/ii, 30–1; iv/i, 235.

[61] RGIA, f.426, op.1, 1894, d.40, ll.3–5.

[62] *IOPDMGI*, iv/i, 235. The expedition was also to locate areas suitable for afforestation (see above, p. 177).

a geologist, a hydraulic engineer, a forester, a farmer, and a topographer. It researched the existing state of water supply and conducted experiments into ways to improve it. They discovered that in the north of the Crimean Peninsula it was not practical to accumulate water by damming gullies as the water seeped through the permeable rock and evaporated due to the high temperatures and strong winds. Instead, they experimented in collecting rain water from the steppe, through pipes buried three or four feet deep into shallow cisterns. The water from the cisterns seeped into the soil and, they concluded, would ensure a supply for crops in times of drought. The cost was 250 roubles per *desyatina*. In addition, the cisterns cost between 1,900 and 3,000 roubles. The expedition maintained that this was the cheapest way to irrigate the Crimean steppes. Glazenap recommended further work, which would cost 800,000 roubles. The minister authorized only 30,000 roubles for a small part of the work. The Tauride provincial *zemstvo* allocated a further 30,000 roubles in loans. As a result, fifty new wells were dug, twenty-two old wells renewed, seventeen gullies dammed to accumulate water in ponds, forty bore holes dug, and three cisterns built. The provincial *zemstvo* continued to petition the government for assistance for irrigation work in the late 1860s and 1870s.[63] In the late 1870s, the ministry also supported experiments with irrigation in Kherson province.[64]

Another substantial landowner in the steppe region which took an interest in irrigation was the Appanage Department. In 1889–91, the department dammed ravines as part of improvements on its estates in Samara and Stavropol' provinces. Up to a hundred earthen dams were built. Over half were washed away by the spring floods, however, but the ponds created by the dams that survived provided water for livestock and human consumption.[65] The dams were not large. Most were around 140–160 feet long and the ponds behind them around a half to three-quarters of a *desyatina* in area.[66]

During the second half of the nineteenth century, the provincial authorities showed increasing interest in irrigation. Among the strongest advocates were the governors of Samara, because the southern part of the province was badly affected by droughts. Rather ominously, in his annual report for 1851 the governor noted that, besides the Volga, the rivers of the province did not have an abundance of water.[67] The shortage of water, recurring droughts, and bad

[63] RGIA, f.426, op.1, 1894, d.40, ll.33, 35–43, 108–9, 195–233ob., 259–72ob., 495–500; *IOPDMGI*, ii/ii, 30–1; iv/i, 235–6; G. P. Sazonov, *Obzor deyatel'nosti zemstv po sel'skomu khozyaistvu (1865–1895 gg.)*, 3 vols (Spb, 1896), iii, 1696–8, 1702–4.

[64] *IOPDMGI*, iv/i, 237.

[65] 'Meropriyatiya udel'nogo vedomstva v bor'be s zasukhami i drugimi klimaticheskimi vliyaniyami, prepyatstvuyushchimi khozyaistvu v yugo-vostochnykh stepnykh imeniyakh', *SKhiL*, 173 (1893), 3rd pagn, 34–5.

[66] GASO, f.43, op.8, d.33. The Appanage Department continued to be involved in irrigation on its estates in Samara province. S. Yu. Rauner, *Iskusstvennoe oroshenie polei v Timashevskom Udel'nom imenii Samarskoi gubernii* (Spb, 1896).

[67] GASO, f.3, op.1, 1851, d.332, ll.52ob.–53.

harvests became regular topics in the annual reports of successive governors of Samara. On the first page of his report for 1880, the governor noted that bad harvests in successive years had been caused by lack of rain and heat waves. Top of the governor's list of measures to deal with the problem was irrigation. He argued that irrigating state land would serve as an example for the local peasant population. He suggested that the Ministry of State Domains could advise them on the simplest and cheapest ways to build ponds with their own resources and whatever loans the government could provide. He also proposed that relief be provided for peasants affected by the bad harvest with public works on irrigation projects.[68] The *zemstva* in southern Samara province also sought support for irrigation. In 1879, the Novyi Uzen' district *zemstvo* petitioned the Ministry of State Domains to send a technician to advise them. The petition was turned down as the *zemstvo* was not willing to cover part of the cost.[69] The government in St Petersburg was, however, about to launch a much wider initiative.

The Zhilinskii expedition

In 1880, the Ministry of State Domains established an 'Expedition for Irrigation (*oroshenie*) in the South of Russia and the Caucasus'.[70] At its head was General Iosef Zhilinskii.[71] The aims of the expedition were: 1. To carry out research in southern Russia into ways of collecting water for human needs, livestock, and to supply it to meadows and fields; 2. To devise hydraulic installations to achieve this; 3. To construct such installations on state land; and 4. To carry out experiments in cultivating crops on irrigated land.[72] The government allocated significant funds to the expedition, ranging between 21,000 and 60,000 roubles a year in the 1880s. It allocated much larger sums, in the form of credits, following droughts and harvest failures. As the governor of Samara had suggested, the money was used for public works to provide relief. In 1881, the government assigned 500,000 roubles for this purpose in Samara, Saratov, and Ekaterinoslav provinces.[73] Zhilinskii had previously been in charge of an expedition to drain the marshes of Podles'e, at a total cost of 5.6 million roubles.[74] Removing water surplus to human requirements in the marshy north-west, however, proved easier than providing water in the semi-arid south-east.

Zhilinskii's expedition conducted a detailed survey of the steppe region. It divided the region into eastern and western parts, with the border running along

[68] GASO, f.3, op.167, 1881, d.89, ll.1, 6–7, 8ob.

[69] Sazonov, *Obzor*, iii, d.1702.

[70] *IOPDMGI*, iv/i, 237–8.

[71] 'I. I. Zhilinskii', *Ezhegodnik otdela zemel'nykh uluchshenii, 1909* (Spb 1910), 1–2.

[72] I. I. Zhilinskii, *Zemledel'cheskie gidravlicheskie raboty* (Spb, 1893), 23–4.

[73] RGIA, f.426, op.1, 1894, d.29, l.174; Vladislav Maksimov, *Ocherki po istorii obshchestvennykh rabot v Rossii* (Spb, 1905), 108–9.

[74] 'I. I. Zhilinskii', 1–2.

the river Volga as far south as Tsaritsyn, and then south-west to the Manych' lake. The eastern part—Samara and Astrakhan' provinces, the south-east of the Don region, north-eastern Stavropol' province, and Ural region—was characterized as very flat, treeless steppe with salty soil that suffered regular bad harvests due to drought. The soil was fertile only if there was sufficient moisture. The western part—Saratov province, most of the Don region, and Ekaterinoslav, Tauride, and Kherson provinces—was described as a system of flat, high steppes bounded by river valleys and gullies, which contained varying amounts of woodland. The soil was mostly very fertile black earth. (These were the two types of steppe landscapes I saw on field trips to the south-east and northern parts of Rostov region—part of the former Don region—in 2003: see above, p. ix.) The expedition's surveyors noted that the west of the region suffered from droughts less frequently than the east. They paid particular attention to the geology, the soil, and the gradient of the rivers and gullies. They estimated the amounts of water available for irrigation in the ground, rivers, and precipitation. Meteorological observations were made in Samara and Ekaterinoslav provinces. In addition, the expedition surveyed the ways of life of the region's inhabitants.[75] Zhilinskii and his staff learned that they needed to take account of local conditions. An attempt to irrigate land on the Kalmyk steppe in Astrakhan' province with water from the river Volga during the spring floods failed as the land turned out to be at least 6–7 *sazheny* (42–49 feet) above the highest water in the Volga.[76]

During the 1880s and early 1890s, Zhilinskii's expedition carried out work to supply water, mostly on state land, in several provinces. It provided water for three different purposes and used different methods for each. The first purpose was for people and livestock, which was achieved by digging wells to tap ground water and damming gullies to retain melt water and rain. For example, on the Kalmyk steppe, the expedition dug thirty-nine wells and constructed ponds. The expedition also built ponds to provide water for people and animals on the Crimean Peninsula and in Samara province. The second purpose was to irrigate meadows and salt flats used to grow grass. The method used was flood irrigation (*limannoe oroshenie*). Dams were built across gullies and streams and parallel to the contours on fields to retain water, especially spring melt water. The water was then released to irrigate the land once at the start of spring. The expedition set up this form of irrigation, for example, on the Kalmyk steppe and on the Valuiskii plot of land in Novyi Uzen' district, Samara province.[77] Zhilinskii was aware of the limitation of flood irrigation: it was little use flooding fields once in the early spring if there was no rain afterwards.[78]

[75] I. I. Zhilinskii, *Ocherk rabot ekspeditsii po orosheniyu na yuge Rossii i Kavkaze* (Spb, 1892), 7–42.

[76] RGIA, f.426, op.1, 1891, l.46.

[77] Zhilinskii, *Zemledel'cheskie*, 26–33. For much more detail, see I. I. Zhilinskii, *Ocherk*, 42–252.

[78] RGIA, f.426, op.1, 1891, d.30, l.65ob.

The third purpose was to irrigate crops in arable fields at the times of the growing season when they needed water, that is, not just once. This was channel irrigation (*pravil'noe oroshenie*), which Zhilinskii favoured, and entailed damming rivers and gullies to retain water, and then channelling water to the fields. Careful surveying was needed to ensure that the topography was suitable. The expedition set up channel irrigation on several plots of state land, including the Velikii Anadol' forestry plantation in Mariupol' district, Ekaterinoslav province, land adjoining the river Malaya Tinguta in Astrakhan' province, on the Berezovskii plot, Nikolaevsk district, Samara province, and the Valuiskii plot, also in Samara province.[79] Zhilinskii reported that on the Valuiskii plot, wheat yields on irrigated land were twice as high as on unirrigated land in 1889, and over three times higher in the dry year of 1890.[80] In the late 1880s, Zhilinskii's expedition identified locations near the Ural river which could be irrigated using dried-up branches of the river to channel spring flood waters. Zhilinskii hoped this would assist the development of grain cultivation, which until that time had suffered from 'almost permanent droughts, which destroy the beautiful shoots of the spring grain'.[81]

The cost of setting up irrigation varied across the region, and depended on local conditions as well as the method used. Zhilinskii reported that flood irrigation cost between 16 and 40 roubles a *desyatina*. Channel irrigation was more expensive, between 57 and 175 roubles per *desyatina*.[82] He noted that due to the topography, it was easier and cheaper to irrigate arable land with channel irrigation in the east of the region, for example Samara province, than the west. Using river water to irrigate land in the west was difficult due to the low gradients of the rivers and because they were in deep valleys, 20–30 *sazheny* (140–210 feet) below the level of the fields. To raise water from the valleys would entail huge and expensive dams. Zhilinskii hoped the development of the local economy and transport to move produce to ports and markets would make such expenditure worthwhile. Until this happened, the expedition relied on water from precipitation and to a lesser extent from springs.[83]

The expedition's work met a favourable response from the region's population. In early 1881, the provincial newspapers in Stavropol' and Samara reported that 'the highest circles of the central government' intended to embark on large-scale work to introduce artificial irrigation of fields in the steppe provinces in areas that had recently suffered crop failures. The newspapers argued that the region needed irrigation, because the climate was getting more arid, and drew attention to irrigation in Central Asia and Transcaucasia as successful

---

[79] Zhilinskii, *Ocherk*, 83–95, 110–18, 122–32, 211–52.
[80] RGIA, f.426, op.1, 1891, d.28, l.48ob.; d.30, l.65ob.
[81] RGIA, f.426, op.1, 1890, d.27, ll.14–17 (quotation l.16ob.).
[82] Zhilinskii, *Zemledel'cheskie*, 33–5.
[83] Zhilinskii, *Zemledel'cheskie*, 26, 36–9; Zhilinskii, *Ocherk*, 374–92.

examples.[84] The governor of Samara was more guarded. In his report for 1881, he recorded that irrigation works were under way in Nikolaevsk and Novyi Uzen' districts. In the first draft of the report, he had added that the installations that had been set up were not large on account of the limited amount of money spent on them, but these words were deleted in the final version.[85]

Zemstva sought assistance from Zhilinskii's expedition. In the early 1880s, the Novyi Uzen' and Nikolaevsk district *zemstva* in Samara province asked the expedition to survey land and assist in setting up irrigation on state and peasant land. The Ministry of State Domains authorized Zhilinskii to carry out some of the work with the assistance of the *zemstva*.[86] Estate owners asked for Zhilinskii's help. In February 1890, Major-General Ivan Ilovaiskii, the owner of Sloboda Ternovaya in the Donskoi district of the Don region, wrote to the Minister of State Domains that he had heard of the 'favourable results of the irrigation works' carried out by the government on the steppes. At the same time, Prince Vya-zemskii, an estate owner in Balashov district, Saratov province, requested tech-nical help. With uncharacteristic haste, perhaps due to the petitioners' high ranks, in March 1890, the government acceded to their requests. Zhilinskii's technical staff showed Ilovaiskii how he could irrigate 160 *desyatiny* with water from precipitation stored in a reservoir. Vyazemskii went on to irrigate 350 *desyatiny* of meadows with river water and 360 *desyatiny* of steppe and meadow with water accumulated in reservoirs. The estate owners bore the costs. The expedition also assisted peasants. Several communities along the Kuma river in arid north-eastern Stavropol' province petitioned the governor for assistance. He arranged for the expedition to regulate the river, releasing water to irrigate vineyards, orchards, and low-lying land.[87]

The case for irrigation became even more pressing in 1891. As the extent of the drought and crop failure became apparent, plans were made both in the affected provinces and St Petersburg for public works—including irrigation—to provide relief for starving peasants.[88] In June 1891, the Samara provincial *zemstvo* established a commission to look into ways to overcome the shortage of water in the south of the province.[89] The initiative came from Ivan Lishin, who had

---

[84] 'Iskustvennoe oroshenie polei (irrigatsiya)', *Stavropol'skie gubernskie vedomosti* (14, 21, and 28 February 1881). The articles were reprinted from *Samarskie gubernskie vedomosti*.

[85] GASO, f.3, op.167, 1882, d.88, ll.2–ob.

[86] Sazonov, *Obzor*, iii, 1707–9, 1712–13. See also I. I. Filipenko, *Vopros obvodneniya stepei: na osnovanii issledovanii proizvedenykh v 1881 godu, po porucheniyu Novouzenskogo zemskogo sobraniya* (Spb, 1882).

[87] RGIA, f.426, op.1, 1890, d.27, ll.5, 6, 8, 52; d.28, l.48.

[88] For an account of the plans for irrigation after the drought of 1891 from the central government's perspective, see V. S. Dyakin, *Den'gi dlya sel'skogo khozyaistva, 1892–1914: Agrarnyi kredit v ekonomicheskoi politike tsarizma* (Spb, 1997), 35–40. For a discussion of the public works, that does not consider irrigation, see Richard G. Robbins, *Famine in Russia, 1891–1892: The Imperial Government Responds to a Crisis* (New York, 1975), 110–23.

[89] RGIA, f.426, op.1, 1894, d.55, ll.52–7.

long taken an interest in irrigation in his native Nikolaevsk district.[90] The commission recommended irrigation and afforestation in southern Samara province, and called on private enterprise and village communities to set up irrigation schemes. Lishin calculated the total cost of the irrigation work, excluding salaries for the technical staff, at 60,000 roubles.[91] The governor of Samara forwarded the commission's report to the Minister of State Domains in November 1891.[92] Similar developments were taking place across the Volga in Saratov province. In June 1891, an extraordinary meeting of the provincial *zemstvo* recommended public works that would benefit the region economically as well as provide relief. At the top of its list was irrigation, in particular on peasant land, to be funded by the government. The *zemstvo* also recommended that credit be extended to estate owners to irrigate their land. The governor of Saratov sent the *zemstvo*'s recommendations to St Petersburg.[93] During the autumn of 1891, the Ministries of Internal Affairs and State Domains agreed to use funds allocated for public works to pay for irrigation work in Samara and Saratov provinces. In November, the Ministry of State Domains instructed Zhilinskii's expedition to expand the areas of irrigated land on plots where they had set up irrigation systems, and to establish irrigation on other plots of state land. The cost was initially set at 215,000 roubles.[94]

In the meantime, at the end of October 1891, the governor of Samara had belatedly submitted his annual report for 1890 to the Ministry of Internal Affairs. He stated that the repeated bad harvests caused by lack of rainfall and heat waves were threatening the welfare of the inhabitants and the viability of farming. He saw artificial irrigation as the main solution, and he called on the government to provide technical advice and credit. With the endorsement of the tsar, the Council of Ministers passed the governor's report to the Minister of State Domains.[95] In the previous chapter, we saw how the governor's insistence on afforestation had led to action. The same was true for irrigation. A special meeting convened by the tsar on 9 February 1892 discussed the matter.[96] The government agreed to allocate further large sums of money for public works on irrigation projects. In March 1892, Zhilinskii worked out an ambitious plan for such works in Saratov and Samara provinces. The latter would cost up to

[90] I. Lishin, *Ocherk Nikolaevskogo uezda (Samarskaya guberniya) v statisticheskom i sel'sko-khozyaistvom otnosheniyakh* (Spb, 1880), 47–9. RGIA, f.426, op.1, 1894, d.55, l.52 ob.

[91] I. A. Lishin, *K voprosu obvodneniya i obleseniya stepnoi polosy Samarskoi gubernii* (Moscow, 1892), 22–5, 33. See I. A. Lishin, *Prilozhenie k zapiske kommissii po obvodneniyu i obleseniyu stepnoi polosy Samarskoi gubernii* (Samara, 1891).

[92] RGIA, f.426, op.1, 1894, d.55, l.31.

[93] RGIA, f.426, op.1, 1894, d.55, ll.8–10.

[94] RGIA, f.426, op.1, 1894, d.55, l.33. See also ll.14, 27–8.

[95] GASO, f.3, op.233, 1890, d.1000, ll.1–ob., 2ob.–3ob.; RGIA, f.387, op.28, 1892, d.1023, ll.5–6; f.426, op.1, 1894, d.55, l.38; f.426, op.1, 1894, d.55, l.43.

[96] RGIA, f.426, op.1, 1894, d.55, ll.44–8.

600,000 roubles, and would be funded by loans from the reserve capital maintained to provide relief in the event of harvest failure. The plan was supported by Minister of Finance Vyshnegradskii (who was replaced by Sergei Witte in August 1892) and the Minister of Internal Affairs.[97] Zhilinskii was assigned just under 500,000 roubles for public works on irrigation projects in Samara province alone.[98] He was allocated 89,000 roubles by the Ministry of State Domains for his expedition's work on state land in 1892.[99] Thus, the government was prepared to spend significant sums of money on irrigation work in the wake of the drought and harvest failure in 1891–2.

Zhilinskii was in charge of the technical side, but management of the public works was assigned to General Mikhail Annenkov.[100] Annenkov had served in Central Asia, where he had been in charge of the construction of the Trans-Caspian railway. In 1889, he had expressed optimism that under Russian rule, the barren lands of Central Asia could be made fertile by irrigation. As a precedent, he cited the transformation of the steppes of southern Russia, from a land that had been considered suitable only for nomads into a productive arable region. He argued that the steppes would become more productive if they were irrigated.[101] Annenkov chaired a commission on irrigating southern Russia in the winter of 1891–2. Zhilinskii and scientists, including Dokuchaev, took part.[102] In April 1892, Annenkov made the case that irrigation was the best solution to the problem of droughts in the steppe region at a meeting of the Moscow Agricultural Society.[103]

Zhilinskii and Annenkov worked together in Samara province in 1892. With labour provided by the public works, they extended the irrigation systems on the Valuiskii plot in Novyi Uzen' district. Two existing dams were increased in size by new earthworks to a combined length of 5½ *versty*. They were over 6 *sazheny*

[97] RGIA, f.426, op.1, 1891, d.29, l.84.

[98] Maksimov, *Ocherki*, 119; RGIA, f.426, op.1, 1894, d.29, l.176ob.

[99] RGIA, f.426, op.1, 1891, d.30, l.74.

[100] RGIA, f.426, op.1, 1894, d.29, ll.9–ob., 20; P. D. Dolgorukov, 'Irrigatsionnye raboty v Samarskoi gubernii', in A. P. Perepelkin (ed.), *Stenograficheskii otchet o soveshchaniyakh pri [Imperatorskom Moskovskom] Obshchestve [Sel'skogo Khozyaistva], s 18-go po 22-e Dekabrya 1892 goda, po obshchestvennym rabotam po obvodeniyu yugo-vostochnoi chasti Rossii, proizvennym v 1892 g. rasporyazheniem zaveduyushchego obshchestvennymi rabotami Generala M. N. Annenkova* (Moscow, 1893), 1st pagn, 128–9. See also Robbins, *Famine*, 112–18.

[101] M. N. Annenkov, 'Srednyaya Aziya i ee prigodnost' dlya vodvoreniya v nei Russkoi kolonizatsii', *IRGO*, 25/4 (1889), 277–93.

[102] Dokuchaev wrote about his involvement in a letter to A. A. Izmail'skii apparently dated 6 January 1891. 'Iz perepiski s A. A. Izmailovskim (1888–1900)', *Sochineniya*, 9 vols (Moscow and Leningrad, 1949–61), viii, 266. This must be a misprint for 1892. Gerservanov, who also took part, dated Annenkov's discussions with Dokuchaev and others to the winter of 1891–2. [V. V. Dokuchaev], *K voprosu o regulirovanii vodnogo khozyaistva v stepyakh Rossii. Beseda v III otdele [Russkogo Tekhnicheskogo Obshchestva], 20 noyabrya 1892 goda* (Spb [1892]), 1. See also V. V. Dokuchaev, 'Nashi Stepi prezhde i teper'', *Sochineniya*, vi, 95.

[103] M. N. Annenkov, 'O merakh k umensheniyu zasukh', *Trudy Imperatorskogo Moskovskogo Obshchestva Sel'skogo Khozyaistva*, 30 (1892), 2nd pagn, 157–74.

(40 feet) high and between two and 3 *sazheny* (14 and 21 feet) in breadth. The area of the reservoir behind the dams increased to 400 *desyatiny*. New floodgates were constructed, and the network of channels to carry water to the fields was increased to a total length of 60 *versty*. The area of irrigated land grew to nearly 4,000 *desyatiny*. This included 1,800 *desyatiny* irrigated by channels: a substantial increase on the previous 253 *desyatiny*. The remaining land was provided with water by flood irrigation. In adjoining Nikolaevsk district, the area of irrigated land on the Kochetkovskii plot was also expanded by increasing the size of the existing dams. Annenkov and Zhilinskii also used the labour provided by the public works to build new installations. A dam two *versty* in length was built on the Shcherbakovskii plot in Nikolaevsk district, creating a reservoir covering 170 *desyatiny*. Almost nine miles of channels were dug to use the water to irrigate between 500 and 700 *desyatiny* of land. In addition, public works were used to irrigate significant areas of peasant land in Novyi Uzen' and Nikolaevsk districts.[104] The work projects provided relief for thousands of peasants.[105]

Annenkov also managed public works in the basin of the river Don. In the spring of 1892, he sent a commission to survey the region. It included the agronomist Pavel Kostychev, and a geologist, transport engineer, and two delegates from the Moscow Agricultural Society. They drew on local knowledge by involving estate owners, *zemstvo* representatives, and peasants. They surveyed ravines with a view to damming them to create reservoirs. The geologists identified areas where the rock was impermeable and so could hold water. The specialists also investigated springs that could provide water, and existing dams and reservoirs. Twelve dams were built on streams flowing into the river Biryug to regulate the water regime in the area, replenish ground water, and reduce erosion. In addition, seventy-nine ravines were dammed to create reservoirs to retain snow melt water to feed the ground water as well as supplying water for irrigation. Two experimental stations were set up with small areas, 18 and 27 *desyatiny*, of irrigated land. Annenkov built dams and ponds on state land in southern and eastern Voronezh province, including the Khrenovskoi plot, which was the location of one of the field research stations on Dokuchaev's simultaneous expedition. The public works programme provided employment for 150,000 working days. Annenkov reported that 90 per cent of the expenditure on irrigation went in wages for peasants.[106]

Annenkov was in charge of all public works in the seventeen provinces affected by the famine. People were also put work reinforcing ravines, on forestry work, constructing grain elevators, and building roads. His total budget was over 12.5 million roubles. Rather less of the money than was intended ended up in the

[104] RGIA, f.426, op.1, 1894, d.29, ll.124–6, 176ob.–177ob.; Dolgorukov, 'Irrigatsionnye raboty', 128–30.

[105] GASO, f.3, op.233, d.1874, ll.75ob.–6.

[106] M. N. Annenkov, 'Zaklyuchitel'nyi doklad o rezul'tatakh proizvedennykh obshchestven. rabot po obvodneniyu', in Perepelkin (ed.), *Stenograficheskii otchet*, 2nd pagn, 24–7, 31–4.

pockets of famine victims. Official figures suggested that only 65 per cent of the money assigned for irrigation work was paid to the workers. Annenkov was reprimanded for misuse of public funds.[107] In his memoirs, Witte remarked that Annenkov was 'capable of deviating from the truth'.[108]

Meanwhile, Zhilinskii continued his work. In 1892, his expedition supported existing irrigation projects and carried out preliminary surveys for new work right across the steppe region.[109] The work met with a positive response from the local authorities and inhabitants of the region. Estate owners, *zemstva*, and peasant communities all over the steppe region sent petitions and requests to St Petersburg asking for government assistance to set up irrigation on their land in the aftermath of the disaster of 1891–2. On 11 February 1892, for example, estate owner Egor Pshenichnyi of Novyi Uzen' district, Samara province, wrote to the Minister of State Domains that he had irrigated part of his estate of Georgievskaya at his own expense. It had shown its worth during the previous year's drought when he had reaped a good harvest from his irrigated land. He requested technical assistance from the Zhilinskii expedition so that he could expand the irrigated area. He stressed that he had irrigated his land not just for his own benefit, but as an example for the 'public good'.[110] His estate adjoined the Valuiskii plot, and technical staff from the expedition advised him how to irrigate a total of 1,150 *desyatiny*.[111] In October 1892, in response to a request for information from the Minister of Internal Affairs, Nikolai Shishkov of the Samara *zemstvo* reported that the population of the province relied almost exclusively on the grain harvest. But the lack of rain and recurring droughts were threatening 'to make agriculture absolutely impossible and complete harvest failures a common occurrence.' He concluded that government spending on public works to expand irrigation schemes would be the most productive use of its resources. This last point was underlined on the document in the archive in St Petersburg, suggesting that it met with some resonance in the central administration.[112] This was confirmed at the highest level shortly afterwards. In his annual report for 1892, the governor of Samara wrote that it was necessary to continue the work on irrigation in order to 'improve agriculture'. Tsar Alexander III wrote in the margin: 'What can be done on this matter?'[113]

The pressure continued from the population. In late 1892 and early 1893, 162 peasant communities set petitions and resolutions to the Samara provincial

---

[107] N. Prokhorov, 'Raboty obshchestvennye', *PERSKh*, viii (1903), 88; Robbins, *Famine in Russia*, 120–3.

[108] [Sergei Yul'evich Witte], *Iz arkhiva S. Yu. Witte: Vospominaniya*, 3 parts in 2 vols (Spb, 2003), i/i, 116.

[109] RGIA, f.426, op.1, 1894, d.29, ll.84ob.–85.

[110] RGIA, f.426, op.1, 1894, d.29, l.71–ob.

[111] RGIA, f.426, op.1, 1890, d.28, l.48.

[112] RGIA, f.426, op.1, 1894, d.55, ll.58–62ob.

[113] RGIA, f.426, op.1, 1894, d.83, l.16.

zemstvo requesting assistance to irrigate their land. The *zemstvo* held a special meeting on 22 February 1893. Shishkov noted that such work could be undertaken properly only after careful surveys of the land, which required special equipment that the *zemstvo* did not have. The *zemstvo* asked the governor to seek help from Zhilinskii's expedition. The *zemstvo* stressed that irrigating the steppes could not be postponed as droughts were intensifying and ground water levels falling. In June 1893, the governor sent the *zemstvo*'s request to the Minister of Internal Affairs. He emphasized the necessity and usefulness of the irrigation systems that had been set up by the expedition in the province. The Ministry of Internal Affairs forwarded the request to the Ministry of State Domains, with a note that it recognized the great value of such work to protect the population from the harmful consequences of recurring droughts.[114]

There was no doubt over the seriousness of the situation faced by some peasant communities in the region, nor over the commitment of the government to support irrigation. Peasant petitions that described their plight and requested assistance to provide water supplies and irrigation continued to flood into the provincial and central administrations. To take just one example, in September 1894 peasants of Aleksandrovo-Gai in Novyi Uzen' district wrote that without artificial irrigation they could not continue growing grain, 'since our locality is year by year becoming more and more like a desert'.[115] The authorities in St Petersburg and the provinces offered assistance in some cases. Officials from the Ministries of State Domains and Internal Affairs as well as the governor of Saratov provided financial assistance to the peasant community of Krasnyi Khutor, in Kamyshin district, Saratov province, to build a new dam to accumulate water for irrigation.[116] The central authorities, moreover, allocated further large sums to Zhilinskii to carry on his work. On 19 April 1893, the new Finance Minister, Witte, authorized 5,300 roubles to pay for technical staff. This was in addition to the 294,000 roubles that had been already allocated for irrigation works.[117]

Meanwhile, on the direction of State Council and the Ministry of State Domains, Zhilinskii had been preparing a plan to expand the work of his expedition.[118] In September 1892, he stressed the success and financial viability of the irrigation systems his expedition had installed on state land. He went on to note that the harvest failure of 1891 had affected a far larger area than that covered by his expedition. Thus, he argued, the entire southern and south-eastern region of Russia needed irrigation. He proposed a survey the whole region, beginning from the shores of the Caspian and Black Seas and working up the

---

[114] RGIA, f.426, op.1, 1894, f.55, ll.49–51. For many more petitions, see RGIA, f.426, op.1, 1895, dd.92–3.
[115] RGIA, f.426, op.1, 1895, d.92, l.104–ob.
[116] RGIA, f.426, op.1, 1895, d.93., ll.1–6. See also 'Po povodu predstoyashchei v 1896 godu deyatel'nosti Departamenta Zemledeliya', *SKhiL*, 181 (1896), 34–5.
[117] RGIA, f.426, op.1, 1891, d.30, ll.145–ob., 162-163ob.
[118] Dyakin, *Den'gi*, 35–6.

river valleys. Noting that the expedition had concentrated mainly on using water from melted snow and rainfall accumulated in ravines to irrigate low-lying land, he added that he wanted to move on to using water from rivers to irrigate fields, where the topography permitted it, through channels. While the survey work was taking place in the west of the region, Zhilinskii outlined more concrete plans to expand the area of irrigated land east of the Volga. He envisaged irrigating 150,000 *desyatiny* of land between the Volga and Ural rivers in southern Samara and northern Astrakhan' provinces. He costed his plans at 700,000 roubles for ponds, 1,300,000 roubles for flood irrigation, and five million roubles for channel irrigation.[119]

Zhilinskii had the support of the new Minister of Agriculture, Aleksei Ermolov. (Ermolov had been recommended to Alexander III by Finance Minister Witte, but he was only Witte's second choice to fill the post.[120]) Zhilinskii and his superiors in the Ministry of Agriculture developed his plans to expand irrigation in the steppe region. Ermolov referred back to the tsar's endorsement of the governor of Samara's request in his report for 1892. In April 1895, Ermolov reported on the expedition's work since 1892. He asserted that their research had shown that the area of land irrigated by flooding and channels could be expanded first to 450,000 *desyatiny* and eventually to 6 million *desyatiny*. Whether this could be achieved, however, would depend on the allocation of funds.[121] Ermolov noted that Zhilinskii and his staff had paid attention to devising effective ways to irrigate land that took account of the topography, and that systems that worked in other parts of the world were not necessarily appropriate on the steppes. Ermolov made expanding the work of Zhilinskii's expedition one of the key components in the ministry's plan for 1896.[122]

In spite of Zhilinskii's and Ermolov's enthusiasm, artificial irrigation was not universally accepted as the best solution to the shortage of water in the steppe region. Specialists continued to raise objections, such as those articulated by Shishkin in 1876 (see above, p. 208). A cogent argument against irrigating the region was made by Gersevanov, who was familiar with Zhilinskii's expedition, at the Imperial Russian Technical Society in 1890. Gersevanov argued that the conditions in the steppe region made channel irrigation of fields impossible as it required rivers with a lot of water in the spring and summer, when the crops needed it, and rivers with steep gradients that would allow water to be channelled onto the fields by gravity. Such rivers existed in the Caucasus and Central Asia, but not in the steppe region due to the flat topography. He further argued that there was not sufficient precipitation to irrigate fields in the region. He calculated

---

[119] RGIA, f.426, op.1, 1894, d.29, ll.173–99; RGIA, f.1152, op.11, 1893, d.213, ll.2–29; Zhilinskii, *Ocherk rabot ekspeditsii*, pp.391–2. Dyakin mistakenly stated that Zhilinskii envisaged only irrigation of fields by flood irrigation, constructing ponds, and digging wells. *Den'gi*, 36.

[120] [Witte], *Iz arkhiva*, i/i, 300.

[121] RGIA, f.426, op.1, 1894, d.83, ll.18–19ob.

[122] 'Po povodu', 33–41.

that to irrigate one *desyatina* of wheat would require collecting the precipitation that fell on 10–15 *desyatiny* of land. Thus, the only viable ways of providing water in the steppe region were irrigating low-lying meadows with water from dammed ravines and gullies, and digging artesian wells to supply water for human and animal use.[123] The disaster of 1891 did not change the minds of the members of the Technical Society. Other specialists were sceptical about the viability of irrigating the steppes in November 1892.[124] Dokuchaev, who had advised Annenkov and devised his own plan to regulate the steppe rivers and provide water for the region, was nevertheless in two minds on the subject. He wrote to Aleksandr Izmail'skii that he was sceptical about Annenkov's and Zhilinskii's work. He felt the costs were out of proportion with the results. Dokuchaev firmly believed, moreover, that more scientific research into the steppe environment was needed before constructing irrigation systems. On the other hand, in a letter to Nikolai Sibirtsev in 1893, he was positive about the work done under Annenkov's direction on the Khrenovskoi plot, where his own expedition was conducting research.[125]

Arguments against the viability of irrigation were also made in government circles. The director of the Geological Committee of the Ministry State Domains had warned Annenkov about the unfavourable conditions in the steppe region in January 1892. He sent Annenkov reports by two geologists that argued that the topography of the Russian plain was unsuitable for irrigation by means of dams as it was too flat, and the gradient of the rivers too shallow. They also pointed out that there was very little water in the rivers on the steppe beyond the Volga, that is, Samara province, in the summer. Hydraulic engineers, moreover, would need to find cost-effective ways to raise water from the river valleys up to the high steppe. One of the reports drew attention to problems in areas with porous rock. For example, the pontic limestone in southern Kherson province was very porous. As a result, water behind a large dam on the estate of Count Stenbok-Fermor had drained away in two-three days. The report recommended damming gullies upstream in northern Kherson province to accumulate water.[126]

Doubts had also been raised in the steppe region about the work carried out by Zhilinskii and Annenkov. The *zemstvo* survey of Nikolaevsk district in Samara province, published in 1889, surveyed the work of Zhilinskii's expedition in the 1880s. It concluded that the attempts to set up channel irrigation of arable land had not lived up to expectations. The dams accumulated sufficient water only for cattle, not to irrigate fields. The *zemstvo* surveyor showed his lack of knowledge, however, by continuing that the 'academic engineers' needed to learn from the

---

[123] Gersevanov, 'Ob obvodnenii, 716. He was in favour of irrigation in the North Caucasus, however, where the topography was different. 'Gersevanov, 'Soobrazheniya ob obvodneniya severnogo kavkaza', *Stavropol'skie gubernskie vedomosti* (16 and 23 February, and 1 March 1880).

[124] [Dokuchaev], *K voprosu*.

[125] Dokuchaev, *Sochineniya*, viii, 291–3, 295, 477.

[126] PFA RAN, f.184, op.1, d.136, ll.39–59; RGIA, f.426, op.1, 1891, d.30, ll.262–80.

experience of other nations, in particular in Central Asia, how to build dams to divert river water to fields.[127] This criticism was unfair since Zhilinskii and his team well knew they needed to devise methods that worked in conditions on the steppes, rather than copying from elsewhere. Zhilinskii had tried, moreover, to deal with the practical problems his expedition encountered.[128]

Reservations about irrigation were expressed at a meeting of the Don Agricultural Society addressed by Annenkov in 1892. The majority of those present recognized the need to improve agriculture in the region and were sympathetic to the work to build dams to store water. Concerns were raised, however, over the cost of Annenkov's public works and whether they were worthwhile. One member of the society pointed to the unfavourable attitude of peasants and cossacks to the construction of ponds. Annenkov replied that in Saratov province he had worked hard to get the peasants' support by showing concern for their welfare and needs.[129] Not all peasants felt their welfare was taken into account. In 1895, Iob Markov Semenchev, who rented land on the Velikii Anadol' plot, in Ekaterinoslav province, complained that members of Zhilinskii's expedition were grazing their horses and cattle on his land, and had occupied all the gullies on the plot leaving the local population with no possibility of storing water. He requested, and received, compensation.[130]

I witnessed an issue similar to the last part of Semenchev's complaint on my visit to the Rostov steppe *zapovednik* in 2003. A local entrepreneur was building dam across a gulley in the buffer zone outside the nature reserve to provide water for an enterprise he planned. If completed, his dam would have cut off one of the main sources of fresh water to the nature reserve. The scientists on the expedition I was with made representations to the local authorities (I was taken along as evidence for the international importance of the *zapovednik*), were interviewed on local television at the scene, and in the end a compromise was reached. This incident brought home to me the value of the scarce supplies of water in the steppe region, and the possibility of serious competition for water, especially in more arid parts such as the location of the reserve.

But in the 1890s, the decisive argument against persisting with large-scale irrigation work in the steppe region was made by Finance Minister Witte in July 1896. In May, Minister of Agriculture Ermolov sent Witte his plans to expand the work of Zhilinskii's expedition over the next few years. Ermolov requested funds to complete the work on the eight plots of state land where the expedition had been working since 1880. He sought additional funds for surveys of the topography, hydrology, meteorology, and other aspects of the geography of

[127] *SSSpSG*, vi, *Nikolaevskii uezd* (1889), 14–16.
[128] For an example in neighbouring Novyi Uzen' district, see RGIA, f.426, op.1, 1895, d.92, ll.44–5ob.
[129] 'Otchet o deyatel'nosti donskogo obshchestva sel'skogo khozyaistva za 1892 god', *SKhiL*, 173 (1893), 13–14.
[130] RGIA, f.426, op.1, 1894, d.111.

the eight million *desyatiny* in the region. The work would take five years and, not counting expenditure on technical staff, would cost at least one and a half million roubles. This was to be followed by two further stages of surveys that would work their way up the river valleys from the coasts. At this precise time, however, Witte was dealing with a request for massive state funding. He was engaged in an argument against a proposal by Tsar Nicholas II to build a naval fleet on the Pacific which would cost hundreds of millions of roubles. Witte was concerned that it could divert funds from building the Trans-Siberian railway, which he favoured.[131]

The embattled Finance Minister seems to have taken out his frustration on his protégé. On 29 July 1896, Witte sent a long memorandum to Ermolov. He explained that irrigation had been discussed several times in the State Council, which had decided to assign priority to Central Asia, to expand cotton cultivation, and then the Caucasus, for the cultivation of 'higher agricultural crops', such as tobacco and tea.

With regard to the southern and certain south-eastern provinces of . . . European Russia—Witte continued—the expediency of releasing further more or less substantial sums of state money for irrigation of land . . . is . . . debateable, and not only because objections of a principled nature may be presented against the timeliness and profitability of irrigation operations in this region, but above all on account of the fact that the practical results are still not known of [Zhilinskii's] experiments in setting up and exploiting artificial irrigation on state, communal [i.e. peasant] and private land, on which over the past fifteen years . . . very considerable sums of money have been spent by the treasury.

There followed thirty pages of closely argued text in which the Finance Minister expanded on this theme and elucidated his reasoning. Irrigation in European Russia was new and experimental. The reports of Zhilinskii's expedition did not demonstrate the economic and agronomical significance of their experiments. Part of the money had been used to set up irrigation on the land of private estate owners as well as peasant and state land. Some of the expedition's work had turned out to be unsatisfactory. The Tengutinskaya dam in Astrakhan' province, which cost 200,000 roubles, had proved not fit for purpose. The Solyanskoe reservoir in Samara province had needed to be reconstructed several times. The work the expedition had done was expensive, but the incomes from irrigated land were not high and also uncertain. Growing grain on irrigated land in the current market conditions (world prices were low) meant that the cost of setting up irrigation could not be repaid. Witte noted the disagreement in the Russian specialist literature—he cited the work of Shishkin amongst others—over the value and practicality of irrigating land in southern Russia. Turning to Ermolov's

[131] Francis W. Wcislo, *Tales of Imperial Russia: The Life and Times of Sergei Witte, 1849–1915* (Oxford), 181–2.

plans for the future work of the expedition, Witte wrote: 'I can not agree with such a programme of irrigation operations at the expense of the Government in these regions of European Russia.' It would be natural, he continued, not only not to increase the area of irrigated land, but to decrease it. To proceed further as the Ministry of Agriculture wanted would be unjustifiable by economic necessity or experience. He was prepared to permit, and assigned 293,000 roubles for, the completion of work on the existing state plots in two years. Then that was to be an end to it. The law on credits for melioration of land, enacted on 6 May 1896, was sufficient for irrigation work on private and communal land. The State Controller wrote to Ermolov in October reiterating Witte's arguments, but with less detail. Ermolov and Zhilinskii replied, more or less agreeing with most of what Witte had written, but seeking five years, not two, to wind up the expedition, and to do a little new work. Witte responded by cutting their funds back further.[132]

Worse was to follow for Ermolov and Zhilinskii's plans. On 7 April 1897, Tsar Nicholas II ratified a decision by the State Council that, every year, 4 per cent of the capital outlay spent setting up the irrigation systems on the plots of state land was to be returned to the treasury.[133] A commission was set up in the Ministry of Agriculture to plan the economic management of the plots. It decided to lease out part of the land to raise money to repay the treasury. The commission rejected expensive ideas to use mechanical pumps to raise water on to the high steppe in favour of continuing to irrigate low-lying land by gravity.[134]

If Witte thought he had settled the future of Zhilinskii's expedition, then he was wrong. The question was revived by Nicholas II. In his annual report for 1897, the governor of Samara, once again, raised the need for irrigation. His province had, once again, been hit by a drought, which had led to another poor harvest, which, once again, was especially serious in Nikolaevsk and Novyi Uzen' districts in the south. The tsar wrote in the margin of the report: 'Irrigation work according to Zhilinskii's plan should be considered.'[135] Nicholas had evidently forgotten the decisions his administration had taken. He seemed not to realize, moreover, that his finance minister considered irrigating the steppes to be 'senseless dreams'. It fell to Anatolii Kulomzin of the Council of Ministers to bring the tsar's note to the attention of the finance minister. In his reply, Witte repeated more succinctly the arguments he had made to Ermolov the previous July. He concluded that to carry out additional irrigation work in Samara province would be 'useless'. Other measures could be used to assist the population, such as giving out grain and horses, and encouraging the Red Cross to help the needy. Ermolov, who was a little bolder than he had been in 1896, made a

---

[132] RGIA, f.426, op.1, 1896, d.114, ll.191–207 (quotation from l.201), 216–25ob., 228–63ob., 301–7ob.; see also RGIA, f.1152, op.12, 1897, d.28, ll.1–102. For a slightly different interpretation, see Dyakin, *Den'gi*, 39–40.

[133] RGIA, f.426, op.1, 1900, d.260, l.31.

[134] PFA RAN, f.184, op.1, d.119, ll.8–13.

[135] GASO, f.3, op.233, 1898, d.1541, ll.2ob.–4, 25ob., 46–ob.

fuller justification of Zhilinskii's expedition. He blamed the high costs in the 1890s on the public works (and by implication Annenkov's mismanagement), and argued that the irrigated land was more profitable than Witte had suggested. He restated his agreement with Witte's decision to wind down the expedition, however, and concurred that other ways could be used to help the population of Samara province. The Minister of Agriculture did increase the amount of money spent on irrigation in Samara province, but used funds originally allocated to other provinces.[136]

Even as it was being wound down, the expedition continued its work and devised ambitious schemes. In 1898, for example, it planned to irrigate two plots of state land in Novyi Uzen' district at a cost of 558,545 roubles 48 kopecks.[137] Ermolov continued to request large sums. On 15 October 1899, Witte had his deputy write to Ermolov to turn down his latest request, repeating the arguments made in July 1896. He underlined his decision by cutting the expedition's funding for 1900 by half, to 100,000 roubles.[138] The last years of the expedition were marred by complaints from peasants. To take just one case: in March 1899, Boris Vasil'ev Kirpa of Kolyshikino in Novyi Uzen' district complained that a dam on neighbouring state land had been breached by the large quantity of water that had accumulated behind it. He added that the dam had not been maintained properly. Kirpa requested 200 roubles in compensation for the loss of his fruit trees, which had been destroyed when the dam burst.[139] Other peasants complained that they had not been paid for work they had done. A survey in 1900 of the Valuiskii plot, which Zhilinskii had been so proud of, revealed a long list of repairs that needed to be done. There were insufficient funds available, however, as the irrigated plots were supposed to be earning money from rents to repay the treasury. This was not happening. In 1902, the Department of Civil Accounting of the State Controller stepped in to request information on the sums that were due. Over the next few years, it sent a number of 'urgent requests' for information, insisting on proper financial management and accountability in the interests of protecting the state treasury. Zhilinskii was still stalling in May 1908.[140] He retired in 1909 for health reasons at the age of 75.[141]

The exchanges over the funding of Zhilinskii's expedition were part of a wider dispute between Finance Minister Witte and Minister of Agriculture Ermolov over what the historian Valentin Dyakin called 'money for agriculture'. Ermolov constantly argued that government spending on the rural economy should be

---

[136] RGIA, f.426, op.1, 1899, d.182, ll.194–8, 199–207.
[137] RGIA, f.453, op.1, 1898, d.11, ll.1–7.
[138] RGIA, f.426, op.1, 1898, d.156, ll.1, 151; d.182, ll.91–93ob.; 329–53; 383–6; d.240.
[139] RGIA, f.426, op.1, 1899, d.182, l.100, see also ll.36, 40, 102–4ob.
[140] RGIA, f.426, op.1, 1900, d.254, ll.4–ob., 7–10ob., 19–21ob., 27–8, 47–8, 71–ob.; d.260, ll.59, 73–4.
[141] 'I. I. Zhilinskii', 3–4.

increased to assist agriculture and the welfare of the people. Witte was firmly of the opinion that financial resources should be concentrated on industry. He feared overproduction of grain and consequent falling prices.[142] In his memoirs (written in 1911) Witte remarked that Ermolov had regularly complained that he did not give him sufficient money. The former minister of finance continued that he thought he ought not to have given him any money at all as he did not know how to manage finances. Witte believed that Ermolov was too concerned to help large estate owners, who had their own resources, rather than the peasantry. Witte also remarked that he considered Ermolov a 'weak' minister, who was much more capable of writing than acting.[143]

Witte had some knowledge of the matter. His father, Yulii, was an agronomist who had experience of the steppe region and the Caucasus.[144] Although born in Tiflis (today's Tbilisi in Georgia), Sergei Yul'evich studied mathematics at the University of New Russia in Odessa, which he entered in 1867. For some years after he graduated, he worked for the state railway in Odessa, where he acquired an understanding of the topography of the region.[145] It may not be a coincidence that at the time he was in Odessa, the regional agricultural society was at best lukewarm about irrigation (see above, p. 217). In 1890, moreover, Witte visited Central Asia, where he was impressed by its economic potential and the development of cotton production.[146]

Zhilinskii's was not the only expedition to the steppe region concerned with irrigation. Dokuchaev's expedition, which began in 1892, was charged with conducting experiments and costing ways to manage the water resources, as well as forests, in the region. Dokuchaev's plan to address the causes of the drought and crop failure of 1891, which formed the basis for his expedition, contained the following points on water resources and irrigation: 1. Regulation of rivers—narrow and straighten courses of the major rivers, reduce spring floods, stop rivers silting up, and dam smaller rivers and upper reaches of larger rivers to regulate flow and retain water in reservoirs; 2. Regulation of ravines and gullies—where appropriate, dam them to create ponds to hold rain and melt water; 3. Regulation of the use of water on the open steppes and watersheds—dig ponds on watersheds to hold melt and rain water and reinforce the banks with trees; elsewhere on the open steppes, plant hedges and build long, low dykes to

---

[142] Dyakin, *Den'gi*, 35, 341.

[143] [Witte], *Iz arkhiva*, i/i, 300–1. See also *Iz arkhiva*, 428–9. On Witte's memoirs as a historical source, see Wcislo, *Tales*, 12–14.

[144] For a study written five years before Sergei Yul'evich was born, see Yu. Witte, 'O sel'skom khozyaistve v Khersonskoi, Tavricheskoi i Ekaterinskoi guberniyakh', *ZhMGI*, 13 (1844), 2nd pagn, 58–75, 101–22. On Yulii Witte, see also below, p. 247.

[145] [Witte], *Iz arkhiva*, i/i, 22–7, 64–102.

[146] [Witte], *Iz arkhiva*, i/i, 199. From the late nineteenth century, textile manufacturers in central Russia and the Finance Ministry advocated irrigation in Central Asia to expand cotton production. Joffe, 'Autocracy, Capitalism and Empire'.

help retain snow, melt and rain water; dig wells to tap the replenished ground water for irrigation.[147]

Dokuchaev's expedition was more concerned with scientific research than Zhilinskii's. Dokuchaev was seeking to learn from what he believed to be samples of virgin steppe environment in devising ways to manage the water resources. To this end, the expedition's scientists carried out detailed research into the hydrology of the plots of state land they were allocated for their work.[148] In addition, Dokuchaev's expedition undertook practical work, digging wells and ponds, damming ravines and gullies to retain water in reservoirs, and using the water to irrigate the land, both meadows by means of flooding once in the early spring and fields by channelling water from reservoirs. The scientists took care to calculate where best to build dams in ravines and gullies, the height and breadth of dams, and the appropriate sizes for reservoirs to ensure they would be filled by the amount of precipitation that fell in the winter. Careful observations were made, moreover, of the water levels in reservoirs over the summer months.[149] Dokuchaev's plans to regulate rivers came up against legal problems (see above, pp. 207–8, 213–16). Like Zhilinskii, Dokuchaev wished to expand his expedition, but this would have required further funding, which, also like Zhilinskii's expedition, was not forthcoming.[150]

SMALL-SCALE IRRIGATION FROM THE 1890S

The withdrawal of government support for research and practical work on large-scale irrigation in the steppe region in the late 1890s did not mean the authorities were set against all irrigation in the region. Rather, there was a switch to smaller-scale work, which to some extent met the continued demand from estate owners, *zemstva*, agricultural societies, and peasant communities for assistance in irrigating their land. To take an extreme example: peasants in Aleksandriya, Novyi Uzen' district, in southern Samara province sent a desperate plea to the Ministry of Agriculture in 1908. They bemoaned the fact that they had rejected an offer to resettle them in 1902 after an outbreak of disease was attributed to the water supply. 'Now', after an outbreak of cholera, they wrote

---

[147] Dokuchaev, 'Nashi stepi prezhde i teper'', *Sochineniya*, vi, 87–96; V. V. Dokuchaev, 'Osobaya ekspeditsiya, snaryazhennaya lesnym departamentom, pod rukovodstvom professora Dokuchaeva', *Sochineniya*, vi, 112–18.

[148] K. Glinka, N. Sibirtsev, P. Ototskii, 'Khrenovskii uchastok', *TESLD, Nauchnii otdel*, 1/1 (1894), 15–18, 33–6, 103–7; I. Vydrin and N. Sibirtsev, 'Starobel'skii uchastok', *TESLD, Nauchnii otdel*, 1/2 (1894), 52–9; P. Zemyatchenskii, 'Velikoanadol'skii uchastok', *TESLD, Nauchnii otdel*, 1/3 (1894), 32–40.

[149] V. Deich, 'Gidrotekhnicheskie raboty 1893 goda', *TESLD, Otdel prakticheskikh rabot*, 2/1 (1894), 1–94; V. Deich, 'Gidrotekhnicheskie raboty 1894–96 godov', *TESLD, Otdel prakticheskikh rabot*, 2/2 (1898), 1–160. Deich referred to the experience of Zhilinskii's expedition.

[150] See RGIA, f.426, op.1, 1891, d.30; PFA RAN, f.184, op.1, d.119, ll.1–7.

'we regret terribly that we acted so thoughtlessly. We are now suffering without water! Save us, Your Excellency!' They stated that they needed a dam with irrigation installations as there was no or insufficient water in their wells and the nearby river. They beseeched the minister, with tears, either to build them a dam or to resettle them somewhere else, 'even in Siberia'. The minister sought further information.[151]

Irrigation was one of the purposes for which the Ministry of Agriculture gave loans to *zemstva*, estate owners, and village communities for 'agricultural improvements' under the law on 'melioration credit' of 1896. Between 1898 and 1910, the ministry lent 1,271,257 roubles for irrigation work. This was over 40 per cent of the total credit extended for land improvements. It was only a little over 100,000 roubles a year, however, which one specialist described as 'insignificant' in comparison with the need for irrigation in parts of Russia.[152] In 1901, for example, the ministry lent 5,000 roubles to a noble, Dmitrii Khristiforov, who owned an estate covering 2,970 *desyatiny*, at Loshkarevka, Ekaterinoslav district and province. Around half the money was to dam a gully to retain water, to dig two wells, and to irrigate a nursery for trees. Water would be supplied to the saplings by a horse-powered apparatus. The ministry awarded Khristiforov the money because it would benefit not just his estate but also the surrounding area.[153]

Zemstva in the steppe and adjoining forest-steppe regions continued to take an interest in irrigation. Some, including the Samara provincial *zemstvo*, set up hydrological bureaus to coordinate the work.[154] In the early twentieth century, *zemstvo* agronomists in Nikolaevsk and Novyi Uzen' districts gave talks and demonstrations to peasants on how to irrigate their land. They paid particular attention to retaining snow and spring melt water. In 1909, V. M. Kuznetsov, a *zemstvo* agronomist in Novyi Uzen' district, reported that farmers who sowed large areas of land were starting to use steam traction engines to pump water to their fields.[155] Use of such advanced technology was rare. In 1911, the Samara provincial *zemstvo* published a pamphlet on irrigation systems. Among the advice offered was that it was best to build a dam in a place where the least amount of earth would need to moved to hold back the largest quantity of water. The engineer provided a formula to assist in the calculations.[156] The Peasant Land Bank, which acquired land for sale to peasants, carried out improvements of the

---

[151] RGIA, f.426, op.1, 1908, d.693, ll.1–2ob. For many more peasant petitions, most less desperate, see RGIA, f.426, op.1, 1894, dd.92–3.

[152] Z. S. Katsenelenbaum, 'Melioratsii i meliorativnyi kredit', *PERSKh*, xii (1912), 707–9; Z. S. Katsenelenbaum, 'Meliorativnyi kredit v Rossii i ego blizhaishie zadachi', *SKhiL*, 234 (1910), 496–7.

[153] RGIA, f.395, op.1, 1901, d.856, ll.3–5.

[154] Katsenelenbaum, 'Melioratsii', 708.

[155] GASO, f.5, op.11, d.102, ll.27ob., 62, 83ob., 98, 101.

[156] K. Levin, *Oroshenie i obvodnenie zemel'nykh ugodii* (Samara, 1911), 3–5. See also GASO, f.5, op.11, d.107, ll.68–70.

land before selling it. In Samara province, the bank introduced irrigation systems to its land. In 1909, the technical department of the Samara section of the bank prepared plans to dig wells and ponds, dam ravines and gullies to create reservoirs, and build dams to retain snow melt water. In 1912, the bank assigned 118,955 roubles in credits to set up and repair irrigation on its land in the province.[157]

There was action on irrigation elsewhere in the steppe region. In the Don region in the late 1890s, K. A. Kartushin advocated artificial irrigation to the Maslakovets commission. He argued that experience had shown the influence of irrigation on crop yields. The water for irrigation was to come from rainfall and melted snow stored in dammed gullies and ravines. Kartushev was aware of the financial constraints. He argued, however, that if cossacks were permitted to hold their land in individual, rather than communal, tenure, then there would be no need to lend them money to install irrigation as they would be able to benefit from any improvements they made. Thus, enterprising farmers would have an incentive to invest in their land. He also urged that outsiders be allowed to buy cossack land if they agreed to irrigate it.[158] Between 1899 and 1903, the Don administration tried to appoint a hydrological engineer called Samonsov. He had drawn up a plan to irrigate land in Astrakhan' province in the 1880s, which had 'brought the land to life'. Crucially, irrigation had increased the rental value of the land more than fourfold, which covered the cost of interest payments on the money borrowed to build the dams. Samsonov turned the Don administration's offer down, twice. The ataman noted in frustration that it was difficult to find experienced people 'in view of the almost complete absence of artificial irrigation works in Russia (the works by the Ministry of Agriculture are insignificant in scale and not always successful due the lack of experienced staff)'. In 1902, on the advice of the minister of agriculture, the Don administration appointed an engineer called Maevskii, who had experience in the steppe region.[159] Members of the Don administration and local scientists continued to advocate irrigation, especially in the drier, south-eastern parts of the region.[160] Irrigation was expanded in the region in the second decade of the twentieth century as a by-product of a scheme to regulate the Don and Donets rivers.[161]

[157] GASO, f.149, op.14, d.19, ll.17–20, 36–37ob., 88–9ob., 123, 288–9; d.13, ll.1–126; op.9, d.84, l.92 ob.

[158] GARO, f.46, op.1, d.3282, ll.1–2. Cossacks held their land in communal and repartitional tenure. Shane O'Rourke, *Warriors and Peasants: The Don Cossacks in Late Imperial Russia* (New York, 2000), 63–76.

[159] GARO, f.301, op.11, d.176.

[160] A. M. Grekov, 'Nuzhdy Dona v trudakh mestnykh sel'skokhoyaistvennykh komitetov', *SOVDSK*, 5 (1905), 37–8; V. V. Bogachev, 'Zadonskie stepi. Pochva i orografiya stepei', *SOVDSK*, 4 (1904), 49–105.

[161] A. A. Pushkarenko, 'Prirodookhrannaya deyatel'nost' v Oblasti Voiska Donskogo vo vtoroi polovine XIX-nachale XX vv.', Candidate's dissertation, Rostov State University, 2000, 96–100. For subsequent plans, see GARO, f.55, op.1, d.717.

CONCLUSION

Over the course of the nineteenth and early twentieth centuries, there was much discussion of artificial irrigation as a solution to the shortage of water in the steppe region. Support for irrigation was particularly strong during and in the aftermath of droughts. By the end of the nineteenth century, Russians had accumulated some experience and expertise of irrigation on land belonging to estate owners, peasant communities, and the state and appanage department. Russian specialists, moreover, had carried out detailed studies of irrigation in other parts of the world.[162] Writing in 1903, governor Alexander Platonovich Engel'gardt of Saratov referred to 'not a few' estates where 'sizeable sums' had been spent on irrigation, which the owners did not regret. Overall, however, Engel'gardt paid little attention to irrigation in comparison with other remedies for the environmental problems facing the steppe region.[163] Over the preceding decades, many estate owners and specialists had decided that artificial irrigation was not their favoured approach. Organizations dedicated to promoting agriculture, such as the Free Economic Society and Southern Russian Agricultural Society had limited interest in irrigation. In July 1896, Finance Minister Witte decided not to allocate substantial funding to large-scale irrigation in the steppe region as he felt it was not a sound investment. Experience elsewhere suggested he may have been right. Profits from irrigated land in British India in the nineteenth century did not cover the cost.[164]

Work to irrigate land in the steppe region, mostly small scale, continued throughout the period. It received a boost towards the end of the nineteenth century from credits for 'melioration' from the Ministry of Agriculture, and from support by *zemstva*, the Peasant Land Bank, and a few other institutions. In spite of its best efforts, however, Zhilinskii's expedition had served only to confirm that large-scale irrigation was not a viable solution in the steppe region. In 1912, Z. S. Katsenelenbaum concluded: 'Irrigation works by government expeditions had been rather unsuccessful and had gone little further than the preliminary stages of investigation.' He argued that irrigation did have a future in Russia, as it allowed the possibility of reducing the harm to agriculture caused by insufficient moisture in the south-east. But, he pointed out that the limited data available indicated that, while irrigating meadows by flooding was economically viable, the same could not be said for irrigating arable land.[165] Experience in other countries, which had been cited as an argument for its use in Russia, was put

---

[162] Much of this expertise was summarized by the specialist in charge of irrigation on appanage estates. S. Yu. Rauner, *Iskusstvennoe oroshenie zemel'nykh ugodii. Posobie dlya russkikh praktikov-orositelei* (Spb, 1897).

[163] Engel'gardt, *Chernozemnaya Rossiya*, 152–3; Prilozhenie, v.

[164] Beinart and Hughes, *Environment and Empire*, 135.

[165] Katsenelenbaum, 'Melioratsii', 705, 708.

forward less frequently by the turn of the twentieth century. Instead, it was increasingly argued that the natural conditions in other parts of the world differed significantly from Russia's steppes. For example, the topography of the region—with water in rivers with shallow gradients in valleys far below the level of fields on the steppes—contrasted sharply with other areas where agriculture needed artificial supplies of water. A Russian study of irrigation in the USA in 1896 noted that American rivers generally had a steeper gradient or flowed through shallow banks. Both made using water from rivers for irrigation easier than on the steppes.[166]

It was other parts of the Russian Empire—Central Asia and the Caucasus—that benefitted from government support for irrigation from the 1890s. Witte felt that investing in growing valuable crops, such as cotton, tea, and tobacco, was better use of government funds than large-scale irrigation to grow grain in the steppe region. From the mid-1890s, Zhilinskii was involved in developing irrigation in Asiatic parts of the empire.[167] Irrigating these regions was also promoted Aleksandr Voeikov. He advocated diverting most of the water from the Syr and Amu Dar'ya rivers, 'now, without use to man, flowing into the Aral Sea, where it evaporates', to provide water for cotton fields.[168] When the Aral Sea did start to dry up, for this very reason, in the late twentieth century, it was an ecological disaster.[169] (Voeikov's view is a reminder not to attribute ahistorical environmentalist views to specialists in the period covered by this book.)

The arguments on the impracticality and uneconomic nature of irrigation in the steppe region of European Russia were repeated at greater length in 1909 by former Minister of Agriculture Ermolov (demonstrating that he had taken on board Witte's arguments in 1896). There was a tone of regret when he discussed irrigation as part of a wider review of measures to avert famines and place agriculture on a firmer basis. He mentioned arid parts of the world, such as India and Egypt, where agriculture was based on irrigation. He stated that he was prepared 'ardently to support the notion of the possible expansion' of irrigation. He expressed reservations about doing so 'in those parts of European Russia, which suffer most of all from harvest failures caused by droughts'. The topography meant that raising the water onto the fields would be possible only by means of long and expensive systems of channels and hydraulic installations. He continued that even in the most arid parts of European Russia there was on average sufficient precipitation to meet the needs of crops. 'But', he pointed out, 'this precipitation is unequally distributed throughout the year—and very often

[166] S. Kizenkov, 'Oroshenie v Soedinennikh Shtatakh Severnoi Ameriki', *SKhiL*, 182 (1896), 367. See also 'O merakh k uluchsheniyu estestvennykh uslovii sel'skogo khozyaistva', *SKhiL*, 209 (1903), 519–20.
[167] 'I. I. Zhilinskii', 3–4.
[168] A. Voeikov, 'Zemel'ye uluchsheniya i ikh sootnoshenie s klimatom i drugimi estestvennymi usloviyami', in *Vozdeistvie*, 106–10 (first published in 1909).
[169] Philip Micklin, 'The Aral Crisis', *Post-Soviet Geography*, 33 (1992), 269–82.

there is none at the precise time when it is most needed by plants.' 'Sometimes from the early spring', Ermolov continued, 'a period of drought starts: the young shoots [of crops] wilt and perish, and the sun is baking, dry winds blow, and everyone starts to pray for rain.' In reviewing various possible methods to overcome the problem by storing water and using it for irrigation, he agreed that everything should be done to put this into practice, but noted that hydraulic installations cost too much to be used for the cultivation of grain, as it did not generate enough income to repay the investment. Irrigation was economically viable only if it was used to cultivate more valuable crops, such as cotton in Central Asia, or if it was feasible more cheaply for orchards, vegetable gardens, and meadows in parts of the steppe region of European Russia.[170]

[170] A. S. Ermolov, *Nashi neurozhai i prodovol'stvennyi vopros*, 2 vols (Spb, 1909), ii, 153–7.

8

Agronomy

INTRODUCTION

Surveying what was to be done to combat droughts and bad harvests, Aleksei Ermolov wrote that for arable land, 'it is necessary to resort not to irrigation, as it cannot repay the cost, but to . . . methods of cultivation directed at the best ways of accumulating, conserving, and using moisture in the soil'.[1] Writing in 1909, the former Minister of Agriculture was echoing what Finance Minister Sergei Witte had explained to him in July 1896:

The practical value of collecting spring flood waters in specially constructed reservoirs . . . to irrigate fields . . . has not been proved, and is disputed by many specialists, who recommend instead deep ploughing and cultivation of the soil as the best and simplest means of making use of the moisture that falls on the steppes.[2]

Witte, in turn, had taken the argument from the agronomist Aleksandr Shishkin, who in 1876 had argued: 'The main means of struggling with droughts is . . . in the way the land is cultivated.'[3] The other great panacea for the shortage of water in the steppe region—planting trees—had started to fall out of favour around the same time. In 1875, S. Lavrent'ev had argued that afforestation as way to prevent droughts had become 'plan B' ('*vtoroi plan*') and been replaced by a more practical measure: deep cultivation of the soil to assist in the accumulation of the moisture needed by plants.[4]

Turning to methods of cultivating the land marked a distinct change of approach to 'combating' the 'problems' caused by the shortage of water and recurring droughts. Rather than trying to transform the steppe environment by artificially supplying water or planting trees—that is, trying to make the steppes more like the homelands of the settlers, authorities, and scientists, or their forebears—efforts were directed instead at working *with* the steppe environment:

---

[1] A. S. Ermolov, *Nashi neurozhai i prodovol'stvennyi vopros*, 2 vols (Spb, 1909), ii, 157. See also James Y. Simms, The Crop Failure of 1891: Soil Exhaustion, Technological Backwardness, and Russia's "Agrarian Crisis", *SR*, 41 (1982), 236–50.

[2] RGIA, f.426, op.1, 1896, d.114, l.199.

[3] A. Shishkin, *K voprosu ob umen'shenii vrednogo deistviya zasukh na rastitel'nost'* (Spb, 1876), 167.

[4] S. Lavrent'ev, 'Po voprosu ob ustranenii stepnykh zasukh', *TVEO*, 3 (1875), 436–7.

seeking the best ways to cultivate the fertile black earth in the largely treeless, semi-arid and drought-prone, flat grassland in which it had formed over time. The change to agronomy was all the more necessary as some settlers were farming the land in ways they or their forebears had done in their previous homes. In 1856, the inspector of agriculture in southern Russia noted that farmers on the steppes were not paying due attention to the need to conserve scarce moisture in the land. His explanation was that Russians who had settled the region came mainly from central Russia (where water was not scarce), and so their customary farming methods were not designed to conserve moisture.[5]

The idea of changing the way farmers cultivated the land to address the problems caused by the vicissitudes of the steppe environment was not new in the second half of the nineteenth century. Attempts to 'improve' agriculture on the steppes dated back to the late eighteenth century. A poor harvest in New Russia in 1789 prompted Grigorii Potemkin to set up an agricultural school near Nikolaev. Potemkin also encouraged more foreigners, especially Germans, to settle on the steppes in the hope that they would provide examples of 'improved agriculture'.[6] One group of foreign colonists, the Mennonites, were very successful in this regard, and went on to devise ways to farm the land that took account of the shortage of water.[7]

The serious drought and harvest failure of 1833 spurred further action by the government. It set up a Committee for the Improvement of Agriculture chaired by Admiral Nikolai Mordvinov, the president of the Free Economic Society, whose members included Count Kankrin, the Minister of Finance, and Count Bludov, the Minister of Internal Affairs. V. I. Veshnyakov, an official in the Ministry of State Domains, later wrote that 1833 was

> remembered in the annals of our economy as the year of one of the most disastrous bad harvests of the present century. It is remembered also because the disaster first impressed on the government the need for serious thought not only about temporary measures to eliminate problems in feeding the population, but also about durable and permanent measures to increase the productivity of the Russian land.[8]

Over the following decades, the authorities and agricultural specialists worked to develop ways to address the problem of recurring poor harvests in the steppe region. Agricultural societies, especially the Southern Russian Agricultural Society, together with the Ministry of State Domains (later Agriculture), the

[5] DAOO, fond 1, opis' 248, 1856, sp.1580, ll.113–ob., 115.

[6] A. Skal'kovskii, *Opyt statisticheskogo opisaniya Novorossiiskogo kraya*, 2 vols (Odessa, 1850–3), ii, 24–7.

[7] See James Urry, *None but Saints: The Transformation of Mennonite Life in Russia, 1789–1889* (Winnipeg, 1989). On Mennonite farmers in Samara province, see Judith Pallot and Denis J. B. Shaw, *Landscape and Settlement in Romanov Russia, 1613–1917* (Oxford, 1990), 79–111.

[8] V. I. Veshnyakov, 'Komitet 1833 g. ob usovershenstvovanii zemledeliya v Rossii', *Russkii vestnik*, 82/7 (1869), 286–320, quotation from 286; *PSZ*, 2, x, 657–62 (no.6567, 24 November 1833).

Appanage Department and, from the late nineteenth century, *zemstva*, and the Peasant Land Bank all supported efforts to devise farming techniques appropriate to the steppe environment. Societies and government agencies sponsored research by agricultural scientists, who set up experiment stations and demonstration fields. From the end of the century, extension services offered agronomical advice to the rural population.[9]

Agronomists sought to understand the processes that were taking place in the soil when it was ploughed up. It was widely believed that yields of crops planted in virgin steppe under the shifting, long-fallow system of farming that prevailed into the nineteenth century declined after a few years due to soil exhaustion. This was one of the reasons farmers left land fallow for many years.[10] In the late nineteenth century, the agronomist and soil scientist Pavel Kostychev argued that the reason yields declined was because weeds spread in the fields, causing the structure of the soil, and crucially its ability to absorb and retain moisture, to deteriorate. In fields left fallow for fifteen–twenty years, he argued, the native vegetation had time to return, eliminate the weeds, and allow the soil to recover its structure and water-retaining characteristics. Leaving fields fallow for fifteen or more years, however, was becoming increasingly unusual in large parts of the steppe region by the late nineteenth century. Farmers were making more intensive use of their land, cutting back the fallow period, or introducing entirely different crop rotations. Kostychev thus advocated cultivating the soil in ways that would assist the accumulation and retention of moisture.[11]

An important centre for research into agriculture in the steppe region was the Bezenchuk agricultural experiment station in Samara province. It was founded by the Appanage Department in 1903 to devise and test farming methods as a basis for advice and instructions to leaseholders of its land. The station's research programme was based on the observation that: 'In southern and south-eastern Russia the basic question is that of accumulation, conservation, and rational use of the moisture that falls on the soil.'[12] The location was well chosen for the purpose of devising methods of cultivation to achieve these goals, since the average precipitation was only around 300 mm a year.[13]

For a long time, however, the main focus of efforts to 'improve' agriculture in the steppe region, and Russia as a whole, was not on experiments conducted in

    [9] See Ol'ga Elina, *Ot tsarskikh sadov do sovetskikh polei: istoriya sel'sko-khozyaistvennykh opytnykh uchrezhdenii XVIII-20-e gody XX v.*, 2 vols (Moscow, 2008).
    [10] See A. S. Ermolov, *Organizatsiya polevogo khozyaistva: Sistemy zemledeliya i sevooboroty*, 5th edn (Spb, 1914), 114.
    [11] P. Kostychev, *O bor'be s zasukhoi v chernozemnoi oblasti postredstvom obrabotki polei i nakopleniya na nikh snega* (Spb, 1893), 6–14. See also above, pp. 112, 161–2.
    [12] GASO, f.832, op.1, d.2, l.1–ob.; I. Klingen and Ya. Zhukov, 'Udel'naya oblastnaya sel'kokhozyaistvennaya opytnaya stantsiya', *SKhiL*, 225 (1907), 179–207; *Podvornoe i khutorskoe khozyaistvo v Samarskoi gubernii. Opyt agronomicheskogo issledovaniya*, 1 (Samara, 1909), 231.
    [13] GASO, f.149, op.9, d.15, l.2ob.

local conditions, but on literature by agronomists and specialists on agriculture in Western Europe.

THE RELEVANCE OF WESTERN EUROPEAN AGRONOMY TO STEPPE FARMING

During the eighteenth and long into the nineteenth centuries, like so many branches of technology, learning and culture, in Russia ideas for improving agriculture and agricultural sciences were heavily derivative on Western Europe. In much the same spirit that had prompted Peter the Great to study shipbuilding in England in the 1690s, a few decades later the Russian authorities dispatched young Russians to rainy and foggy Albion to study the latest developments in farming. In 1776, Catherine the Great sent Ivan Komov—who had just returned from the Academy of Sciences expeditions to the steppes of 1768–74—on a further expedition, this time to England to study agricultural sciences. He spent eight years there, and took the opportunity to audit courses on natural sciences at Oxford University, study under the agronomist Arthur Young, become a member of the Bath and West of England Society for the Encouragement of Agriculture, Arts, Manufactures and Commerce, and travel extensively studying such innovations as crop rotations that included root vegetables for fodder. On his return to Russia, he taught agronomy under the auspices of the Free Economic Society, organized an experiment farm near Moscow, and wrote an important study on agriculture. He was a firm advocate of drawing on the experience of other countries as well as Russia. He asserted that Russia had 'almost all European climates and there was not one vegetable, grass or tree in Europe that would not grow in [Russia's] northern or southern provinces'. He was keenly aware of the central importance of water for plant growth, the role of cultivation of the soil in raising productivity, as well as crop rotations that were appropriate to Russian conditions.[14]

Potemkin also looked to English expertise. In 1788, he ordered the manufacture of a thousand 'English' ploughs and harrows to be distributed to estate owners and settlers on the steppes of New Russia.[15] Throughout the period down to the twentieth century, moreover, articles on agriculture and agricultural sciences in Western Europe were regularly published in Russia. For example, the influential book by the German agronomist Albrecht Thaer (1752–1828) *Principles of rational agriculture* (*Grundsätze der rationellen Landwirthschaft*) of 1809–12 was published in Russian translation in 1830. From the 1860s, Russian

---

[14] Elina, *Ot tsarskikh sadov*, i, 162–7; I. F. Kopyl', 'Iz istorii russkoi agronomii XVIII v. (I. M. Komov o zemledelii)', in V. I. Shunkov (ed.), *Iz istorii opyta sel'skogo khozyaistva SSSR: Materialy po istorii sel'skogo khozyaistva i krest'yanstva SSSR*, 7 (Moscow, 1969), 84–98.

[15] Ol'ga Eliseeva, *Grigorii Potemkin* (Moscow, 2006), 366.

students of agricultural sciences routinely spent time in Germany, France, or Britain to study the latest European theory and practice.[16]

Relying on the agricultural experience and expertise of Western Europe in the steppe region was, however, inconsistent with the contrast that most observers— since the time of Herodotus—had made between the environment of the steppes and other parts of Europe. To take just one example, in 1807, Engel'man argued that the climate of the steppes was different from other parts of Europe on the same latitude: the winters were more severe, and the summers much hotter and drier. He further noted the shortage of water, but very fertile soil.[17] It became increasingly apparent to farmers and those involved in promoting agriculture on the steppes, moreover, that agricultural sciences, techniques, and crops from Western Europe were not necessarily appropriate to the steppe environment (or in many respects to Russia as a whole). This was the view of Mikhail Pavlov, who was sent to Germany in 1818 to study under Thaer. Pavlov had experience of the northern steppes, since he was the son of a priest from Voronezh province and spent a year at Khar'kov University. He came to recognize the need for different agricultural systems for different climates and soils in Russia, and rejected the suitability of some foreign methods for Russian conditions.[18]

Whether improved agricultural techniques from Western Europe were appropriate in Russian conditions was discussed by the Committee for the Improvement of Agriculture, whose chairman, Mordvinov, was an anglophile. The committee read a paper by Senator Mechnikov, who surveyed the state peasantry of Slobodsko-Ukraine (later Khar'kov) and Kursk provinces in the drought year of 1833. He drew also on his experience as an estate owner in Slobodsko-Ukraine and Voronezh provinces, where long-fallow farming had already been replaced by the three-field system. Mechnikov wrote:

For more than five years in succession all the southern provinces have experienced bad harvests of grain. It is notable, moreover, that these almost complete harvest failures have gradually worsened, and in 1833, reached the final stage, placing the inhabitants of these provinces in a very impoverished position.

He further noted that the harvest had also failed in years that had been rainy, cold, hot and utterly dry. He concluded—and this was contrary to the views of most commentators on crop failures in the steppe region—that the bad harvests were not due to the atmosphere and temperature. He attributed the failures to system of crop rotation and poor cultivation of the soil. 'Our teacher, Europe' ('*Uchitel'nitsa nasha Evropa*'), he continued, could serve as an example as it had replaced the three-field system with more productive rotations. He explained

---

[16] Elina, *Ot tsarskikh sadov*, i, 168, 178, 196–7; ii, 459.

[17] Engel'man, 'O zavedenii v stepi sel'skogo khozyaistva', *TVEO*, 59 (1807), 181–3.

[18] Mikhail Pavlov, *O glavnykh sistemakh sel'skogo khozyaistva, s prinarovleniem k Rossii* (Moscow, 1821); Elina, *Ot tsarskikh sadov*, i, 167–9.

how he had tried to introduce the 'Thaer system' on his estate, but had experi-enced difficulties due in part to 'our climate', but also 'ill-intentioned' attitudes to innovation. The 'Thaer system' entailed sowing fodder grasses in the fallow field. This is what created the problem. The local peasants and estate owners thought sowing grass was 'foolhardy', because 'grass grows by itself' ('*sama roditsya*'). Therefore, he recommended a version of the Thaer system adapted to Russian conditions (see below, pp. 252–3). The committee concluded that introducing improved agriculture was difficult as it required 'sound knowledge', and that 'all farming methods employed in alien regions ('*chuzhie krai*') must in future be adapted to the climate and localities of Russia by careful thought and experiments.[19]

Nevertheless, the Russian government remained interested in farming tech-niques and agronomy in other European countries. In 1834, a number of junior officials and graduates of the Forestry Institute were sent to study under the agronomist Professor Schmaltz in Dorpat University in Livonia. Six were then sent to complete their studies at an agricultural institute near Dresden in Saxony. Some of these students went on to play a role in the steppe region. Yulii Witte was assigned to work for the Ministry of State Domains in Saratov province, where in the early 1840s he managed the model farm in Novyi Uzen' district (which became part of Samara province in 1851). He was then assigned to Tiflis, in Georgia, where his son (the future Minister of Finance) was born in 1849. The elder Witte wrote a detailed study of agriculture in New Russia in 1844. Karl Tsin, another of the students, studied the success of Mennonite farming in Tauride province. A third graduate of the scheme was assigned to the Lugansk training farm in Slavyanoserbsk district, Ekaterinoslav province.[20]

In 1837, Pavel Kiselev, head of the new Ministry of State Domains, asked Russian representatives in European countries to collect information about agriculture and the management of state lands. He produced a long list of questions concerning field systems, crop rotations, crops, implements, livestock, education, and other topics. Kiselev was not interested in blind imitation. In his initial report to the tsar, he stated that agriculture had developed quickly in European states as a result of the combined efforts of governments and private landowners with the assistance of science. It would be useful, he continued, to

[19] RGIA, f.398, op.83, 1831–8, d.4, ll.16ob.–17, 149–ob., 156ob.–8, 169ob., 205ob.–6; f.1287, op.2, 1833, d.147, ll.1–2ob. See also Basil Dmytryshyn, 'Admiral Nikolai S. Mordvinov: Russia's Forgotten Liberal', *RR*, 30 (1971), 54–63.

[20] RGIA, f.398, op.83, d.148; Yu. Witte, 'Kratkii ocherk golshtinskogo khozyaistva i sravnenie ego s khozyaistvom meklenburgskim', *ZhMGI*, 1 (1841), 2nd pagn, 79; Yu. Witte, 'O sel'skom khozyaistve v Khersonskoi, Tavricheskoi i Ekaterinskoi guberniyakh', *ZhMGI*, 13 (1844), 2nd pagn, 58–75, 101–22; K. Tsin, 'Otchet ob uspekakh sel'skogo khozyaistva v mennonitskom kolonial'nom okruge za 1843', *ZIOSKhYuR*, 2 (1844), 7–20. On Yulii Witte, see Francis W. Wcislo, *Tales of Imperial Russia: The Life and Times of Sergei Witte, 1849–1915* (Oxford, 2011), 25–7; A. M. Fadeev, 'Vospominaniya', *Russkii arkhiv*, 5 (1891), 40–1. I am grateful to Professor Wcislo for this reference.

gather information that was appropriate to the climate, soil, and other conditions that could be used in Russia. Foreign Minister Nesselrode sent out Kiselev's list of questions, and replies came in from various European states.[21]

The issue of the applicability of Western European agronomy to conditions in Russia, especially the steppes, remained the subject of discussion during the rest of the century. Experience demonstrated the shortcomings of Western European farming in the steppe region. In 1846–7, for example, an English variety of winter wheat—'Oxford parish'—was sown on a farm in Slavyanoserbsk district, Ekaterinoslav province. The wheat was not able to cope with the rigours of the steppe climate.[22] A. Skal'kovskii, the author of a study of New Russia published in 1853, argued that due to the difference in soil and climate, 'grain cultivation [in New Russia] cannot be similar to farming in Germany or England. . . . Consequently, the science of agriculture which has been deepened and refined in the West is of no use here'. He added that conditions in New Russia also differed from those in Asia. He further noted that ploughs imported from Western Europe were of little use on the steppes, and that local implements, even if more primitive, were better suited.[23]

In a speech in Odessa in the same year, the Orthodox priest turned agricultural specialist Ivan Palimpsestov characteristically argued strongly against relying on German science:

You have heard . . . that most farmers in our fatherland have received German agricultural science coldly. Why is this? It is because it does not conform with our climate and soil, our abundance of land, political culture (*grazhdanstvennost*), and particular economic demands. . . . The example I have given tends to confirm the idea that a country which differs sharply from others, such as our fatherland, and more particularly its southern region, must have its own economic rules (*pravila khozyaistva*).[24]

There is more than a hint of slavophilism in Palimpsestov's writings. Many better-known slavophiles, such as Aleksandr Koshelev and Yurii Samarin, however, took a keen interest in Western European agriculture. Both, moreover, owned estates in the steppe region.[25]

A number of specialists repeated the argument against the relevance of German, and more broadly European, agronomy to the steppes. In 1873, Aleksei Ermolov visited the agricultural exhibits at the World Fair in Vienna. He found little relevant to Russia. When he moved from the German and Austrian exhibits

   [21] RGIA, f.398, op.83, d.74, ll.1–4, 7–28ob., 64, and *passim*.

   [22] Or. Shuman, 'Opyt poseva ozimoi angliiskoi pshenitsy v Slavyanoserbskom uezde', *TVEO*, 1 (1848), 3rd pagn, 162–4.

   [23] Skal'kovskii, *Opyt*, ii, 54–5, 66–7.

   [24] I. Palimpsestov, 'Vstupitel'naya beseda o sel'skom khozyaistve Novorossiiskogo kraya', *ZhMGI*, 48 (1853), 2nd pagn, 92. See also I. Palimpsestov, *Otchet o deistviyakh Imperatorskogo Obshchestva sel'skogo khozyaistva yuzhnoi Rossii* (Odessa, 1855), 10–11.

   [25] Elina, *Ot tsarskikh sadov*, i, 184–8; E. A. Dudzinskaya, *Slavyanofily v obshchestvennoi bor'be* (Moscow, 1983), 60–98.

to the Russian, he felt that 'a rather different world was presented'.[26] At around the same time, S. A. Zabudskii, a member of the Kazan' Economic Society, argued that what was needed was instructions on how to farm the land based on Russian experience of Russian labour on Russian soil.[27] A decade later, Kostychev argued:

Western European agricultural science cannot be fully applied to our agriculture, in particular on the black earth, a soil that is almost unknown in Western Europe. Therefore, there is a need for our own observations and research of our soils, our climatic peculiarities, and our entire economic order.[28]

This was also the view of the soil scientist Vasilii Dokuchaev. He opposed the uncritical application of Western European systems of agronomy to Russian soil:

We should be ashamed of having applied German agronomy in Russia to true Russian chernozem.... [S]pecific Russian agronomic techniques and methods must be evolved for the individual soil zones of Russia, in strict accordance with local pedological [soil], climatic, as well as socio-economic conditions.[29]

This was in line with Dokuchaev's theory of soil formation, which understood soils as a product of the environment in which they had formed.

In the plan he drew up in 1892 to address the problems caused by recurring droughts in the steppe region, Dokuchaev identified the need to work out: norms for relative areas of arable land, meadows, forest, and water in conformity with local climate, ground, and soil conditions, as well as agriculture. In addition, he wanted to identify ways to cultivate the soil that made the best use of the available moisture, and the most appropriate varieties of crops to grow in the local soil, climatic, and hydrological conditions. The remit of his scientific expedition to the steppes in the 1890s, which was funded by the Forestry Department of the Ministry of State Domains, was limited to testing and costing methods of managing the forestry and water resources on the steppes in three locations.[30] He wanted to do more, and requested permission from the Forestry Department to establish two further research stations and carry out experiments with agriculture. He also wanted to produce essays on agriculture for a popular readership. His request was passed to the Department of Agriculture and Rural Industry of

---

[26] A. Ermolov, *Sel'skokhozyaistvennoe delo Evropy i Ameriki na venskoi vsemirnoi vystavke 1873 goda i v epokhu ee* (Spb, 1875), 58.

[27] S. A. Zabudskii, 'O zasukhakh na yuge i o sredstvakh k sokhraneniyu i uvelicheniyu syrosti v nashikh stepyakh', *TVEO*, 1 (1870), 8–10. See also A. Nikol'skii, 'Nekotorye dannye k voprosu o travoseyanii v Novorossiiskom krae', *TVEO*, 1 (1875), 20.

[28] Quoted in A. Bychikhin, 'Kratkii obzor nauchnoi i pedagogichestkoi deyatel'nosti Pavla Andreevicha Kostycheva', *ZIOSKhYuR*, 11–12 (1895), 4.

[29] Quoted in the introduction to V. V. Dokuchaev, *Russian Chernozem*, trans. N. Kaner (Jerusalem, 1967), 2.

[30] Dokuchaev, 'Nashi stepi: prezhde i teper'', V. V. Dokuchaev, *Sochineniya*, 9 vols (Moscow and Leningrad, 1949–61), vi, 87–96, 112–18.

the ministry, which turned it down. The official response noted pointedly that Dokuchaev had ignored the existence of the department, which had already identified the issues he raised.[31] What the official who rejected his request may not have appreciated was that Dokuchaev wanted to base his proposed work on agriculture on the detailed research by his expedition's scientists into the native steppe environment. He wanted to devise a steppe agriculture that, in so far as possible, emulated what he considered the 'natural' environment of the region. Thus, he recommended expanding the area of meadow land, i.e. land with cultivated fodder grasses, as this was the closest crop to wild steppe grasses.[32] This would have represented a partial return to the previous pattern of land use in the region when it was the domain of nomadic pastoralists.

Over the course of the nineteenth century, Russian agronomists increasingly recognized that agricultural systems needed to take account of local conditions, in particular the soil and climate, and could not be the same everywhere.[33] But they also drew on experience and research elsewhere, including elsewhere in Europe. In the 1870s and 1880s, for example, the Southern Russian Agricultural Society published a number of articles on the key issue of cultivating the land to ensure the retention of scarce moisture by, or that drew on, the work of German scientists.[34] Writing the society's journal in 1876, M. Borovskii suggested drawing on the experience of 'rational crop rotations' in Hungary, as the conditions were similar to Kherson province.[35] As the nineteenth century went on, Russian specialists and 'improving' farmers aimed not to simply to copy science or techniques from other parts of Europe, but to learn from them and adapt them to conditions on the steppes.[36]

---

[31] RGIA, f.426, op.1, 1891, d.30, ll.51ob.–56. See also N. S. Tsintsadze, 'Vzglyady V. V. Dokuchaeva na ekologicheskie aspekty agrarnogo razvitiya evropeiskoi chasti Rossii vo vtoroi polovine XIX-nachale XX vv.', *Istorichestkie, filosofskie, politicheskie i yuridicheskie nauki, kul'turologiya i iskusstvovedenie. Voprosy teorii i praktiki*, 5 (2011), 201–3.

[32] Dokuchaev, 'Soobshcheniya o lektsiyakh V. V. Dokuchaeva "Ob osnovakh sel'skogo khozyaistva", *Sochineniya*, vii, 216–26.

[33] See D. N. Pryanishnikov, *Izbrannye sochineniya*, 3 vols (Moscow, 1965), i, 27. (Text of lecture delivered in 1890s.)

[34] 'Opyty nad vysykhaniem pochvy pri razlichnoi stepeni razrykleniya pakhatnogo sloya', *ZIOSKhYuR*, 2 (1876), 110–20; G. Vol'nii [Wollny], 'Vliyanie obrabotki, udobreniya, ukatyvaniya i rastitel'nosti na isparenie i soderzhanie vlagi v pochve', *ZIOSKhYuR*, 1 (1881), 1–12; S. M. Tanatar, 'O vliyanii razrykhleniya i uplotneniya pochvy na ee vlazhnost' (na osnovanii materialov nemetskoi literatury po voprosu o fizicheskikh svoistvakh pochvy), *ZIOSKhYuR*, 8 (1884), 550–62.

[35] M. Borovskii, 'Sposoby vedeniya pravil'nogo khozyaistva v Khersonsoi gubernii', *ZIOSKhYuR*, 2 (1876), 191–5.

[36] This argument has been made for the adaptation of Western European agronomy to the central non-black-earth region. S. A. Kozlov, *Agrarnye traditsii i novatsii v doreformennoi Rossii (tsentral'no-nechernozemnye gubernii)* (Moscow, 2002).

THE DEVELOPMENT OF STEPPE FARMING IN PRACTICE

Some farmers in the region had been conducting experiments into ways of farming the land from at least the start of the nineteenth century. A few drew on and sought to adapt to local conditions techniques from other parts of Europe. New Russia was particularly well suited to such a combination of approaches as the population included settlers from the German lands and south-eastern Europe as well central and northern Ukraine and Russia.[37] The relationship between farmers and farming methods from other parts of Europe and the steppe environment is nicely illustrated by the experiences of Jean Demole ('Ivan Demol'' in Russian), a Swiss who managed farms of the military settlements in the region. He was also a founder member of the Southern Russian Agricultural Society.[38] It was the failure of Demole's attempt to use imported 'strongly praised Belgian ploughs' in 1832 that Skal'kovskii cited in his discussion of the superiority of local ploughs. Demole, who replaced his Belgian ploughs with local models, was initially sceptical about the prospects for grain cultivation in the steppe environment, but changed his mind after he experimented with new crop rotations based on practices in Western Europe, which he adapted to the steppe environment.

The best example of the combination of settlers from outside Russia adapting farming methods from other parts of Europe to conditions on the steppes is the group who, by general agreement, were the most successful farmers in the region: the Mennonites. Introducing an article on their methods of cultivating grain in 1853, Baron Rosen—the head of the Guardians' Committee that oversaw foreign colonists—wrote: 'The remarkable fact that the Mennonites ... farm the land more successfully than other settlers prompts me to bring these farmers to the attention of others as an example.'[39] The Mennonites of the colony of Molotschna, in eastern Tauride province, were under the energetic leadership of Johann Cornies, the chairman of the Mennonites' Agricultural Society. The colony had a reading society and library of books and periodicals on religious, historical, and economic topics. They subscribed to journals, including German as well as Russian agricultural periodicals.[40] It may have been his reading of works by German agronomists that prompted Cornies to deride the old system

[37] See V. M. Kabuzan, *Zaselenie Novorossii v XVIII-pervoi polovine XIX veka (1719–1858 gg.)* (Moscow, 1976).

[38] His article was summarized in 'Russkie khozyaistvennye periodichestkie izdaniya', *ZhMGI* 3 (1841), 2nd pagn, 217–33. On Demol', see *Listki Imperatorskogo Obshchestva Sel'skogo Khozyaistva Yuzhnoi Rossii*, 1 (1838), 1st pagn, 9.

[39] Filipp Vibe [Philipp Wiebe], 'Khlebopashestvo Menonitov yuzhnoi Rossii', *ZIOSKhYuR*, 4 (1853), 153 (introduction by Rozen) (first published in *Unterhaltungsblatt für deutsche Ansiedler im Südlichen Russland*, 1852). On Rosen, see Urry, *None but Saints*, 147.

[40] I. Kornis, 'O sostoyanii khozyaistva v Molochanskikh Menonistskikh koloniyakh v 1842 g.', *ZhMGI*, 8 (1843), 2nd pagn, 77–8. See also above, pp. 176–7.

of shifting agriculture, which he associated with the nomadic peoples of the steppes, as a 'lottery'. He frequently asserted that it was time to abandon the system, and persuaded his colony to do just this.[41] Skal'kovskii, who doubted the relevance of Western European agricultural techniques on the steppes, was prepared to concede that they were appropriate for the Mennonites, because their allotments of 50–60 *desyatiny* were relatively small (in comparison with large noble estates), and so operated in similar conditions to farmers in Western Europe.[42]

During the nineteenth and early twentieth centuries, farmers in the steppe region—with the Mennonites often in the vanguard—and agronomists devised and tested various ways of farming the fertile soil to make more intensive use of the land to maximize yields, but also to reduce the risk of harvest failures in drought years. The latter aim meant making the most effective use of the limited supplies of moisture. In the next section of this chapter, attention will focus on field systems and crop rotations; techniques for cultivating the soil, in particular deep ploughing; and the practice of keeping the fallow field clear of vegetation or 'black'.

Field systems and crop rotations

The move away from shifting, long-fallow farming was risky as this system, however inefficient, allowed the land time to recover, for the native vegetation to return (and replace weeds), and, crucially, for the soil to regain its structure that would enable it to retain moisture. As farmers and agronomists gradually became aware, long-fallow farming succeeded in this regard only if it was indeed long fallow: fields needed to be left for at least fifteen years, until the feather grass returned. Yet the increasing pressure of population on the land and greater opportunities for marketing grain during the nineteenth century meant that in much of the steppe region this was no longer possible or appropriate.

The Committee for the Improvement of Agriculture set up in 1833 considered the three-field system, which had already been introduced in the north of the steppe region, to be inefficient and a contributory cause of the crop failure. Senator Mechnikov, who farmed in the north of the region, advocated an improved rotation based on one devised by the German agronomist Thaer. Mechnikov adapted it for Russian conditions by replacing sowing fodder grasses with '*toloka*'—using the fallow field for pasture. The land was divided into six fields, in which only one-sixth of the land was not sown with crops each year (in comparison with one-third under the three-field system). Mechnikov proposed the following rotation: 1. Winter rye or wheat; 2. *Toloka*; 3. Barley; 4. Vegetables;

[41] G. L. Gavel', 'Sravnitel'nye ocherki sel'skogo khozyaistva i agrarnogo polozheniya poselyan v nekotorykh mestakh Rossii', *SKhiL*, 117 (1874), 67.
[42] Skal'kovskii, *Opyt*, ii, 55, 63.

5. Oats; 6. Buckwheat. He recommended peas, beans, potatoes, and beets in the vegetable field, since agronomists knew that they enriched the soil and crucially, assisted it retain moisture.[43]

In 1837, Cornies ordered the Mennonites of Molotschna to introduce a four-field crop rotation in place of long-fallow agriculture.[44] This was only four years after the 'great drought' of 1833, and little over a decade after Molotschna had suffered from two successive harvest failures, caused in part by drought, in 1824 and 1825.[45] Under the new rotation, each field followed the sequence: 1. Barley; 2. Spring wheat (girka or arnautka); 3. Winter rye or oats; and in the fourth year, the field was left fallow.[46] Peter Köppen, an official of the Ministry of State Domains who inspected Tauride province in 1837, reported: 'Out of 43 Mennonite colonies, 23 have already completed the introduction of four-field agriculture (*vierfelder Wirtschaft*).' He added that he had 'invited' more Mennonites to follow suit in 1838.[47]

In 1843, on the farms of the military settlements, Jean Demole introduced new, multi-field crop rotations—up to eight fields in settlements with sufficient land—including sowing grass ('*travoseyanie*'). Before his innovations, the duration of the fallow period had been cut to only five–ten years. Demole also advocated sowing early to protect seed from spring droughts. His innovations were based on the experience of French and Swiss farmers, but he adapted them to conditions on the steppes. His improved agriculture, like that of the Mennonites, was promoted by the Southern Russian Agricultural Society.[48] Following the example of the Mennonites and Demole, a few estate owners in the region introduced crop rotations that paid attention to the crucial issue of moisture retention. In the 1860s, Sergei Bulatsel', who owned an estate in Slavyanoserbsk district, Ekaterinoslav province, devised four- and six-field rotations. They included short fallow, sown grasses, and other fodder crops, such as clover, which could resist drought. He had taken the environmental conditions—in particular the fertile soil but dry climate with easterly winds—into account, and described his rotations as 'most appropriate . . . practical and rational for the locality'.[49]

During the mid- and later decades of the nineteenth century, many farmers in the region moved away from long-fallow agriculture to make more intensive use

[43] RGIA, f.398, op.83, 1831–8, d.4, ll.160–1.
[44] John R. Staples, *Cross-Cultural Encounters on the Ukrainian Steppe: Settling the Molochna Basin, 1783–1861* (Toronto, 2003), 121. See also H. L. Dyck, 'Russian Servitor and Mennonite Hero: Light and Shadow in Images of Johann Cornies', *Journal of Mennonite Studies*, 2 (1984), 9–28.
[45] DAOO, f.6, op.1, 1824, sp.1774, ll.51–62.
[46] Sergei Dobrovol'skii, 'Obzor khozyaistva Menonitov Tavricheskoi gubernii', *ZIOSKhYuR*, 8 (1849), 491.
[47] RGIA, f.383, op.29, 1837–8, d.609, l.38ob.
[48] Dmitrii Osten-Saken, 'O neobkhodimosti v Novorossiiskom krae samykh rannikh posevov, o rastitel'nom udobrenii zemli i o travoseyanii', *ZIOSKhYuR*, 3 (1848), 143–60.
[49] Sergei Bulatsel', 'Zemledelie v Slavyanoserbskom uezde, Ekaterinoslavskoi gubernii', *TVEO*, 1 (1866), 333–6, 343–9.

of the land. Surveying agriculture in New Russia in 1873, Shishkin lamented: 'On most farms in New Russia not only do crop rotations not exist, even the word itself is unknown.' He recommended multi-field rotations that included sowing grasses, fallow for up to eight years, and sowing maize (*kukuruza*) in addition to the customary cereal crops.[50] Many farmers objected to the introduction of crop rotations, because they sowed such a large proportion of wheat—the main cash crop—that it was difficult to find another crop to replace it in a rotation.[51] Nevertheless, the authorities tried to promote crop rotations appropriate to the environment. In the 1880s and 1890s, the governor of Samara urged farmers in the fertile but drought-prone south of the province to move away from monoculture of grain and introduce rotations, with rye and potatoes, which were less valuable than wheat, but better able to withstand shortages of water. State and appanage land in the province was leased out on condition that farmers introduced such rotations.[52]

In the early twentieth century, the Appanage Department tested crop rotations on the Bezenchuk experiment station in Samara province with the aim of enforcing them for leaseholders on its land. Starting in 1904, on seven plots of land, the station's agronomists set up four-field rotations: 1. Fallow; 2. Winter grain; 3. Grain with intertillage crops; 4. Spring crop. On three of the plots, experiments were conducted with fertilizers. On a further three, they tested different ways of cultivating the land. On the seventh plot, they tried different intertillage crops, for example root vegetables and varieties of American maize. And, on all the plots, different winter and spring grains were tested. On a further three plots, twelve-field rotations were set up with grain crops, fallow, intertillage crops, and sown grasses. Preliminary reports indicated that fertilizers improved yields by 20–33 per cent. They identified the varieties of grass that gave the highest yields. The root vegetables sown between rows of grain, however, were destroyed by weevils. During the years 1904–7, the methods tested had a marked impact on grain yields: they were almost three times higher than those of local peasants. Significantly, the difference was greatest in the drought year of 1906. Tests showed that yields were in direct proportion to the amount of moisture in the soil, which was precisely what the methods were designed to increase.[53]

The Appanage Department's estates in Samara province, amounting to 432,569 *desyatiny*, were acquired by the Peasant Land Bank in 1908. Most of the land was in the steppe south of the province and much had been exhausted by 'irrational' farming. The estates included the Bezenchuk experiment station, and the bank continued the policy of testing crop rotations. The bank leased estates

[50] A. Shishkin, 'Sel'skokhozyaistvennyi ocherk Novorossii', *SKhiL*, 113 (1873), 2nd pagn, 282, 306.
[51] Skal'kovskii, *Opyt*, ii, 62.
[52] GASO, f.3, op.167, 1881, d.89, l.7; op.233, d.1000, l.3ob.
[53] GASO, f.149, op.9, d.15, ll.2–6ob.; Klingen and Zhukov, 'Udel'naya', 187–98.

until they were sold to peasants, and leaseholders were obliged to maintain the crop rotations. Not all did so, however, and the most common infringement was sowing spring wheat rather than less valuable winter rye. Other infringements included ploughing up meadows and pastures and sowing fields out of rotation.[54] In May 1912, the bank approved new crop rotations, which included spring and winter grains, sown grasses, and fallow for up to seven years. They were designed to make more intensive use of the land, but without exhausting it. The bank official responsible, Boris Skalov, thought deeply about agricultural methods and was well informed about the science behind his proposals. He considered the impact of ploughing up virgin steppe on yields, selecting varieties of wheat best suited to the environmental conditions, and—echoing Dokuchaev—the need to link exploitation of land to its natural history.[55]

In a manual for Russian farmers of 1914, S. S. Bazhanov made a series of recommendations to make farming less reliant on the amount of rainfall in south-eastern Russia. In an argument that clearly reflected Kostychev's research, he argued that the move from long-fallow farming had reduced the moisture retention capabilities of the soil. He recommended 'correct' rotations that would ensure each crop was planted in soil that was not exhausted and was free of weeds, and that the crops sown were appropriate to the local climate and soil conditions. Bazhanov advised multi-field rotations including grains, sown grass, fallow, and intertillage crops. The best rotations were designed to ensure that 'all rain water would be retained in the soil and, therefore, in dry years it would be possible to depend on obtaining a harvest'. They were also more profitable.[56]

There was another solution to the problem of the soil becoming less productive with the introduction of more intensive systems of farming. In the Don region, the cossack administration tried to prevent land from its reserves that it rented out from being used more intensively. In 1894, they asked the Scientific Committee of the Ministry of State Domains for advice on whether increasing the proportion of the land that leaseholders were permitted to plough from 1/6th to 1/3rd would exhaust the soil. The committee recommended that land be used accordingly: 1/3rd ploughed up; 1/3rd left fallow for six years; and 1/3rd for twelve years. It concluded: 'There was no basis to suppose that such use of the land could exhaust it; on the contrary, . . . soil left fallow for twelve years would fully recover its original fertility.'[57] In 1903–4, however, the cossack authorities leased land in the Second Don district with the right to plough half of it. It was

---

[54] GASO, f.43, op.10, dd.59–60; f.149, op.1, d.296, l.20, 46–ob., 53; op.9, d.84, ll.17ob., 18ob.

[55] GASO, f.149, op.1, d.84, ll.47–51; d.296, ll.131–5ob., 156–59ob. On Skalov, see N. A. Ustina, *Krest'yanskii pozemel'nyi bank v srednem povolzh'e (1885–1917 gg.)* (Samara, 2003), 38.

[56] S. S. Bazhanov, 'Novye sposoby vedeniya polevogo khozyaistva v yugo-vostochnykh stepnykh guberniyakh', in P. N. Sokovnin (ed.), *Nastol'naya kniga russkogo zemledel'tsa*, 2nd edn (Spb, 1914), 33–41.

[57] RGIA, f.382, op.2, 1894, d.1291, ll.5–8.

more cautious with land in Sal'sk district in the more arid south of the region: leaseholders were restricted for the most part to ploughing only 1/6th of the land. Supervisors were to fine any who violated this stipulation.[58]

Throughout the steppe region, farmers chose the crops they sowed on the basis of both market and environmental conditions. They were sometimes torn between sowing crops, for example wheat, that could earn them high prices, and less profitable crops that were more likely to survive climatic fluctuations, especially drought. The Mennonites were more inclined to experiment than other farmers. In 1837, Köppen noted that they were starting to replace the traditional *arnautka* (a hard, spring-sown durum wheat) with red wheat from the Crimean Peninsula as it was in greater demand in the nearby ports of Berdyansk and Mariupol'.[59] Farmers on the peninsula preferred the red wheat, which was a winter wheat, because it was resistant to drought. Mennonites to the north of the peninsula were initially reluctant to sow it, as it suffered from early spring frosts, until they worked out a way to protect the young shoots by harrowing soil over them. They expanded the cultivation of the hard, red, winter wheat, which they called '*Krymka*', from the 1860s and 1870s, to take advantage of its market demand and drought resistance.[60]

Experiments with crop varieties best suited to the steppes were conducted on the Ministry of State Domains' training and experimental farms, for example the Lugansk farm in Ekaterinoslav province, from at least the 1840s.[61] The quest for drought-resistant and high-yielding crops for which there was demand intensified after droughts. In the discussions in the Free Economic Society at the end of 1891, Ermolov recommended sowing crops other than the traditional cereals—he singled out maize and sunflowers—as they survived droughts better. Later in the discussion, Filipenko advocated Asiatic rather than European strains of wheat.[62] In 1892, the Ekaterinoslav provincial agronomist reported that some farmers were experimenting with millet, maize, and sunflowers, and seeking drought-resistant varieties of grain.[63] In Samara province, from 1904 the Bezenchuk experiment station conducted tests to find the 'varieties of grain that were most suited to local conditions'. They showed, for example, that winter wheat, which was grown near the north coast of the Black Sea, could not survive the harsher winters on the Volga.[64] By the early twentieth century, Russian

[58] GARO, f.301, op.11, d.324; d.323, 1903–6, ll.7–ob., 55–ob.

[59] RGIA, 383, op.29, 1837–8, d.609, ll.37ob.–8.

[60] David Moon, 'In the Russians' Steppes: The Introduction of Russian Wheat on the Great Plains of the United States of America', *Journal of Global History*, 3 (2008), 216–18.

[61] 'Otchet o raznykh khozyaistvennykh opytakh i nablyudeniyakh na Luganskoi ferme za 1840 god', *ZhMGI*, 3 (1841), 2nd pagn, 333–42.

[62] 'Besedy v I Otdelenii Imperatorskogo Vol'nogo Ekonomicheskogo Obshchestva po voprosu o prichinakh neurozhaya 1891 goda i merakh protiv povtoreniya podobykh urozhaev v budushchem', *TVEO*, 1 (1892), 86, 120.

[63] *Otchet i doklad po agronimicheskomu byuro ekaterinoslavskomu gub. zemskomu sobraniyu* (Ekaterinoslav, 1892), review in *SKhiL*, 172 (1893), 54–6.

[64] GASO, f.149, op.9, d.15, l.2ob., 5ob.

scientists were turning to selection and hybridization to breed crops suitable for the steppe environment. From 1909, the Southern Russian Agricultural Society sponsored experiments with selection on the Odessa experimental field. Scientists at Bezenchuk followed suit.[65]

An important element of many new crop rotations, despite initial hostility, was sowing fodder grasses in the fallow field. The original intention was to speed up the natural regeneration of grasses, which took fifteen years or more, by sowing grasses artificially. There was much discussion over the value of different types of fodder grasses, such as timofeevka, lucern, esparet, wheat grass, and clover amongst others, both with regard to their yields and drought resistance. In time, in line with the findings of Kostychev and others, agronomists recommended sowing grasses also as a way of assisting the soil regain its structure, and hence ability to retain moisture, more quickly. Thus, artificially-sown grasses became part of the 'struggle with droughts'.[66]

In spite of the significance of varieties of crops and grasses and the rotations they were part of, most specialists attached more importance to the cultivation of the soil.

Cultivation of the soil: deep ploughing

There was much discussion of the best ways to prepare the soil for sowing to assist the accumulation and retention of scarce moisture. Debate focused on the value of deep ploughing. In the forest-heartland of Russian settlement, for centuries farmers had used the light, horse-drawn wooden plough—the famous *sokha*—with which they ploughed to a depth of 2–3 *verskhi* (3.5–5.15 inches). Settlers from the heartland found their wooden ploughs and ploughing techniques of little use on the steppes. The black earth was deeper (the topsoil was 1–2 feet deep), as well as more fertile, than the soils in the heartland. Wooden ploughs could not cut through the roots of the steppe grasses in virgin land or long-fallow fields. Ploughing to only the shallow depths possible with wooden ploughs left the soil liable to dry out in the hotter, drier, and windier climate of the steppes. Instead, settlers adopted heavier, wheeled ploughs used by Ukrainians, or *sabans* used by Tatars (i.e. peoples with longer experience of cultivating black earth), pulled by several pairs of oxen. Ukrainian and Tatar ploughs could deal with the steppe grasses and plough to a depth of about 4 *vershki* (7 inches). In the 1840s, the Southern Russian Agricultural Society held

[65] For a fuller discussion, see Elina, *Ot tsarskikh sadov*, i, 281, 310–34. See also DAOO, fond 22, op.1, 1912, sp.481.

[66] For examples of the large literature, see Dmitrii Osten-Saken, 'O neobkhodimosti v Novorossiiskom krae samykh rannikh posevov, o rastitel'nom udobrenii zemli i o travoseyanii', *ZIOSKhYuR*, 3 (1848), 143–60; A. Nikol'skii, 'Nekotorye dannye k voprosu o travoseyanii v Novorossiiskom krae', *TVEO*, 1 (1875), 19–32; 2 (1875), 13–27; Kostychev, *O bor'be*, 80–2; Ermolov, *Organizatsiya*, 26–27; Bazhanov, 'Novye sposoby', 34–5.

258 Combating the Steppe Environment?

two competitions to find the ploughs best suited to the region. Implements that ploughed to depth of less than 6 inches (3.5 *vershki*) were ineligible. With an eye to implements that peasants with limited draft power could use, the conditions stipulated that ploughs for breaking virgin soil should need no more than four pairs of oxen, and for land that had already been cultivated, no more than two pairs. The competitions were won by modified Ukrainian ploughs, rather than imported implements.[67]

Nevertheless, in the second half of the nineteenth century, many steppe farmers bought heavier, steel ploughs that were capable of cutting furrows to a depth of over 5 *vershki* (8.75 inches). In practice, as Shishkin noted in the 1870s, many farmers ploughed to a depth of between 2½ and 4 *vershki* (4.375 and 7 inches). The move away from shifting, long-fallow agriculture and the expansion of the area under cultivation had important consequences for ploughing. There was less virgin or long-fallow land that needed heavy ploughs, and farmers sought to minimize the time and expenditure of labour and draft power in ploughing in order to cultivate more land. Some farmers ploughed the field for the spring crops the previous autumn. But in the following year, after the spring grain had been harvested, they sowed the winter crops in the same field without further ploughing. They used lighter implements—ralos, extirpators or bukkers (the last a Mennonite invention)—to prepare more land for sowing and cover the seeds with less effort.[68]

There was a persistent view among steppe farmers that ploughing was of little importance. In 1839, Andrei Leopol'dov noted 'the system of ploughing has little influence on the harvest, which more than repays the labour everywhere'.[69] A similar view was reported by N. Nal'tsov in 1876. He was advocating deep ploughing, but explained that, because of the unreliability of the rainfall, many estate owners had a careless and fatalistic attitude to cultivating the soil: if the rains came, then there would be a bumper harvest and they would become rich; if the rains failed, so would the harvest, and they would be ruined. Estate owners could see little reason to invest more time and energy into ploughing.[70] In the mid-1880s, a *zemstvo* study of Buzuluk district in Samara province reported 'cultivation [of the soil] is very primitive ... and has little significance in ensuring good harvests, which are dependent on the weather.' Many peasants elsewhere in

---

[67] DAOO, f.6, Op.1, 1840, sp.5632; Skal'kovskii, *Opyt*, ii, 66–7.

[68] For discussions by historians who tried out some of the implements, see David Kerans, *Mind and Labor on the Farm in Black-Earth Russia, 1861–1914* (Budapest, 2001), 17–27, 133–40; Leonard Friesen, *Rural Revolutions in Southern Ukraine: Peasants, Nobles, and Colonists, 1774–1905* (Cambridge, MA, 2009), 158–64. See also S. Lavrent'ev, 'Polevodstvo v okrestnostyakh Elizavetgrada', *TVEO*, 1 (1855), 2nd pagn, 60–1; Shishkin, 'Sel'skokhozyaistvennyi ocherk Novorossii', 278, 282–3.

[69] A. Leopol'dov, *Statisticheskoe opisanie Saratovskoi gubernii*, 2 vols (Spb, 1839), i, 116.

[70] N. Nal'tsov, 'Glubokaya vspashka i ee znachenie dlya chernozemnoi polosy', *TVEO*, 3 (1876), 118. See also Arkhilles Alferaki, *O polozhenii sel'skogo khozyaistva v yugo-vostochnom krae* (Spb, 1879), 7, 16.

the province doubted the land needed deep ploughing and continued with their customary shallow ploughing.[71]

Others were less complacent, or perhaps had the resources to improve the way they cultivated their land. As early as 1807, Engel'man considered the importance of ploughing in the steppe region.[72] As agronomists and some farmers came to understand, the crucial issues in tilling the black earth were removing weeds and, above all, facilitating the accumulation and retention of moisture. Discussions were fed by the latest ideas of Western European agronomists, the accumulated experience of steppe farmers and, in time, experiments conducted in the region. It may come as no surprise that among the advocates and practitioners of deep ploughing were the Mennonites of Molotschna. After they introduced their four-field rotation in 1837, they used Saxon ploughs drawn by four horses or heavy ploughs pulled by three pairs of oxen to plough their fields deeply, and carefully, to assist in accumulating moisture. In the late summer, they ploughed the fields for the winter crops deeply, and then harrowed them to help absorb moisture as well as cover the seeds to protect them from frost. Specialists, such as Tsin, as well as the Mennonites themselves believed deep ploughing contributed to their success.[73]

The experience of droughts in the region seemed to confirm the value of deep ploughing. In the wake of a drought in the summer and autumn of 1839, experiments were conducted on the Lugansk farm. Contrary to local practice, the farm manager ploughed deeply and harrowed the field for the winter rye twice, both before and after sowing, with the aim of protecting the seeds by burying them more deeply in the soil. Neighbouring estate owners were sceptical. The winter was very severe with a lot of snow, and the spring of 1840 was cold with further snow. As a result, in the district as a whole, the rye was in a poor condition or did not grow at all. Many estate owners ploughed the fields again and sowed spring grain to replace the crop that had been lost. In contrast, on the Lugansk farm, the rye grew and gave a satisfactory harvest.[74] In the drought year of 1855, the inspector of agriculture in southern Russia noted that the results of deep cultivation on grain and other crops was 'especially striking'. Farmers near Odessa who ploughed to a depth of 7 *vershki* (12.25 inches) obtained yields of 1:18, whereas shallow-ploughed fields barely returned the seed. Grain crops could sink deeper roots in friable and fertile soil, he argued, and thus use water that had accumulated deep in the ground in the autumn, winter, and early spring. He went on to demonstrate that deep ploughing was economical. The extra cost of using more draft animals—five rather than three pairs of oxen—was

---

[71] *SSSpSG*, iii, *Buzulukskii uezd* (1885), 60–4; *SSSpSG*, vi, *Nikolaevskii uezd* (1889), 47–50.

[72] Engel'man, 'O zavedenii', 199–207.

[73] See Tsin, 'Otchet ob uspekakh', 11; Sergei Dobrovol'skii, 'Obzor khozyaistva Menonitov Tavricheskoi gubernii', *ZIOSKhYuR*, 8 (1849), 495–8; Vibe, 'Khlebopashestvo', 154–5.

[74] 'Otchet o raznykh khozyaistvennykh opytakh i nablyudeniyakh na Luganskoi ferme za 1840 god', *ZhMGI*, 3 (1841), 329–31.

cancelled out by the income earned from the higher yields. Deep ploughing, moreover, did not need new implements as traditional Ukrainian ploughs could plough to depth of 6–7 *vershki.*[75]

Over the following decades, there was much debate over deep ploughing in agricultural journals. The agronomist Reidemeister advocated ploughing to a depth of less than 4 *vershki* (7 inches) in most cases, better to assist in accumulating and retaining moisture, and more deeply only to bring fresh soil to the surface to prevent soil exhaustion. Writing in 1856, however, A. Zherebko argued that ploughing more deeply than the customary 3–4 *vershki* (5.25–7 inches) allowed moisture to penetrate further and remain for longer to be used by plants as it was less likely to evaporate. On the other hand, he noted that deep ploughing was not appropriate on land where the topsoil was only 3–5 *vershki* (5.25–8.75 inches) deep as it would bring less fertile subsoil to the surface. Both men argued against deep ploughing at times of year, such as the late spring and summer, when drought, heat, and winds were likely to cause evaporation.[76]

Proponents of deep ploughing included Lavent'ev, who felt it was needed in northern Kherson province.[77] Palimpsestov argued in favour of deep ploughing. Uncharacteristically, he cited the work of the German agronomist Thaer as well as the experience of steppe farmers in support.[78] Nal'tsov, who was also informed by German studies of moisture conservation, argued in favour of deep ploughing in southern Russia, but pointed to the need for care to avoid bringing up infertile subsoil. He urged experimentation.[79] In the 1870s, Shishkin advocated that farmers replace their Ukrainian ploughs with imported implements, plough more carefully, and more deeply, to a depth of 5 *vershki* (8.75 inches). He concluded that 'deep cultivation of the land assists greater penetration of moisture into the soil and reduces evaporation, partly because the water that has seeped [into the soil] is better protected against evaporation, and partly because the friable soil better retains moisture'. He cited studies by the German scientist Pfaff in support.[80] Shishkin's view was important politically as it was used by Witte to argue in favour of cultivation techniques, rather than irrigation, in the struggle with droughts (see above, p. 232).

A. I. Umissa, an estate owner in New Russia, reported his experiences on his estate since the early 1870s. He had ploughed his fields to a depth of no more than 5 *vershki,* and sowed them every year without rest. Not surprisingly, yields

[75] DAOO, f.1, op.248, 1856, d.1580, ll.57–72ob.

[76] K. Z. Bunitskii, 'Osnovye pravila stepnogo khozyaistva', *ZIOSKhYuR* (1855), 336–41 (translation of a work by Reidemeister); A. Zherebko, 'Koe-shto o glubokoi obrabotke zemli', *ZIOSKhYuR* (1856), 41–6.

[77] S. Lavrent'ev, 'Polevodstvo', 63.

[78] I. Palimpsestov, 'Glubokaya pashnya—plug saka', *ZIOSKhYuR* (1859), 277–309.

[79] Nal'tsov, 'Glubokaya vspashka', 113–25.

[80] Shishkin, 'Sel'skokhozyaistvennyi ocherk Novorossii', 302–3; A. Shishkin, 'Neskol'ko slov ob ustranenii stepnykh zasukh', *SKhiL*, 117 (1874), 242–4; Shishkin, *K voprosu*, 166.

began to decline. In 1883, he purchased big, Sakka ploughs and ploughed to a depth 8 *vershki* (14 inches). His yields improved, which he believed was because deep ploughing had brought up new soil to replace the exhausted upper layer. He recognized that no ploughing could return fields to the state of virgin land or long-fallow fields, but concluded 'deep ploughing also has a huge influence on harvests . . . because it is connected with the . . . accumulation of reserves of moisture [and] . . . it is the only important means we have to do this.'[81] The value of deep ploughing was also recognized by *zemstva*. In 1883, a study of Samara district noted that deep and timely cultivation was essential for a good harvest as it allowed crops to sink deep roots and the soil to retain moisture.[82]

The drought and crop failure of 1891 led to further support for deep ploughing. An official of the Ministry of State Domains from Samara province noted that experience had shown good harvests were more likely on land that had been ploughed well and deeply—to a depth of 6 *vershki* (10.5 inches)—from the previous autumn.[83] In Kherson province, Umissa took the opportunity to reiterate his advocacy of deep ploughing, adding that it destroyed weeds that used up water needed by crops. He continued that rolling (*ukatyvanie*) fields formed a protective layer on the surface that reduced evaporation.[84] Several participants in the discussions in the Free Economic Society at the end of the year referred to deep ploughing. Agricultural specialist F. N. Korolev pointed out that estate owners who had ploughed their fields deeply had obtained better yields than peasants who did not. Ermolov noted that deep ploughing followed by shallow ploughing had been shown to assist in accumulating and conserving moisture in Poltava province. The agronomist Valerian Chernyaev attributed the crop failure in part to poor cultivation of the soil, and pointed the finger at farmers in Samara and Orenburg provinces who ploughed up as much land as they could without regard to the quality of their work.[85] Relevant experience from other parts of Europe supported the argument for deep ploughing. In 1892, the Ministry of State Domains printed a report from the Hungarian Ministry of Agriculture on the effectiveness of deep ploughing (to a depth of 25–30 or even 40 cm; 10–12 or 20 inches) in increasing yields. It was, apparently, the almost universal view among Hungarian farmers that deep ploughing was especially effective in dry years. Hungary, it was noted, had a continental climate and experienced regular droughts.[86]

The arguments about techniques for cultivating the soil were getting more nuanced. In the Free Economic Society in late 1891, Kostychev argued that it

[81] A. I. Umissa, 'Istoshchena li pochva nashei stepi?', *ZIOSKhYuR*, (1884), 443–9, 529–33.
[82] *SSSpSG*, i, *Samarskii uezd* (1883), 1st pagn, 46.
[83] RGIA, f.398, op.75, d.22, ll.112–13.
[84] *Sbornik khersonskogo zemstva 1891 g.* (Kherson, 1891), review in *SKhiL*, 167 (1891), 2nd pagn, 1–6.
[85] 'Besedy', 81, 86, 95–8.
[86] 'K voprosu o glubokoi pakhote', *SKhiL*, 170 (1892), 54–7.

was better to plough fields in the autumn, and then cultivate them to keep the soil friable over the summer, rather than plough fields in the summer months, which was the custom in northern Russia. Land should be ploughed only to a shallow depth in the summer to combat weeds, and, he argued, ploughed for a second time only after good rainfall. The key to his argument, of course, was moisture retention. Deep ploughing at the wrong time of year could increase evaporation.[87]

Experiments in the steppe region, for example on an experimental field in Khar'kov province in 1892–3, confirmed the importance of deep ploughing in the autumn to assist the accumulation of moisture over the winter. The tests also showed that harrowing the soil from the spring to form a friable surface layer helped reduce evaporation.[88] Similar conclusions were reached by Aleksandr Izmail'skii, on the basis of his research in Poltava district over the years 1886–93. He found the best way to make full use of all precipitation was to plough the fields deeply and early in the autumn. This resulted in the moistest soil in spring. On the other hand, if there had been no rain since June, then no methods of cultivation could preserve moisture in upper layer of soil to ensure winter grain sprouted in good time. Some methods, e.g. rolling, could prevent deeper layers of soil from drying out. In such circumstances, Izmail'skii recommended not deep ploughing, but light ploughing and immediate harrowing so that soil presented the least surface area to reduce the drying effects of the sun and wind.[89]

Further experiments at the Plotyanskaya experiment station in Podolia province in the 1890s and the Bezenchuk experiment station in Samara province during the following decade indicated that deep ploughing improved yields by assisting in the accumulation of water. They also demonstrated that there was little to be gained by ploughing to depth of 6 *vershki* (10.5 inches) rather than 4 *vershki* (7 inches). Experiments in the Odessa experimental field in 1896–1907, moreover, raised doubts over whether deep ploughing did have any benefits as no difference was observed in the length of roots of crops sown in fields ploughed to depths of 2 *vershki* (3.5 inches) or six. The director further noted that since ploughing tended to be done at dry times of the year—in April, July, and September—shallow ploughing was better as it helped reduce evaporation.[90]

Thus, as time went on and experience was accumulated, attention came to focus on the timing of ploughing, as well as the depth, and the importance of

    [87] 'Besedy', 112–13. See also Kostychev, *O bor'be*, 28–9.
    [88] *Izvestiya Petrovskoi sel'skokhozyaistvennoi akademii*, 16/2–3 (1893), reviewed in *SKhiL*, 176 (1894), 3rd pagn, 1–8.
    [89] A. A. Izmailovskii, *Vlazhnost' pochvy i gruntovaya voda v svyazi s rel'efom mestnosti i kul'turnym sostoyaniem poverkhnosti pochvy* (Poltava, 1894), review in *SKhiL*, 178 (1895), 3rd pagn, 79–81. See also above, pp. 152–7.
    [90] S. Kizenkov, 'Sel'skokhozyaistvennye voprosy v russkoi pechati za 1898 g.', *SKhiL*, 191 (1898), 673–706; GASO, f.149, op.9, d.15, l.4, 6; K. G. Man'kovskii, 'Parovaya obrabotka po dannym Poltavskogo opytnogo polya', *SKhiL*, 229 (1909), 739–56.

cultivating the surface of fields during the spring and summer to assist in the retention of scarce and valuable moisture by reducing evaporation. To some extent, moreover, the results of the experiments with different depths of ploughing and ways of cultivating the soil at different times of the year confirmed the views of some local estate owners and peasants who were suspicious of deep ploughing. In the Free Economic Society in 1891, A. E. Filipenko echoed his comment about choosing Asiatic crops by arguing that it would be better to follow the 'Asiatic' practice of frequent, shallow ploughing in the summer.[91]

Many of these issues about ways of cultivating the land to assist in the accumulation and conservation of moisture in the steppe environment had also been discussed and tested with regard to fallow fields, in particular, the practice of black fallow.

Black fallow

The Mennonites of Molotschna introduced 'black fallow' (*schwarze Brache, chernyi par*) as part of their new four-field crop rotation in 1837 in the aftermath of the drought of 1833. Before 1837, the Mennonites had planted grass in the fallow fields and used them as pasture. Cornies 'ordered householders to prevent livestock from grazing in fallow fields and to plough them regularly throughout the summer to prevent the growth of grass or weeds.' He was aware that grass and weeds depleted the soil of nutrients and moisture. Black fallow entailed more labour, but Cornies characteristically justified this with reference to the admonition in Genesis: 'In the sweat of thy face shalt thou eat bread.'[92] Over time, however, they reduced by the burden by developing appropriate agricultural implements.[93] Further, they located their fields as near their houses as possible so that they did not waste time travelling. Philipp Wiebe (Cornies's son-in-law and successor as chairman of the Agricultural Society) explained further that furrows left in the fallow field during the winter were to run from north to south, to retain snow blown by the prevailing easterly winds, which would be absorbed when it melted. The furrows were destroyed in the spring, and the fallow field harrowed to make it smooth and firm, to prevent evaporation. In addition—and this was unusual in black-earth regions of Russia—the Mennonites manured their fallow fields.[94]

The results of the new, four-field rotation and black fallow were higher and more reliable harvests. In 1851, Wiebe presented data on yields obtained by

---

[91] 'Besedy', 119–20.

[92] See Staples, *Cross-Cultural Encounters*, 118–22. On the Mennonites' attitude to agriculture as a 'religious duty', see August von Haxthausen, *The Russian Empire: Its People, Institutions and Resources*, 2 vols, trans. Robert Farie (London, 1856), i, 423, 428; Urry, *None but Saints*, 39, 138.

[93] Gavel', 'Sravnitel'nye ocherki', 67.

[94] Vibe, 'Khlebopashestvo', 154–7. On Wiebe, see Urry, *None but Saints*, 148.

Table 8.1. Average yields (expressed as a ratio of seed to harvest) on Mennonite land

Decade	Molotschna	Chortitza
1809–18	1: 6 $7/10$	1: 6 $1/10$
1819–28	1: 5 $2/3$	1: 4 $1/4$
1829–38	1: 9 $3/7$	1: 5 $3/4$
1839–48	1:13 $2/3$	1: 6 $1/2$

Source: Filipp Vibe, 'Khlebopashestvo Menonitov yuzhnoi Rossii', *ZIOSKhYuR*, 4 (1853), 159

Mennonite farmers in Molotschna and neighbouring Chortitza district (see Table 8.1).

Thus, yields in Molotschna were higher after the introduction of the new crop rotation and black fallow, and higher than in Chortitza, where the inhabitants introduced black fallow later. The introduction of black fallow also reduced the fluctuations in yields from year to year. Before the change, yields in individual years in Molotschna fluctuated between 1:1⅓ and 1:18⅖. After 1838, they varied from 1:8 to 1:17⅘. Wiebe further noted that in 1849, when there was a serious drought, they obtained a yield of 1:5, which was far higher than would have been achieved without black fallow.[95] He concluded that black fallow brought a special advantage to their region as it allowed moisture to penetrate so deeply that grain could withstand drought and give a good harvest in years when other fields barely returned the seed.[96]

The Mennonites may have found out about the practice from literature on agronomy in their library. According to a later Russian source, 'black fallow' had been devised at the turn of the nineteenth century on farms in England, from where it was adopted by farmers in continental Europe. The original purpose was to control weeds in the fallow field, but it also assisted in absorbing and retaining moisture.[97] Intriguingly, in 1901, a Russian agronomist also gave a Turkish name—'*kara-saban*'—for black fallow, hinting that it may have had its origins among the region's former inhabitants.[98] In the early 1840s, Cornies presented the Mennonites' success as an example of what could be achieved by 'hard work and thrift'.[99] He also drew attention to the fact that their farming techniques were based on experience and knowledge, rather than, as in the past, 'luck'.[100]

[95] [F.] Vibe, 'O chernom pare v stepnykh khozyaistvakh', *TVEO*, 1 (1851), 2nd pagn, 78–86. See also Urry, *None but Saints*, 115–16.
[96] Vibe, 'Khlebopashestvo', 159.
[97] I. Shulov, 'Par', *PERSKh*, vi (1902), 896–7.
[98] Ya. Neruchev, 'Byvshie "stepi" i—shto ot nikh ostaetsya', *SKhiL*, 200 (1901), 605.
[99] Kornis, 'O sostoyanii khozyaistva . . . v 1842 g.', 64.
[100] I. Kornis, 'O sostoyanii khozyaistva v Molochanskikh Menonistskikh koloniyakh v 1843 g.', *ZhMGI*, 11 (1844), 2nd pagn, 129.

Wiebe later concluded: 'Black fallow is the key factor of our steppe farming, without which a long time ago we would already have collapsed and grain farming in the Mennonite colonies would never have reached such a blossoming condition.' The Molotschna Mennonites were convinced that if black fallow was practiced everywhere, then 'even in the driest years there would be no need to fear complete harvest failure'.[101] Wiebe doubted that estate owners in southern Russia would introduce black fallow, however, since they owned land in such large quantities that they did not pay attention to how it was cultivated and, in any case, keeping the fallow fields clear of weeds required twice as much work.[102] Indeed, estate owners in the region did object to the extra work, in spite of attempts to persuade them otherwise.[103] Skal'kovskii argued that while the practice was possible for the Mennonites, who owned relatively small areas of land, it was hardly possible for owners of large estates, with 500 or 1,000 *desyatiny* of land under crops.[104]

There were further reasons why it was difficult for peasants in the steppe region to carry out the regular work required black fallow. Some were discussed by the Committee for the Improvement of Agriculture in 1833–4. Mechnikov recommended that settlements contain between 250 and 2,000 inhabitants. They should not be too large, he argued, as the fields would be too far from the villages, which would make it difficult for peasants to work on them. On the other hand, settlements that were too small were 'absolutely evil' as it was harder for the police to maintain surveillance over the inhabitants to ensure they fulfilled their obligations and paid their taxes.[105] (This indicates the authorities' order of priorities.) In any case, state peasants in the steppe region tended to live in large settlements, containing several hundred households, as they located them near scarce sources of water. Earlier settlers had lived in large settlements for protection against raids by the indigenous nomads. The average population of foreign colonists' settlements in Tauride province in the 1840s was 120; state peasant villages were four times the size. Thus, foreign colonists had to go only a few kilometres to their land, while state peasants had to travel 20 or more kilometres.[106] An additional reason why it would have been difficult for peasants to keep their fallow fields 'black' was that many households had insufficient draft animals to pull their ploughs. Households shared oxen and used them one after the other, rather than at the precise time the land needed ploughing.[107] Moreover, peasants had less land than the Mennonites, and so needed to use their

---

[101] Vibe, 'Khlebopashestvo', 158–9.
[102] Vibe, 'O chernom pare', 79.
[103] Dmitrii Osten-Saken, 'O letnom pare', *ZIOSKhYuR*, 5 (1849), 332.
[104] Skal'kovskii, *Opyt*, ii, 65.
[105] RGIA, f.398, op.83, 1831–8, d.4, l.159.
[106] See Friesen, *Rural Revolutions*, 24, 58–9, 214.
[107] RGIA, f.398, op.83, 1831–8, d.4, ll.18ob.–19. This was also the case among Don Cossacks. GARO, f.46, op.1, d.1347, l.685.

fallow fields to graze their livestock. The increased grain yields that would result from the introduction of black fallow would not compensate for the loss of grazing.[108]

Palimpsestov discussed black fallow in 1855. He summarized Wiebe's arguments in favour based on the Mennonites' experience since 1837. Palimpsestov acknowledged that black fallow helped increase the amount of moisture in the soil. On the other hand, he asserted that all that glittered was not gold, and in this case in time it would turn into an ordinary, rusty metal. He argued that black fallow had such a strong influence on the productivity of the land that it hastened the exhaustion of the soil. He doubted the Mennonites could maintain their success for long. He noted that some were applying manure to their fields, which he adduced as evidence for soil exhaustion. In conclusion, he cited the experience of a landowner in Belorussia (i.e. a region with higher rainfall where moisture retention was less critical) who found he needed three times more labour to maintain a *desyatina* of black fallow than ordinary fallow.[109]

Palimpsestov, as a patriotic Orthodox Russian, may have been biased against black fallow because introduced by foreign, protestant colonists. Nevertheless, similar concerns were made later by other specialists. In the late 1880s, the agronomist A. Filipchenko analysed the experience of the improving landowner I. I. Shatilov on his estate of Mokhovoe, in Tula province in the forest-steppe region.[110] Shatilov advocated black fallow for the central black-earth region. Filipchenko strongly disagreed, arguing that it was inappropriate in the northern part of the black-earth region, because leaving the soil unprotected by vegetation from the elements for prolonged periods created conditions in which the minerals in the soil, so important for its fertility, were leached out by precipitation, leading to soil exhaustion.[111] In the steppe region, and other parts of Russia, moreover, some farmers believed that land with plant cover conserved moisture better than land left black, as vegetation protected the soil from the sun's rays and wind which caused evaporation.[112]

Black fallow seems to have been used mainly by Mennonite and German settlers on the steppes.[113] Some other farmers adopted similar practices. In 1892, V. M. Borkovskii, the agronomist of the Ekaterinoslav provincial *zemstvo*, found that a few 'practical farmers' were increasing their productivity and obtaining higher yields. He attributed this to good choice of seed, careful and timely preparation of the fields to preserve moisture, and energetic struggle with weeds.

---

[108] A. Chelintsev, 'Obzor russkoi literatury po sel'skomu khozyaistvu', *SKhiL*, 228 (1908), 157–8. See also Pallot and Shaw, *Landscape*, 110–11.

[109] I. Palimpsestov, 'O chernom pare', *ZIOSKhYuR*, (1855), 207–14.

[110] Elina, *Ot tsarskikh sadov*, i, 183.

[111] A. Filipchenko, 'Pol'zovanie chernym parom', *SKhiL*, 161 (1889), 161–2, 167. See also Ermolov, *Organizatsiya*, 354–5.

[112] Shishkin, *K voprosu*, 122.

[113] Ya. Neruchev, 'Byvshie "stepi"', 605.

On basis of trial, experiment, and observations, moreover, some farmers had started to plough the fields for the winter grain not, as was customary, at the end of July or start of August, but in June and late May. They had also started to plough the spring fields the previous May, rather than in August or September, thus in effect, turning the fields into black fallow for spring wheat. On other farms, however, Borkovskii found agriculture in the province in a poor condition.[114]

Regardless of these objections and despite the practical reasons why it was difficult for peasants to introduce black fallow, the specialist literature, further studies, and experience supported the contribution of the Mennonites' innovation. In the mid-1870s, Shishkin pointed out that plants both drew moisture from the soil and transpired it into the atmosphere. Experiments had shown that more moisture was lost from land occupied by plants than bare of vegetation. Thus, 'black fallow' assisted moisture conservation better than fallow with plant cover. The drier the climate, the greater the difference between the amount of moisture retained by 'black fallow' and land with plant cover. Shishkin recommended 'black fallow' in a list of measures for 'the struggle with droughts'.[115] He drew heavily on the work of agronomists from Western Europe, but he had also surveyed agriculture in the steppe region.[116] Tests conducted in the rather different environmental conditions of the Rothamsted Experimental Station in Hertfordshire, England, in 1878 confirmed the efficacy of black fallow in making nutrients and moisture available to plants, especially in drought years. The results were duly reported in Russia by the Ministry of State Domains.[117] In the wake of the drought and crop failure of 1891, moreover, Kostychev noted the effectiveness of black fallow in conserving moisture.[118]

Zemstva began to conduct tests into the ways to cultivate the land that were most suited to the steppe environment. In 1894, for example, experiments were conducted into the efficacy of different sorts of fallow at the Kherson agricultural college. They revealed an 'unusual phenomenon for the steppe region: with the assistance of black fallow a surplus of water was accumulated'. The soil was moist to a depth of 32 *vershki* (56 inches), compared with between 7 and 20 *vershki* (12.25–35 inches) for fallow with vegetation. The black fallow fields gave the highest harvests.[119] The result was not a fluke. Fields that had been 'black fallowed' consistently gave higher yields in experiments on the Kherson experimental field during the 1890s.[120] Similar experiments were conducted at the

---

[114] *Otchet i doklad po agronimicheskomu byuro ekaterinoslavskomu gub. zemskomu sobraniyu* (Ekaterinoslav, 1892), reviewed in *SKhiL*, 172 (1893), 54–6.

[115] Shishkin, *K voprosu*, 73, 119–33, 166.

[116] Shishkin, 'Sel'skokhozyaistvennyi ocherk Novorossii', 265–315.

[117] 'Vliyanie chernogo para na plodorodie pochvy', *SKhiL*, 164 (1890), 2nd pagn, 34–8.

[118] 'Besedy', 113; Kostychev, *O bor'be*, 45–57.

[119] G. P. Sazonov, *Obzor deyatel'nosti zemstv po sel'skomu khozyaistvu (1865–1895 gg.)*, 3 vols (Spb, 1896), iii, 1225–6 (also i, 347, 375, 407).

[120] S. Kizenkov, 'Sel'skokhozyaistvennye voprosy v russkoi pechati za 1898 g.', *SKhiL*, 191 (1898), 692–4.

Bezenchuk experiment station in Samara province. The fallow field was ploughed early and kept 'black' by constant cultivation to destroy weeds and prevent evaporation. In 1906, a year of drought and bad harvests, the yields on land after black fallow were six-times higher than on peasant land, where the fallow field was used as pasture. The experiments thus confirmed the value of black fallow in conserving moisture and controlling weeds. The station received many visitors, including peasants, who came to see the results of the experiments. This emphasized the importance of taking measures to bring 'agronomical help' to the peasant population.[121] Similar results were obtained in experiments at agricultural experiment stations across the steppe region.[122] In 1912, the Peasant Land Bank in Samara decided in favour of keeping fallow fields 'black' as it ensured the best harvest.[123] By 1914, manuals aimed at wide audiences recommended black fallow.[124] Thus, the efficacy of 'black fallow' was accepted in theory, if not adopted very widely in practice.

The panoply of agricultural techniques that was devised and tested on the steppes—from crop rotations to black fallow—was an entire system of farming aimed at accumulating, conserving, and making the most effective use of water in fertile, but semi-arid and drought-prone regions. By the end of the period, scientists were testing the system at experiment stations such as Bezenchuk. Nikolai Tulaikov, the director of the station between 1910 and 1916, became a leading specialist on what may be termed 'dry farming'.[125]

SPREADING THE WORD

The various techniques of 'dry farming' had been devised by a few improving farmers, in particular the Mennonites, and agricultural specialists on experiment farms in the steppe region. In order to make a real difference in the 'struggle with droughts' they would need to be adopted by farmers throughout the region. The same institutions that supported the development of agricultural techniques appropriate to the environment—including the central and provincial government, agricultural societies, and *zemstva*—were also involved in spreading the word.

The Committee for the Improvement of Agriculture of 1833–4 recommended spreading theoretical and practical information about improved agriculture by

---

[121] GASO, f.149, op.9, d.15, l.4; Klingen and Zhukov, 'Udel'naya', 195–6, 203.

[122] A. Chelintsev, 'Obzor russkoi literatury po sel'skomu khozyaistvu', *SKhiL*, 228 (1908), 155–8. See also Ermolov, *Organizatsiya*, 352–5.

[123] GASO, f.149, op.1, d.296, l.95.

[124] Bazhanov, 'Novye sposoby', 34.

[125] GASO, f.832, op.1, d.2; f.149, op.9, d.15; *Podvornoe i khutorskoe khozyaistvo v Samarskoi gubernii. Opyt agronomicheskogo issledovaniya*, 1 (Samara, 1909), 229–43; N. M. Tulaikov, '"Sukhoe" zemledelie (sistema Kembellya)', *PERSKh*, xxii (1912), 1262–7; N. M. Tulaikov, 'Agriculture in the Dry Regions of the U.S.S.R.', *Economic Geography*, 6 (1930), 54–80.

publishing a newspaper, establishing agricultural schools with 'experimental fields' to train famers, including peasants, and setting up a factory to make improved implements. In the first instance, only a newspaper was published. The State Council rejected the rest. Finance Minister Kankrin raised all sorts of objections, including the practical details of building schools and educating peasants. The authorities were alarmed about the social consequences, fearing peasants would get ideas above their station in life. The authorities seemed more concerned about this than periodic crop failures and famines, even on the scale of 1833.[126]

The criticism of government should not be taken too far. Veshnyakov argued that Kankrin's objections were motivated more by the pressing need to sort out government finances, and that, in a longer-term perspective, the Committee of 1833–4 was the start of government efforts to improve agriculture in Russia. As we have already seen, the Ministry of State Domains, founded a few years later in 1837, took a keen interest in agricultural development.[127] There was still a long way to go. In 1839 and 1840, the ataman of the Don Cossacks asked the government in St Petersburg for an agricultural experiment station to be established in his territory to help raise the 'primitive' level of farming. He was turned down, and advised that the Lugansk farm in adjoining Ekaterinoslav province should suffice, and that children could be sent to the Gorygoretskaya agricultural school (far-off to the west in Belorussia).[128] On 2 June 1841, however, the government authorized the establishment of five new 'training farms' for the 'further improvement' of agriculture, in different regions to reflect variations in climate, soil, and the way of life of the population. For the steppe region, one farm was to serve the south-eastern region, comprising Saratov, Asktrakhan', and Orenburg provinces. The existing Lugansk farm was to serve the Don Cossack territory, as well as Kherson, Ekaterinoslav, and Tauride provinces, and the Caucasus region.[129]

The recent historiography has emphasized the origins and gradual development of official support, by the Appanage Department as well as the Ministry of State Domains, to improve agriculture and promote agricultural education, rather than what was not achieved. Recent research has also emphasized the work done by *zemstva*.[130] Activities to achieve these can be divided into education; publications; and above all, direct advice to farmers through extension services.

[126] RGIA, f.398, op.83, 1831–8, d.4, ll.29–41, 346–7. See also B.A. Val'skaya, 'Zemledel'cheskaya gazeta i zemledel'cheskaya geografiya v Rossii v 30-kh gg. XIX veka', *IRGO*, 125/5 (1993), 41–7.

[127] Veshnyakov, 'Komitet 1833 g.', 286–320.

[128] GARO, f.46, op.1, d.497, ll.41–2.

[129] 'Ob uchrezhdenii uchebnykh ferm v Rossii', *ZhMGI*, 3 (1841), xv–xxix.

[130] See, for example B. N. Mironov, *Blagosostoyanie naseleniya i revolyutsii v imperatorskoi Rossii: XVIII-nachalo XX veka* (Moscow, 2010), 342–5; N. G. Koroleva (ed.), *Zemskoe samoupravlenie v Rossi, 1864–1918*, 2 vols (Moscow, 2005), i, 294–348; ii, 159–207; Elina, *Ot tsarskikh sadov*; James W. Long, 'The Volga Germans and the Zemstvos, 1865–1917', *JGO*, 30 (1982), 336–61.

A start had been made to agricultural education in Russia by the early nineteenth century. Courses in higher education were offered by a number of universities, including Dorpat in Livonia, as well as specialist institutions such as the Petrovskaya academy near Moscow from 1857, and the Novo-Aleksandriiskii institute near Lublin in Russian Poland from 1869. The numbers studying agriculture at all levels remained low until the late nineteenth century. Between 1844 and 1869, in the Russian Empire as a whole, 1,372 pupils completed courses in lower agricultural schools run by the Ministry of State Domains. By 1865, only 569 students had completed the course at the Gorygoretskaya agricultural school.[131] (The students included Palimpsestov, who studied there in 1843–6.[132]) Agricultural education continued to develop only slowly after the establishment of *zemstva* in 1864. This was due to shortage of funds, and also the low level of agronomical knowledge.[133] But the pace increased from the 1890s, spurred in part by the drought and harvest failure of 1891. Between 1893 and 1913, the numbers of institutions of agricultural education in the empire as a whole grew from 68 to 360.[134]

In the steppe region, the Kherson provincial *zemstvo* was one of the first pay attention to agricultural education. In 1874, it set up an agricultural college with 200 *desyatiny* of land. From 1882, it was offering a six-year course with practical work. In the early 1890s, it had a farm, tree nursery, vegetable garden, meteorological station, laboratory, and library. The treasury allocated the college 7,800 roubles a year. By 1892, it had graduated 128 students.[135] Elsewhere, the Samara provincial *zemstvo* made an early start in providing agricultural education. Overall, however, progress was slow until the end of the nineteenth century. It was not until the second decade of the twentieth century that there were significant numbers of institutions and students in the steppe region.[136] In the Don region in 1916, for example, a concerted effort was made to provide agricultural education. The region's administration spent 7,700 roubles on short-term agricultural courses in schools.[137] The numbers of graduates with higher education in agriculture was also increasing. The Moscow Agricultural Institute graduated 165 students in 1912 and 248 in 1915. Many went to work as agronomists for *zemstva* or taught in agricultural schools.[138]

The volume of publications on agriculture, for specialist and wider readerships, also developed slowly in Russia. (This was one of the reasons for the

[131] Elina, *Ot tsarkikh sadov*, ii, 40–8; Mironov, *Blagosostoyanie*, 345.

[132] DAOO, f.22, op.1, 1852, sp.229, l.19–ob.

[133] Koroleva, *Zemskoe samoupravlenie*, ii, 160–1.

[134] A. A. Kaufman, *Agronomicheskaya pomoshch' v Rossii: Istoriko-statisticheskii ocherk* (Samara, 1915), 7.

[135] N. Kolyupanov, 'Chto sdelano zemstvom dlya podnyatiya sel'skogo khozyaistva', *SKhiL*, 174 (1893), 1st pagn, 213.

[136] Koroleva, *Zemskoe samoupravlenie*, ii, 163–4, 193, 202.

[137] GARO, f.46, op.1, d.3510, l.107.

[138] Koroleva, *Zemskoe samoupravlenie*, ii, 193–4, 197, 201.

continued importance and influence of publications on agricultural sciences from elsewhere in Europe.) A start had been made by the Free Economic Society, which published a journal from 1765. The Southern Russian Agricultural Society published a journal from 1830. On the initiative of the Committee for the Improvement of Agriculture of 1833–4, the newspaper *Agricultural Gazette* ('*Zemledel'cheskaya gazeta*') appeared from 1830s. And, from 1841 the Ministry of State Domains published a monthly journal. There was a rapid increase in the number of agricultural periodicals in the early twentieth century. By 1912, there were 162 such publications, and by 1915 the number had nearly doubled to 310.[139]

The numbers of books on agriculture published in Russian also grew steadily. In 1868, for example, the Southern Russian Agricultural Society published a collection of articles on key practical issues, including deep ploughing and black fallow. The collection became widely known and contributed to raising the level of agricultural knowledge in New Russia.[140] In the early twentieth century, a twelve-volume encyclopedia on Russian agriculture was published with articles on a full range of subjects by Russian authors who drew largely on Russian specialist literature.[141] The encyclopedia made it way to the steppe region. In 1910, for example, the Bugul'ma district *zemstvo* in Samara province had a copy.[142] I first came across it, almost a century later, in the library in Rostov-on-Don. However, it was one thing to reach the relatively small numbers of educated Russians, including estate owners, scientists, *zemstvo* activists, and officials of the provincial and central governments. In researching this book, I have been very conscious that I have been delving largely into the world of such people. To convey the findings of research in agricultural techniques appropriate to the steppe environment and the experience of improving farmers to a wider audience, including the peasants and migrant labourers who worked on the land, was rather a different matter.

There were many attempts at reaching this wider, and important, readership. Such initiatives encountered problems, from low levels of literacy among the peasantry, if indeed they had the time, resources, and inclination to read such works, to censorship and anxieties about educating peasants on the part of the authorities. For a long time, there was a shortage of literature written for a wider readership. In 1845, the Southern Russian Agricultural Society set the task of producing a handbook for peasants, to include such topics as loyalty to the faith, throne, and authorities, as well as agriculture. By 1854, however, it had no

[139] A. A. Bychikhin, *85-letie 'zapisok' Imperatorskogo Obshchestva sel'skogo khozyaistva yuzhnoi Rossii, 1830–1915* (Odessa, 1916), 8–9.
[140] I. Palimpsestov (ed.), *Sbornik statei o sel'skom khozyaistve yuga Rossii, izvlechennikh iz Zapisok Imperatorskogo Obshchestva sel'skogo khozyaistva yuzhnoi Rossii s 1830 po 1868 god* (Odessa, 1868); Bychikhin, *85-letie 'zapisok'*, 13–14.
[141] *PERSKh.*
[142] GASO, f.5, op.11, d.107, l.56.

received a satisfactory compositions.[143] With more success, in 1846 the Scientific Committee of the Ministry of State Domains set the task of writing an exposition of agriculture applicable to the conditions of peasant life in all regions of Russia. It received one on agriculture in the steppe region, entitled 'A flourishing agriculture is the wealth of the fatherland' ('*Eine bluehende Landwirtschaft ist des Vaterlands Wohl*'). The author was the agronomist Reidemeister, who drew his experience of farming in the steppe region, rather than theoretical literature from Germany. The Southern Russian Agricultural Society had it translated into Russian by a specialist on steppe farming and estate owner in Ekaterinoslav province, and published it in 1855.[144] Reidemeister later wrote a textbook on agriculture for the Southern Russian Agricultural Society.[145]

The numbers of publications on steppe agriculture aimed at a popular readership grew from the 1890s. The increase was prompted by the disaster of 1891, and also by the growth in popular literacy and readership.[146] In 1894, a book on the struggle with droughts was approved by the Ministry of State Domains, with some reservations, for use in parish schools.[147] In the early twentieth century, a much fuller popular study of steppe agriculture was published, which explained many of issues discussed in this chapter, such as deep ploughing, fallowing etc.[148] In 1903, Aleksandr Platonovich Engel'gardt donated the earnings from his book on black-earth Russia to the Saratov provincial *zemstvo* to fund popular brochures on agriculture.[149] A key issue in bringing agricultural techniques to the attention of a wider, peasant, readership was language, and not just a simple, straightforward style for people with limited formal education. Between 1897 and 1903, the agricultural innovator and Ukrainian activist Yevhen Chykalenko published a series of pamphlets on steppe agriculture in Ukrainian under the title *Rosmovy pro selske khoziaistvo* (*Conversations about Agriculture*). He drew on his experience of farming in Kherson province, and works by specialists such as Kostychev. It is indicative of the importance the government attached to spreading the word about farming techniques in the steppe region that it made an exception to the ban on publication in Ukrainian: the native language of most peasant farmers in the western part of the steppes.[150] Further east, in the Don

---

[143] DAOO, f.22, op.1, 1845, sp.346, ll.3–4ob., 65.

[144] Bunitskii, 'Osnovye pravila', 312–44, 353–92.

[145] DAOO, f.22, op.1, 1874, sp.425.

[146] See B. N. Mironov, 'Gramotnost'v Rossii 1797–1917 gg.', *Istoriya SSSR*, 4 (1985), 137–53; Jeffrey Brooks, *When Russia Learned to Read: Literacy and Popular Literature, 1981–1917* (Princeton, NJ, 1985).

[147] RGIA, f.382, op.2, 1894, d.1321.

[148] P. N. Sokovnin, *Shto nuzhno znat' zemledel'tsu, shtoby uspeshno borot'sya s neurozhayami ot zasukhi: obshchedostupnoe posobie dlya sel'skikh khozyaev chernozemnoi polosy Rossii*, 2nd edn (Spb, 1911).

[149] V. A. Skripitsyn, *Voistiny chelovek: iz vospominanii ob Aleksandre Platonoviche Engel'gardt* (Spb, 1903), 13.

[150] D. B. Saunders, 'The Russian Imperial Authorities and Yevhen Chykalenko's *Rozmovy pro selske khoziastvo*', *Journal of Ukrainian Studies*, 33–4 (2008–9), 417–27.

region, in 1916 the ataman reported that his administration was meeting the need for accessible literature on farming by publishing the journal *Farming on the Don* (*Khozyaistvo na Donu*), and distributing popular-scientific books, brochures, and posters.[151] Concerns were expressed about the value and the results of attempts at bringing the latest advice about steppe farming to a mass readership. A book entitled 'How to obtain a harvest of winter [grain] even during a drought', published in Rostov-on-Don in 1909, was reviewed very critically in an official agricultural periodical. The reviewer noted that it would not be suitable for uneducated peasants.[152]

Practical example could get through where the written word could not. From the late nineteenth century, agricultural societies, *zemstva*, and provincial and cossack authorities expended a lot of effort on demonstration fields and exhibitions to bring the success of innovations and improvements to wider notice. They also paid attention to extension services in which agronomists offered practical advice directly to farmers. The first *zemstvo* to hire agronomists was Kherson in the late 1880s. Others followed, especially after 1891. Spending on agronomists remained very low, however, until the early twentieth century, when most *zemstva* and cossack authorities began to provide agronomical advice. Agronomists went to the villages to offer advice on new techniques, such as crop rotations, sowing fodder grasses, and new crop varieties.[153] To take one example, in 1916, the ataman of the Don Cossacks reported that agronomists gave lectures to and held discussions with the rural population. He also reported on a major reorganization and expansion of demonstration farms to make them more relevant to needs of average cossack farmers. The existing 205 demonstration farms were supplemented by a further 84, at cost of over 84,000 roubles. The main tasks were to show farmers how to cultivate the land in ways that facilitated the accumulation of moisture in the soil, combated weeds, and provided fodder for livestock by sowing grasses.[154]

Did the word get through to the mass of the farming population of the steppes? In 1916, the editor of the Southern Russian Agricultural Society's periodical questioned the impact of the journal, and of the scientific research and practical experience on which it was based. 'Justice requires us to note', he wrote, 'that what has been achieved is a long way from what is needed.' He continued that the journal had tried very hard to increase its readership among

---

[151] GARO, f.46, op.1, d.3510, ll.106ob.–7.

[152] E. Robuk, *Kak poluchit' urozhai ozimogo dazhe pri zasukhe* (Rostov-on-Don, 1909) reviewed in *SKhiL*, 231 (1909), 191.

[153] Koroleva, *Zemskoe samoupravlenie*, i, 331–44; N. Kataev, 'Zemskaya sel'skokhozyaistvennaya i ekonomicheskaya deyatel'nost'', *SKhiL*, 229 (1909), 630–60; K. Matsuzato, 'The fate of agronomists in Russia: their quantitative dynamics from 1911 to 1916', *RR*, 55 (1996), 172–200; M. V. Loskutova, 'Lyubiteli i professionaly: estestvoznanie v rossiiskoi provintsii vtoroi polovine XIX—nachala XX vv.', *VIET*, 2 (2011), 45–66.

[154] GARO, f.46, op.1, d.3510, ll.106–7.

the agricultural population, but that growth was very slow. Attempts to bring it to the attention of farmers involved in working the land, rather than thinking about it, had not been successful.[155] The argument that attempts to 'improve' peasant agriculture had little success has persisted in the historical literature. In his analysis of agricultural co-operatives in the decades after 1861, Yanni Kotsonis drew attention to the cultural gulf between the leaders and activists in the movement, who came from educated society, and the mass of the peasantry. Many activists were convinced of their ability to 'transform a population that they believed could not conceive of transforming itself'. He called his book *Making Peasants Backward*, however, since many agronomists disregarded peasant 'knowledge' and, in the process, undermined their own efforts to promote agricultural development.[156]

In a forthright assessment of peasant agriculture in Tambov province, in the forest-steppe region, David Kerans asserted that peasants had limited competence as farmers. They were not able to move beyond their existing systems, he argued, because they had limited mental capacities. He attributed this to the 'magico-religious world' of Russian villages, child-rearing practices, but also to a physical environment—an abundance of fertile land in the recent past—that had long encouraged extensive rather than intensive farming. He concluded that 'village culture produced relatively few individuals with an inclination to techno-logical exploration and experimentation'.[157] Kerans' interpretation, however, could also be applied to other sections of the farming population. In the early 1880s, a *zemstvo* study of Samara district noted that there was little demand on private, that is, noble, estates for people with specialized education in agriculture or agronomy. Estate administrators were too busy with 'other matters'.[158]

It is easy to find evidence for the farming population's reluctance to change their ways. Resistance to change among peasants, especially those living near the margins of subsistence, is often interpreted as an aversion to risk, or to additional labour that is perceived as unnecessary.[159] Commentators on agriculture in the steppe region noted that peasants were suspicious of experiments and preferred their own experience.[160] Official reports over the nineteenth century from the Don region regularly referred to the 'primitive' level of agriculture among the cossacks. 'Improved' agriculture was practised by only a few estate owners and leasers of large estates.[161] The Maslokovets commission that investigated the

---

[155] Bychikhin, *85-letie 'zapisok'*, 12–13.

[156] Yanni Kotsonis, *Making Peasants Backward: Agricultural Cooperatives and the Agrarian Question in Russia, 1861–1914* (Basingstoke, 1999), quotation 95.

[157] Kerans, *Mind and Labor*, quotation 184.

[158] SSSpSG, i, *Samarskii uezd* (1883), 2nd pagn, 69–70.

[159] See James C. Scott, *The Moral Economy of the Peasant: Rebellion and Subsistence in South East Asia* (New Haven, CT, 1976).

[160] Nal'tsov, 'Glubokaya vspashka', p.125.

[161] GARO, f.46, op.1, d.522 (1844), l.89ob.; d.639 (1859), l.26ob.; d.985 (1869), l.40; d.3164, 1890, l.57ob.

cossacks' condition in 1898–9 reported that they were still using the long-fallow system. While agriculture in the Don region had become more orientated to the market since the 1870s, the cossacks' main motivation was subsistence and the need to support their arduous military obligations. The commission believed the latter were holding back economic development. The system of communal land tenure, moreover, made it difficult for cossacks to introduce improved crop rotations.[162] A *zemstvo* study of Novyi Uzen' district in Samara province in 1890 noted the 'absence of agronomical knowledge' among the peasants as a reason for the poor condition of agriculture. The study described peasant farming as 'rapacious' (*'khishchnicheskoe'*).[163] In his report for 1891, the governor of Samara reported that in the southern districts of his province, peasants were borrowing money to sow high quality varieties of wheat on as much land as possible in the hope of enriching themselves after one or two good harvests. 'The cultivation of the land in such circumstances', he wrote, 'is inevitably very poor, and the prospects for good harvests are declining with every year.' The peasant economy in southern Samara province, therefore, was on a 'very unsound basis'. And, in 1891, disaster struck.[164]

The picture may not have been quite as bleak. Ilya Gerasimov has recently offered a new interpretation of relations between agronomists and peasants in the decade after 1905. In the last years of the old regime there was a massive increase in the number of agronomists and other rural professionals employed by *zemstva*. On the basis of archival research, Gerasimov argued that the agronomists in particular began to establish contact with what he termed 'new peasants': those who had benefitted from the wider opportunities for education. 'Probably for the first time in modern Russian history', he argued, 'peasants eagerly reacted to the initiative of the educated elite to change their ways, which made their interaction a dialogue, and not the usual "discursive dictate" of modernizers over an "objectified class".'[165]

Further evidence for Gerasimov's argument can be found in Samara province. In Nikolaevsk district in 1909, for example, a *zemstvo* agronomist explained to peasants the advantages of changing from their two-field to a four-field rotation with sown grasses to use the land more profitably. The peasants, he reported, 'listened attentively, discussed sowing grasses seriously, . . . and came to the conclusion that it would be useful . . . to do it.' The village assembly agreed to introduce the new rotation on communal land. Elsewhere in the same district in 1909, an agronomist gave talks on techniques to conserve moisture, including

---

[162] RGVIA, f.330, op.61, d.1948, ll 48–52. I am grateful to Dr Shane O'Rourke for a copy of a microfilm of this file. See also Shane O Rourke, *Warriors and Peasants: The Don Cossacks in Late Imperial Russia* (New York, 2000), 90–2.

[163] *SSSpSG*, vii, *Novouzenskii uezd* (1890), 52.

[164] GASO, f.3, op.233, 1892, d.1060b, ll.3–5.

[165] Ilya V. Gerasimov, *Modernism and Public Reform in Late Imperial Russia: Rural Professionals and Self-Organization, 1905–30* (Basingstoke, 2009), quotation 104.

regular cultivation of the fields to keep weeds down, and black fallow. He reported that peasants attended his talks willingly and in numbers ranging from forty to two–three hundred. '[T]hey always listened . . . attentively, like children listening to a good folktale, only from time to time interrupting to ask something or to share their own observations.' The agronomist backed up his talks with examples of techniques, for example sowing grasses, in demonstration fields. I am aware that we have only the agronomists' own reports on their success in getting through to the peasants, nevertheless their accounts deserve to be taken seriously. The peasants may have paid attention to the agronomists as they had suffered the effects of several successive bad harvests caused by droughts, which had compelled them to plough up and sow as much land as possible in the hope of a good harvest that would enable them to repay their debts. On the other hand, rich peasants were buying agricultural machinery, including seed drills, recommended by the agronomists not to intensify production on their existing land, but to extend their farming to land they had rented cheaply. Some complained the seed drills were too 'slow'.[166] Peasants in the steppe region, it seems, were prepared to adopt innovations if they could see that they were necessary, and successful.[167]

CONCLUSION

By the early twentieth century, agriculture in parts of the Russian Empire, in particular the fertile steppe region, was becoming more productive. Data on per-capita production and consumption of grain for the European part of the empire as a whole show rising trends from the early 1880s. There were still short-term fluctuations, most dramatically in 1891 but also in 1906 and other years caused by droughts, but the overall trend was upwards. Farmers had turned the steppe region into the breadbasket not just of the Russian Empire, but parts of Europe. The Russian Empire led the world in grain exports.[168] This was achieved in two ways. Most farmers—including peasants and estate owners—were prepared to take a gamble on the weather and plough up and sow as much land as they could as cheaply as possible in hope of reaping a bumper harvest. Most sowed wheat as it was the most profitable crop. Most did not adopt 'black fallow' or other expensive and labour-intensive methods of accumulating and conserving mois-ture in the soil. They were motivated more by market conditions than aversion to

---

[166] GASO, f.5, op.11, d.102, 1909, ll.21ob.–22, 95, 98–102.

[167] See Friesen, *Rural Revolutions*, 192.

[168] See Friesen, *Rural Revolutions*, 193–5; B. K. Goodwin and T. J. Grennes, 'Tsarist Russia and the World Wheat Market', *Explorations in Economic History*, 35 (1998), 405–30; Paul R. Gregory, 'Grain Marketings and Peasant Consumption in Russia, 1885–1913', *Explorations in Economic History*, 17 (1980), 135–64.

risk. But some did take heed of agronomists' advice and their own experience in adapting their farming techniques to the steppe environment.[169]

In 1884, the agricultural specialist S. M. Tanatar wrote:

It is rare to find a place where the harvest depends to such a degree on the amount of water in the soil as southern Russia. . . . The peasant and estate owner and every farmer in the [region] is already accustomed to stake his entire well being on the rain. . . . At certain times, all eyes turn to the sky, looking for . . . clouds on the horizon; in towns and villages, public prayers are offered to be granted a little rain, and every drop at the right time is literally a gold coin falling from the sky.

The first duty of every southern farmer, he continued, was to ensure that he increased the amount of water in the soil by cultivating the land in such a way that it retained most of the water that fell on it.[170]

Thus, in the late nineteenth century, Tanatar was advocating farming methods that had been devised for the steppe environment. Nevertheless, for some decades Russians had looked to 'improved' farming in Western Europe, where shortage of water was not the key factor, as a model for 'improved' agriculture. The Russian government studied Western European farming, and invited settlers from elsewhere in Europe to the steppes in the hope that they would become model farmers. From the early nineteenth century, however, growing numbers of agricultural specialists, such as Pavlov, Palimpsestov, Kostychev, and Dokuchaev, argued that what was needed was not imported agricultural sciences devised in the very different conditions of Western Europe, but an agronomy developed in and for the conditions on the steppes.

Farming methods appropriate to the steppe environment were devised during the nineteenth century by a combination of practical experience, trial and error, and experimentation by farmers, agricultural societies, agencies of the central and provincial government, and *zemstva* in the steppe region. All were advised by Russian agricultural specialists and scientists, who drew on both Western European specialist literature as well as the accumulated experience of steppe agriculture. This process of drawing on ideas and experiences from both the steppe region and other parts of Russia and Europe was assisted by the mixed population of the region, which comprised migrants and descendants of migrants from these geographical origins. This combination of ideas and people from elsewhere in Europe and practical experience on the steppes was best exemplified by the Mennonites, whom most specialists regard as the most successful steppe farmers.[171] They took a justifiable pride in their achievement. In 1843, the redoubtable Cornies wrote

---

[169] See RGIA, f.426, op.1, 1898, d.156, l.12; I. M. Rubinow, *Russia's Wheat Surplus; conditions under which it is produced* (Washington, DC, 1906).
[170] Tanatar, 'O vliyanii razrykhleniya', 550.
[171] On reasons for their success, see Friesen, *Rural Revolutions*, 55–9 and 103.

It is joyous to behold how in our colonies the population and the improvement of economic life are increasing with every year . . . thirty or even twenty years ago, we often endured harvest failures and loss of livestock, which occurred from lack of diligence in managing our farms; now . . . there are fewer harvest failures; we may hope that our grandsons, having inherited clearer opinions on the interrelationship between our localities, resources, and needs . . . and adding their own observations to our experience, will cease to be impoverished by harvest failures, and will extract more sources of enrichment from economic activity than their ancestors.[172]

Almost two generations later, an article written in 1889 to mark the centenary of the arrival of the first Mennonites in the Russian Empire claimed that they had transformed the 'yellow, arid steppe' into fields of wheat that 'billowed in the gentle spring wind', and had replaced a 'horrible wilderness' with 'neat, orderly, well laid-out villages, surrounded by dark green, mature trees'. James Urry pointed out that the steppe had not been quite as unsettled and uncultivated before the arrival of the Mennonites, but continued that Russian visitors wrote 'lyrically of the sense of wonder they experienced on encountering a Mennonite colony after journeying across the open steppe and passing through squalid peasant villages.'[173]

---

[172] Quoted in Tsin, 'Otchet ob uspekakh', 9.

[173] Urry, *None but Saints*, 274–5. I experienced a similar sense of order and modest prosperity (but not surrounding squalor) when I encountered the municipality of North Newton, which had been founded by Mennonite migrants from the steppes, while driving across Kansas in 2009.

Conclusion

The agricultural settlement of the steppes after their incorporation into the Russian Empire may be seen as colonization, both human and ecological. The settlers who migrated to the steppes, the authorities who governed them, and the specialists who advised them aimed to transplant their largely agricultural way of life, based on growing grain, to the steppe region with its very fertile soil. They had little regard for the indigenous population, who had lived mainly by nomadic pastoralism, and gradually drove them out. As the settlers ploughed up the steppes and grew grain, however, they became aware of the vagaries of the steppe environment, in particular the semi-arid climate and recurring droughts that harmed their way of life. For many decades, the authorities, specialists, and some settlers considered planting trees and artificial irrigation to be the best ways to deal with the barriers to arable farming presented by the steppe environment. The intention—either implicit or explicit—was to change the steppe environment to make it more like the forested and more humid environments of central and northern Russia and Ukraine, and Central Europe where many of them or their forebears came from. It was from these regions, moreover, that the settlers brought their agricultural way of life and practice of using forest products for many everyday purposes, from timber to firewood. Most Russian and Ukrainian peasant settlers, however, were happier to fell trees than plant them.

The urge among settlers in new environments to use the land in familiar ways and to make it familiar was not confined to the Russian Empire. Thomas Dunlap emphasized how 'Anglo' settlers in North American and Australasia 'made themselves at home on the land'. They did so perhaps to a greater extent than settlers on the steppes, importing song birds and animals they enjoyed hunting, as well as their livestock, crops, and trees, from their homelands. In seeking to understand the new environments, the Anglo settlers were guided by the science of natural history, which they also brought with them, and thus also thought about the new lands they had moved to in familiar ways. By the late nineteenth and early twentieth centuries, however, the scientists who advised the Anglo settlers had devised new ways of understanding the environments, which crossed the boundaries between scientific disciplines, such as botany, geology, and zoology, and had at their heart the interrelationship between the component parts of the environment. This was the new science of ecology.[1] Libby Robin has argued that ecology was a 'science of empire' and one of the 'sciences of "settling"' in new environmental conditions. Throughout much of the world of Anglo settlement, moreover, the new ways of understanding the environment were closely related to the 'difficulty of establishing European agriculture . . . within pre-existing non-European ecosystems' that differed from those familiar to the settlers back home. Robin also noted the emergence of ecology in the context of the development of agriculture on the North American grasslands.[2]

The story told in this book offers parallels the Anglo settlers in North America and Australasia. In the eighteenth century, Russians used natural history to understand the new world they found on the steppes. The Academy of Sciences expeditions of 1768–74, led mostly by German or German-trained naturalists, are the best examples of this. As the settlement and expansion of agriculture in the steppe region developed over the following decades, however, it became increasingly apparent that ideas and practices from elsewhere in Europe about how to understand the environment and farm the land were not appropriate. Specialists in Russia sought new approaches based in part on their own experience on the steppes. Like their Anglo counterparts, Russian specialists and scientists were also influenced by Alexander von Humboldt, who sought interconnections between different parts of the natural world on a global, not European, scale. To some extent, a start in understanding the steppe environment in new ways was made by men such as Ivan Palimpsestov in the mid-nineteenth century. Over the course of the second half of the nineteenth century, a new generation of university-trained scientists in Russia went further. They studied the specific conditions of the steppe region. In the process, they came to understand the interconnections between the component parts of the steppe environment, and the impact of human activity on it. These new ways of understanding the environment prompted new ways of working with it. Russian scientists and other specialists made significant innovations based on the specific conditions in the steppe (and adjoining forest-steppe) regions.

The most important was genetic soil science, devised by Vasilii Dokuchaev and his colleagues on the basis of studies of the black earth in the 1870s and 1880s. This provided a strong scientific rationale for the idea of working with, rather than against, or combating, the steppe environment in order to put arable farming on a more solid and sustainable basis. Dokuchaev's genetic soil science showed conclusively that the black earth, the chief natural resource for farmers in

---

[1] Thomas Dunlap, *Nature and the English Diaspora: Environment and History in the United States, Canada, Australia, and New Zealand* (Cambridge, 1999), 19–70, 139–63.

[2] Libby Robin, 'Ecology: A Science of Empire?', in Libby Robin and Tom Griffiths (eds), *Ecology and Empire: Environmental History of Settler Societies* (Edinburgh, 1997), 63–75. See also William Beinart and Lotte Hughes, *Environment and Empire* (Oxford, 2009), 203–8.

the steppe region, had formed as a result of the environment as a whole—the flora (steppe grasses) and fauna, climate, topography, and parent rock, over time. The Russian soil scientists had revealed the underlying paradox for farmers in such regions: the fertile soil that produced bumper harvests in years with sufficient rainfall had formed in conditions of a semi-arid and drought-prone grassland. To change these 'soil forming factors' by planting trees or providing artificial irrigation, however, would, over time, change the soil. The implication was that it was better to study how the steppe environment had evolved and, on the basis of this understanding, work *with* it. This was what Dokuchaev advocated in the aftermath of the drought and crop failure of 1891–2. In his expedition to the steppe region in the 1890s, his team of scientists studied what they believed to be samples of 'virgin' nature. They then sought to develop ways to use the land that would do less harm and emulate natural processes.[3]

Parallel to the development of new ways of understanding the steppe environment, during the nineteenth and early twentieth centuries some settlers and agronomists, supported by the authorities and advised by scientists, devised new methods of cultivating the land to make effective, and indeed sustainable, use of the natural resources. They sought to make the most of the fertile soils and hot summer temperatures, while accumulating and conserving in the soil the limited supplies of moisture that were so essential for crops. Thus, these methods aimed to work *with* the steppe environment, rather than combat or struggle against it. This agronomical approach to dealing with the vagaries of the steppe environment from the point of view of arable farming was an alternative to afforestation and artificial irrigation. By the end of the nineteenth century, in a marked change of approach, agronomy had partly replaced planting trees and providing water by artificial means in 'combating droughts' in the steppe region.

The changes were reflected in government policy. In 1900, Minister of Agriculture Aleksei Ermolov sent a long memorandum to the governor of Samara in reply to his latest request for assistance after the most recent drought and harvest failure in his province. The minister contrasted northern and southern Russia. In the north, the main issue was increasing the fertility of the soil by applying manure as fertilizer. In the south, however, the main issue was the climatic conditions and the need to ensure sufficient moisture for crops. Ermolov considered afforestation and irrigation as remedies. But he also considered the work of agricultural experiment stations in the steppe region and Dokuchaev's scientific expedition of the 1890s. Ermolov recommended to the governor that the best way to deal with the recurring droughts was to cultivate the land in ways that assisted in the accumulation and conservation of moisture.

---

[3] See David Moon, 'The Environmental History of the Russian Steppes: Vasilii Dokuchaev and the Harvest Failure of 1891', *Transactions of the Royal Historical Society*, 6th series, 15 (2005), 149–74; V. A. Vergunov, 'Vossozdanie istoricheskikh etapov razvitiya sel'skokhozyaistvennoi nauki Rossii', *VIET*, 1 (2010), 170–1.

The minister also advocated education to spread knowledge of such techniques among the population.[4]

Trees were still planted, however, but for more specific purposes: binding drifting sands; in shelterbelts to protect the land from the drying and eroding impact of the wind; and to reinforce the sides of ravines to arrest water erosion. Areas of sandy soils and ravines, moreover, were two of the locations in the steppe region where trees grew naturally. The hopes that had been expressed earlier in the nineteenth century, by men such as Palimpsestov, that large-scale tree planting could make the region's climate less extreme and wetter, had largely evaporated. Planting trees in such large numbers was not feasible. As forestry specialists and scientists came to understand, the conditions in parts of the region, in particular the alkaline subsoil, were not conducive to trees. Indeed, such conditions went some way to explaining the limited extent of woodland on the steppes.

The attention to artificial irrigation culminated in Zhilinskii's state-funded expedition to conduct trials in southern Russia and the Caucasus in 1880–1902. What Zhilinskii's expedition and pioneers of irrigation in the region showed, even if some were reluctant to admit it, was that supplying water artificially to arable fields on a large scale was impractical and very expensive. In the late 1890s, Finance Minister Sergei Witte put a stop to significant government investment in extensive irrigation of arable land in the steppe region. Smaller-scale irrigation, for example of low-lying meadows where water could be supplied by gravity, continued because it was more practical and much cheaper. The government sponsored larger-scale irrigation in the Caucasus and Central Asia, where it was used to grow more valuable crops.

From the 1890s, *zemstva* in the provinces and the Ministry of Agriculture in St Petersburg made funds available on credit to estate owners and peasant communities in the steppe region to support such work as planting trees to restrict erosion and irrigation. In other regions of Russia, they supported other types of work, for example draining marshes in areas where there was too much, rather than too little, water. The government described such work as 'melioration' of the land. A leading specialist defined 'melioration' as 'such improvements that are connected with changing the soil and water conditions in farms and that require . . . large capital outlays'. It covered such ambitious projects as Zhilinskii's irrigation expedition. Over time, however, funds were directed at smaller-scale work on the land of individual estate owners and peasant communities. There was a subtle change, moreover, in the meaning of 'melioration'. In temporary regulations issued in 1896, it was conceived as fundamental improvements in the soil, that is, changing the environment. In a new law of 1900, however, the concept was broadened to include improvements of an economic character—the way the

---

[4] GASO, f.3, op.233, d.1541, ll.47–63ob.

land was cultivated.[5] Thus, the change in the meaning of 'melioration' reflected the transition from combating to working with the environment.

The strategies to manage the steppe environment also reflected the evolving understandings of who or what was to blame for changes that were being observed in the environment. There was no doubt that the local population was responsible for the destruction of the small areas of woodland in the region. The inhabitants were also clearly responsible for ploughing up vast areas of virgin steppe, thus removing the native grassy vegetation. With the passage of time, scientists and others came to suspect that, as in other parts of the world such as Europe's overseas colonies, deforestation and the removal of native vegetation were having wider consequences. Many drew a direct link between deforestation and climate change. In particular, it was widely believed that the droughts that afflicted the steppe region were recurring more frequently, and that this was due to human action, or anthropogenic. Towards the end of the nineteenth century, however, based in part on observations of the steppe climate and the work of climatologists in Russia and elsewhere in the world, a new consensus emerged. Climate change was taking place. But it was taking the form of cyclical changes that could be predicted. And it was caused by factors outside human control, that is, it was autogenic. It was generally accepted that human activity could have an impact on local micro-climates, however, and deforestation was blamed for removing natural barriers to the easterly winds that dried out the soil.

When scientists and other contemporaries looked at changes in the land, they assigned blame to both autogenic and anthropogenic factors. Over the course of the nineteenth century, and in contrast to debates over climate change, there was a move towards attributing blame to human rather than natural factors. The causal connection between felling trees and removing the native vegetation, on the one hand, and the alarming spread of drifting sands on the other was fairly clear cut. Dust storms were caused by a combination of natural factors, in particular the wind, and human action, especially clearing woodland that had sheltered the land. Until the late nineteenth century, most scientists understood the formation and expansion of ravines as natural phenomena. By the end of the century, however, they attributed a greater role to human action. Aleksandr Izmail'skii and Dokuchaev, moreover, showed that the steppes were drying out under the influence of removing the native vegetation. There was less agreement on whether, and if so why, the soil was loosing its fertility. In the wake of the disaster of 1891–2, anxieties about desertification became widespread. As a result of the changes they observed in the steppe environment, scientists and the authorities developed ways to use the natural resources of the region in ways that would conserve, rather than harm them.

[5] Z. S. Katsenelenbaum, 'Zemel'nye melioratsii v Rossii', *SKhiL*, 233 (1910), 255–80; id., 'Meliorativnyi kredit v Rossii i ego blizhaishiya zadachi', *SKhiL*, 234 (1910), 479–505; K. Verner, 'Melioratsii', *PERSKh*, v, 616–18.

The recognition that people could and did damage the environment was as important as the awareness of the interconnectivity of the different parts of the steppe environment, in particular the formation of the soil, in the change in strategy from working against to working with the environment. Thus, as in settler and colonial societies elsewhere in the world, Russians became 'environmentally aware' as result of their encounter with a new environment, and a gradual recognition that their activities were harming it. Richard Grove traced this process in Europe's overseas colonies, especially on fragile 'tropical island edens' between the early seventeenth and mid-nineteenth centuries. He also traced the consequent development of ways of exploiting natural resources that aimed also to conserve them.[6] Thus, societies where settlers have encountered and adapted their ways of life to different environmental conditions have proved fertile ground for innovation in understanding and managing the relationship between the human and non-human worlds.

A key difference between the story told here and that of Grove and other specialists on Europe's overseas colonies was that the settlers on the steppes of the Russian Empire had not sailed long distances from their homelands to encounter completely different and remote worlds. The Russian and Ukrainian settlers, if not those from German lands, had travelled much shorter distances to encounter a different environment. The sense of otherness so apparent in most descriptions of the steppes from the time of Herodotus to the Academy of Sciences expeditions of 1768–74 and beyond, however, began to change. As late as 1865, the botanist L. Chernyaev (quoted in the Introduction to this book), described the steppes as a 'separate world'. Over time, however, with mutual adaptations, the authorities and inhabitants in the Russian Empire came to incorporate the steppe region into their political, social, and economic structures. They also came to incorporate it into their cultural understanding of their homeland.[7]

By the late nineteenth century, generations of settlers had been born in the steppe region. By this time, moreover, studying the steppe environment had come to play a large role in Russian science. Specialists seeking to draw on 'local knowledge', moreover, reported the views of 'old timers' among the settlers who could look back to how they remembered, or perhaps imagined, changes in their homeland—the steppes—over their lifetimes. Russians and other settlers from outside the region may have 'naturalized' the steppes, but they had a bifurcated image of them. They saw the steppes as either a source of anxiety and concern over environmental change, at worse expressing fears that the region was turning into a desert. Such images came to the fore in years of drought, such as 1833 and 1891. On the other hand, in good years, when the rains came they saw the

[6] See Richard Grove, *Green Imperialism: Colonial Expansion, Tropical Island Edens and the Origins of Environmentalism, 1600–1860* (Cambridge, 1995).

[7] See Christopher Ely, *This Meagre Nature: Landscape and National Identity in Imperial Russia* (DeKalb, IL, 2002).

steppes as an immensely fertile region that yielded bumper harvests for sale on the domestic and export markets. The American historian Willard Sunderland concluded that, by 1900

it was clear that the grasslands north of the Black and Caspian Seas belonged to the outsiders who had colonized them, reinvented them, and so naturalized their possession that it seemed hard to believe that the plains could ever have belonged to anyone else.[8]

The experience of the expansion of arable farming on the steppes of the European part of the Russian Empire, and addressing the periodic droughts and crop failures, proved useful in assisting the expansion of farming on the steppes further east. From the late nineteenth century, growing numbers of agricultural migrants moved east of the Ural river and Ural mountains to southern Siberia and today's northern Kazakhstan. The settlers found fertile soil, but climatic conditions more extreme than on the steppes further west. They also encountered an indigenous population comprising mostly nomadic pastoralists. In the early years, livestock husbandry was an important part of the settlers' economy. As they came to terms with the environmental conditions, however, arable farming developed on the eastern steppes, which became a major grain-growing region over the twentieth century.[9]

FROM THE STEPPES TO THE GREAT PLAINS

The history of agriculture and environment on the steppes of the Russian Empire had a parallel half way round the world, where settlers from wetter, forested lands were ploughing up and cultivating the fertile soil of a similar, treeless, semi-arid, flat environment: the Great Plains of North America. American farmers experienced similar environmental constraints to the development of agriculture on their grasslands as their counterparts on the steppes. Plains farmers also experienced periodic droughts and dust storms, which culminated in the 'Dust Bowl' of the 1930s.[10] By the late nineteenth century, some Russians came to realize that they could learn from the American experience on the prairies and Great Plains. Russians learned from the American network of agricultural

[8] Willard Sunderland, *Taming the Wild Field: Colonization and Empire on the Russian Steppe* (Ithaca, NY, 2004), 228.

[9] V. A. Ostaf'ev, 'Ocherk akmolinskoi oblasti', *SKhiL*, 172 (1893), 1st pagn, 249–64. See also Donald W. Treadgold, *The Great Siberian Migration: Government and Peasant in Resettlement from Emancipation to the First World War* (Princeton, NJ, 1957); George J. Demko, *The Russian Colonization of Kazakhstan, 1896–1916* (Bloomington, IN, 1969); Virginia Martin, *Law and Custom in the Steppe: The Kazakhs of the Middle Horde and Russian Colonialism in the Nineteenth Century* (Richmond, UK, 2001).

[10] For contrasting interpretations, see Geoff Cunfer, *On the Great Plains: Agriculture and Environment* (College Station, TX, 2005), 143–63; Donald Worster, *Dust Bowl: The Southern Plains in the 1930s*, 25th Anniversary edn (New York, 2004).

experiment stations and more advanced agricultural machinery. Some American manufacturers set up factories in the steppe region.[11]

An underlying theme in this book has been the development in Russia of scientific ways of understanding the steppe environment, and how Russian specialists developed ways of dealing with the environmental constraints on arable farming based on scientific studies of the environment. Thus, they accumulated a great deal of experience of farming and forestry in the conditions of the steppe region. These ways of understanding and exploiting the resources of the steppes entailed a partial rejection of scientific theories and practices of agriculture and forestry from elsewhere in Europe. Thus, Dokuchaev and his colleagues devised genetic soil science. Farmers, agronomists, and forestry specialists came up with ways of planting trees that suited the steppe environment and specific purposes for doing so, such as shelterbelts. Steppe farmers and agronomists identified varieties of crops that grew best in the region, and techniques of cultivating the land that assisted in accumulating and conserving the scarce moisture. A key role in practical developments was played by Mennonite farmers.

Over time, American farmers, the scientists who advised them, and the authorities they elected came to realize that they could learn from the Russian experience on the steppes. The transfer of science, expertise, and experience, therefore, was not just one way. The Russian experience on the steppes only gradually attracted interest in the USA. Russian genetic soil science was slow to come to the attention of American soil scientists, who persisted with older ways of understanding soils. In 1928, however, Curtis F. Marbut, the new chief soil scientist of the US Department of Agriculture's Bureau of Soils, lectured to the Department's Graduate School. He explained how soils were formed as a result of several forces, including natural vegetation, temperature, rainfall, geological formations, and topography. Marbut continued:

That is fundamentally the character of the work done in Russia in the late 70s and 80s of the nineteenth century, and on the basis of which the science of pedology [soil science] as it is now understood was built.

In the following lecture, he explained how it was in studying the black earth of the grasslands that the Russians had worked out 'the relation of soil character to the character of the physical environment in which the soil developed'. He went on to analyse the soils of the American prairies and Great Plains, and used the Russian term '*chernozem*' (black earth).[12] The previous year, at the First International Congress of Soil Science in Washington, DC, Marbut praised the work

---

[11] See Ol'ga Elina, *Ot tsarskikh sadov do sovetskikh polei: istoriya sel'sko-khozyaistvennykh opytnykh uchrezhdenii XVIII-20-e gody XX v.*, 2 vols (Moscow, 2008), ii, 65–71; Norman E. Saul, *Concord and Conflict: The United States and Russia, 1867–1914* (Lawrence, KS, 1996), 148–51, 275–9, 410–1.

[12] C. F. Marbut, *Soils: Their Genesis and Classification* (n.p., 1951), 17–18, 25, 128–30. See also C. F. Marbut, 'Soils of the Great Plains', *Annals of the Association of American Geographers*, 13/2 (1923), 41–66.

of the 'Russian delegation', which included Dokuchaev's former student Konstantin Glinka.[13] Marbut was instrumental in Russian terms such as *chernozem* being adopted as the standard international terms for soil classification. They were used on US government soil maps produced under Marbut's direction.[14] At around the same as Dokuchaev was devising his theory of soil formation, however, in a similar continental-sized laboratory—North America—Eugene W. Hilgard independently came up with a similar theory. Hans Jenny, an American soil scientist, argued strongly that Hilgard should share credit with Dokuchaev for genetic soil science. Nevertheless, it was Russian soil science that Marbut drew on.[15]

In his memoir published in 1947, the prominent American forester and conservationist Gifford Pinchot recalled his train trip across Russia in 1902. He described how, after travelling for several days from Moscow 'unwashed in a second-class railroad carriage', they found themselves in a 'wonderfully fertile agricultural country', and the next day 'in a region of rich black soil like our own prairies'. He noted that the 'Russians had . . . begun the planting of shelter belts [of trees] . . . , whereby they beat us by some forty years'.[16] The chapter was based on more detailed, unpublished notes Pinchot made at the time of his visit. His itinerary included a 'tree planting preserve' called 'Stone Steppe' (*Kamennaya step'*). (This was one of the research stations of Dokuchaev's expedition to the steppes in the 1890s.) Pinchot described the methods Russian foresters used to plant 'shelterbelts' on the steppe. He noted:

The purpose of all this plantation is double, to supply timber, and to afford protection to agricultural crops. Careful measurements are in progress, of strips ten feet wide parallel to the plantations, to ascertain the effect of protection from wind. There are no final results as yet, but the indications are strong that the crops vary in quality with their nearness to the shelter belt.

He had reservations about the costs of the Russian techniques, but noted that one—planting trees and shrubs in a ratio of two shrubs for every tree—'has great

---

[13] Marbut translated the German edition of Glinka's book that built on Dokuchaev's work. K. Glinka, *The Great Soil Groups of the World and their Development*, trans. C. F. Marbut (Ann Arbor, MI, 1927).

[14] C. F. Marbut, 'Fifth Commission. Classification, Nomenclature, and Mapping of Soils', and id., 'Sub-Commission II. Classification, Nomenclature, and Mapping of Soils in the United States', *First International Congress of Soil Science: A Summary of the Scientific Proceedings. Soil Science*, 25/1 (1928), 51–70; *Atlas of American Agriculture* (Washington, DC, 1936). See also Douglas Helms, 'Early Leaders of the Soil Survey', in Douglas Helms, Anne B. W. Effland, and Patricia J. Durana (eds), *Profiles in the History of the U.S. Soil Survey* (Ames, IO, 2002), 19–64; I. A. Krupenikov, *Istoriya pochvovedeniya ot vremeni ego zarozhdeniya do nashikh dnei* (Moscow, 1981), 169, 172, 211, 224–41, 286.

[15] Hans Jenny, *E. W. Hilgard and the Birth of Modern Soil Science* (Pisa, 1961). Russian scientists disagree. See Krupenikov, *Istoriya*, 172, 181, 270–1.

[16] Gifford Pinchot, *Breaking New Ground* ([1947] Washington, DC, 1998), xiii, 213–16.

advantages for planting in the Western United States . . . I believe it will have important use at home'.[17]

The reason Pinchot singled out 'shelterbelts' in his memoir was that in 1934 President Franklin D. Roosevelt had launched an ambitious plan to plant shelterbelts on the Great Plains in a band from Texas to the Canadian border as part of the measures to deal with the 'Dust Bowl' of the 1930s. One of the strongest advocates of the plan was a protégé of Pinchot named Raphael Zon.[18] Zon was born in Simbirsk on the mid-Volga on the edge of the steppe region. He migrated to the USA, where he trained as a forester, and worked for the US Forest Service. In helping plan Roosevelt's shelterbelt project, he drew on Russian experience of steppe forestry.[19]

By the 1930s, varieties of wheat that had been imported from the steppes were of enormous importance on the Great Plains. In the central and southern plains, the variety of hard, red, winter wheat, known as 'Turkey Red', was planted on over two-thirds of the land sown with wheat. On the northern plains, hard, durum wheat was sown on around a quarter of the land under wheat. The import of these varieties from the steppes had been had been organized by the US Department of Agriculture around the turn of the twentieth century. In large part, it was due to cereal scientist Mark Alfred Carleton, who made two trips to the steppes. The value of varieties of wheat from the steppes had first come to his attention when he came across them in the fields of Mennonite migrants from the steppes in Kansas in the 1890s. The Mennonites' wheat, which they had imported from their previous homes in Tauride province, had proved to be drought and disease resistant on the American grasslands. At home, they had called their variety '*Krymka*'. The durum wheats were similar to *arnautka*, which was a staple of steppe farming.[20]

---

[17] Library of Congress, Washington, DC, Manuscript Division, Gifford Pinchot Papers, Box 715, File: 'Notes taken by Mr Pinchot on his trip through Russia and Siberia. Prepared by Mr Pinchot 1902', ff.49–61. See also above, p. 192.

[18] See W. H. Droze, *Trees, Prairies, and People: Tree Planting in the Plains States* (Denton, TX, 1977); Edgar B. Nixon (ed.), *Franklin D. Roosevelt and Conservation, 1911–1945*, 2 vols (Hyde Park, NY, 1957), i, 200–3. See also Pinchot Papers, Box 587, File 'Program proposal to Franklin D. Roosevelt', Zon to Pinchot, 2 December 1932, Pinchot to Zon, 5 December 1932, Box 330, General Correspondence, File: 'Zon, Raphael, 1934', Zon to Pinchot, 26 September 1934, Copy of letter from Zon to F. A. Silcox, 25 September 1934, Pinchot to Zon, 3 October 1934.

[19] See P. O. Rudolf and S. R. Gevorkiantz, 'Shelterbelt Experience in Other Lands', in *Possibilities of Shelterbelt Planting in the Plains Region* (Washington, DC, 1935), 59–76. Most of the chapter was on Russian experience. Zon was the director of the forest experiment station in St Paul, Minnesota, that produced the volume. Roosevelt wrote to F. A. Silcox, the Chief of the US Forest Service, to thank him for the volume. Silcox sent a copy of the letter to Zon. Minnesota Historical Society, St Paul, P1237, Raphael Zon papers, Box 9, Folder 5, Roosevelt to Silcox, 13 February 1936; Silcox to Zon, 19 February. 1936. On Zon, see Jeremy Cameron Young, 'Warrior of Science: Raphael Zon and the Origins of Forest Experiment Stations', *Forest History Today*, 16/1–2 (2010), 4–12.

[20] See David Moon, 'In the Russians' Steppes: The Introduction of Russian Wheat on the Great Plains of the United States of America', *Journal of Global History*, 3 (2008), 203–25; Thomas

Around the same time as Carleton realized the value of the wheat varieties the Mennonites had imported from the steppes, Russian specialists were noticing other parallels between the two regions. Nikolai Tulaikov, who travelled to the USA to observe developments there, paid a lot of attention to a system of 'dry farming', which had been developed in South Dakota by Hardy Webster Campbell in the 1890s. Its features were summarized in an article written by a Russian agronomist, V. Benzin, which was published in a Russian journal in 1913. Among the features of Campbell's system he singled out were: black fallow; deep ploughing; and regular cultivation of fields to assist in retaining moisture. Some Russian specialists commented on the similarities between American and Russian dry farming. A. N. Chelintsev suggested the two systems may have developed independently.[21] In the USA, Carleton noted that the 'methods of culture' the Mennonites had brought with them from the steppes in the 1870s included black fallow, deep ploughing, their crop rotations as well as, his main interest, their wheat.[22] Thus, dry farming on the Great Plains may also owe its origins to the steppes. The value of Russian experience on the steppes across the Atlantic, however, has diminished over time. In the aftermath of the 'Dust Bowl', farmers on the American grasslands tapped water for irrigation from the vast Ogallala aquifer that lies under much of the Great Plains. Since the 1960s, centre-pivot irrigation, using up water from the aquifer, has transformed the landscape and ecology of plains farming.[23]

THE STEPPES IN THE SOVIET AND POST-SOVIET PERIODS

While aspects of the Russian experience on the steppes in the main period covered by this book experienced a curious afterlife on the Great Plains of North America, arable farming in the steppe region—which does not have an aquifer underneath it—had very mixed experiences in the twentieth and early twenty first centuries. Agriculture in the steppe region was badly hit by the First World War. The Ottoman and German Empires blockaded Russia's ports on the Black and Baltic seas and almost ended its export trade in grain. The mass conscription of men and horses from rural areas during the war dealt further

D. Isern, 'Wheat Explorer the World Over: Mark Carleton of Kansas', *Kansas History*, 23/1–2 (2000), 12–25.

[21] V. Benzin, 'Sukhoe zemledelie', *SKhiL*, 241 (1913), 492–504; (1913), 691–708; 242 (1913), 3–19; (1913), 137–61; A. N. Chelintsev, 'Obzor russkoi literatury po sel'skomu khozyaistvu', *SKhiL*, 229 (1909), 622; N. Tulaikov, '"Sukhoe" zemledelie (sistema Kembellia)', *PERSKh*, xii (1912), 1262–7.

[22] Mark Alfred Carleton, 'Successful Wheat Growing in Semiarid Districts', *Yearbook of the United States Department of Agriculture 1900*, 538–42. See also J. S. Otto, 'From the Russian Steppes to the North Dakota Prairies: The Agricultural Practices of a Russian-German Family', *Journal of the American Historical Society of Germans from Russia*, 7/1 (1984), 37–44.

[23] See Cunfer, *On the Great Plains*, 164–200.

blows to agricultural production. The dislocation of the economy caused by the war upset trade between the agricultural and industrial sectors of the economy. As a consequence, the area of land sown with grain, and thus the size of harvests, fell in the steppe region. In contrast, the Great Plains experienced a boom as its farmers brought more land into cultivation and took over Russia's export markets.[24] On the steppes, the area of land under cultivation continued to decline as a result of the mounting chaos of the revolutions of 1917 and Civil War of 1918–21. When combined with drought in the Volga region in 1921, the result was a catastrophic famine on a scale that dwarfed those of the tsarist period.[25] Another consequence of the chaos was a second wave of emigration by Mennonites from southern Ukraine. Around 25,000 left the Soviet Union in the 1920s. Most went to Canada or South America.[26]

The sown area in the steppes did not return to pre-war levels until the end of the 1920s. At this point, the Soviet government launched the collectivization of agriculture. It set high targets for bringing virgin steppe into cultivation in the Five-Year Plans that started in 1928. The planned targets were not fully achieved. But large, new state and collective grain farms were established on former pasture land in the south and south-east of the steppe region. For example, the large, mechanized state farm 'Gigant' (Giant) was founded on virgin black earth in the Sal'sk district south-east of Rostov-on-Don in 1928. The American soil scientist Marbut visited in 1930. He reported that it covered 427,000 acres, of which 280,000 were sown with grain in 1930.[27] Marbut saw what the Soviet authorities wanted him to see. Forced collectivization of agriculture provoked what amounted to civil war between the Soviet regime and much of the rural population. The conflict was greatest in the most fertile regions, the steppes, where the drive for collectivization was most intense.[28]

The return of drought in 1931 and 1932, combined with the chaos unleashed by collectivization, led to poor harvests and shortages of food. The Soviet authorities prioritized access to scarce food to cities and workers over rural areas and peasants. The result was a famine on a horrific scale, greater even than that of 1921–2. Worst hit was Ukraine, where the famine is known as the

---

[24] See Peter Gatrell, *Russia's First World War: A Social and Economic History* (Harlow, 2005), 154–75; Norman E. Saul, *War and Revolution: the United States and Russia, 1914–1921* (Lawrence, KS, 2001), 19.

[25] See M. Wehner, 'Golod 1921–1922 gg. v Samarskoi gubernii i reaktsii sovetskogo pravitel'stva', *Cahiers du Monde Russe*, 38 (1997), 223–42; Bertrand M. Patenaude, *The Big Show in Bololand: The American Relief Expedition to Soviet Russia in the Famine of 1921* (Stanford, CA, 2002).

[26] 'Migrations', in Bert Friesen (ed), *Global Anabaptist Mennonite Encyclopedia Online* (1989), <http://www.gameo.org/encyclopedia/contents/M542ME.html> (accessed 6 May 2012).

[27] C. F. Marbut, 'Russia and the United States in the World's Wheat Market', *Geographical Review*, 21/1 (1931), 15, 20.

[28] See R. W. Davies, *The Socialist Offensive: The Collectivisation of Soviet Agriculture, 1929–1930* (London, 1980); *The War Against the Peasantry, 1927–1930. The Tragedy of the Soviet Countryside*, ed. Lynne Viola, V. P. Danilov, N. A. Ivnitskii, and Denis Kozlov (New Haven, CT, 2005).

'*Holodomor*' (the 'hunger killing'), but famine was not confined to Ukraine: the North Caucasus was badly hit. Kazakhstan suffered a catastrophic famine as a result of Soviet policies of denomadization and grain requisitions. Historians disagree sharply on the relative importance of the size of the harvest and the actions of the Soviet authorities in causing the famine, and whether or not they were deliberate or directed specifically at Ukraine. Nor do they agree on the numbers of dead, but estimates vary between 5 and 8 or more million.[29]

Agriculture in the steppe region slowly recovered after the disaster, only for the region to become one of the major theatres of military action in the Second World War on the eastern front. In 1941–2, the invading armies of Nazi Germany and its allies drove right through Ukraine and the Don region, before separating into two spearheads. One pushed deep into North Caucasus, reaching the mountains (including the territory of the Teberdinskii *zapovednik* I visited in June 2003). The other spearhead reached the Volga at Stalingrad (formerly Tsaritsyn, today's Volgograd). The treeless, flat steppes proved ideal terrain for tank warfare. A few months after the Soviet victory at Stalingrad in the winter of 1942–3, the largest tank battle in history was fought on the steppe near Kursk.[30] The eventual expulsion of the invading armies by 1945 left the steppe region devastated.

A further consequence was the final dispersal of the Mennonite and German colonists from the steppe region. In August 1941, in advance of the German invasion, the Soviet authorities deported around one million ethnic Germans (including Mennonites) from the Volga region, Ukraine, and the North Caucasus to Central Asia and Siberia. The invading Wehrmacht found around 35,000 Mennonites still in southern Ukraine. The German authorities sent them back whence they had come, a century and a half earlier, to the Vistula region (which had been annexed to the Reich from Poland). At the end of the war, two-thirds of the relocated Mennonites were forcibly returned to Soviet territory, while the remainder managed to join their co-religionists in North and South America.[31] Thus, the descendants of the Mennonite and German colonists

---

[29] For contrasting interpretations, see Robert Conquest, *The Harvest of Sorrow: Soviet Collectivization and the Terror-Famine* (London, 1986); Mark B. Tauger, 'Natural Disaster and Human Actions in the Soviet Famine of 1931–1933', *The Carl Beck Papers in Russian and East European Studies*, 1506 (2001); R. W. Davies and Stephen G. Wheatcroft, *The Years of Hunger: Soviet Agriculture, 1931–1933* (Basingstoke, 2004). On Kazakhstan, see Sarah Cameron, 'The Hungry Steppe: Soviet Kazakhstan and the Kazakh Famine, 1921–1934', Ph.D. dissertation, Yale University, 2010.

[30] See Evan Mawdsley, *Thunder in the East: The Nazi-Soviet War, 1941–1945* (London, 2007).

[31] See J. Otto Pohl, *Ethnic Cleansing in the USSR, 1937–49* (Westport, CT, 1999), 27–60; 'Migrations', *Global Anabaptist Mennonite Encyclopedia*. Many of the Mennonites remaining in the Soviet Union left for West Germany or North America in the 1970s–80s. Many people of Volga German descent left for Germany or elsewhere in the 1980s and 1990s. See Philip Jones, 'Recent Ethnic German Migration from Eastern Europe to the Federal Republic', *Geography*, 75/3 (1990), 249–52; Andrew Brown, 'The Germans of Germany and the Germans of Kazakhstan: A Eurasian Volk in the Twilight of Diaspora', *Europe-Asia Studies*, 57 (2005), 625–34.

no longer live in the steppe region. My first encounter with the descendants of the Mennonite farmers who played such a large part in this book took place in Goesell, Kansas, in the spring of 2007.[32]

The devastation of the steppe region and its population by the Second World War was exacerbated by the return of drought in 1946, which led to harvest failure. In a tragic repetition of 1932–3, the Soviet authorities turned crop failure into the famine of 1946–7.[33] In the 1930s, however, the Soviet government had made plans for a renewed 'struggle with droughts'. The plans included large-scale afforestation and planting shelterbelts on the steppes. Implementation of the plans was interrupted by the war. In 1948, in the aftermath of the latest drought, crop failure, and famine, The 'Great Stalin Plan for the Transformation of Nature' was announced. It envisaged planting nearly 6 million hectares of trees with the goal of changing the climate of the forest-steppe and steppe regions. The trees were to be planted in shelterbelts along rivers and roads and around collective farms. The aim was to shelter the land from the drying impact of the winds from Central Asia. The ultimate aim was to end the recurring droughts. Some historians, for example Douglas Weiner, have seen the plan as evidence of the Stalinist regime treating 'nature' as 'counter-revolutionary', and trying to make it conform the designs of the Communist Party. '[A]narchic first nature' was to be replaced by '"planned" second nature'. The guiding force behind the Plan, for Weiner, was the pseudo-scientist Trofim Lysenko.[34]

Stephen Brain has argued that the plan was a more complex attempt to 'restore the Russian countryside to an idealized but more diverse earlier state'. The plan had its antecedents in the work of Dokuchaev, and more specifically the plan he drew up in 1892, and researched in his expedition to the steppes, in the wake of the drought, and harvest failure, and famine of 1891–2. The Soviet authorities made the link between the Stalin Plan and Dokuchaev's work explicit. Indeed, it was prepared at the Agricultural Research Institute at Kamennaya Steppe, which had been one of Dokuchaev's field research stations in the 1890s.[35] However, the Stalin Plan emphasized only one side of Dokuchaev's work. In the words of a Soviet biographer of Dokuchaev in 1950 (i.e. at the time of the Stalin Plan), Dokuchaev 'studied the soil so that it could be subjugated to man, in order to give reliable methods to take it into the possession of its native people.'[36] As we

---

[32] On their Mennonite Heritage and Agricultural Museum, see <http://skyways.lib.ks.us/ museums/goessel/index.html> (accessed 7 June 2012).

[33] See V. F. Zima, *Golod v SSSR 1946–1947 godov: proiskhozhdenie i posledstviya* (Moscow, 1994); Nicholas Ganson, *The Soviet Famine of 1946–47 in Global and Historical Perspective* (New York, 2009).

[34] Douglas R. Weiner, *A Little Corner of Freedom: Russian Nature Protection from Stalin to Gorbachev* (Berkeley, CA, 1999), 88–93.

[35] Stephen Brain, 'The Great Stalin Plan for the Transformation of Nature', *Environmental History* 15 (2010), 670–700, quotation 673.

[36] I. Krupenikov and L. Krupenikov, *Vasilii Vasil'evich Dokuchaev* (Moscow, 1950), 3 (see also 183–9).

have seen in this book, Dokuchaev's approach was more ecological. He aimed to learn from how nature worked. In practice, Lysenko's influence prevailed in implementing the Stalin Plan. The techniques he recommended for planting trees failed. Other scientists, such as Vladimir Sukhachev, tried to intervene to retrieve the situation, but with limited success. Brain concluded that the Plan did not meet its aims. Only half the trees were planted, and more than half of these had died by 1954. Some of the shelterbelts did grow, but the plan itself died with Stalin in 1953.[37]

Russian steppe ecologists, however, contrast the Stalin Plan with what happened next, Nikita Khrushchev's 'Virgin Lands' campaign of 1954. It called for the ploughing up of 'virgin or idle [i.e. long-fallow] land' on the steppes in the south and south-east of European Russia, southern Siberia, but mainly in northern Kazakhstan. These were regions where the rainfall was lower than further west and the conditions were marginal for arable farming. The initial target was to plough up 13 million hectares, but by 1960, this had been increased to 33 million. There was investment in machinery and seed, and agronomists developed techniques appropriate to the environment. The 'virgin lands' yielded bumper harvests in 1956 and 1958, when there was sufficient rain. Success was short lived: there was not sufficient equipment; the agronomists recommendations were disregarded; and, in spite of the lessons of the previous century, the migrants cultivated the soil in ways that were more appropriate to the regions with more rainfall they came from. In dry years, such as 1957 and 1963, there were poor harvests, accompanied by soil erosion and dust storms. Vast areas were ruined. The outcome resembled the 'Dust Bowl' on the southern plains of the USA in the 1930s.[38]

Khrushchev's fall in 1964 led to a change in agricultural policy. Extensification of cultivation in the steppe region was replaced by intensification on existing agricultural land. The Soviet government invested money in mechanization and chemical fertilizers. Crop rotations and use of fallow, which had been dispensed with on the Virgin lands, were reintroduced. New techniques of cultivation were introduced in the steppe region, based on experience on the Canadian prairies, which shared similar environmental conditions. Deep ploughing was replaced by ploughing without turning over the soil (by using ploughs without mouldboards). This allowed the soil to retain its structure and left stubble in the fields. The risk of erosion was reduced and the retention of snow, to provide melt water in the spring, improved. From the late 1960s, moreover, there was investment in planting trees, in particular shelterbelts, and irrigation. Artificial irrigation was set up in southern Ukraine and the valleys of the rivers Don and Kuban, as well as

[37] Brain, 'Great Stalin Plan'. See also S. V. Zonn and A. N. Eroshkina, 'Ucheniki i posledovateli V. V. Dokuchaeva', *Pochvovedenie*, 2 (1996), 124–38.

[38] See Martin McCauley, *Khrushchev and the Development of Soviet Agriculture: The Virgin Land Programme, 1953–1964* (London, 1976); A. A. Chibilev and S. V. Levykin, 'Tselina, razdelennaya okeanom (aktual'nye zametki o sud'be stepei severnogo polushariya)', *Stepnoi Byulleten'*, 1 (1998), <http://savesteppe.org/ru/archives/5591> (accessed 9 September 2011).

in Central Asia. Nevertheless, droughts continued to afflict the steppe region. Two of the worst, which hit grain production, occurred in 1972 and 1975. Some contemporaries, possibly exaggerating, compared these droughts with those of 1891 and 1921.[39] In the aftermath of the collapse of the Soviet Union in 1991, there was a decline in the sown area in the steppe region. In the early twenty-first century, however, land that had been left fallow was once again ploughed up, and the long-term trend of expansion of cultivation of the grasslands continued.[40]

During the twentieth and early twentieth-first centuries, there was a massive expansion in the proportion of land that was ploughed up in the steppe region east of the Urals. On the other hand, west of the Urals, the area under cultivation grew less dramatically from approximately 50 per cent at the turn of the twentieth century. In 2004, two scientists calculated the current proportion of arable land in the Eurasian steppe—from Moldova to eastern Siberia—to be 57 per cent. In the European part of the steppe region the proportion was higher: 60 per cent or more in Ukraine, the North Caucasus, and the Urals. In the central black-earth region—in the forest-steppe—a colossal 83 per cent of the land had been converted to arable. The proportions of land with black earth, the most fertile land, that had been ploughed up were even higher.[41] To put these figures in perspective, on the Great Plains of the USA, the proportion of the total area converted to arable land has never exceeded 31 per cent. It reached this level in 1935 after a steady increase from 1880. For the rest of the twentieth century, the proportion varied between 25 and 29 per cent. O the eastern plains the proportion was higher. In central Kansas, for example, it exceeded 50 per cent in 1920, but was 45 per cent in 1997. The main determinants of the proportion of land under crop cultivation on the Great Plains have been the availability water, either from precipitation or irrigation, temperature, and soil quality.[42] On the steppes, in spite of the slightly less favourable climatic conditions for arable farming, the proportion of land ploughed up has, thus, been much higher. This has been due, in part, to the lack of alternative land.

CONSERVATION, INDIGENOUS KNOWLEDGE, AND NATURE'S AGENCY?

The loss of virgin steppe started to attract serious attention in the mid-nineteenth century, at the time of the big plough-up to grow grain for export. In 1859, a native of Kherson province wrote:

[39] Nikolai M. Dronin and Edward G. Bellinger, *Climate Dependence and Food Problems in Russia, 1900–1990* (Budapest, 2005), 223–5, 245–52.
[40] A. Chibilev and S. Levykin, 'Virgin Lands divided by an Ocean: The Fate of Grasslands in the Northern Hemisphere', trans. David Moon, *Nova Acta Leopoldina, Neue Folge* (forthcoming).
[41] A. A. Chibilev and O. A. Grosheva, *Ocherki po istorii stepevedeniya* (Ekaterinburg 2004), 34–5.
[42] Cunfer, *On the Great Plains*, 5–6, 16–36, 200, 236.

I was born in the New Russian region; I saw with my own eyes the growth of towns and villages; before my very eyes the face of the steppes has started to change: there where once over vast expanses there was grey feather grass, [now] fields of grain have started expand . . . The pristine beauty of the steppes, the dense grassy vegetation that clothed it, has disappeared.

His words were quoted in 1901 by Ya. Neruchev, who opened his article 'What is Left of the Former Steppes' with:

Our steppes, both the sense of a landscape and in the agricultural sense are changing more and more; and recently so quickly that future generations will be able to form an impression of them only from tales; and only a few remnants will be around to help reconstruct a picture of their former state.[43]

Concerns about human impact on the steppe environment engaged a wider public. In his semi-fictionalized family chronicle written in the 1840s and 1850s, Sergei Aksakov looked back almost a century to the time when his grandfather had established a new estate in the forest-steppe near Buguruslan, in Orenburg province:

How wonderful in those days was that region, in its wild and virginal richness! It is different now; it is not even what it was when I first knew it, when it was still fresh and blooming and undeflowered by hordes of settlers. . . .

He related how in the early years crop yields on the black earth had been 'fabulous'. His imagined descriptions of the environment in his grandfather's time and recollections from his childhood at the start of the nineteenth century emphasized an abundance of trees, water, birds, and fish (he was keen hunter and fisherman).[44] Images of the despoliation of nature in the forest-steppe and steppe regions recurred in literature and art in the late nineteenth century, for example in plays by Anton Chekhov and paintings by Ilya Repin.[45] As the grasslands succumbed to the plough and the small areas of woodland to the axe, and as the climate seemed to be changing and soil erosion increasing, there was a growing awareness in nineteenth-century Russia that human action could have an impact, at times quite considerable, on the environment. The destruction of the fragile steppe environment brought this home to Russians as starkly as the devastation of the 'tropical island edens' had to European colonizers over the preceding period.

By the late nineteenth century, Russian scientists had developed an understanding of the steppe as a distinct landscape, defined by its vegetation, climate, landscape, and soil. Thus, the destruction of the steppes meant the loss of

[43] Ya. Neruchev, 'Byvshie "stepi" i—shto ot nikh ostaetsya', *SKhiL*, 200 (1901), 597.
[44] Sergei Aksakov, *A Russian Gentleman*, trans. J. D. Duff (Oxford, 1982), 9–11; Sergei Aksakov, *Years of Childhood* (Oxford, 1983), 205–9; Aksakov, *A Russian Schoolboy* (Oxford, 1983), 53–5. Buguruslan district became part of Samara province in 1851.
[45] See above, pp. 170, 110–11.

something valued by science, as well as of immense importance in a country where agriculture was the largest part of the economy. This was recognized in particular by Dokuchaev, who also realized the importance of preserving samples of 'virgin steppe' as a scientific and economic resource. In 1892, at the start of his expedition to the steppes, he set up three field research stations on locations selected to include typical features of steppe environment and various types of land use, including forestry plantations. Above all he selected locations with what he believed to be virgin, or unploughed, land. These were sites of detailed scientific research to understand the natural processes that took place in the 'virgin steppe' so that systems of farming the land that best emulated them could be developed. The samples of virgin steppe were to serve as baselines, or controls, for experiments into ways of overcoming the environmental constraints on arable farming in the region. Dokuchaev designated the areas of 'virgin steppe' as protected from all human disturbance besides scientific research.[46] At least one still existed at the end of the twentieth century.[47]

These Dokuchaevian principles of inviolable management were the basis for a network of scientific nature reserves (*zapovedniki*), where 'models of nature' (*etalony prirody*) were preserved for scientific research. They were set up throughout the major environmental regions of Russia and the Soviet Union over the twentieth century. The Soviet authorities conducted periodic 'offensives' against the nature reserves, the scientists who worked in them, and the principles of nature protection they stood for. Nevertheless, the network of nature reserves survived the Soviet regime and the economic crises that accompanied its passing.[48] Nature reserves in the steppe and forest-steppe regions, however, have been few and small. This reflected the extent to which the fertile land of the steppes had been ploughed by the turn of the twentieth century. In the early twenty-first century, *zapovedniki* in the steppe region comprised only 0.4 per cent of the total area of such protected land in the Russian Federation. Most steppe *zapovedniki*, moreover, were in Ukraine, for example Askaniya Nova, and Kazakhstan. Russian scientists campaigned to establish *zapovedniki* on small areas of unploughed steppe that still existed in Russia. In 1989, the Orenburg *zapovednik* was set up in sections covering 21,700 hectares.[49] In 1996, a smaller *zapovednik*, less than half the size, was set up on land that had been used for grazing and meadows in south-east Rostov region.[50] This was the reserve I visited in 2003.

[46] Moon, 'Environmental History of the Russian Steppes', 168–9.
[47] V. E. Boreiko, 'Starobel'skii stepnoi zapovednyi uchastok, vydelennyi V. V. Dokuchaevym,–sushchestvyet!', *Stepnoi Byulleten'*, 2 (1998), <http://savesteppe.org/ru/archives/5504> (accessed 9 September 2011).
[48] F. Shtilmark, *The History of Russian Zapovedniks, 1895–1995*, trans. G. H. Harper (Edinburgh, 2003), 10–13. See also D. R. Weiner, *Models of Nature: Ecology, Conservation and Cultural Revolution in Soviet Russia*, 2nd edn (Pittsburgh, PA, 2000); Weiner, *A Little Corner*.
[49] Chibilev and Grosheva, *Ocherki*, 107–19.
[50] V. A. Minoranskii and O. N. Demina, 'Priroda gosudarstvennogo stepnogo zapovednika "Rostovskii"', *Stepnoi Byuleten'*, 1 (1998), <http://savesteppe.org/ru/archives/5591> (accessed

The scientific importance of protecting areas of unploughed steppe is immense. Ploughing up 'virgin' grassland, which has evolved over several thousand years, removing the native vegetation of plant communities, and replacing them with cultivated crops is, in the words of leading steppe ecologist Aleksandr Chibilev, the 'unjustifiable annihilation of the steppe landscape, the destruction of flora and flora'.[51] Ploughing also destroys the structure of the soil. Scientists on the Great Plains concur. Cunfer described ploughing the grassland quite simply as 'ecological genocide'.[52] These were lessons that farmers and scientists gradually learned from practical experience during the nineteenth century. Experiments on *zapovedniki* have replicated the conclusions that Izmail'skii reached in the 1880s and 1890s that ploughing land and removing the native vegetation caused the land to dry out (see above, pp. 152–7). The water regime in virgin land is in balance: the amount of water coming in is equal to the amount going out.[53] Chibilev summed it up with the title of one of his books: *Nature Knows Best.*[54] From this perspective, therefore, the plow did break the steppe.

The protection of small areas of steppe, however, raises the question of what is being preserved. It became clear to scientists by the mid-twentieth century that the steppe environment had been shaped partly by the nomadic pastoralists who for millennia had lived there, burned the steppe, and kept their herds on it (see the Introduction to this book). The indigenous population had not only helped fashion the environment, but had also learned to live in it. They grazed their livestock on the luxuriant grasses that grew on the fertile soil. Crucially, they moved their livestock between pastures with the seasons, using pastures that were best at particular times of year, and leaving them to recover while they were away.[55] The farmers who migrated to the region and displaced the nomads, in marked contrast, settled in one place and did not move around with the seasons. Thus, they were more prone to the effects of droughts as they could not drive their crops off to land with more water if the rains failed. Moreover, the farmers removed not only most of the previous population and their herds, but also much of the native vegetation: the wild grasses and small areas of woodland. This seemed to exacerbate the vagaries of the steppe environment, such as soil erosion, the impact of the hot winds that dried out the land, and possibly even the climate.

The indigenous nomadic peoples have been largely absent from this book, since the authors of the sources on which it is based largely excluded them. When

---

9 September 2011); V. A. Minoranskii and A. V. Chekin, *Gosudarstvennyi stepnoi zapovednik 'Rostovskii'* (Rostov-on-Don, 2003).

[51] A. A. Chibilev, *Priroda znaet luchshe* (Ekaterinburg, 1999), 173.

[52] Cunfer, *On the Great Plains*, 16.

[53] *Biosfernyi zapovedni 'Askaniya-Nova' imeni F. E. Fal'tz-Feina UAAN: Tipchako-kovyl'naya step'* (Kherson, 2007), [4].

[54] Chibilev, *Priroda znaet luchshe*.

[55] See A. M. Khazanov, *Nomads and the Outside World*, trans. Julia Crookenden (Cambridge, 1984). See also Shepard Krech III, *The Ecological Indian: Myth and History* (New York, 1999).

they do mention the nomads, they mostly disparaged them and their way of life. Palimpsestov and others 'blamed' them for destroying the woodland on the steppes. I came across only a few cases in which settlers, specialists, and scientists acknowledged that the nomads' accumulated knowledge of the steppe environment may have had some value, and some cases this was implicit rather than explicit. In 1841, Jean Demole, the Swiss manager of the farms on the military settlements in the steppe region, almost despaired of the prospects for arable farming face of droughts and locusts. He concluded that 'southern Russia' was a 'land of pastures', that was suitable mainly for livestock.[56] In the 1890s, Dokuchaev recommended seeking an appropriate balance between different forms of land use, including arable and pasture,[57] which implied controlling the rapid expansion of arable land and a recognition that pasture was a more appropriate form of land use in the steppe environment. The strongest explicit statement I came across that the nomads' way of using the land was more appropriate to the steppe environment was by D. L. Ivanov, who wrote a devastating indictment of the impact of Russian colonization of the North Caucasus on the basis of his survey of the region during the drought year of 1885 and whose observations have been cited in several chapters of this book.[58] Ivanov's argument implying the superiority of the nomads' way of life in the steppe environment and the damage inflicted on it by migrants from wetter environments anticipated that of the US Federal Government in the wake of the 'Dust Bowl' in the 1930s, which contrasted the impact of the Plains Indians' way of life with that of the seters from east of the Mississippi. The US government went further, however, in making provision to take land out of cultivation and resettle the population.[59] I have come across no similar recommendations on the steppes in the period under consideration; on the contrary, set backs caused by droughts have been followed by plans to combat them by the various means described in part three of this book.

This brings us back to the the issue raised in the Introduction concerning whether 'nature' has 'agency' in history, or if the non-human world somehow plays an active role in the history of the interaction between human societies and the environments they live in. In his recent book, John McNeill reached the measured conclusion that 'almost all human history is really a co-evolutionary process involving society and nature. But the degree to which this is true varies greatly from context to context'.[60] He argued that in the world of the

---

[56] 'Russkie khozyaistvennye periodichestkie izdaniya', *ZhMGI*, 3 (1841), 2nd pagn, 230.

[57] Dokuchaev, 'Soobshcheniya o lektsiyakh V. V. Dokuchaeva "Ob osnovakh sel'skogo khozyaistva"', id., *Sochineniya*, 9 vols (Moscow and Leningrad, 1949–61), vii, 216–26.

[58] D. L. Ivanov, 'Vliyanie Russkoi kolonizatsii na prirodu Stavropol'skogo kraya', *IRGO*, 22/3 (1886), 225–54.

[59] US Great Plains Committee, *The Future of the Great Plains* (Washington, DC, 1937).

[60] John McNeill, *Mosquito Empires: Ecology and Water in the Greater Caribbean, 1620–1914* (Cambridge, 2010), 7.

Greater Caribbean between 1620 and 1914, the quest for wealth and power by European and North American empires changed the ecologies of the region, and ecological changes in turn shaped the fortunes of empire, war, and revolution. In particular, the ecological changes brought about by the plantation system 'improved breeding and feeding conditions for . . . mosquito species, helping them become key actors in the geopolitical struggles of the early modern Atlantic world . . .'[61] The argument for co-evolution fits the history of the steppes under the domination of the nomads: their pastoral way of life influenced the landscape, by grazing their livestock and burning the steppe, and in turn they adapted their economic activities to the environment. The largely treeless environment, moreover, was inhospitable to the forest peoples from the north, who coveted the fertile soil but relied on woodland for many of their everyday needs and for shelter to protect their settlements against raids by the nomads.

Once the balance of power between settlers and nomads, and forest and steppe-based states had switched decisively in favour of the former, however, another picture emerges. The waves of incoming settlers transformed the steppe environment and endeavoured to reshape it to their needs. This proved rather more difficult than they might have imagined. While the environment had very fertile soil, it lacked the woodland they depended on and the reliable supplies of the water their crops needed. The steppe environment seemed at times to defy their efforts to plant trees and was the wrong shape for artificial irrigation, with fertile land on the high steppes and water in river valleys far below them. The settlers therefore had to adapt their designs to what the steppe environment would allow. The settlers' encounter with a different environment, displacement of the indigenous inhabitants, and attempt to persist with the ways they had used the natural resources in their previous homes, in time led to conceptual innovations in how they understood the new environment and practical innovations in how they managed their interaction with it. The most important innovation in the way they understood the new environment was genetic soil science. This explained that the component parts of the steppe environment—organic matter, climate, parent rock, relief—were interconnected and, over time, had formed the fertile soil. This realization then shaped approaches to using the land in ways that worked with 'nature' rather than against it in order to make arable farming viable. Over a similar period, and in advance of the scientific developments, some settlers in the region, especially but not solely the Mennonites, developed ways of cultivating the land and identified the most appropriate varieties of crops that aimed to conserve the scarce moisture in order to achieve more reliable, and indeed sustainable, harvests. As we have seen, moreover, both the science and the farming methods had wider applications in similar grassland environments outside the Russian Empire, in particular on the Great Plains.

---

[61] McNeill, *Mosquito Empires*, 2–3.

The more sustainable ways of farming the land, however, were adhered to by only a minority of steppe farmers in the last decades before the First World War. In the subsequent periods of Soviet power and post-Soviet regimes, moreover, there have been recurring 'offensives' to plough up ever more grassland. Thus, to return to the suggestion by environmental historian Linda Nash quoted in the Introduction to this book, the 'conversation' between the human and non-human worlds about the 'possibilities of existence' on the steppes since the advent of large-scale agricultural settlement has been more of a battleground. It may even offer an ecological parallel to the great tank battles in the region during the Second World War. In years of adequate and timely rainfall, and when they have adhered to the recommendations of agronomists, the farmers have advanced across the steppes, armed with their ploughs to break them, grain to sow in their fertile soil, and harvesters to reap the fruits. But, in years of drought, crop failure, and soil erosion, they have had to retreat, and rely on their 'intelligence services' (scientists and agronomists) for advice on how to take on their persistent adversary. If human history is also environmental history, and humans—even settlers from regions with different natural conditions—are also part of the environment, then the continuing interaction, and indeed struggle, between farmers and the steppe is the latest stage in the environmental history of the grasslands of Russia, Ukraine, Kazakhstan, and also North America.[62]

---

[62] See David Moon, 'The Grasslands of North America and Russia', in J. R. McNeill and Erin Stewart Maudlin (eds), *A Companion to Global Environmental History* (Oxford, 2012), 247–62.

Epilogue

In May 2011, with a party of scientists and naturalists, I drove south from the city of Kherson, in southern Ukraine, across the river Dnepr. On the flood plain to the south-east (i.e. on the left bank) of the river, we passed through the natural woodland (*poimennyi les*) that grows in such locations. Then, after the town of Tsyurupyns'k (formerly known as Aleshki), we entered a starkly anthropogenic environment: row upon row of Scots and Crimean pine and black locust trees. The trees had been planted on the sandy soil from the 1940s in an attempt to undo the damage caused by over-grazing sheep. The sheep had eaten the grasses down to their roots, rendering the thin layer of topsoil liable to erosion, exposing the sand underneath, which drifted over the surrounding land. The plantations form a ring of trees around a huge area of sand dunes: as we explored them, I felt we were in the Sahara desert.[1]

In the nineteenth century, with similar consequences, local estate owners, such as the Faltz-Feins, had also grazed vast herds of sheep on this fragile land. The sand had already begun to drift, inundating fertile fields and settlements, as a result of actions by settlers who had moved to the steppes from the north after the former Khanate of Crimea, of which it was a part, was annexed by the Russian Empire in 1783. The settlers had gradually felled the native woodland that grew on the sandy soil and had held it in place. Thus, I was not in the Sahara desert, but the location of the woodland described two and half millennia earlier by Herodotus as 'Hylaea'. Ironically, scientists are now concerned that planting trees has gone too far and is endangering rare species of plants that grow on the sand. A compromise has been reached and part of the sands has recently been designated by the Ukrainian government as a national park called Oleshkivs'ki pisky (Aleshkovskie peski in Russian).[2]

It is not far from the first nature reserve (*zapovednik*) in the steppe region, Askaniya Nova, which I also visited in May 2011. It was founded in late nineteenth century by local estate owner Friedrich Faltz-Fein, from the same family that had grazed its sheep on sandy land to the west. He was alarmed by the rapid loss of the native, unploughed grassland. In 1888, anticipating Vasilii Dokuchaev, he

---

[1] See the location on Google Earth: the centre of the sandy area is at 46° 30' N, 33°E.
[2] I am grateful to Dr Ivan Ivanovich Moysiyenko of Kherson State University for information on the national park.

protected an area of virgin steppe on his estate against human intervention. A decade later, on the advice of the botanist I. K. Pachoskii, he chose a more suitable location and protected an area of around 500 *desyatiny*. He anticipated later principles of protected land, moreover, by designating a buffer zone around it. Faltz-Fein acted just in time. In the late 1920s, V. K. Fortunatov wrote that until a few years earlier there had been thousands of *desyatiny* of unploughed land scattered around the steppe. But, as a result of the land reform that followed the October Revolution of 1917, former noble estates had been broken up and distributed among the peasant population. Peasants then ploughed up the parcels of virgin land. Only Askaniya Nova, which had its protected status confirmed by the new Soviet government, remained on the entire expanse of steppe between the Dnepr and Don rivers. One peasant remarked that there was only enough feather grass—which had once covered the seemingly endless steppe—to make a bouquet.[3] Askaniya Nova survived the big plough up during collectivization in the 1930s, but lost an area of land to the plough when the Soviet authorities redesignated land on nature reserves in 1951.[4] I visited the surviving protected, unploughed, steppe at the right time of year to see the silvery-grey spiklets on the feather grass blowing in the wind, creating the illusion of waves on the sea.[5]

When I explored the protected steppe in the company of a botanist one afternoon, I recalled my first excursion to the steppe, further to the east, to the Rostov steppe nature reserve several years earlier (see above, p. ix). Then, everything had seemed alien. I had felt disorientated, exposed, and overwhelmed by the vastness of the sky overhead, and lost my sense of distance. Now, more accustomed, I didn't worry about the distance, and concentrated on my discussion with the botanist on the types of plants and soil, the connection between them, and the history of the reserve. She also explained her research into different regimes for protecting steppe. Some exclude all human intervention, besides scientific research. Others allow grazing animals and controlled use of fire to mimic the processes, including the actions of the nomadic inhabitants, that had assisted in the evolution of the steppe environment over the millennia.

After we returned to the research institute, with time before dinner, I visited the beautiful dendropark, an artificial woodland designed for Faltz-Fein in the German romantic manner in the 1880s. It offered a contrast to both the natural woodland on the floodplain of the Dnepr and artificial plantations around the Oleshkivs'ki sands. In this semi-arid environment, Faltz-Fein supplied water to his woodland park by an elaborate system of artesian wells and irrigation

   [3] B. K. Fortunatov, 'Stepnoi zapovednik', in M. N. Kolod'ko and B. K. Fortunatov (eds), *Stepnoi zapovednik Chapli-Askaniya Nova* (Moscow and Leningrad, 1928), 30–49.
   [4] Vladimir Evgen'evich Boreiko, *Askania-Nova: Tyazhkie versty istorii (1826–1993)* (Kiev, 1994).
   [5] See the official website of Askaniya Nova, <http://askania-nova-zapovidnik.gov.ua/index.php?lang=ua> (accessed 13 May 2012).

channels. As I strolled around his park, chatting with other visitors, admiring the artificial lake and the trees that were now tall and imposing, I thought that relaxing in the cool shade of the woodland after an afternoon exploring the exposed steppe would be a fitting end to this book.

David Moon
Odessa

List of Archival Collections Cited

Derzhavnyi arkhiv Odes'koi oblasti (DAOO) (Odessa)

Fond 1   Kantselyariya Novorossiiskogo i Bessarabskogo General-Gubernatora
Fond 6   Popechitel'nyi komitet ob inostrannykh poseleniyakh yuzhnogo kraya Rossii
Fond 7   Upravlenie glavnogo nachal'nika yuzhnykh poselenii
Fond 22   Obshchestvo sel'skogo khozyaistvo yuzhnoi Rossii

Gosudarstvennyi arkhiv Rostovskoi oblasti (GARO) (Rostov-on-Don)

Fond 46   Kantselyariya voiskogo nakaznogo atamana
Fond 55   Popov, Khariton Ivanovich (lichnyi fond)
Fond 243 Ul'yanovy, Donskie kazaki-dvoryane
Fond 301 Oblastnoe pravlenie oblasti voiska donskogo
Fond 309 Kalmytskoe pravlenie
Fond 353 Oblastnoi voiska donskogo statisticheskii komitet
Fond 801 Voiskovaya kommissiya narodnogo prodovol'stviya pri Voiskovom pravlenii

Gosudarstvennyi arkhiv Samarskoi oblasti (GASO) (Samara)

Fond 3   Kantselyariya Samarskogo gubernatora
Fond 5   Samarskaya gubernskaya zemskaya uprava
Fond 43   Upravlenie Samarskogo udel'nogo kontora
Fond 112 Samarskoe upravlenie gosudarstvennykh imushchestv
Fond.149 Krest'yanskii pozemel'nyi bank
Fond 329 Zaveduyushchii rabotami po ukrepleniyu sypuchykh peskov i ovragov v Samarskom, Stavropol'skom i Buzulukskom uezdakh, Samarskoi gubernii
Fond 332 Zaveduyushchii rabotami po ukrepleniyu peskov i ovragov po Samarsko-Orenburgskomu peschanomu-ovrazhnomu okrugu
Fond 832 Bezenchukskaya udel'naya opytnaya stantsiya
Fond 834 Samarsko-Ural'skoe upravlenie zemledeliya i gosudarstvennykh imushchestv

Gosudarstvennyi arkhiv Stavropol'skogo kraya (GASK) (Stavropol')

Fond 80   Stavropol'skii gubernskii statisticheskii komitet
Fond 101   Kantselyariya Stavropol'skogo gubernatora
Fond 146   Upravlenie gosudarstvennykh imushchestv Stavropol'skoi gubernii

Sankt-Peterburgskii filial arkhiva Rossiiskoi Akademii Nauk (PFA RAN) (St Petersburg)

Fond 3   Kantselyariya Akademii Nauk
Fond 184   Dokuchaev, V. V. (lichnyi fond)

Rossiiskii Gosudarstvennyi Istoricheskii arkhiv (RGIA) (St Petersburg)

Fond 91   Vol'noe Ekonomicheskoe Obshchestvo
Fond 379   Departament gosudarstvennykh imushchestv Ministerstva finansov
Fond 382   Uchenyi komitet Ministerstva zemledeliya
Fond 383   Pervyi Departament Ministerstva Gosudarstvennykh imushchestv
Fond 387   Lesnoi Departament, Ministerstva Zemledeliya i Gosudarstvennykh imushchestv
Fond 395   Otdel sel'skoi ekonomii i sel'skokhozyaistvennoi statisiki Ministerstva Zemledeliya i Gosudarstvennykh imushchestv
Fond 398   Departament Zemledeliya Ministerstva Zemledeliya i Gosudarstvennykh imushchestv
Fond 426   Otdel zemel'nykh uluchshenii Ministerstva Zemledeliya i Gosudarstvennykh imushchestv
Fond 453   Ekspeditsiya po orosheniyu na yuge Rossii i Kavkaze 1881–1902
Fond 1152 Departament Gosudarstvennoi Ekonomii Gosudarstvennogo Soveta
Fond 1263 Komitet ministrov
Fond 1281 Sovet ministra vnutrennikh del
Fond 1284 Departament obshchikh del, Ministerstva vnutrennikh del
Fond 1287 Khozyaistvennyi Departament Ministerstva vnutrennikh del

Rossiiskii Gosudarstvennyi Voenno-Istoricheskii arkhiv (RGVIA) (Moscow)

Fond 330   Glavnoe Upravlenie Kazachikh Voisk

Library of Congress, Manuscript Division (Washington, DC)

Gifford Pinchot Papers

Minnesota Historical Society (St Paul, MN)

P1237   Raphael Zon papers, 1887–1957

Index

Don, river ix, 8, 11, 35, 40, 48, 54, 58, 68, 73, 100, 107, 150, 193, 212, 238, 293
Don agricultural society 201, 231
Don Cossack territory (Don region from 1870) 8, 19, 44, 58, 68, 71, 72, 73, 75–6, 77, 88, 96, 99–100, 101, 104, 106–7, 113, 122, 124, 127, 134, 144, 150, 151, 157, 160, 165, 167, 175, 182, 183–4, 190, 191, 197, 203, 216, 221, 223, 238, 255, 269, 270, 272–3, 274–5, 291
Don forestry plantation 190
Don region, *see* Don Cossack territory
Donets district, Don region 201
Donets, river 39, 54, 58, 100, 102, 104, 226, 238
Dorpat Universities, *see* Universities, Dorpat
drifting sands 74–5, 139–44, 283, 301
  binding sands 5, 194, 195–8, 203, 282
droughts 1, 3, 4, 6, 7, 18, 23–4, 29, 42–3, 53, 54, 59, 65–8, 100, 109, 118, 120, 122, 124, 125, 126–7, 130–4, 136, 144, 152, 160, 162, 164, 167–9, 173, 179, 183–4, 189, 207, 208, 210, 213, 214, 220, 221, 222, 239, 242, 259, 260, 270, 279, 281, 283, 285, 290–1, 292, 294
  see also crop failures
dry farming 268, 289
Dunlap, Thomas 279
'Dust Bowl' 23–4, 90, 146–7, 285, 288, 289, 293, 298
dust storms 4, 6, 23–4, 25, 67, 74, 137, 139, 144–8, 198, 201, 283, 293
Dyakin, Valentin 234

l'École forestière de Nancy 192
ecology 279–80
education (agricultural) 247, 269–70, 272, 282
  see also Forestry Institute; Moscow Agricultural Institute; Novo-Aleksandriisii Agricultural Institute; Petrovskaya Agricultural Academy; Universities
Egypt 35, 206, 240
Ekaterinoslav province 8, 21, 44, 54, 98, 104, 106, 109, 126, 135, 144, 145, 150, 175, 185–6, 198, 201, 220, 221, 237, 256, 266, 268
Elina, Olga 161, 170
Elizavetgrad district, Kherson province 115, 199
El'ton, lake 211
Engel'gardt, Aleksandr Nikolaevich (1832–93, chemist) 50
Engel'gardt, Aleksandr Platonovich (1845–1903, official and provincial governor) 91, 125, 143, 149, 179, 194, 239, 272

Engel'ke, K. (German colonist, Saratov province) 66, 125
Engel'man (member of Free Economic Society) 246, 259
environmental determinism 13, 27
Eriks, Mikhail (hydralic engineer) 214
Eristov, ataman of the Terek Cossacks 210
Ermolov, Aleksei (1846–1917, statesman, Minister of Agriculture, 1894–1905) 67, 91, 132, 157, 179, 198, 229, 231–5, 240–2, 248, 256, 261, 281
erosion 4, 23–4, 73–5, 90, 93, 109, 139–52, 156, 162, 165, 173, 178, 193, 194, 202, 210, 226, 282, 293, 295, 301
  see also drifting sands; 'Dust Bowl'; dust storms; gullies; ravines
Eruslan, river 143
Eurasian steppes 6–7, 11, 15
European colonialism 22, 279–80, 283, 284, 295, 299
evaporation 7, 70, 72, 128, 136, 147, 152–3, 155, 178, 186, 192, 198, 200, 208, 210, 218, 219, 260, 261, 262, 263, 266, 267
  see also precipitation; water, shortage of
Evtuhov, Catherine 15
extension services, *see* agronomists, extension services

Falck (Fal'k), Johann Peter (1725–74, Swedish naturalist) 48, 63, 72, 75, 76, 102, 103
fallowing 111–15, 158, 252–7
  See also black fallow; crop rotations; shifting, long-fallow agriculture
Faltz-Fein, Friederick (1863–1920, estate owner and pioneering conservationist) 301–2
  see also Askaniya Nova
famine relief 66, 168–9, 171, 202–3, 220, 223, 224–5, 226–7
feather grass (*kovyl'*) 5, 7, 31, 41, 62, 63, 64, 76, 77, 83, 95–6, 111–15, 155, 252, 295, 302
fences 104
Feodotova, Anastasiya 63
fertilizer (including lack of need for in black-earth region) 75, 86, 158, 159, 160, 161, 254, 263, 266
Filipchenko, A. (agronomist) 266
Filipenko, A. E. (participant in Free Economic Society debate, 1891) 157, 256, 263
Finland x, xi, xii, 59, 180, 195
fire 7, 44, 60, 88, 105, 111, 183, 184, 188, 302
firewood 95, 98, 105–6, 108, 124, 173, 176, 177, 182, 187, 191
First World War (1914–18) 289

Vorontsov, Count (1782–1856, statesman, Governor-General of New Russia) 51
Vorskla, river 125
Vyazemskii, Prince (estate owner) 223
Vyshnegradskii, Ivan (1831–95, statesman, Minister of Finance 1888–92) 225
Vysotskii, Grigorii (1865–1940, forestry scientist) 54, 57, 60, 62,147, 175, 180, 181, 187, 188, 189, 192, 193, 200, 201, 204–5

water law, *see* law on water
water, shortage of xii, 1, 2, 3, 4, 7, 23, 25, 31, 43, 59–60, 76, 83, 90, 109, 122, 152–7, 162–4, 165, 167, 168, 175, 187, 205, 208, 211, 212, 213, 217, 219, 223, 230, 231, 242–3, 254
  see also droughts; evaporation; moisture retention or conservation; treelessness
weeds 67, 96, 111–15, 116, 161, 181, 184, 189, 244, 255, 259, 261, 262, 263, 265, 266, 268, 276
Weiner, Douglas 14, 292
wells 154, 155, 157, 206, 209, 211, 218, 219, 221, 230, 235, 237, 238, 302
Western European agricultural and forestry sciences, relevance of to Russian conditions 153, 160–1, 170–1, 173–5, 245–50, 251–2, 253, 259, 260, 267, 277–8, 280, 286
wheat, *see* crops, wheat
Wiebe, Philipp (1816–70, chairman of Mennonite Agricultural Society) 263–5, 266
wild flowers 62–5, 89, 114, 115
William of Rubruck (13th century Franciscan friar) 37, 39, 41, 42, 43
winds 42, 54, 59, 60, 65, 66, 67, 69, 72, 74–5, 109, 118, 120, 121, 122, 123, 125, 127, 128, 134–7, 139, 144–8, 153, 164, 173, 177, 178, 183, 186, 187, 192, 193, 196, 198–202, 208, 214, 219, 253, 283, 287, 292
Witte, Sergei (1849–1915, Finance Minister 1892–1903) 171, 225, 227, 228, 229, 231–5, 239, 240, 242, 260, 282
  memorandum to Minister of Agriculture Ermolov of 29 July 1896 232–3, 242
Witte, Yulii (1814–67, agronomist, father of Sergei) 235, 247
Wollny, Ewald (1846–1901, German scientist) 154 n.64, 250 n.34
woodland, see forest
worms 80
Worster, Donald 24

Wrangel', Baron (official of Baltic German origin) 174
Wüst, Eduard (1818–1859; German protestant pastor) 6

Yaik Cossacks, *see* Ural (Yaik) Cossacks
Yaitsk, *see* Ural'sk/Yaitsk
Young, Arthur (1741–1820, English specialist on agriculture) 245
Yuzhakov, Sergei (1849–1910, philology graduate) 212–13

Zablotskii-Desyatovskii, Andrei (1808–81; official of Ministry of State Domains) 5–6, 120, 140
Zabludskii, S. A. (estate owner and agricultural specialist) 2, 153, 249
Zaporozhian Cossacks 41
zapovedniki ix, 14, 28, 55, 296–7
  see also Askaniya Nova *zapovednik*; Orenburg *zapovednik*; Rostov steppe *zapovednik*; Teberdinskii *zapovednik*; Zhigulevskii *zapovednik*
Zelenskii, P. A. (official of Kherson *zemstvo*) 203
zemstva xviii, 25, 47, 51, 70, 108, 113–14, 116, 134, 136, 153, 159, 169, 194, 197, 198, 202, 202–3, 219, 220, 223, 224, 226, 227–8, 237, 239, 261, 266, 267, 269, 270, 271, 272, 282
Zemyatchenskii, Petr (1856–1942, scientist) 53, 145
Zherebko, A. 260
Zherebtsov estate 216
Zhigulevskii *zapovednik* ix
Zhilinskii, Iosef (1834–1916, civil engineer) 209, 220–36, 239, 240
Zhilinskii expedition for irrigation in the south of Russia and the Caucasus 209, 220–36, 282
  see also Berezovskii plot, Nikolaevsk district, Samara province; Kochetovskii plot, Nikolaevsk district, Samara province; Malaya Tinguta, river; Shcherbatovskii plot, Nikolaevsk district, Samara province; Sol'yanskoe reservoir, Samara province; Tengutinskaya dam, Astrakhan' province; Valuiskii plot, Novyi Uzen' district, Samara province
Zon, Raphael (1874–1956, Russian-born American forester) 288
Zuev, Vasilii (1754–94, naturalist) 48, 58, 74, 98, 209